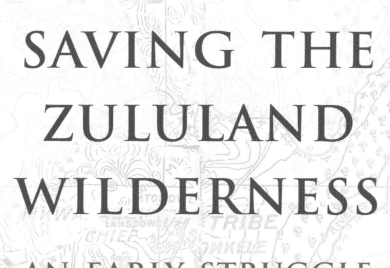

SAVING THE
ZULULAND
WILDERNESS

AN EARLY STRUGGLE
FOR NATURE CONSERVATION

SAVING THE ZULULAND WILDERNESS

AN EARLY STRUGGLE
FOR NATURE CONSERVATION

Donal P. McCracken

JACANA

DEDICATED TO

BRUCE HOPWOOD

OF MTHUNZINI, ZULULAND

First published by Jacana Media (Pty) Ltd in 2008

10 Orange Street
Sunnyside
Auckland Park 2092
South Africa
+2711 628 3200
www.jacana.co.za

ISBN 978-1-77009-596-0

Design and layout by Jenny Young
Set in Minion
Printed by Tien Wah Press, Singapore
Job No. 000775

See a complete list of Jacana titles at www.jacana.co.za

CONTENTS

6   Preface

7   Acknowledgements

7   Notes on nomenclature

SECTION I:
THE ZULULAND WILDERNESS

11   1. Arcadia: the game

31   2. The forests

SECTION II:
THE HUNTERS' ROAD: THE DESTRUCTION OF GAME

43   3. The white hunters

59   4. White residents

65   5. African society

79   6. Guns and roads

SECTION III:
CONSERVATION

93   7. The Zululand wilderness revealed

111   8. Back from the brink: rules and regulations

119   9. The game reserves

129   10. Running the conservation system

SECTION IV:
TROUBLE IN ARCADIA

141   11. Enforcing the conservation laws

153   12. Trouble in arcadia

161   13. Postscript: white settlers and white elephants

171   Bibliography

175   Index

PREFACE

Piles of elephant tusks were once a common sight at the landing place at Port Natal, the town which in 1836 was renamed Durban. Following a struggle with the Boers for hegemony, in 1845 this region of south-east Africa known as Natal became a province of the Colony of the Cape of Good Hope, and then in 1856 a British colony in its own right. We know that in the half-century from the British annexation some 880 000 kg of elephant ivory were logged as having been shipped out of Durban Bay. The preceding 20 years must bring that total up to at least a million kilograms, or about a thousand tons – the equivalent of a thousand oxwagons lined up, each laden down with 40 tusks, representing the slaughter of 20 000 elephant.

And that was not all – rhino horn; antelope horn; buffalo, hippopotamus and wildebeest hide; lion, leopard and wildcat skin; as well as live wild animals, all were shipped out of the subtropical paradise that was Durban in the nineteenth century. Some of the cargoes had originated from far inland and had been brought over the uKhahlamba-Drakensberg mountain range. Much of it, however, came directly from a hundred kilometres or more up the north coast – from the last surviving great African kingdom in southern Africa, Zululand, and from its satellite territory of Maputaland.

This book is about the onslaught on the three pillars of the Zululand and Maputaland wilderness and the efforts made to preserve them from the destruction that seemed imminent and inevitable. These pillars were the wild game of Zululand, which included what today is referred to as the Big Five: elephant, Cape buffalo, leopard, lion and hippopotamus. Then there were the avifauna and in particular the game birds, which included the spectacular secretary bird and ground hornbill. Even today Zululand boasts the greatest number and diversity of bird life in South Africa. Third, there were the indigenous forests. These existed on the slopes of the higher ridges and in the deep gullies or krantzes, where the hefty yellowwood and stinkwood reigned. There were also the coastal forests, where the canopy was not so high, but where the range of species was considerable.

It is easy to criticise what was done 110 years ago and indeed sometimes even the motivation for what was done. But the fact remains that had the pioneers of Zululand conservation not embarked on this early conservation movement, the Zululand wilderness with its tremendous diversity of fauna and flora would have disappeared completely in the opening decades of the twentieth century and, with it, one of South Africa's brightest jewels.

ACKNOWLEDGEMENTS

I should like to thank the staff of the following archives and libraries:

Arquivo Histórico Ultramarino, Lisbon, Portugal

Don Africana Library, Durban

Ezemvelo KwaZulu-Natal Wildlife Library, Pietermaritzburg

Killie Campbell Collections, University of KwaZulu-Natal

KwaZulu-Natal Herbarium, Durban

National Botanical Institute, Pretoria

Natural History Museum, Durban

Natural History Museum Library, London

National Museum of Ireland, Natural History Division

National Zoological Gardens of Ireland

Percy FitzPatrick Institute of African Ornithology

National Archives, London

Royal Botanic Gardens, Kew (Archive and Library)

Royal Geographical Society Library, London

South African National Archives (Cape Town, Durban and Pietermaritzburg)

South African National Biodiversity Institute, Pretoria

South African Department of Water and Forestry, Eshowe, Pietermaritzburg and Ulundi

University of KwaZulu-Natal

Zoological Society of London Library

Specific individuals I wish to thank for their help are Dr David Allan, Dr Hamish Campbell, Greg Davies, William Forgrave, Liezel Hannemann, Crispin Henson, Bruce Hopwood, Dr David Johnson, Emeritus Professor J.L. McCracken, Patricia McCracken, Lord Murton of Lindisfarne, Joan Read, Professor Sihawukele Ngubane, Mkhipheni A. Ngwenya, Margaret Sandwith, Dr Bheki Shabane, Shelagh O'Byrne Spencer, Adrienne Weerheim and the Earl of Perth.

NOTE ON NOMENCLATURE

KwaZulu-Natal, unlike some other parts of South Africa, is fortunate in having a large number of places retaining their original or slightly modified Zulu names. In recent years there has been a move to de-anglicise some of these names. This process is not yet complete with the result that in a few years' time some of the names in this volume will have changed. The changing or altering of names which have been spelt in a particular fashion for over 150 years will take some time to be used fully by many members of the general public. Examples of game reserves that have had their name changed recently include:

• Imfolozi, changed from Umfolozi (it should be noted that the river is spelt Mfolozi)
• Mapalana, changed from Mapelane
• Mkhuze, changed from Mkuze
• Ndumo, changed from Ndumu

Other examples of name changes include Ongoye forest in southern Zululand, which used to be spelt Ngoye, and the former 'Lower Umfolozi' magisterial division, which is now the Empangeni magisterial district. The River Thukela is still widely spelt as Tugela, though this will no doubt change with time.

In this volume I have employed the old names of the Zululand game reserves in their historical context, and the former spellings of Zululand names in historical quotations. I have used the nomenclature Tsonga rather than the sometime preferred Thonga.

The Zululand Wilderness

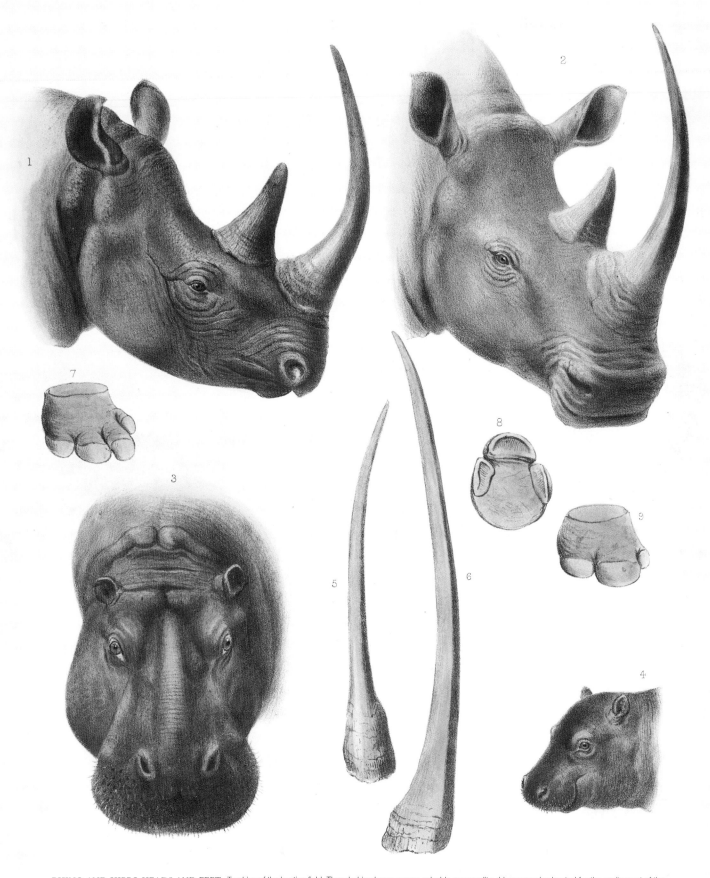

RHINO AND HIPPO HEADS AND FEET Trophies of the hunting field. Though rhino horns were a saleable commodity, rhino were also hunted for the excitement of the chase. Hippo ivory, hide (for whips) and fat (for cooking and candles) were all valuable items too. As well as mounting stuffed heads of rhinos, feet of rhino, hippo and even elephant were sometimes preserved as curiosities or even table legs. WARD, *GREAT AND SMALL GAME OF AFRICA*, 1899

CHAPTER 1

Arcadia: the game

This side of Umhlatusi lies
Of Zululand the paradise
A land of forest, streams, and plains,
Of verdant meads, and gentle rains:
Beyond – to Hlabatini's vale
Poor soil, and stony ridge prevail.[1]

THE PANGOLIN OR 'SCALY-EATER'
Rarely seen or mentioned by travellers and hunters, the pangolin nonetheless was to be found in Zululand.
PARKER GILLMORE, *THE HUNTER'S ARCADIA*, 1886

This is a story of survival: the overcoming of terrible odds and the laying of a foundation upon which the conservation of Zululand's indigenous forest, bush, game and birdlife would grow. It takes us back a hundred years to when the Zululand wilderness still existed, yet even then was already greatly fragmented from what it had been just fifty years earlier.

Fortunately, the concept of game reserves in the territory was well established even outside these reservoirs, though much game still survived, especially in remote, hot and disease-riddled Maputaland, described in 1904 as 'a howling wilderness of sandy flats and swamps … the deadliest hole for civilised man to get into'.[2] Three major onslaughts threatened this outpost of nature with extinction: disease, borne by game and tsetse fly; the impact of powerful hunting rifles; and the introduction of white commercial farming.

Yet despite all this, the white rhino, the leopard, the wildebeest and the mamba have survived to this day, as have the yellowwood and the stinkwood trees. The tale is not a pleasant one. It is studded with slaughter and exploitation. But it was a battle worthy of the fight and a saga that should not be forgotten, lest this remnant of arcadia is threatened again.

Game on the move
In 1929 R.C.A. Samuelson confidently asserted which animals had been found where in the Zululand wilderness of the past:

Their [hyenas'] homes, however, and where they were noted to be somewhat fierce and aggressive, were Ivuna, across the Black Mfolozi, and at Emandwe, in the valley of the Mhlatuze … The Riet-bucks, Steen-bucks, Duikers, Bush-buck and Ree-buck were quite common everywhere then, and were for a long time thereafter. The Riet-bucks were to be found, even in respectable herds, in that part of Zululand lying between the Tugela River, Ndulinde range, Eshowe, Mtunzini and the sea. The lions and tigers [leopards'] district was from Ntumeni, Ingotye range, down Eshowe, Mhlatuze, Mfolozi valleys away to the Ubombo and Ngwavuma, and downward to the ocean. The buffalo favoured the same areas, as did the koodoo. The elephant and black rhinoceros were found in the country from Mhlatuze valley and onward, along the coast, away to the Ubombo and onward. Wild pigs innumerable in Mhlatuze valley and away onward along the coast. Baboons, the ordinary ape and the large blue skinned ape were numberless. Wild dogs were found in the midlands. Snakes and reptiles seemed to be the weeds of Zululand in these early days; rivers abounded in crocodiles along the whole coast parts. Hippopotami were also numerous in the coast parts of the rivers.[3]

But such lists, especially written from memory, have to be treated with caution. Even when looking at contemporary mid-nineteenth-century accounts by hunters, the quantity of game in a specific area clearly varied greatly from year to year. The simple truth is that many species of animal moved, some on a regular basis.

Even when firearms were primitive and the battle between people and beasts in Zululand less one-sided, wild animals had to be cautious, not least to protect themselves from predators. The vegetation of Zululand with its extensive wetlands, its reedbeds and its bush was ideal for many species. Within these jungles, animals hid away, lived and died. The hunter William Drummond wrote of the 'vegetable cave' where these creatures sheltered. There were hidden tunnels in the thorn bush and the reeds, where even elephant could pass undetected – and woe betide the hunter who entered these domains, especially after dark.

But as the persecution of game increased, even these sanctuaries came under threat, and some species, such as elephant, buffalo and kudu, forsook these bastions and retreated before the onslaught. In any case, some species had a natural urge to roam over wide ranges, and being forced into this by natural factors was, of course, not a new phenomenon either. The difference from the late 1850s was that the animals would, in many cases, out of caution and fear, not return to their old haunts.

The landscape of eastern Zululand allowed for natural avenues of migration or, to put it another way, escape corridors for animals in search of food sources. These migrations might be seasonal or due to drought. Many hunters' accounts talk of travelling through areas where there was next to no game. Another factor was fire, destroying grazing in the winter months.

In 1850 one diarist in Zululand noted, 'This part of the country, which on our way up looked so bare and barren is now the reverse up to our knees in fine Grass.' The writer then goes on to talk about buffalo hunting in the area.[4] A generation later, in 1891, writing from his isolated post on the top of the Lebombo Mountains, Charles Saunders commented: 'As a consequence of the winter setting in the trees are commencing to shed their leaves and the whole country will soon present a very parched appearance. The grass is commencing to burn & as soon as it is all burnt in the low country …'[5]

Game also altered their ranges in response to a dramatic increase or decrease in the African cattle herds. The Zululand cattle herds were severely hit by disease in the 1850s, the mid-1870s and the 1890s. Generally, less pressure from domestic cattle on grazing land benefited the game, except, of course, when the game themselves were affected by disease, as with rinderpest in the 1890s which wiped out perhaps as much as three-quarters of the cattle herds of Zululand.

The third reason for animals to move was because of over-hunting. In the 1830s Captain Gardiner commented that 'The chief employment of the Europeans at Port Natal is in hunting the elephant and buffalo'.[6] While it is likely that they first shot out most of what was in the hinterland before turning their attentions to regions further afield, hunting did also take place across the Tugela, where the Zulus themselves also regularly hunted. We know, for example, that in 1826 Henry Francis Fynn hunted in the Umlalazi region of Zululand, bagging 50 hippo and returning to Port Natal with 144 kg of elephant ivory. But that said, the pressure on big game around Port Natal must have been such that elephant in particular retreated away from the white settlement.[7]

A generation later, persecution by hunters in Zululand itself frequently led to elephant or buffalo herds retreating into the fastness of the thick thorn bush. There is no shortage of references to hunters remarking on the game being 'scarce and wild' or 'wild and shy'.[8] And the elephant were wont to set off in haste for distant country known to them where people were few and tsetse fly plentiful. T.E. Buckley commented in 1876: 'When Elephants are disturbed by shooting now, they often go great distances, passing through a large extent of thirst-land to a distant water; so fearful are they of firearms.'[9]

Elephant might travel for over 40 miles (60 km) at a stretch to get away from danger or to find food or water. One route they and other migrating animals took was between the northern end of Lake St Lucia and the Lebombo Mountains. This funnelled wildlife north on to the Maputaland plains, east into the lakes system, or to the thornveld of the rivers and streams leading into that system. Then there was the thick thorn on the western side

THE AARDVARK Like the pangolin, the aardvark or antbear was not in the firing line for the visiting hunter and was generally unmolested by them.
PARKER GILLMORE, *THE HUNTER'S ARCADIA*, 1886

of the Lebombo Mountains and the east–west valley system, such as the Mfolozi and the Phongola rivers. The north–south–running Swaziland lowveld was another escape valve for game. Here as late as 1905 it was reported that there were no white inhabitants and very few Africans, though hunters did enter the area in winter.[10]

A great crescent of eastern game lands stretched from southern Zululand right up either side of the Lebombo Mountains into the present-day Mpumalanga and Mozambique lowveld. One of the key factors in Zululand retaining a large amount of game into the late nineteenth-century was that this range of movement remained long enough to enable such large game as kudu, elephant and buffalo to survive much longer than they did in Natal or most of the Cape.

The extent of wild game in Zululand is mirrored by the volume and nature of exports of wildlife products out of Lourenço Marques (Maputo) and Port Natal (Durban), the latter founded only in the mid-1820s. In particular we have some idea of the extent of exploitation of wild animals in Zululand from the export figures from Port Natal, with continuity from 1845. Of course, not all wild-animal products were exported; a fair proportion were sold in the Durban and Pietermaritzburg markets. Here in the mid-1840s the prices were in the region of:

- A wildebeest skin – 1s. 6d.
- A rhino horn – 6s.
- An eland skin – 8s.
- A lion skin – £1 3s.
- A buffalo hide – £1 3s. 3d.

In the early 1850s the prices could range as follows:

- A 'spotted cat' skin – £2 to £4
- A 'yellow cat' skin – £1 to £2
- A springbok skin – 15s. to £1
- A leopard skin – £3 5s.[11]

Not all the elephant ivory exported from Durban would have come from Zululand. Ivory from the interior, known as the Overberg trade, was shipped out of Natal as well as out of the Cape. There were periods when the Overberg trade in wildlife products was brisk, but equally there were times when the Zululand trade dominated. In 1854 the *Natal Mercury* noted, 'The Ivory exported is chiefly provided from Panda's country [Zululand] by basters and hunters of this District.'[12]

When Zululand was in crisis – whether political, military or epidemiological – the statistics clearly show an increase in the export of some commodities, such as ivory. No doubt the

THE CARNAGE OF THE ELEPHANT HUNT This title-page image from Faulkner's book on elephant-hunting vividly illustrates the carnage caused by ivory-hunters.
HENRY FAULKNER, *ELEPHANT HAUNTS*, 1868

disruption of everyday agriculture led to a need to supplement incomes by exploiting wild resources, as well as liquidating stockpiles saved for a crisis. It is also perhaps an indication of an increase in some species due to decline in cattle numbers.

The victims

The various accounts of hunting in nineteenth-century Zululand are striking as much for the species of animal omitted as those mentioned. Reading these reports one would never imagine that Zululand contained any species of bat, let alone the red squirrel, porcupine, aardwolf, caracal, serval, polecat, civet, aardvark and pangolin. The hunters' focus was purely on what they were out to kill, or on those species such as lion, hyena and jackal that were a nuisance. Whether the unmentioned species got off more lightly than the target victims we cannot know. Even those few accounts that do mention one or two of these species are frequently devoid of any useful information on the animal.

This approach also bedevils the attempt to pinpoint geographical detail, reference to specific recorded sites being usually vague, general or simply unspecified. The task of constructing a location map of wild game in Zululand is hampered by this as well as by the fact that animal populations varied greatly due to hunting, weather and food supply. Nevertheless, there is sufficient information from mention in the diaries and reports of hunters, naturalists and officials to compile status assessments for the main trophy and target species.

Elephant

In the 1840s and into the 1850s elephant were to be found in many parts of Zululand. Herds still roamed the undulating southern bush lands. They were also found in the wetlands and great reedbeds of the low-lying areas in the east, as well as in the bush and reeds of the rivers flowing from the Zululand highlands in the west. Further north, elephant were to be found both to the west of the Lebombo Mountains and in Maputaland.

There were areas where elephant were to be found in large numbers, such as the valleys of the Black and the White Mfolozi rivers, and greater St Lucia. Robert Plant, writing in 1852, remarked of the St Lucia region, 'Elephants seem in great plenty all over this district, as we frequently saw herds of them.' The reedbeds of the lake and lake lands were so extensive that large numbers of elephant could hide there largely unmolested. William Cowie wrote from Richards Bay to Joe Cato in July 1853 about 20 elephant they saw not far from their outspan: 'They remained all day so that we had a good look at them feeding etc. we could not get at them on account of the mud swamps, reeds and bushes.' The reedbeds were dangerous places for people to venture even with guns. Within them were mazes of 'cave like gloomy avenues' where animals could move around out of view of the hunters.[13]

The bastion for elephants, and the sanctuary to which they retreated, was to the north. Here the matriarch could lead the herd for mile upon mile without risk of encountering much in the way of human settlement. It was not a land completely devoid of human settlement, but the population was not great and most of the firearms available to the local population were generally ancient and fairly ineffectual against these colossi. While assegais, pits and dogs took their toll, the slaughter was restricted, and if necessary the Phongola and Usuthu rivers also had the sanctuary of extensive reedbeds offering good cover to the animals.

Even so, by the late 1860s the elephant population of Zululand had been decimated by hunting. A few still held out in the St Lucia–Mfolozi area. Only north of the Phongola were they to be found in any numbers. Here in summer they ate the marula fruits, 'retiring to their fastnesses in the interior at the approach of winter'.[14] By 1880 Ludlow states, 'a herd of elephants, numbering about twenty' was still roaming the Lower Umfolozi district.[15] A remnant of this herd survived into the second decade of the twentieth century, when the last surviving elephant in the Dukuduku region was shot in 1916.

The elephants still held out in northern Maputaland. An evocative account by a local trader has survived of his encounter with a herd on the banks of the Maputa River in the 1890s:

Elephants along the Maputa I only came across once or rather they came across me and that was on a bright moonlight night. The boat had that evening with a heavy load of mealies [maize] struck a sandbank close to a particular steep bank with overhanging trees and for that reason I had decided to sleep in the boat on the mealie bags. These were fairly weevilly and therefore I was kept from sleep.

Subsequently I was kept awake pretty well the whole night, when at about 10 o'clock a herd of elephants came onto the scene. It was a grand sight I thought at first, when I saw them coming down to the river, drinking and spouting themselves. What advantage they have with their natural shower baths, I thought. Then the idea occurred to me that having quenched their thirst, they might feel hungry and perhaps take a fancy to my mealies, if the wind would veer round from me to them. I now still wonder what might have occurred that night, had such been the case as the only weapon I possessed was a shotgun. I had already selected one of the overhanging branches up which to climb if necessary. But after a few hours of breaking and cracking of branches they went across the river, bodies submerged, the periscope of their trunks above water like submarines and I felt very much relieved.[16]

TUSKERS It is difficult to give an average weight to the elephant tusks coming out of nineteenth-century Zululand. It might have been in the region of 24 kg per tusk but there are many examples of considerably heavier elephant tusks. In 1848 William Cowie wrote to Donald Moodie:

I shot 15 large Elephants in the vicinity of the [St Lucia] Bay – in the Beach bush – had several very narrow escapes. Once a large Elephant ran over me and broke my gun. I had shot him [so] that [he] fell but got up again, his Tusks measure about 7 feet [2.1 m] and weigh about 90 lb [40 kg] each. The ivory I have brought is as fine a lot as has been brought to Natal by any hunter. I was only 2 months across the Tugela – 3 of my people are still there to look after some wounded Elephants. I could not stay longer as the oxen got sick and some of them died.[17]

The old elephant that lived alone in the Maphelana/Dukuduku forest lands when shot in 1916 was said to have tusks weighing 129 and 131 lb (58 and 59 kg). The heaviest elephant tusk known to us was that given by Cetshwayo to Lord Chelmsford as a peace offering in 1879. It weighed 150 lb (68 kg), was 7 ft long (2.1 m) and about 18 in. (46 cm) in circumference.[18]

IVORY EXPORTS In addition to Port Natal, Zululand wildlife products were also shipped out of the European enclave at Delagoa Bay, which at different times was Portuguese-, Dutch- and Austrian-controlled. By the early nineteenth century Delagoa Bay was Portuguese. Here, under the red cliffs, they possessed a ramshackle fort and tiny settlement called Lourenço Marques. But their tenure was insecure and their sovereignty over the surrounding territory, in the early period, pretty well non-existent.

It is uncertain exactly how much ivory was shipped out of Delagoa Bay in the eighteenth and nineteenth centuries. But we know, for example, that after a lengthy lull in the trade, during the 'Austrian' occupation of Delagoa Bay in the late 1770s and early 1780s, there was an upsurge in the export of ivory. Six shipments between 1777 and 1780 amounted to about 14 650 elephant tusks weighing 111 360 kg. One account for July 1786 listed 37 consignments of ivory that numbered 2 435 tusks weighing 39 901 lb (18 075 kg) in total.

TABLE 1

IVORY EXPORTS FROM DELAGOA BAY

YEAR	KILOGRAMS OF IVORY
1800	680
1823	9 000
1824	9 450
1825	48 370

A further lull in the trade occurred in the 1790s, but with the Portuguese again in control, at least in name, there was a revival in the first quarter of the nineteenth century. In 1808, for example, 4 375 tusks were exported out of Quelimane, constituting 48 per cent of the town's exports. Slave exports constituted another 18 per cent of trade, and gold dust 9 per cent.[19] The exponential growth of ivory exports out of Delagoa Bay can easily be seen from Table 1.[20]

The Delagoa Bay ivory came from a large hinterland to the north and west as well as from Maputaland and Zululand, and in the earlier period also from Natal. From the works of Hedges and of Smith, it is clear that considerable amounts of ivory were traded by the early Zulu kings with Delagoa Bay. As the nineteenth century progressed there was a seesaw of the ivory exports between Lourenço Marques and Durban. But the healthier and better-organised port of Durban steadily gained the upper hand. Two major economic factors counted against Delagoa Bay. Coinage was under-valued at Delagoa Bay with the guinea exchanging for only 16s. Secondly, the price of ivory was usually higher in Durban. In 1846 when ivory was fetching 1s. 6d. to 2s. per pound weight at Delagoa Bay, in Natal one could expect to receive between 3s. 6d. and 4s. per pound.[21]

So it was that the export of ivory out of Durban gradually built up in the 1840s and 1850s, reaching its peak in the early 1860s, after which it began to decline. In the fifty years from 1844 to 1895, some 869 tons of ivory, valued at just over half a million pounds sterling, was exported out of Durban. Much of this, especially in the late 1840s and the 1850s, came from Zululand and Maputaland, which had also been the principal supplier of ivory exports from Port Natal (Durban) in the 20 years prior to 1844. By the late 1880s the Natal ivory trade was all but dead. So were most Zululand elephants.

FIGURE 1

IVORY EXPORTS FROM DURBAN (1844-94)

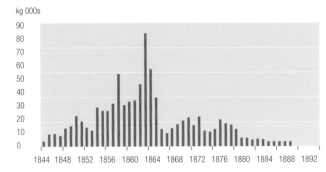

kg 000s

Buffalo

It was not just ivory that was exported out of Durban, as can be seen from the tables at the end of this chapter. In the nineteenth century, Durban increasingly usurped Lourenço Marques' position generally in the trade of wildlife products. By the 1890s it could be reported that there was only one surviving establishment buying animal skins at Delagoa Bay: 'cat, monkey, wildebeest, blesbok, springbok, buffalo, gnu, quagga, ox and cow' – and occasionally leopard and lion, 'which are exceedingly dear'. The latter comment is strange, for lion were plentiful in parts of Mozambique well into the twentieth century.[22] But as far as the hunters in Zululand were concerned, the second prize after elephant was not cat skins but buffalo.

In the early days of white hunting, the buffalo occurred in most parts of Zululand, certainly in the lower-lying eastern part. Herds were sometimes large, numbering over a hundred beasts. David Leslie recalled one sighting of buffalo: 'I never saw so many in one place; they were like cattle over the country. We stood on

WILDEBEEST AND BUFFALO HEADS In the 1850s great herds of buffalo and of blue wildebeest were to be found in Zululand. These species were hunted remorselessly, their skins fetching high prices.

WARD, *GREAT AND SMALL GAME OF AFRICA*, 1899

a high conical hill, and whichever way we looked we saw game.' Another time, near the Phongola River, Leslie took part in the massacre of a large number of a herd of buffalo he estimated to be 300 strong, which were driven into the river:

> the bellowing and madness of the game, the whole pond being in one whirl of constant motion – the buffaloes being bad hands at the water. You would see one old bull facing defiantly three or four enemies who were pegging away at him, up to their shoulders in water … at last, however, we stood upon a sandbank, thoroughly exhausted, and, because we really couldn't help it, allowed the remainder of the herd to go. They struggled up, one here, one there, completely blown; and in a quarter of an hour all was again silent on the river, and except for our trophies, there was nothing to indicate that there had so recently been 'a buffalo hunt in the water'.[23]

Buffalo were to be found in the thick bush, the savannah land and often in the thick reedbeds along rivers and in wetland areas. Their enemies were people and lion. Some hunters thought buffalo hunting gave the best sport. It had all the elements that appealed to the colonial huntsman: buffalo were powerful, determined and brave creatures. The males protected the herd, the bulls forming up in front to confront danger and often charging down on the hunter 'like a troop of cavalry'. William Drummond was probably correct when he said that more lives were lost annually from hunting buffalo than any other species, adding, 'but then for one man who especially goes after elephants, rhinoceros or other game, there are ten who make buffaloes their sole object'.

Buffalo horns were also sold as trophies, the largest from Zulu-land recorded in the nineteenth century being 39 in. (99 cm). And with buffalo hides fetching £1 each on the Durban market, a wagonload could bring in a respectable profit from a hunting trip.

We do not have a complete record of the export of buffalo hide, though from 1854 to 1876 some 18 139 buffalo hides valued at £13 075 were shipped out of Durban. These do not, of course, include hides used locally or those transported overland to the Cape. The destruction of buffalo in the 1840s and early 1850s must have been tremendous, averaging perhaps over a thousand animals killed per annum. Again in the late 1860s and early 1870s destruction was considerable when more powerful rifles began being used for hunting in Zululand. By then, however, the hunter had to travel much further north to find his prey, and where once herds of hundreds of buffalo had roamed, now only groups of ten could commonly be found, hiding in the thickest bush and in the reedbeds. Like the elephant, the buffalo for all its ferocity was a sensitive animal and, when persecuted, it retreated north to where people were fewer and less well-armed.[24]

By 1876 T.E. Buckley observed that the Cape buffalo was to be found only in Zululand, though 'even there it is getting very scarce'. A quarter of a century later, the 21-year-old son of an African chief in the Hlabisa district reported on the killing by two game conservators of a buffalo that had chased them beside the Pofana stream, a tributary of the Hluhluwe River. He commented, 'This is the first buffalo I have ever seen in our neighbourhood. It was not known by our kraal that the animal was at the Pofana.'[25]

Hippopotamus

The third most sought-after species of game by white hunters was the hippopotamus, or sea cow, as they were often called.[26] Hippo were also hunted by the local African population, who dug hippo traps with sharpened spikes embedded in the pit.[27] Hippo were widely distributed especially in the eastern lowlands along rivers, in wetlands and in lakes. In the 1830s large numbers were

FIGURE 2

EXPORT OF HIPPO HIDES FROM DURBAN (1862-72)

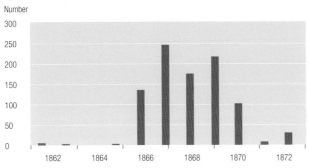

Because of the hippos' tendency to graze on crops and their aggression to humans, the local inhabitants were sometimes hostile to the beasts and, as will be seen later, in colonial Zululand British magistrates were constantly being asked for permission to shoot them. These requests were sometimes granted, but not always. Civil Commissioner Charles Saunders, commenting on a request from a chief in Lower Umfolozi, noted, 'I do not see what necessity there is for these people planting near the lakes … if they will plant where the Sea Cow can get at their gardens they must take the risk.'[33] On the other hand, the local African population might on occasion report the illegal killing of a hippo.[34]

The last of the famous hippo hunters was Frank Green, who for many years ran a trading store near to Ongoye forest. Even in the 1890s and into the new century Green would pay his £10 licence fee and set off annually to shoot a hippo, from which he made what were reputed to be excellent soap and sjamboks.[35]

There were four products that might be extracted from a slaughtered hippo. The meat was eaten by the hunters, as well as being fed to the party's pack of hunting dogs. The Boers were very partial to *zeekoespek*, or hippo bacon. Then the fat could be melted down and used for cooking, for candles and even as a form of moisturiser for the leathery skin of the hunters. Hippopotamus hide made excellent whips and full hippo hides were sometimes exported. The export statistics show that 892 hippo hides were shipped out of Durban between 1866 and 1870, the period when breech-loading rifles were becoming more common in Zululand.[36]

The most profitable element of hippo hunting, though, was the sale of hippo ivory. The largest hippo tusk recorded in Zululand was extracted from a beast shot at St Lucia by Charles Ellis. On the outside curve it measured 30 1/2 in. (77 cm) long and was 9 in. (23 cm) in circumference.[37] How much of this hippo ivory was shipped out of Durban is unclear. Between 1868 and 1875 this appears to have amounted to 28 238 lb (12 791 kg), which would have been considerably less than 20 years earlier when the hunting onslaught was at its peak.[38]

In the 1840s Delegorgue wrote, 'Without a doubt, it [the hippopotamus] is the first animal which is destined to become extinct because the resources with which nature has provided it are insufficient to protect it from man.'[39] His fears are understandable, yet he had not taken into consideration what a sanctuary their natural home in the great wetlands of Zululand would prove for the persecuted hippo. When measures were finally taken in the 1890s to protect the big game of Zululand, of all the royal game that was not buck, it was the hippo, albeit with drastically reduced numbers, that emerged best from the 60-year age of carnage. Neither Zulu impi nor British regiment, road builder nor refugee could invade their territory with ease.

concentrated along the Tugela, the Umhlathuze lagoon complex (Richards Bay) and in the greater St Lucia area. Hippo were also reported by William Baldwin on the Umhlathuze, Black Mfolozi, Matikulu, Nseleni, Mkuze (Mkhuze) and Phongola rivers.[28] And as with the other big game, Maputaland remained a refuge long after the bastions of southern Zululand had fallen to the hunter's gun, though in the 1890s anthrax was reported to have killed large numbers of hippo in northern Maputaland.[29]

The fact that hippo were concentrated in specific areas meant that hunters, white and black, knew where to come to kill them. Yet, the swamps and vleis in those areas were notoriously difficult to traverse. They were also very dangerous places. Here elephant could be found as well as crocodiles in vast numbers. And there was the ever-present disease-carrying mosquito. Small boats were occasionally used to hunt hippo, but these seem to date from only the 1850s onwards and were not commonly used. It was something of a Herculean task bringing an upturned boat to Zululand on top of a wagon.

The target, the hippo itself, was a fearsome adversary, killing any hunter who might come within reach. Moreover, the hippo hide and thick layer of fat below meant that the low-velocity shot used in the 1840s and 1850s was often ineffective. Regularly, when a beast was killed, a large number of shots were found embedded in the fat from previous hunters' attempts to kill it.[30]

Despite all these difficulties, the hippo population declined fast. As early as 1842 Adulphe Delegorgue estimated that on a three-league (13 km) stretch of the Tugela River, the 100 hippo he encountered were hardly a tenth of the number which had been there just three years earlier in 1839.[31] Ten years later, in the early 1850s, the hippo of southern and central Zululand were fleeing the hunters' guns and becoming reclusive, hardly surprising when one reads of the numbers of hippo killed.[32] John Dunn would boast of shooting 203 hippo in a season, 23 in one morning, 'before 10 o'clock'.

Rhinoceros

In the Zululand context many nineteenth-century hunters did not regard the rhinoceros as primary targets. William Baldwin stated quite bluntly in 1856, 'they do not pay to shoot'. Baldwin also thought the white rhino 'stupid things, and easy of approach, if met with alone, they generally keep near quaggas [zebra], wildebeests, or buffalo, who give them the alarm'. When rhino were hunted, the white was preferred over the black, which was considered more aggressive. But F.R.N. Findlay questioned the reputation of the black rhino as being 'fierce, irascible, and vindictive', claiming it gave chase because people ran away,

> To fly the boar before the boar pursues,
> Were to incense the boar to follow,
> And make pursuit where he did mean no chase.

William Drummond, though, who regarded the rhino as the most dangerous wild animal, was of the Baldwin school, believing that the black rhino was shot out of malice because of its 'evil disposition and vicious propensities' and that 'their cunning is only equalled by their viciousness'.[40]

This ferocity in attack earned the rhino respect. It was said that one animal had killed four African hunters before falling with a mass of spears in its side. Charles Barter paid tribute to the beast in 1897:

> The black rhinoster too, he'd face;
> Few steeds can beat his headlong pace
> When in straight course, with horns depress'd
> Like an arm'd knight, with lance in rest
> He dashes madly at his foes;
> None his dread onslaught may oppose.
> Firm as a rock Ketshwayo stands,
> His ready rifle in his hands,
> A shower of spears upon his ear
> Have turn'd the beast in mid career;
> A bullet lodges in his brain;
> The horns lie harmless on the plain.[41]

Occasionally references to rhino are even sympathetic – such as a wounded animal searching for its mate, a young calf defending the slain body of its mother, or a rhino charging into camp and stamping out the campfire with its feet.

Both species of rhino were to be found scattered across Zululand where suitable habitats existed. In the 1860s there were concentrations of black rhino in the valley of the Black Mfolozi, around St Lucia, in the thorn country lying between the Mkhuze River poort and the Mbuluzi, and in the Nhlophenkulu great flats. The white rhino was also at the Mfolozi junction as well as in the expanse of thorn country in the upper Mkhuze River. By 1903 black rhino were still to be found in the Lower Umfolozi,

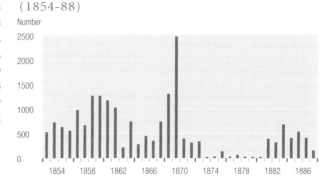

FIGURE 3

EXPORT OF RHINO HORN FROM DURBAN (1854–88)

Hlabisa, Ndwedwe and the Ubombo districts, but the white was restricted to the Umfolozi (Imfolozi) Game Reserve and its vicinity.[42] The extension of the reserve in 1907 was a laudable attempt to bring these outlying animals into the protective net. The existing black rhino in the present-day Hluhluwe and Mkhuze game reserves are original stock, as are the white rhino in Umfolozi and Hluhluwe.[43]

Rhino were also to be found to the north, though references are few. Vaughan-Kirby noted a white rhino and her calf existing in the Sabi–Crocodile area in 1895. In 1900 he commented, 'I have not heard of their being killed since.' Sadly, this last outpost of the white rhino was not to survive.[44]

Rhino meat was an acquired taste and rarely eaten by white hunters. Drummond, however, tells of one 'half-mad' hunter who did enjoy a rhino steak and would go to extremes to protect a rhino carcass from scavengers, including on one occasion even sleeping in the carcass.[45] Then as now, though, the rhino horn was both a valuable trophy and a source for ornamental knife handles.

The largest trophy horn of a Zululand black rhino up to the late 1890s was 41½ in. (105.41 cm), extracted from an animal shot by Lieutenant-Colonel the Honourable W. Coke. The white rhino record, also shot by Coke, was 31 in. (78.74 cm).[46] Between 1854 and 1888, 17 245 rhino horns, valued at £12 558, were exported out of Durban, many of which would have come from Zululand.

The rhino, like the hippo and the eland, did not retreat away from the hunter's rifle. As a result, already by the mid-1870s the white rhino was rare. In 1876 T.E. Buckley reported to the Zoological Society in London of the white rhino, 'Owing to incessant persecution these animals are now getting scarce, eight Rhinoceroses only having been seen by our party. At one time they must have been extremely common, judging from the number of skulls seen lying about.'[47]

Buck

Large antelope were most keenly sought after by the huntsmen with particular targets being wildebeest, eland, kudu and, when they could find them, nyala. Of the smaller buck, the duiker species, reedbuck, steenbuck, bushbuck, klipspringer and impala were readily shot, the last two being regarded by 1889 as rare.[48] There is a reference to a blesbok being shot in Zululand in 1863 by General Ellis.[49] Equally rare are references to the tiny suni. Though scientifically discovered in Mozambique in the 1840s by the extraordinary German naturalist Dr Wilhelm Peters, it is only from the late 1890s that references to the little buck are found.[50]

Hartebeest – 'one of the fastest antelopes in Africa, and possess[ing] such strength' – were common only on the grasslands to the north-west of Zululand. Of all the buck, the reedbuck species was most prized for its venison, making them a target for the pot-hunters. The plucky bushbuck was also frequently hunted for its meat – a taste shared by people and leopard alike – but bushbuck numbers seem to have held up better than those of reedbuck. By the time a degree of conservation was being imposed in the 1890s the reedbuck was so endangered in many parts of Zululand that it was not uncommon for a magistrate specifically to exclude reedbuck from hunting licences.

Kudu could be found in wooded, low-lying areas of Zululand, often in considerable numbers. They were especially plentiful in the thornveld to the west of the Lebombo Mountains. They were regarded as excellent sport and, as such, were consistently pursued. In 1876 T.E. Buckley noted:

> Here [Zululand] it [kudu] yet holds its ground in spite of the yearly persecution of the hunters, by who it is killed on account of the value of its skin, which is fine, but at the same time tough and durable ... the finest specimens come from the Zulu country, even animals killed near the Zambesi not having such fine horns; possibly this may be accounted for by the Zulu country possessing better pasturage.[51]

The kudu generally responded to this persecution by retreating north, though many remained in southern Zululand for quite some time. By the 1890s their bastions, however, were the watersheds of the Usuthu and Mkhuze rivers.[52]

Eland, the largest of the South African buck, occurred in Zululand in very large number, often on higher and more open ground. Sometimes herds well in excess of 100 animals were reported. Drummond claimed to have seen a herd of 150, including 30 calves. In 1852 Cato saw a herd of about 130 near the Umlalazi River.[53]

Eland had a reputation among hunters for nobility; it was said individual animals did not desert a herd member that had been shot. They also sometimes stood head-on to face their persecutors, only to be shot down. They were shot for their hides, which were said to be better even than those of buffalo. The flesh could be eaten and the horns, like those of the kudu, were prized as trophies. William Baldwin had an additional use for the eland:

> I had to return to camp seven or eight miles in a woeful plight, minus my hat, and my shirt torn to ribbons, exposed to a fearful hot sun, and my whole body blistered and sunburnt, giving me great pain, and my throat and tongue parched up for want of water. I was well greased with eland fat from head to foot, which was a great relief to me, but for several days I could rest in no position from the frightful extent of the sun-burns, than which I know nothing more painful, as every atom of skin peels off. I found my eland nearly eaten up, but I brought his horns back as a trophy.[54]

Considering their popularity as a target with hunters there are surprisingly few references to the blue wildebeest. William Baldwin, for instance, has only passing references to the animal that, with their ever-trusty companions, the zebra, was shot in great numbers. In January 1871 the *Natal Mercury* noted that 173 340 wildebeest and zebra skins 'have helped to swell our outward-bound cargoes during the year! What a vision of wholesale slaughter is thus presented.' These were not all, of course, from Zululand; some would have been brought from the interior.[55] In 1876 T.E. Buckley noted the presence of the blue wildebeest in Zululand but gave no details. They seem to have been fairly widespread, and today the specimens in Mkhuze and Hluhluwe are original populations.[56]

William Drummond clearly had a soft spot for the forlorn-looking wildebeest. He considered it the toughest of the wild game he had encountered but also recounted a terrible thunderstorm in Zululand when a group of wildebeest stood huddled together in a mass, 'their heads together and their sterns outwards'. He talked of wildebeest herds of up to a hundred animals, and speculated on an old bull that moved the herd on out of danger from his waiting guns – 'Could it have been that instinctive knowledge of something wrong which we call presentiment … or was he merely thirsty, and wanting to take the herd to water?' Drummond nevertheless did not hesitate to shoot the old bull.[57]

Drummond commented that waterbuck were 'extremely fine animals, and so plentiful that there are, perhaps, more of them shot than of any of the other large antelopes'. However, it was said that the flesh of the animal was 'coarse, poor, and tasteless'. They were plentiful along the Msunduzi and Phongola rivers and in the general region west of the Lebombo Mountains. Their range seems to have stretched to only just south of the Umfolozi area.

By the early twentieth century, however, waterbuck numbers had dwindled considerably. In 1907 Magistrate Fynney commented on an application to hunt in the Ubombo region, 'I think the application as regards water buck & reedbuck should be refused, these buck being very scarce still in this Division,' a recommendation supported by his superior, Charles Saunders.[58]

Nyala were unknown to science until well into the nineteenth century when George French Angas discovered the animal for science in 1847. He had not only come across the species just north of St Lucia but had also met up with a party of Boer hunters that had shot a specimen. They were, however, unwilling to part with the carcass or skin in the name of science.

Not surprisingly the nyala was prized for its beauty, but the pursuit of that beauty came at a price. As William Drummond observed: 'I should fancy that more people have caught fever by hunting this antelope than by the pursuit of any other animal in Africa, except perhaps, the elephant.'[59]

The nyala was found only in the lowland from St Lucia northward, partially protected because the thick bush where they lived was difficult to penetrate as well as being in the heart of malaria and nagana country. Nonetheless, the appeal of this attractive buck was such that in the 1890s even the great Selous came in search of it for specimens to send to the British Museum.

The nyala was particularly numerous in the bush near the confluence of the Usuthu and Phongola rivers near the present Ndumo Game Reserve. They could also be found around the Mkhuze poort, in the extensive woodland bordering Lake Sibaya and north of the Nyalazi River that flows into the southern end of False Bay. In 1892 the magistrate and trophy hunter A.H. Newmann claimed nyala to be 'fairly plentiful on the Mkuze River'.[60]

Selous recalled that the African population had told him that the nyala ram was very savage when wounded. Because they were excellent eating, the nyala was frequently snared by the local population and, as such, was a wary animal and often difficult to find.[61]

The carnivores

Big cats were generally not hunted for sport. Their fur was, however, a saleable product in Durban or Lourenço Marques, and various cat products were used in African society for regalia or for charms. In 1883, for example, the export of dressed cat skins and monkey skins out of Delagoa Bay numbered 17 713, and from Inhambane further north 4 430 skins. These were probably mostly the skins of the small cats, though lion and leopard were still numerous in northern Zululand, Maputaland and Mozambique at the time. References to cheetah in Zululand are not common.

References to cats in contemporary accounts generally relate to those species that hunters had shot. This means that many of the smaller species passed unmentioned in the various texts. Not surprisingly lion feature in some accounts, not so much because they were hunted but because of their strength and determination. Usually they were stumbled upon by accident rather than by design. One unknown hunter in Zululand in 1850 wrote in pencil in his notebook:

> And the Germans went out together after Elands, fancied they saw 2 coodos on the side of a hill & went after them … went up the hill & Mr B at right angle to intercept them as they ran down. He heard a roar in the Bush but did not like to call out for fear of frightening the Coodoo, shortly Mr Richard the German hailed him when he said (Thems not Coodoos them Beggars be lions). They however went towards them but they made off.

Lion were regarded as extremely dangerous and many an African homestead in Zululand had elaborate defences of thorns in an attempt to prevent lion entering the cattle kraal or the huts. African farmers would try clattering tin dishes to frighten off a lion attack. But such efforts did not always work and lion sometimes took dogs, goats and even humans, though Drummond said that lion rarely went out of its way to attack people. This is possibly true, as in Maputaland where cattle were fewer and lion more numerous, lion were less feared. Indeed, Baldwin observed of the Tsonga, 'the lions were their friends, and provided them constantly with flesh, and they would take no part in molesting them'.

Nor were the white hunters' camps immune from these night attacks. In September 1853 William Baldwin and his companion Lieutenant Clifton were attacked in camp by five lion which ignored warning shots, one 'brute striking me in the chest with his head'. On another occasion, on his way north to St Lucia, Baldwin saw a fine black-maned lion.

LION ATTACK AT NIGHT, 1853 The hunters' camp at night could be a dangerous place. Attack might come from several quarters with hyena and leopard being particularly troublesome. Rhino sometimes rushed into camp, stamping out the fire – but the most feared intruder were lion which wanted the oxen.
BALDWIN, *AFRICAN HUNTING*, 1863

Lion were particularly numerous from central Zululand northwards, though they were encountered also in the south, as indeed they were in Natal. Even the Durban Botanic Gardens had a visit from a roaring lion as late as July 1854. William Drummond recorded: 'The most likely places in the [Zululand] bush country in which to find lions, as far as my experience goes, are the ukaku thorns, the dense evergreens which line the rivers,

and during summer, the reeds on the margin of lagoons or streams, while in the open flats any patch of reeds or tall grass suffices to conceal them.'

Areas in Zululand specifically mentioned as abounding in lion were west of St Lucia and Maputaland. As late as March 1897, a colonial official commented in a letter: 'Mr Peniston is mistaken in thinking that lions and leopards can only be found in this particular reserve [Umfolozi] as these animals are numerous in the Ubombo District. Lions have been constantly seen in that district lately.'

The last two residential lion in the Umfolozi Game Reserve were shot by a poacher in 1915, yet for decades afterwards lion would occasionally visit the reserve, probably from the Maputaland thornveld.

The 'favourite dishes' for lion were, according to Drummond, first zebra; second, a fat rhino – though lion could not kill a mature and healthy rhino, they would travel immense distances to a rhino carcass – and third, a fat buffalo. Drummond added, 'soft succulent fat is what the lion probably considers most toothsome'.[62]

'Tiger' generally referred, and in some parts of Zululand even today still does refer, to leopards, which were found throughout Zululand. Baldwin's 1854 reference to a tiger-cat in a tree may, however, mean a wildcat or genet. Leopards were also occasionally referred to as panthers. William Drummond was sympathetic towards the leopard, saying that they were retiring and secretive, and did not attack humans unless provoked.

Drummond's friend David Leslie thought otherwise and gave an example of a leopard breaking into a hut one night, killing two people and wounding three others. Leopards were certainly the main culprits when it came to killing hunters' dogs. Leopards were sometimes shot because of this nuisance value as well as occasionally for their skins. But they were not easy to shoot as Robert Struthers discovered in 1853: 'Raining all day – we had a carcase lying at the landing place, and today a beautiful leopard made his appearance on it. But the house being visible, whenever one of us came outside he was off. Got a long shot at the Leopard today but missed him, he bounced off growling.'[63]

PREDATORS' HEADS Leopard, 'jungle cat', caracal, hyena, aardwolf and wild-dog heads. Of these, only the leopard was prized as a prime hunting trophy, the rest being regarded as nuisances or vermin.

WARD, *GREAT AND SMALL GAME OF AFRICA*, 1899

Reptiles

The only reptiles mentioned regularly in nineteenth-century writings on Zululand are crocodiles and snakes. Both were regarded as extremely dangerous.[64] In 1832 Andrew Smith noted that crocodile were abundant at the Tugela River, basking in the sun on the sandbanks in the middle of the river. Twenty years later Cato claimed to have seen a crocodile at Umhlathuze Bay that was between 25 and 30 ft (7.6 and 9.1 m) in length – 'He was much longer than the boat.' More realistic was Drummond's record of a female crocodile shot at the Phongola River which was 12 ft 9 in. (3.9 m) in length.[65]

There are cases of crocodile taking hunters' dogs – 'his favourite morsel' – and even oxen. People were not safe either, especially when there was flooding and rivers had to be crossed.[66] Crocodile were particularly plentiful around Lake St Lucia and the pans along the Phongola River. They were usually shot as a security measure or out of simple hatred. But sometimes they were also targeted because various parts were prized by African society, as well as for their fat – 'which burns brilliantly' – and their leather. In the 1860s crocodile skin was in demand in Natal, where it was used for women's boots, being soft and flexible and taking a high polish.[67]

The 'alligator menace' prompted the introduction of a bounty system in Natal, where 10s. might be picked up for the destruction of a crocodile. This noxious animal status was in force in Zululand by the 1890s, with the result that there was widespread killing of the reptile. One trade-store owner boasted killing 151 crocodiles in northern Maputaland in one month.[68]

Snakes feature less than one might expect in nineteenth-century accounts of Zululand. There are occasional comments, but nearly all refer to the danger snakes posed rather than to a scientific interest in them as species. In November 1842, for example, at the Umlalazi River Johan August Wahlberg 'trod on a snake, which bit at my shoe'. Twenty-two years later Baldwin recorded: 'Killed three snakes out of a rotten tree, all different kinds of tree-snakes. They all came out of the same hole, while I was cutting out two bullets.'

David Leslie remarked, 'At the black Umvelose I saw nothing but snakes.' Forty years later a report noted that 'Snakes are numerous, especially along the Lebombo [Mountains]'.

In the 1890s the trader Von Wissell had a handyman named George Thomas at his northern Maputaland store who made extra pocket money trapping snakes: 'by catching them round the neck with a sling attached to a short fishing rod, then grabbing them with a pair of tongs and removing the poison fangs, packing them in boxes and sending [them] away for export.'[69]

In 1907 the *Zululand Times* carried a letter from 'Snake catcher', someone who had been dealing in live snakes in Zululand for 25 years. He was keen to find an 'indhlondhlos' (*indlondlo*), which he had never seen. He listed, however, three places where the legendary serpent resided: near the Ulundi drift of the Mfolozi River; north of Umsundusi; and at the mouth of the Umhlathuze lagoon. By 1907 snakes, like the rest of Zululand's wildlife, were under sustained attack. There was even a bounty on them with the government offering from half a crown to 8s. 6d. per head for pythons, puff-adders and mambas.[70]

Giraffe

Some of the wildlife products exported out of Durban were clearly the product of trade with the interior. Giraffe were rare in Zululand, so the export of over 25 000 giraffe bones from Port Natal in the 20 years from 1858 to 1878 reflects trade with the highveld rather than being an indicator of the species' existence and exploitation in Zululand. Giraffe may have existed in Zululand at one time and were possibly one of the animal victims of King Shaka's expansionist Mfecane.

Tradition has it that giraffe were killed near the junction of the Black and White Mfolozi rivers in a great hunt organised by Shaka in August 1819.[71] The Zulu certainly had a name for the giraffe – *indlulamithi*. But none of the naturalists/hunter-writers such as Delegorgue, Wahlberg, Baldwin, Struthers or Drummond mention the giraffe as occurring in Zululand. Indeed, Captain Gardiner, writing of northern Zululand in the 1830s, observed: 'Wild animals abound, and, besides those common in this part of the country, they have the rhinoceros and tiger [leopard]: they appear to know nothing either of the ostrich or cameleopard [giraffe]. The eyland is the only large animal they hunt, being fearful to approach the elephant, although aware of the value of its tusks. Alligators [crocodiles] abound in the rivers …'[72]

If giraffe survived into the nineteenth century, it would probably have been in Maputaland. A British report into the region in February 1887 noted that 'Elephants and Giraffes are found'.[73] There is also a reference to three giraffe being sighted in northern Maputaland in the 1890s, but the location of the report has been challenged, with the suggestion that it was, in fact, Swaziland. But it is possibly accurately placed as the upper Maputa River area, for no other reason than that the memoir is almost entirely based in northern Maputaland and because of the fact that the sighting of the giraffe was regarded by the writer, a local storekeeper, as a great curiosity.[74]

Jackal, hyena and wild dog

Though less likely to threaten people, jackal, hyena and wild dog were still regarded as both a menace and a pest. Few comments survive on the two species of jackal, the side-striped and the black-backed. Of the former, Drummond remarked, 'They are

GIRAFFE HEADS Giraffe existed in the wild in Zululand as late as the 1890s, but they were never common and references to them in contemporary accounts are rare.

WARD, *GREAT AND SMALL GAME OF AFRICA*, 1899

pretty little creatures whose only use to the hunter is to indicate the proximity of lions.'[75] There is more on the hyena, or 'wolf', Drummond going into some detail on the spotted hyena, not having encountered the brown hyena. The spotted hyena has great powers of scent and hearing, he said, and immense strength – 'there is no animal so universally hated, or that causes more trouble and annoyance'. Drummond also observed that old hunters declared the numbers of hyena to have increased greatly in the hunting districts of Zululand – 'there is every reason to think that they find man a better purveyor than the lion, and increase accordingly'.[76] When Baldwin crossed the battlefield of Ndondakusuka in 1856, he commented that 'A vast horde of hyena and jackals were engaged in cleaning up the debris'.

The hyena had a reputation for stealing and eating nearly anything it could scavenge. This included Wahlberg's halter and harness. The animals staked the hunter's camp at night, fighting with the hunter's dogs and causing great annoyance. Frequently hyena were killed just because of the nuisance they created.[77]

Before the 1890s there are relatively few references to wild dog. They were certainly in Zululand and a few were shot for their beautiful skins. Of the wild dog Drummond comments, 'It is a marvellous sight to see a pack of them hunting.'

The wild dog moved far and wide. Just after the colonial era Vaughan-Kirby observed, 'these animals are the most pronounced wanderers of all the mammal fauna of Zululand, never remaining more than two or three days at a time in one locality'.

Despite Drummond's admiration, as the nineteenth century drew to its close the early game conservators of the 1890s regarded wild dog as the principal vermin they had to confront. One colonial official was clearly disturbed when he wrote in 1896, 'In the Umfolozi valley our camp was one day surprised by wild dogs.' By 1901 there was a bounty of £1 on the head of every wild dog shot in Zululand. Their days were numbered.[78]

Other victims

There were a few other victims of the hunters' gun and spear. The innocuous zebra, often referred to as quagga, was fairly widespread, especially in northern Zululand. But they were shot in large numbers for their attractive skins, which were then exported. Those zebra in the present-day Hluhluwe–Imfolozi Park are original stock.[79]

The zebra's flesh was also regarded as a delicacy by the local African population, though T.E. Buckley was not attracted by the smell of the dark meat or by the yellow fat.[80] Lion also preyed on the zebra. Catherine Barter was touched by the sight of a herd of zebra in an expanse of thornveld:

To the extreme right was the grey wood, skirting the sea; and nearer to us, in a deep fertile valley, were herds of game of various kinds, and troops of quaggas.

These were in numbers, and on scrutinizing them carefully with the glass, I could see them frisking and galloping about, and the little foals running up to their mothers and playing with them.[81]

It is not always clear when writers refer to wild boar or wild pig if they are speaking of the bushpig or the warthog. Both were common in Zululand and both were hunted for their meat. According to Drummond, the warthog (indhlovudwane) was not met with south of the 29 °S latitude (about Umlalazi) and was not plentiful before the 30° latitude (about St Lucia). He warned about the ferocity of the warthog, describing one specimen as the size of a rhino calf that killed his dog Leauw ('lion') and wounded Drummond in the leg. He also commented on the warthog's technique of retreating down a burrow: 'A fair proportion used to escape into the innumerable hyena, ant-eater, and porcupine holes, and though I sent for a couple of spades from the wagon, I seldom succeeded in getting them out.'[82]

Monkey were hunted for their skins, which were used especially by African hunters as a trading commodity. The Lebombo Mountains were famous for both the samango monkey and for baboon, the latter, according to Findlay, 'attain[ing] a tremendous size'. The baboon features more than monkeys in hunters' accounts as they could be very dangerous and were treated with caution.[83] The skin of the ant-bear was also of value, being said to be superior to the best pigskin.

Sea animals received even less attention from the writers of hunters' diaries and British government reports. But in 1889 Dr G.D. Trevor-Roper noted of the Sodwana Bay coast: 'Turtle in some numbers are found on the shore, as also a few edible oysters; fish are plentiful. The rock-cod and red *Holocentrum ruber* (Swainson) [*Holocentrus rubrum*] are the most common.'

In the 1860s and 1870s David Leslie found that those African people who lived by the lakes caught plenty of fish. A War Office report dated 1905 remarked on the '"fish kraals", basket-work fences stretching across the bay [Kosi Bay], in which the fish are left by the receding tide'. Hunters also ate fish, usually barbel, when they could catch them. Baldwin has an interesting reference to the area just north of the Tugela River mouth when he was there in April 1854: 'Hunted the strand bush unsuccessfully, bathed in the sea, but had to beware of the ground sharks. Played whist until a late hour, finished the grog, and wound up by a soaking wet night (from the heavens, I mean).'[84]

TABLE 2[85]

WILDLIFE PRODUCT EXPORTS FROM DURBAN, 1844–1904 (I)

DATE	IVORY (KG)	SKINS (NO.)	KAROSS (PACKETS)	SPECIMENS OF NATURAL HISTORY (PACKETS)	DATE	IVORY (KG)	SKINS (NO.)	KAROSS (PACKETS)	SPECIMENS OF NATURAL HISTORY (PACKETS)
1844	3 947	160		(£1 036)	1875	10 856	194 443		39
1845	8 885	187		(£16)	1876	13 159	109 782	24	33
1846	9 543	439		(£40)	1877	19 576	56 852	38	33
1847	8 402	61		(£44)	1878	16 860	43 156	1	25
1848	13 311	41			1879	15 504	22 550		14
1849	14 972			(£24)	1880	13 107	7 623		15
1850	22 464			(£60)	1881	6 340	9 367	2	41
1851	18 576			(£240)	1882	6 669	8 144	4	19
1852	14 320			(£372)	1883	5 341	7 378	17	12
1853	11 655			(£328)	1884	5 529	10 278	250	25
1854	29 151	95		(£102)	1885	5 353	8 726	101	18
1855	26 490	20		(£426)	1886	3 562	409	33	53
1856	26 446	42		(£25)	1887	1 752	396	40	22
1857	31 466	485		61	1888	2 521	447	8	24
1858	53 419	371		42	1889	50			19
1859	30 534	138		88	1890	114	20	1	8
1860	33 457	81		31	1891	61	44	1	6
1861	34 297	25		32	1892-3	14	26		5
1862	45 861	46		27	1893-4	43	20	1	4
1863	83 088	60		34	1894-5	1 075			13
1864	57 147	39	1	36	1896		72		22
1865	36 045	1 591	6	51	1897	(£79)		1	19
1866	13 047	2 076	7	34	1898				5
1867	9 815	1 879	3	22	1899		3		5
1868	13 479	197	1	21	1900	0.5	3		3
1869	16 330	53 924	7	51	1901		3		52
1870	18 980	174 340	2	28	1902		6		8
1871	21 280	314 446	2	55	1903		(£126)		
1872	15 721	417 014	3	31	1904		(£99)		(£522)
1873	22 184	345 009	1	16					
1874	11 693	222 728		54	**Totals**	**883 491**	**2 015 246**	**555**	**1 256**

TABLE 3

WILDLIFE PRODUCT EXPORTS FROM DURBAN 1844–1904 (II)

DATE	WILD ANIMALS (NO.)	GIRAFFE BONES (NO.)	BUFFALO HIDES (NO.)	HIPPO HIDES (NO.)	BUCK HORNS (NO.)	RHINO HORNS (NO.)	DATE	WILD ANIMALS (NO.)	GIRAFFE BONES (NO.)	BUFFALO HIDES (NO.)	HIPPO HIDES (NO.)	BUCK HORNS (NO.)	RHINO HORNS (NO.)
1844			717				1875	3	5 377	4 444		16	(8 kg)
1845			996				1876	4	218	1 299		175	15
1846			1 615				1877	304	700			19	116
1847			669				1878		900			34	9
1848	1		18				1879	3				6	42
1849							1880					100	13
1850							1881	1					11
1851							1882					2	376
1852					(£734)		1883						303
1853							1884	1	(1 829 kg)			95	679
1854	9		163			536	1885	3				56	402
1855	14		134			712	1886	5				279	519
1856	4		250			623	1887	3				4	395
1857	27		616			544	1888	248				5	133
1858	6	3 057	671			982	1889						
1859	5	(711 kg)	91		2	642	1890						
1860	11	(711 kg)	n/a			1 267	1891	1				54	
1861	4	(324 kg)	70			1 263	1892–3					28	
1862	32		27	8		1 161	1893–4					33	
1863	8	(178 kg)	73	8	124	1 019	1894–5	1				14	
1864	12		n/a			201	1896					113	
1865	11		671	7	5	735	1897					1	
1866	25	133	172	138	54	282	1898	1				42	
1867	40	59	468	251	14	433	1899					18	
1868	1 620	686	584	178	108	348	1900					3	
1869	217	1 451	935	221	62	727	1901					16	
1870	25	3 727	1 098	104	36	1 289	1902					8	
1871	19	6 653	1 206	9	84	2 470	1903					25	
1872	8	2 254	760	32	28	371	1904					(£241)	
1873	7	413	1 154		73	310	**Totals**	**2 683**	**25 753**	**22 154**	**956**	**1 739**	**19 245**
1874		125	3 253		3	317							

REFERENCES

1 Barter, *Stray memories*, p. 45.

2 Letter written by Friend Addison, quoted in *Delimitations commission*, 1905, p. 276.

3 Samuelson, *Long, long ago*, pp. 10–11.

4 KZNA, Morewood papers, A 1273, anonymous diary, 4 December 1850.

5 KZNA, 1/UBO, 3/1/1, fortnightly report, 165/1891, 15 June 1891.

6 Gardiner, *Journey to the Zoolu country*, p. 110.

7 On African uses for ivory, see Papini, 'Some Zulu uses for the animal domains', p.185; and Van Jaarsveld, *Mtunzini*, p. 28.

8 See for example, Baldwin, *African hunting*, pp. 33, 54, 57, 69; *Report of the Zululand boundary commission*, 1880, D4; and KZNA, ZA 19, 1880.

9 T.E. Buckley, 'The geographical distribution of South African mammals', *Proceedings of the Zoological Society of London*, 1876, p. 280.

10 See for example, Hackel and Carruthers, 'Swaziland', p. 8; Hedge, 'Trade and politics in southern Mozambique and Zululand', p. 54; KZNA, ZA 43, letterbook 1890–1891, April 1891, fol. 201; and *Swaziland, Tongaland and northern Zululand*, War Office, p. 73.

11 *Natal Independent*, 15 December 1853.

12 *Natal Mercury*, 8 November 1854. See also *Natal Independent*, 16 February 1854; *Natal Mercury*, 18 October 1854; *Natal Times*, 14 November 1851; and *Natal Witness*, 22 November 1850, 21 November 1851 and 10 December 1858.

13 Drummond, *The large game*, p. 181; and Killie Campbell Collections, Cowie to Cato, 30 July 1853.

14 Drummond, *The large game*, pp. 213–14. See also Buckley, 'Geographical distribution of large mammals of South Africa', p. 280.

15 Quoted in Bryant, *The Zulu people*, p. 364.

16 Killie Campbell Collections, Miller papers, Von Wissell, 'Reminiscences', fols. 36–37.

17 KZNA, SGO, III/1/2, Cowie to Moodie, 26 July 1848; and ZGH 695, minute paper, 2154/1885, 16 December 1885.

18 Harrison, *Matubatuba*, p. 93; and Ward, *Records of big game*, p. 290.

19 National Archives, London, ADM 1/22269, Captain Owen's account.

20 For information on the volume of ivory shipped out of Delagoa Bay see Arquivo Histórico Ultramarino, Lisbon, India Maço, 137, Processo da Feitoria Austriaca, fols. 61, 92, 109, 125; Hedges, 'Trade and politics in southern Mozambique and Zululand', p. 129; SAAC, CO 3941, fols. 445–47; *Natal Witness*, 10 May 1850; and Pridmore, 'The impact of the European traders on Port Natal 1824–1834', pp. 4–6. See also Smith, 'The trade of Delagoa Bay in Nguni politics, 1750–1835', pp. 173–89.

21 *De Natalier*, 7 July 1846; *Natal Mercury*, 25 June 1857; *Natal Times* 12 March 1852; and Natal *Witness*, 26 June 1846, 17 December 1847 and 15 March 1850.

22 Monteiro, *Delagoa Bay*, p. 156.

23 Leslie, *Among the Zulus and Amatongas*, pp. 12, 22, 138–41. A few years earlier Baldwin had also seen a herd of 300 in the same area. For Baldwin's comments on buffalo, see *African hunting*, pp. 35–6, 40, 43–5, 53, 60, 66, 88, 104, 108–9, 120, 122–3, 128, 139.

24 Drummond, *The large game*, pp. 28, 50, 66, 110, 163, 362.

25 Buckley, 'Geographical distribution of large mammals of South Africa', p. 289; and KZNA, 1/MTB, 3/2/2, statement, 20 February 1903.

26 See *Natal Mercury*, 22 December 1863.

27 Du Plessey, 'Past and present geographical distribution', p. 302; and Isaacs, *Travels and adventures in eastern Africa*, 2, p. 261; and Webb (ed.), *Adulphe Delegorgue's Travels*, p. 159.

28 Du Plessey, 'Past and present geographical distribution', p. 67.

29 Killie Campbell Collections, Miller papers, Von Wissell 'Reminiscences', fol. 76.

30 Killie Campbell Collections, Captain Garden papers, Cato's trip, 1852, 'Mnhlatuzi', 2 August 1852; and *Zululand Times*, 2 August 1907.

31 Webb (ed.), Adulphe *Delegorgue's Travels*, p. 156.

32 See Baldwin, *African hunting*, pp. 57, 83. See also other Baldwin references to hippo, pp.19, 57, 65, 69, 84, 88–9, 109–11, 119, 121.

33 KZNA, 1/EPI, minute paper, R 2075/1901, 2 December 1901.

34 A few of the many requests to kill hippo are: KZNA, 1/EPI, letter book, 27 July 1887, fol. 4, 26 September 1887, fol. 45, and minute paper, R 2485/1893, 7 November 1893; 1/UBO, minute paper no. 41, monthly report of resident commissioner, fol. 5; and ZGH 769, minute paper, R 1512/1896, 14 April 1896.

35 KZNA, 1/EPI, minute papers, LU 116/1895, 8 April 1895 & LU 153/99, April 1899; *Natal Witness*, 14 August 1899; *Zululand Times*, 2 August 1907; and Van Jaarsveld, *Mtunzini*, p. 9.

36 Findlay, *Big game shooting*, p. 226; and Gardiner, *The Zoolu country*, p. 85.

37 Ward, *Records of big game*, p.300.

38 Stuart and Malcolm (eds.), *Diary of Henry Francis Fynn*, p. 42.

39 Webb (ed.), *Adulphe Delegorgue's Travels*, p. 156.

40 Baldwin, *African hunting*, pp. 105–107, 109, 125, 127–9, 218; Drummond, *The large game*, pp. 97, 111, 120–1, 128; and Findlay, *Big game shooting*, pp. 190–1.

41 Barter, 'Stray memories', pp. 46–7.

42 Findlay, *Big game shooting*, p.188.

43 Du Plessis, 'Past and present geographical distribution', pp.10–11, 20–1; and Rowe-Rowe, *The ungulates of Natal*, pp. 2–4.

44 Natural History Museum, London, Vaughan-Kirby, 'Report upon the Sabi-Krockodile District Division of Leydenburg, Transvaal as a Game Reserve, 1900', DF 232/6, fol. 240.

45 Drummond, *The large game*, p. 282.

46 Ward, *Records of big game*, pp. 285, 289–90. See also KZNA, ZGH 759, minute paper, Z 684/1894.

47 Buckley, 'Geographical distribution of large mammals of South Africa', p. 280. It is uncertain whether Buckley is talking about Zululand or Zimbabwe, but either way his comment holds true.

48 KZNA, ZA 42, no. 32. For these buck see Baldwin, *African hunting*, pp. 52, 65, 79, 108, 14–15, 125–7, 131; Buckley, 'Geographical distribution of South African mammals', pp. 283–5; Drummond, *The large game*, pp. 325, 330, 351, 379, 386–90, 392, 396–8; Du Plessis, 'Past and present geographical distribution', pp. 84, 88, 91, 99, 107, 112, 117, 120–8, 133, 139, 157, 198, 219, 226, 246; and Findlay, *Big game shooting*, p. 201.

49 Ward, *Records*, p. 84.

50 Du Plessis, 'Past and present geographical distribution', p. 117.

51 Buckley, 'Geographical distribution of large mammals of South Africa', p. 284.

52 KZNA, ZA 27, report, 1896; and ZA 46, diary, 13 August 1895. See also, Baldwin, *African hunting*, pp. 32, 39, 40, 42, 53–6, 60–3, 66, 108, 117, 128–9, 131, Drummond, *The large game*, pp. 341, 342–4, 346; and Du Plessis, 'Past and present geographical distribution', p. 269.

53 Drummond, *The large game*, pp. 146–7; and Killie Campbell Collections, Cato papers, 17 October 1852.

54 Baldwin, *African hunting*, p. 44.

55 Baldwin, *African hunting*, pp. 42, 128; and *Natal Mercury*, 12 January 1871.

56 Buckley, 'Geographical distribution of large mammals of South Africa', p. 287; and Rowe-Rowe, *The ungulates of Natal*, p. 9.

57 Drummond, *The large game*, pp. 341, 361, 363–6.

58 Baldwin, *African hunting*, pp. 120–1; Buckley, 'Geographical distribution of large mammals of South Africa', p. 284; Drummond, *The large game*, pp.237, 341–2, 367–9; Du Plessis, 'Past and present geographical distribution', p. 145; Findlay, *Big game shooting*, p. 203; Rowe-Rowe, *The ungulates of Natal*, p. 27; and KZNA, 1/UBO, minute paper, June 1907.

59 Drummond, *The large game*, pp. 378–9.

60 Baldwin, *African hunting*, pp. 77, 92, 117, 120; Buckley, 'Geographical distribution of large mammals of South Africa', p. 285; Du Plessis, 'Past and present geographical distribution', pp. 254–5; Findlay, *Big game shooting*, pp. 206–7, KZNA, 1/UBO, minute paper, UB 48/1892; and KZNA, ZA 27, report, 1896, fol. 23.

61 Killie Campbell Collections, Miller papers, Von Wissell 'Reminiscences', fols. 21–2; and Ward, *Great and small game of Africa*, pp. 455–60.

62 Drummond, *The large game*, pp. 15, 46–8, 55, 102 and Chapter 5. On lion, see also Baldwin, *African hunting*, pp. 20, 32, 48, 78, 115, 118–19, 126, 132; (Barter), *Alone among the Zulu*, p. 101, 114; Killie Campbell Collections, Durban, Miller papers, Von Wissell 'Reminiscences', fol. 71; KZNA, Morewood papers, A 1273, anonymous diary, 5 November 1850; ZA 46, diary, 17 August 1895; ZGH 789, Ingwavuma report, 29

September 1895; and ZGH 835, no. 25, Peachey to Green, 30 March 1897; Struthers, *Hunting Journal*, p. 26; Vincent, 'Umfolozi', pp. 8, 36; and Vincent, *Web of experience*, p. 91.

63 Struthers, *Hunting journal*, p. 34. See also, Baldwin, *African hunting*, pp. 34, 62; Craig and Hummel (eds.), *Wahlberg*, p. 93; Drummond, *The large game*, pp. 289, 298, 300–2, 305; Gardener, *The Zoolu country*, p. 123; Leslie, *Among the Zulu and Amatongas*, pp. 26, 30; Rowe-Rowe, *The carnivores of Natal*, pp. 19–20; and KZNA, 1/EPI, Lower Umfolozi letter book, report for August 1900.

64 Baldwin, *African hunting*, pp. 9–13, 100–1, 130; and Brooks, *Natal*, p. 126.

65 Kirby (ed.), *Andrew Smith and Natal*, p. 45; Killie Campbell Collections, Cato papers, 1852; and Drummond, *The large game*, p. 239.

66 Gardiner, *The Zoolu country*, p. 372.

67 *Natal Herald*, 2 July 1868.

68 *Natal Herald*, 23 April and 16 July 1868; and Killie Campbell Collections, Durban, Miller papers, Von Wissell 'Reminiscences', fols. 19–20.

69 Baldwin, *African hunting*, pp. 69, 99, 110, 120; Bryant, *The Zulu people*, pp. 353–63; Craig and Hummel (eds.), *Wahlberg*, p. 95; Killie Campbell Collections, Miller papers, Von Wissell 'Reminiscences', fols. 70–71; Leslie, *Among the Zulus and Amatongas*, pp. 27–28; Stuart & Malcolm (eds.), *The diary of Henry Francis Fynn*, pp. 310–11; and *Swaziland, Tongaland and northern Zululand*, War Office, p. 9.

70 *Zululand Times*, 11 January and 8 November 1907.

71 Du Plessis, 'Past and present geographical distribution', pp. 75–6.

72 Gardiner, *Journey to the Zoolu country*, p. 167.

73 KZNA, ZGH 704, Report on Tongaland, 7 February 1887, fol. 3.

74 Killie Campbell Collections, Durban, Miller papers, Von Wissell 'Reminiscences', fol. 71; and P.S. Goodman and A.J. Tomkinson, 'The past distribution of giraffe in Zululand and its implications for reserve management', pp. 28–32.

75 Drummond, *The large game*, pp. 315–16.

76 Drummond, *The large game*, pp. 306–8, 311.

77 Baldwin, *African hunting*, pp. 46–7, 62, 116, 118–21, 125, 127; and Craig and Hummel (eds.), *Wahlberg*, p. 89.

78 Baldwin, *African hunting*, p. 120; Bryant, *The Zulu people*, pp. 350–3; Craig and Hummel (eds.), *Wahlberg*, p. 31; Drummond, *The large game*, pp. 311–12; Findlay, *Big game shooting*, p. 203; KZNA, ZA 27, 1896 report, fol. 23; KZNA, 1/EPI, letter book, 1896, fols. 703–4 and 1900, fol. 38, 1/MEL, minute paper, R 1626/1903, 1/MTB, minute paper, H 343/1901, & 1/MTU, minute paper, R 2177/1901; and Vaughan-Kirby, 'Game and game preservation in Zululand', pp. 385–7.

79 Drummond, *The large game*, pp. 281–2, 367; and Rowe-Rowe, *The ungulates of Natal*, pp. 4–5.

80 Buckley, 'Geographical distribution of South African mammals', p. 282.

81 (Barter), *Alone among the Zulu*, p. 140.

82 Drummond, *The large game*, pp. 105, 335–7. See also Baldwin, *African hunting*, pp. 45, 53, 61, 128.

83 Baldwin, *African hunting*, pp. 52, 128; Bryant, *The Zulu people*, pp. 363–4; Drummond, *The large game*, pp. 338, 389–90; Findlay, *Big game shooting*, p. 232; Leslie, *Among the Zulus and Amatongas*, p. 21; KZNA, 1/UBO, minute paper, R 2459/1902; and KZNA, ZA 27, 1896 report, fol. 23.

84 Baldwin, *African hunting*, pp. 19, 62; Drummond, *The large game*, p. 317; Leslie, *Among the Zulu and Amatongas*, p. 258; and *Swaziland, Tongaland and northern Zululand*, War Office, p. 99.

85 Statistical information for the two tables of exports from Durban compiled from the following sources:
For the year 1844: *The Cape of Good Hope Almanac and Annual Register for 1846*, p. 136.
For the year 1845: *Natal Witness*, 10 April 1846.
For the years 1846 to 1848: *Natal Witness*, 2 February 1849.
For the year 1849: *Natal Witness*, 15 March 1850.
For the years 1850, 1852, 1854 to 1859 and 1861: KZNA, NAC 7/1/1-9.
For the 1851: *Natal Mercury*, 30 January 1852 and *Natal Witness*, 30 January 1852.
For the year 1853: *Natal Government Gazette*, 1 August 1854.
For the year 1860: *Natal Government Gazette*, 15 January 1861.
For the year 1861 et seq: *Natal Blue Books*.

Statistics for the period prior to 1845 have not come to light. One source states that in the period 1830 to 1835, 40 000 lb (18 120 kg) of ivory were shipped from Port Natal to the Cape. See Leverton (ed.), *Records of Natal, volume three, August 1835–June 1838*, p. 21.

MOUTH OF THE UMVOTI As this illustration shows, in the 1840s the road to Zululand along the Natal north coast could be as much an adventure as being in Zululand itself. Lion, leopard and elephant could all be found on the week-long wagon trail to the Tugela River. ANGAS, *KAFIRS ILLUSTRATED*, 1847

CHAPTER 2

The forests

NKANDLA FOREST IN THE 1880S One of the great mist-belt forests of Zululand, Nkandla was both a source of wood and fuel for black and white people, and also a place of refuge for Africans in times of crisis.

It was not just animals that were under threat in nineteenth-century Zululand. The region, like Natal, had tracts of indigenous forest: high mist-belt forest and 'stunted, gnarled and crooked' coastal forest. There was, however, one major difference between the forests of the two regions by the time the British conquered Zululand in 1879: timber from Natal's forests had been commercially exported for a generation. Large areas of Natal's indigenous forests had either been sold off as 'timber farms' or been included in areas allocated as African locations and left to their fate in increasingly overcrowded reserves. In 1904, when white settlement came to Zululand, most of the forestland remained Crown land, though not all. In 1922, commenting on some forest at Nsingabantu, about 6 km north-east of Qhudeni, a forester noted, 'It is surprising how these forests with their surviving glades could ever have passed out of the hands of the crown.'[1]

This is not to say that the Zululand forests had not seen white sawyers in them, especially those on the periphery of the territory. There was also forest exploitation by the indigenous population. But despite all this, the forests of Zululand were in 1880 generally in a better condition than those south of the Tugela.[2] The principal forests of Zululand are listed in Table 4.[3]

TABLE 4

PRINCIPAL FORESTS OF NINETEENTH-CENTURY ZULULAND

FOREST NAME	CONTEMPORARY ESTIMATES OF FOREST SIZE
Qhudeni	1 800–2 700 ha 1891: [seven portions of forest] 'These forests are certainly the finest in Zululand.'
Nkandla	1 700–2 800 ha 1891: 'I do not think they possess so much yellowwood [as Qhudeni] nor that the timber is so fine, but they are in a sense virgin; they have not suffered at all from the spoilers in the shape of sawyers, but licensed pole-cutting has been going on to some extent.' 1898: '8 or 10 miles by 4 or 5 miles wide & more compact than Qudeni.'
Entumeni	564 ha 1891: 'The timber in these forests is inferior to that of the Qudeni and Nkandla ... there is only a moderate supply of white pear, stinkwood and Umbaba [*Bowkeria verticillata*], but milk-wood, saffron-wood (Umbomoane), red-currant (Umhlakoti), and white ivory are plentiful.'
Dhlinza	200 ha 1891: 'These [Eshowe forests] are not very extensive ... [mainly white ironwood, wild plum and coast silver oak (maduli)]. Great havoc has been made of many of these woods [by the British army].'
Ongoye	800–1 000 ha 1891: 'What has saved the forest from spoliation by sawyers is its inaccessibility ... this forest is very rich in timber. Umsimbite [umzimbeet] abounds; it furnishes, I am told, blocks 4 feet in diameter and 20 feet in length [1.2 x 6 m]. Bastard or Outeniqua yellow-wood is plentiful, but very little of the real or upright kind, and milk-wood, white pear, and sneeze-wood are to be found.' 1904: 'Full of hard wood, which is valuable.' 1914: 'The general impression left ... is one [forest] from which much timber has been removed.'
Useme Hill	Small
Mpembeni Hill	–
Nhlatu Hill	–
Eome Hills	'The timber grows to a good height.'
Ezibayeni Hill	–
Nkwankwa Hill	Small
Ceza Hill	400 ha 1891: 'Composed of the usual high timber forest trees, but they are said to be of small size.'
Ngome	3 300 ha [NB: From 1884 to 1903 Ngome forest was politically not part of Zululand]
'Nbonauiti', Lower Umfolozi	1893: 'A fine group of between two and three hundred large yellowwood timber trees.'
Dukuduku	2 000–3 500 ha [7 300 ha of woodland, 2 000 ha of grassland and 450 ha of swamp] 1911: 'very badly cut into' – 'waterwood forest with some red els and knobwood.'
Hlathikhulu	800–1 200 ha
Manguzi	500 ha

Of the coastal forests, the Lower Umfolozi magistrate wrote in 1891:

> The range of Sand Hills near the sea both North & South of the Umfolozi River mouth are almost entirely clothed with coastal forest. In these forests there are various kinds of trees some of which are large & high. The Idukuduke [Dukuduku forest] which is on the North of the Umfolozi River & some miles in extent is also a coast forest, & there are similar patches of forest between the Mbater stream & the sea.

In this area was the low-lying Manjo forest, 2 miles long by ½ mile wide (3.2 km by 800 m), in which were 'some splendid yellowwood trees'. In 1898 Maphelana forest, which stretched for 6 miles (9.6 km) along the right bank of the Mfolozi River, contained 'large quantities of wood used in wagon making'.[4]

'THE HAUNT OF BUFFALO', 1860s A good impression is conveyed in this drawing of the thick thornbush that existed in many parts of Zululand and where buffalo, black rhino and other large and dangerous beasts lurked. It was a brave hunter who entered this domain at all – and a foolish one who did so after dark.   BATES, *ILLUSTRATED TRAVELS*

Information on Dukuduku forest was particularly scanty even well into the second decade of the twentieth century. Difficult to approach, regarded as unhealthy and full of wild beasts, Dukuduku was protected by its bad reputation.

As well as these larger forests there were more isolated areas of forestland, especially in kloofs and along river banks. In the 1890s the banks of the Phongola and Usuthu rivers were said to be well timbered. At the coast, in the estuarine lakes, were mangroves, those at Sodwana Bay were in 1889 said to be 'exceedingly tall'. Kosi Bay had 'densely wooded shores'. In 1848 William Cowie described Lake St Lucia as 'an immense Body of water surrounded for the most part with bush (large timber), it receives the waters of five rivers'.[5] The area to the west of False Bay appears to have been particularly heavily wooded.

In his report on Maputaland in 1896, Bosman observed: 'From the foot of the Ubombo Mountains to the coast the country is one vast sandy plain thickly wooded chiefly with soft timber and mimosa thorns.' The two largest forests in Maputaland were the low-lying Manguzi forest, where Cuthbert Foxon established himself in 1896 when appointed British Resident for the new Tongaland Protectorate, and Hlathikhulu, on the eastern slopes of the Lebombo Mountains north of the Phongola Poort. Hlathikhulu was a large forest, stretching north for some 20 km and about 4 km in width. It was at the edge of this forest that King Dingane was buried.

It is possible that Hlathikhulu was the forest in which Robert Plant found a superb collection of orchids on his fateful expedition in 1857. Fifty years later a military officer noted that 'The wood itself is almost impenetrable owing to the tangle of thorny creepers interlacing the trunks of the trees. There are numerous springs in the interior and deep kloofs and ravines.'[6]

In addition there were vast areas of thornveld. In Lower Umfolozi in 1891 it was said that 'The Thorn bush extends through the whole district & I do not recommend its preservation. It is spreading & soon grows up where it has been cleared for cultivation.'[7] Catherine Barter's account of her adventure in Zululand in 1855 mentions the lion-infested thornveld as well as the wooded country north of the Umfolozi River: 'The plain, too, is full of mimosa thorn, the branches of which will need to be lopped away as you go, to allow space for a wagon to pass. Beyond the river and the plain you will come to a wood; a day's journey through that wood will bring you to the kraal.'[8]

An interesting description of the wooded nature of the Makhathini Flats, still the haunt of elephant, was penned by the local magistrate in February 1896:

> over flat country among scattered lala trees we went along a large open grassy place between two belts of forest, the forest and bush occasionally closing in and again widening out on

THE FORESTS

park side, then through some fairly thick bush with lala trees and tall palms to an open bit of country, where there was a large pan. [Later on] we passed on through open places between strips of forest trees, and through two places of forest with good timber trees such as yellow wood and at 6 p.m. arrived at Bashhlazi's kraal.[9]

A particular area of coastal forest was to be found at Kosi Bay. It was here or possibly nearby beside Lake Amanzimnyama around 1907 that Cuthbert Foxon is said to have collected the seed of the giant raphia palm, *Raphia australis*. It was Foxon who in 1916 planted the first of the raphia palms at Mthunzini, which are now a national monument. In the winter of 1920 R.D. Aitken and G.W. Gale, respectively the assistant and student of Professor John Bews, professor of botany at Natal University College, visited the Kosi Bay area. Their account ran as follows: 'There is a great wealth of varied vegetation, no single species being dominant, including a number of ferns, among which is *Lygodium scandens* … In the heart of this forest we made the interesting discovery of a species of Raphia, probably new, but not identical with *R. vinifera*.'[10]

The Zululand high forests were not dramatically different from those in Natal, though some of them tended to have fewer of the stinkwood and yellowwood species and more varieties such as black ironwood (*Olea capensis*), lemonwood (*Xymalos monospora*), and knobwood (*Zanthoxylum davyi*) in Qhudeni, and umdoni (*Syzygium gerrardii*) in Ngome. Different species could dominate different sections of a forest and the presence of Cape beech in the interior of a forest was said to be a strong indicator of previous heavy felling. This is confirmed by the few early reports we have of Zululand forests. For example, in 1891 it was said of Qhudeni forest that 'both Outeniqua and upright [yellowwood] abound'. Such a comment could not have been made 20 years later.[11]

Only two steam sawmills operated in colonial Zululand, one in Nongoma and the other in Qhudeni forest. A logbook from the latter covering the years 1903 to 1910 has survived from which the information in Table 5 is extracted concerning the major species of tree felled.[12]

'EARLY MORNING ON THE BANKS OF THE NKWAVUMA'. This attractive illustration showing a reedbuck, a giant sycamore fig tree, palms and a euphorbia tree on the banks of the Ingwavuma River in Maputaland appeared in William Drummond's book about hunting in Zululand and Maputaland, *The large game and natural history of south and south-east Africa* (1875). Drummond was the younger son of the Scottish Earl of Perth. His book is superior to many other contemporary hunting volumes, dealing with the game according to species rather than simply being an account of general slaughter.

TABLE 5

TYPES AND NUMBERS OF TREES RECORDED AS FELLED IN QHUDENI FOREST, 1903–10

SPECIE OF TREE	NUMBER OF TREES FELLED	% OF TOTAL FELLED
lemonwood	421	24
33 species where under 40 trees per species were cut in the period	402	23
yellowwood	316	18
black ironwood	226	13
'wattles'	117	7
spek [wild peach (Kiggelaria africana)]	63	4
knobwood	57	3
white stinkwood	47	3
sneezewood	47	3
tungwane [umthongwane, (Englerophytum natalense)]	44	2
Total	**1 740**	**100%**

The woodcutters

The Victorian image of a sawyer as being 'strong in the arm and thick in the head' might be applied to some of the woodcutters who made a meagre livelihood in the forests of Natal and Zululand. Their methods of extraction were certainly wasteful: felling the best trees, felling high and crowning low, as well as causing damage to saplings by clearing undergrowth and creating slip paths out of the forest. They were rough and tough. In 1860 Father Justin Barret recounted a visit to a group of Irish woodcutters in the forests of the Drakensberg mountains: 'They are not generally the "cream" of society … but … the cream of hard drinking fellows, frequently living in sin. But, say you, these poor Protestants! Not at all. They are good Catholics, of Irish blood, who devoutly read the Bible, pray at Mass as if they were angels, and would give their lives for the Pope!'[13]

In Zululand white sawyers were fewer in number but no less colourful characters. In the north the great Ngome forest, which had once fallen under the control of the Zulu king, had the greatest number of sawyers, with about 60 at the end of the era of Boer control.[14] These sawyers were mainly Afrikaners. Nothing was done by the Boers' New Republic to check either their methods of extraction or the quantity of timber they took. The only regulation enforced related to the purchase of a licence to use a saw for a specific period of time. Boers were also prone to cross the border from the New Republic into Zululand to cut timber illegally.[15]

In southern Zululand John Dunn cut timber in Ongoye forest and for a while in Qhudeni and possibly in Nkandla forests.

These last two mountain mist-belt forests also had resident white woodcutters in them, in Qhudeni's case from the early 1870s. We know little of them, but a few names have survived. There was Edmund Aureal Woodroff, a former African levy leader during the Anglo-Zulu War. He turned his hand to such things as cattle ranching and trading with homes at Rorke's Drift and Qhudeni. Other interesting characters of the forest were William Reid and William Law, the latter a British army deserter who lived in a small cabin in Qhudeni forest.

In 1883 the British put Woodroff in charge of Qhudeni forest, where he lived in a wood-and-iron house with his Zulu wife. Licences were issued at a rate of £1 per saw per month. In 1883 and again in 1887 he boldly, and perhaps foolishly, claimed ownership of the forest for himself. The authorities would have none of this, correctly pointing out that 'the Zulu king could not

LICENCE TO CUT WOOD, 1892 The Zululand magistrates were determined to protect the forests of Zululand and insisted that all, including the missionaries, had to obtain a licence before any timber could be cut. Both black and white people who cut timber illegally were prosecuted when caught. The result was that while much damage was inflicted on the Zululand forests, nevertheless they remain today in a finer state of preservation than most of those in the rest of KwaZulu-Natal.
KWAZULU-NATAL ARCHIVES (ZGH 750, Z263/1893)

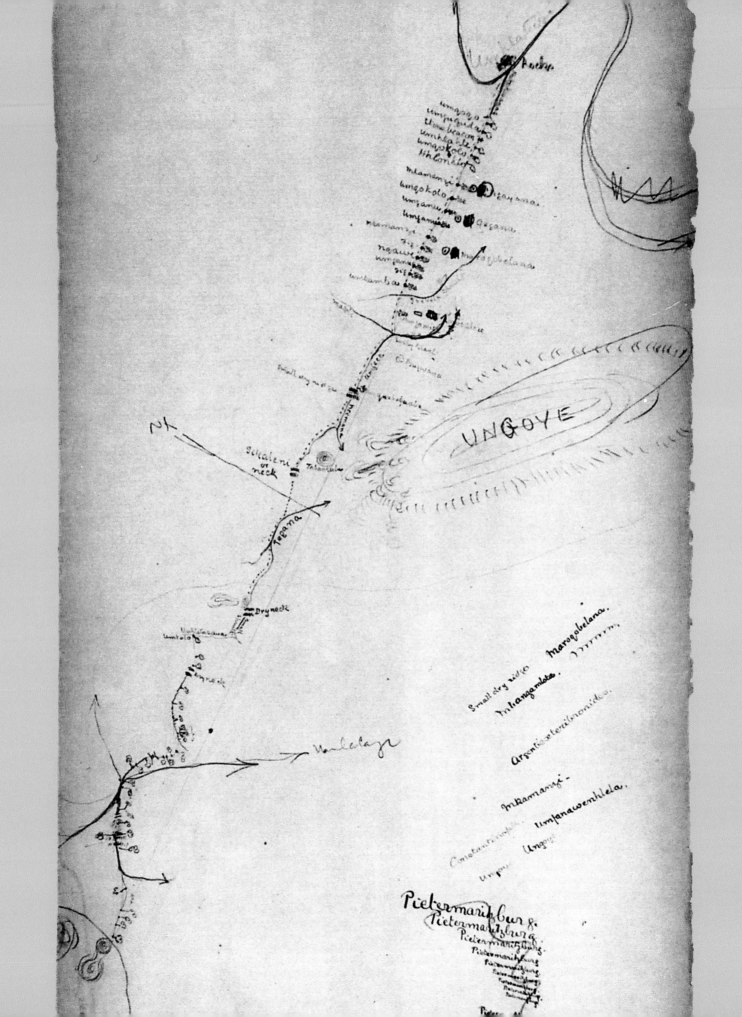

UNGOYE

Nk

Selkaleni
or neck

Tegana

Dryneck

Umlalaze

Small dry vlei to   Marogobelana.
        Mkangamlote.
            Argentesterilnomides.
                Mkamanzi.
    Constantinihn   Umfanawenhlela.
            Ungwe.

Pietermaritzburg.
    Pietermaritzburg.
        Pietermaritzburg.
            Pietermaritzburg.

in his own right alienate the land'.[16] Indeed, these sawyers were regarded by the British authorities as squatters with no right of settlement or of ownership of the forest land. By the Edwardian period any woodcutter who had a house on forestland in Zululand had to pay the authorities £2 a year or provide 40 days a year labour to the forestry department.

Needless to say, there were endless disputes and constant acrimony between sawyer and forester. The main complaint of the woodcutters was that the foresters selected and marked trees for them to fell that were damaged or partly rotten. In 1904 one sawyer complained that 40 per cent of all timber cut was a quarter rotten.[17] The sawyers were also often confined by the local forester to a section of the forest. The other great complaint of the woodcutters was the difficulty of transporting sawn timber to Natal. The usual route from the Qhudeni–Nkandla forests was along a bad dirt road to Dundee. The 'killing cost of cartage to Dundee' perhaps did more than other factors to reduce the extent of the commercial exploitation of the southern Zululand forests. But on top of transport costs were the wages that had to be paid to those sawyers employed by the sawmill. At 15s. a day this was as much as 50 per cent more than was paid to sawyers in some parts of Natal. As William Law said in 1904, 'We only make [a] bare living.'

When Zululand was subjected to white settlement, the fate of the old sawyers varied. Many woodcutters were evicted from Ngome, whilst those at Qhudeni seem to have survived. At that time it was said that 17 to 20 wagonloads of umdoni (*Syzygium cordatum*) were being extracted daily from Ngome forest.[18]

The sawmills

In the latter part of the nineteenth century and possibly the early twentieth century there was some collecting of rubber by the local African population in Maputaland. This was extracted from the indigenous shrub or woody climber, umbungwa (*Landolphia kirkii*), and sold in Lourenço Marques. Umbungwa grew in large quantity in the Phongola bush and was harvested carefully, as the local African population also ate the fruit of the vine. At the end of the colonial period there was some commercial exploitation of this rubber vine in Maputaland, but this did not prove financially viable and the enterprise came to an end in 1914.[19]

More successful were a couple of sawmills that operated in colonial Zululand, but even these had shaky existences and were not commercially viable in the long run. In the 1890s a sawmill operated at Nongoma. Little is known of its operations. We do, however, know a little about the sawmill in Qhudeni forest, which existed under various owners from 1897 to 1915. It was the presence of this sawmill that prompted the Natal government in

THE UNDERSIGNED is a purchaser for cash, of—

IVORY

Wool,

Yellow Wood Deals.

JOHN BROWN.

Port Natal, 1st Sept., 1853.

ADVERTISEMENT FOR IVORY, WOOL AND YELLOWWOOD TIMBER, 1854 Advertisements for the purchase of ivory in Durban and Pietermaritzburg newspapers not only attracted hunters returning from Zululand but also encouraged others to venture there in the hope of earning some cash. Hunting profits, however, were not always great. *NATAL INDEPENDENT*, 9 DECEMBER 1854

1898 to appoint G.H. Davies as the first professional forester in Zululand. He was based at Qhudeni forest.

H. Swanfield's sawmill complex, erected in 1897 on the ridge of Qhudeni overlooking the forest, comprised a mill with two circular saws, one bandsaw, one log-frame saw with a capacity for logs 1.2 by 9 m, spoke-making equipment, and lathes, buffing and planing machines. There was a shed with a 24-horsepower steam engine, a blacksmith's shop, a drying kiln, workmen's quarters and a house for Swanfield, who as well as being a partner in the Qhudeni Saw Mills Company was manager of the sawmill. The initial capital outlay was in the region of £6 000.

Later Swanfield erected a small bushmill, complete with horizontal and circular saws, on the lower slopes of the forest. Four thousand pounds was spent on building a 3 km wooden tramline with a narrow gauge of 760 mm – 'now spanning kloofs nearly 100 ft deep and then creeping along the faces of precipitous krantzes'. Near the tramway terminus a wire cable dropped 76 m down to the bushmill, logs being raised up the precipice on hooks attached to the cable band, which was moved by the bushmill's engine. An observer in 1904 described the system of tramway and cable as 'a marvel of engineering skill and ingenuity'.

The venture, however, was not a success, with Swanfield accusing the forest department of overcharging him for timber and singling out second-grade trees for him to fell. The restrictions on using draught animals to counter the spread of East Coast fever also made transporting timber difficult and, as always, a wage bill had to be paid. On top of this, there was a

ZULULAND'S FIRST BOTANICAL MAP, 1885 This fascinating sketch map marks an 1885 unfenced boundary in southern Zululand near Ongoye forest. The beacons include the main Eshowe wagon road, the Umlalazi and Umhlathuze rivers, as well as 43 marked trees. KWAZULU-NATAL ARCHIVES (ZGH VOL. 694)

THE FORESTS

downturn in the economy in the later Edwardian period. In 1909 Swanfield cut his losses and sold out. Several owners came and went until finally in 1916 most of the machinery was removed, the last being taken out in July 1918. After that, the sound of steam-driven saws was heard no more in Qhudeni forest.[20]

In the immediate post-colonial period, from about 1911 to 1919, the Ngoya Forest Company, owned by Messrs Johnston and Carmont, operated in Ongoye forest. It is said to have extracted some 25 000 m³ of timber from the forest, mainly in the form of pit props for the mines on the Rand.

Other culprits

The activities of the British army in Zululand after 1879 impacted on several forests, especially around the military headquarters at Eshowe. That said, by the late 1880s there is some evidence that the colonial authorities were clamping down on unbridled cutting of timber for fuel, building and disselbooms by the army. In his 1891 Zululand forest report Colonel Cardew commented on the destruction of indigenous timber, 'in which the troops were as much to blame as anyone else'. Governor Mitchell did not permit even the legal cutting of timber unless it was supervised. The magistrates followed suit and there were some frosty exchanges between the military and civil authorities on the issue.[21]

By 1880 there were 17 Christian mission stations in Zululand, all of which required timber for building and for fuel. These missionaries occasionally fell foul of the authorities over forest matters. There were three elements to this. First, there were the requests to be exempt from the forest regulations and in particular the payment of licence fees for cutting timber. Such impositions they thought 'unfair'. The magistrates, however, would have none of this and strongly opposed such requests on the ground that to grant concessions 'would create a dangerous precedent'.

In 1889 the administrative secretary of Zululand, William Windham, wrote to the military authorities in Eshowe: 'Unless a close check is kept upon the cutting of wood, His Excellency fears that the forests in Zululand, which have already been seriously damaged, will fast be destroyed.' On another occasion Governor Mitchell made it clear that 'all Europeans requiring wood from the forests of Zululand, whether for missionary or other purposes, must pay the usual fees for licence to cut such wood'. That did not, however, rule out a grant in aid being made later to help with building costs.

Disputes over forestland between the ecclesiastics and the military around Eshowe also occurred. And related to these was a lengthy dispute over ownership of part of Entumeni forest. Eventually the saga was ended by the missionaries being awarded

WILLIAM COWIE'S SKETCH MAP OF LAKE ST LUCIA, 1848
This early map of the St Lucia complex is interesting, for as well as human habitation it marks those areas where there was forest or bush.
KWAZULU-NATAL ARCHIVES (SGO III/1/2)

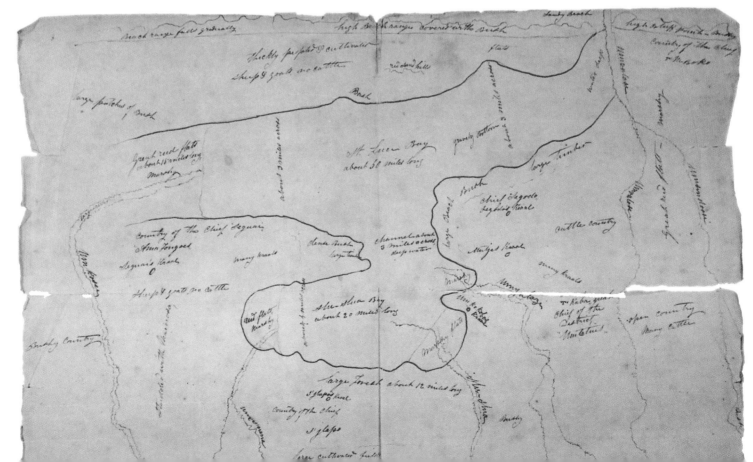

about half of the land they claimed. But interestingly, the government specifically excluded the main belt of forest from this award.[22]

Afforestation

The threat to the wilderness from exotic vegetation was not recognised until very late in the day. Because white commercial farming was for security reasons delayed deliberately by the British authorities, effectively until the late Edwardian period, commercial agriculture and silviculture only became a noticeable feature of the Zululand landscape in the post-colonial era after 1910.

Even the battle against noxious weeds, such as the burr-weeds *Xanthium spinosum* and *Xanthium strumarium*, was not taken seriously until after 1901, when the Zululand Police, or Nongqai as the locals called them, were instructed to enforce rigorously the anti-burr weed regulations. But even then the Nongqai had more to worry about than harassing headmen about some weeds on old kraal sites. This is not to say that there was no environmental degradation prior to white settlement. The fluctuating fortunes of an at times enormous national cattle herd in Zululand cannot but have affected the environment, as did concentrated farming in some areas of population density, and to a lesser extent iron-smelting using charcoal. But the introduction of white commercial agriculture had by the 1930s effected a dramatic impact on parts of the Zululand landscape.

In the 1890s talk was already under way about establishing exotic stands of timber forest trees, very much a feature of present-day Zululand. The purpose of such plantations was not just purely commercial but also to provide fuel and building materials to the local African population and to the British military. Following the intervention of Governor Mitchell in 1891, Colonel Cardew was acquiring blue gum (*Eucalyptus*) and black wattle (*Acacia mearnsii*) seeds, the eucalyptus being twelve times more expensive than the acacia. This was for distribution by magistrates to the African population.

By 1895 a proposal was being discussed to establish exotic plantations at Nondweni, Nquthu, Ntingwe and Empangeni, and the following year £800 was placed on the Zululand estimates for afforestation. A small military plantation was established in 1896 in the Nquthu district near Qhudeni. But it was not until the new century that the Zululand afforestation scheme got off the ground with the establishment of the Empangeni nursery in 1902 and the beginnings of what would become a large forestry enterprise at Port Durnford from 1904 onward. So seriously was this enterprise taken that the infamous 1903 forest proclamation, as well as listing 52 reserved species of indigenous tree, extraordinarily also included a general prohibition on cutting any exotic tree without a licence.

The Dukuduku forestry scheme did not begin to get off the ground until the late 1920s and early 1930s. In the colonial period sugar cane and exotic timber plantations were not an environmental factor in Zululand.[23] In fact, it was not until 1935 that revenue exceeded expenditure for the forestry department in Zululand.

REFERENCES

1   Forestry Department Archive, Eshowe, Report for November, V 2100/600, Z 1970/25, 9 December 1922.

2   For the forests of Zululand see Marwick, *Kwamahlati*; McCracken, 'The indigenous forests of colonial Natal and Zululand'; and McCracken, 'Qudeni'. See also McCracken, 'A history of indigenous timber use in South Africa'.

3   As colonial Zululand forests were not properly demarcated or surveyed, and as contemporary estimates of forest size in some instances vary considerably, these figures must be regarded as rough estimates.

4   KZNA, 1/ER1, letter book, report, 26 December 1898, fol. 406.

5   KZNA, SGO, III/1/2, W. Cowie to D. Moodie, 26 July 1848.

6   KZNA, ZA 27, R 4451/96, Report on Tongaland, 24 December 1896, fol. 10; and *Swaziland, Tongaland and Northern Zululand*, War Office, 1905, p. 108.

7   KZNA, EPI/1, letter book, 3 February 1891, fol. 242.

8   (Barter), *Alone among the Zulus*, p. 101.

9   See KZNA, 1/UBO, 3/1/3, 29 February 1896, fol. 333.

10 See Van Jaarsveld, *Mtunzini*, pp. 163–9; and Aitken and Gale, *Botanical survey of Natal and Zululand*, pp. 12–13. Foxon did not know of the giant raphia palm when he wrote a report on Maputaland in 1896. See KZNA, ZGH 796, report, point 6, 1896.

11 See Cardew, *Report on the forests of Zululand*, p. 4; and Forestry Department Archive, Eshowe, File Y 3010/600, N 976/70/11, 25 May 1921 and Z 326/16, 29 April 1921.

12 Department of Forestry and Water Affairs, Ulundi, Qhudeni forest logbook. It should be noted that this logbook is incomplete so the figures must be considered to be conservative. They do, however, give an impression of what was being cut and in what volume.

13 St George, *Failure and vindication*, pp. 221–3.

14 Pooley and Player, *KwaZulu-Natal*, p. 302.

15 KZNA, 1/MEL, minute paper, PB 43/1887, 10 June 1887.

16 See KZNA, ZA 38, 10 March 1883; and ZGH 682, 10 March 1883, and ZGH 829, fol. 184, 13 March 1883. It must, however, be pointed out that there were occasions when forest land was alienated by the Zulu king, such as Chorway forest in 1859. See ZGH 705, grant of farm to Ephraim Frederick Rathbone, 23 November 1859.

17 Forestry Department Archive, Eshowe, Qhudeni, Y 3010/600, 23 July 1904.

18 Forestry Department Archive, Eshowe, L 2000/615, 1905; and Natal Government Notice No. 75 of 1905.

19 Marwick, *Kwamahlati*, pp. 27–33. For an earlier reference, see Leslie, *Among the Amatonga*, p. 258; Campbell Collections, Miller papers, Von Wissell 'Reminiscences', fol. 46; KZNA, 1/ING, minute paper, R 715/1901 and R1553/1904; and KZNA, ZGH 793, report, 2 September 1896, fol. 2.

20 See McCracken, 'Qudeni', pp. 71–80.

21 Cardew, *Report on the forests of Zululand*, pp. 4–5; KZNA, 1/ESH, letter book, 24 August 1889, fol. 283 and 6 November 1890, fol. 387; and minute papers, R 494/1892 and R 2647/1894.

22 KZNA, 1/ESH, minute papers, R 1781/1889, R 778/1895 and R 1309/1898 and 1/MEL, minute paper, R 1965/1891; KZNA, ZGH 750, minute paper, Z 263/1893, ZGH 716, minute paper, Z 775/1888 and ZGH 778, minute paper, Z 637/1897; and *Delimitations commission*, pp. 100 *et passim*.

23 Forestry Archive, Eshowe, L 200/600; Marwick, *Kwamahlati*, Chapter 4; and KZNA, ZGH 741, minute papers R 2389/1891 and R 2640, ZGH 766, minute paper R 2546/1895 and ZGH 835: 25, 20 August 1895. See also *Zululand Times*, 27 December 1912.

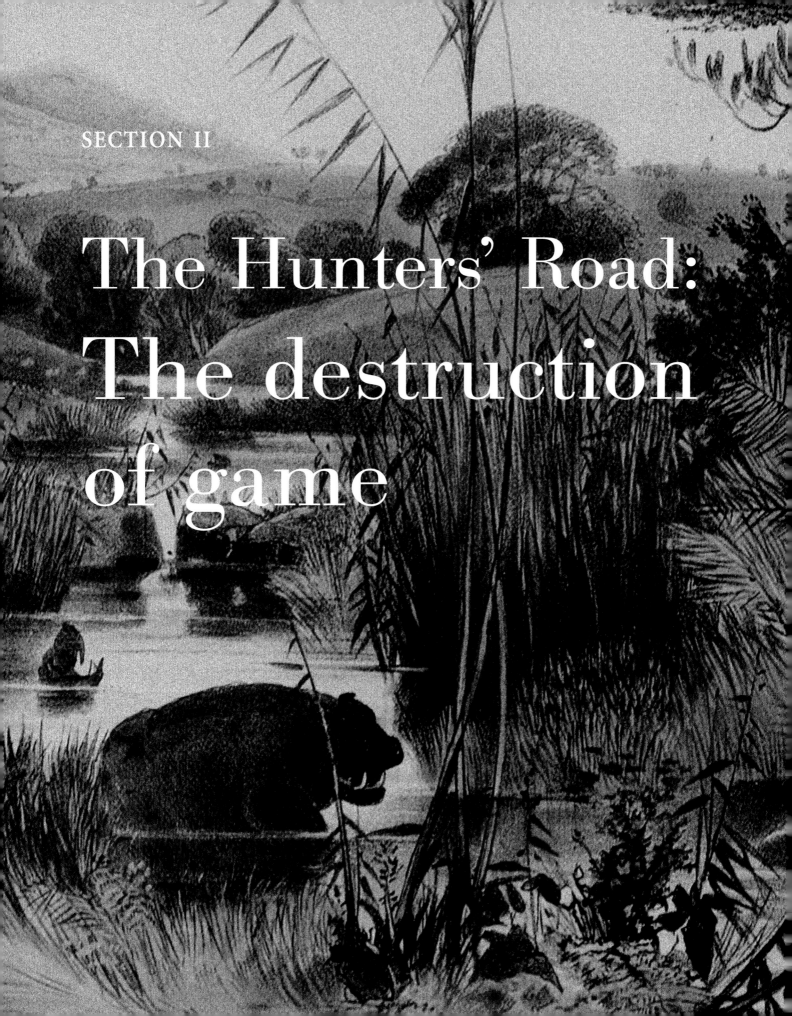

The Hunters' Road: The destruction of game

'ALONE AMONGST THE ZULUS' (AND WILDEBEEST) This illustration was published in *Alone among the Zulus, by a plain woman: The narrative of a journey through the Zulu country, South Africa.* This was published in London about 1866, the author's name not being given. The book was in fact written by Catherine Barter, who ventured into northern Zululand to rescue her brother who was seriously ill. Of the wildebeest Barter wrote, 'On this day I first came in sight of the gnu (*Catoblepas gnu*). It is a horned animal of about the same size as an ox, with a mane and tail something like those of a horse. The herd was not far off, and the creatures stood and stared at us for some time, and then suddenly started off at an awkward gallop.'

CHAPTER 3

The white hunters

STALKING A BUFFALO IN ZULULAND, 1856   William Baldwin's book *African hunting and adventures from Natal to the Zambesi* was published in 1863 with a less lavish French edition appearing in 1868. The illustrations by James Wolf and J.B. Zwecker are better than many appearing in contemporary hunting accounts.

In the mid-1890s there was a controversy in Britain as to who was killing most of Africa's game. Sir Graham Bower put the blame, in descending order of destruction, on white market hunters, black inhabitants and irresponsible white sportsmen.[1] In Zululand the first two categories hunted, but the professional sportsman was rare. A Maputaland trader recounted with glee a Russian prince, whom he called Xetetinsky, coming to hunt nyala. He had a professional double-barrelled heavy express rifle, silk-lined double-flapped tents and several cases of pint bottles of champagne. He also hunted on horseback rather than on foot as

was the normal practice in Zululand – and he failed to shoot a single nyala.[2]

In 1894 one disgruntled overseas visitor, A.J. Brandon, complained that he had spent £250 on a wagon, oxen and 'outfit' only to find that hunting was closed in Zululand. No doubt the locals were greatly amused. Hunting was for locals, not English toffs. Be that as it may, Mr Brandon eventually not only got his way but, as can be seen from Table 6, was one of those few gentlemen who hunted in Zululand and bagged a record specimen.[3]

TABLE 6

WARD'S ZULULAND TROPHIES RECORDED UP TO 1899

SPECIES	HUNTER	LOCATION	SIZE OF HORN LENGTH OF OUTSIDE CURVE OF HORN
Blesbok	Maj. Gen. Arthur Ellis (1863)	Zululand	15¼ in. [38.1 cm]
Buffalo	A.J. Brandon	Zululand	39 in. [99.06 cm]
Bushbuck	A.H. Newmann (collector for British Museum)	Zululand	15¾ in. [40 cm]
Duiker (grey)	Capt. L.O. Williams	Zululand	5¼ in. [13.33 cm]
Elephant	Gift of King Cetshwayo to Lord Chelmsford	Not specified	7 feet [2.13 m] Greatest cir. c.18 in. [45.72 cm]
Hippopotamus	Hon. Charles Ellis	St Lucia	30½ in. [77.47 cm]
Kudu	Hon. Charles Ellis	Lebombo Mts	Under 60 in. [Under 1.52 m]
Kudu	C.D. Rudd	Zululand	55 in. [1.397 m]
Nyala	Hon. Walter Rothschild	Zululand	28½ in. [72.39 cm]
Nyala	G.F. Angas	St Lucia (1847)	Specimen measured by Angas; under 22 in. [55.88 cm]
Reedbuck	F.R.N. Findlay	Zululand	under 15 in. [40.33 cm]
Reedbuck (mountain)	A.H. Newmann	Zululand	7 in. [18.74 cm]
Rhino (white)	Lt. Col. Hon. W. Coke	Zululand	31 in. 78.74 cm
Rhino (white)	C.H. Varndell	Zululand	29¾ in. [♀75.56 cm]
Rhino (black)	Lt. Col. Hon. W. Coke	Zululand	41½ in. [1.054 m]
Steenbuck	Capt. L.O. Williams	Zululand	4 in. [11.12 cm]
Suni	A.H. Newmann	Northern Zululand	3¹⁄₁₆ in. [9.20 cm]
Waterbuck	Capt. L.O. Williams	Zululand	31¹⁄₁₆ in. [80.64 cm]
Wildebeest (blue)	Lt. Col. Hon. W. Coke	Zululand	29 in. [73.66 cm]

The hunter-traders from Port Natal

Although there is no shortage of references to the early traders in Port Natal in the 1820s and 1830s, there are relatively few comments concerning their hunting activities across the Tugela River.[4] This is in part because they often traded in ivory rather than hunted the elephant themselves, at least that far north. Sources might comment on Francis Farewell having stocks of ivory of up to 800 lb (360 kg) at a time, but much of that was the result of barter. Only in the late 1830s and early 1840s, after the Boer–Zulu conflict, does there emerge as a distinct entity the independent trader who sets off in an oxwagon with the purpose of both bartering and hunting in Zululand. By the early 1850s the wagon tracks up the Natal north coast to the Tugela were well worn.

In October 1854 it was said that there were as many as 50 white traders in Zululand.[5] Their trade was by barter and, assuming permission was granted by the king to trade and hunt, it was a fairly straightforward matter. It was, however, foolish to trade without the king's permission. William Cowie remarked of two traders operating without permission: 'they are stupid [being] there till permission comes from the Black Prince'. After the British reorganised the administration of Zululand in the mid-1880s, trading was permitted to continue but from then on only the local chief's

permission had to be sought.[6] By then all importation of goods into Zululand by sea was forbidden. And as early as 1848, under Natal Ordinance No. 4 of that year, anyone leaving Natal to trade in Zululand had to obtain a licence from a magistrate.[7]

Captain Ludlow, writing in the early 1880s, left an evocative picture of the Zululand hunter-trader, in rough flannel shirt, corduroy riding breeches, long riding boots in the top of which was stuck a hunting knife, and carrying a heavy riding whip. Such men were usually bearded with bronzed weather-beaten faces and wore a broad-brimmed, hard felt billycock hat, into the band of which were placed an assortment of bird feathers. They wore small earrings.

All transport riders, traders and hunters are as a rule very incommunicative. They rarely speak during a meal beyond asking a few questions such as: 'How is trade up-country?' 'What are the prices of hides?' 'Is there much cattle sickness among the cattle?' After the meal they smoke their pipes and drink their coffee in silence. They know little about the outside world, read neither books nor newspapers and have forgotten how to write a letter long ago. They often lose a good deal of their language, speaking the various native dialects fluently, and these they use in conversation with each other. They are commonly good natured, generous, cool, daring, facing danger daily. Their wants are simple. They have lost many of the refinements of civilisation.[8]

The merchandise their wagons carried as they forded the Tugela River into Zululand included cotton and lambswool blankets, calico and salempore cloth, brass and copper wire, and coloured glass beads. But other commodities such as pick handles were not uncommon, and sometimes a gun or some gunpowder might be smuggled in to enhance profits.[9]

These traders are sometimes termed hunter-traders. To an extent, the description is correct, in that many hunters also traded and, equally, traders sometimes hunted and bartered wildlife products. But by the 1850s most traders were primarily interested in cattle. On their journey home, if all went well, there might indeed be some wild game products in the wagon – especially buffalo and wildebeest skins, rhino horn, hippo teeth or elephant tusk, as well as some hippo fat. Cat and monkey skins were also desirable commodities.

When in December 1856 some Natal traders found themselves, their cattle and their wagons on a sandbar in the middle of the Tugela River in the midst of an inter-Zulu conflict, the battle of Ndondakusuka, wisely they abandoned their possessions and swam for the Natal bank. Their subsequent claim for compensation is an invaluable source of information for the historian. Six of the claimants included wildlife products such as monkey skins, cat skins, mersimber skins, rhino horn, buffalo horn, feathers and buck skins in their inventories, but these were valued at only £78. It was the bartered Zulu cattle that were the major loss – worth £3 680.[10]

Conversely, some men who would describe themselves as hunters also traded extensively for cattle. In 1849 William Cowie said he had brought out of Zululand 120 head of cattle, and claimed another man named Jan Meyer had brought out about 400 cattle. William Baldwin used Arthur Eastwood's farm Brindle to fatten up these Zulu cattle before selling them off.[11] In the mid-1870s, however, such trading expeditions were not so easy. As guns became more plentiful certain species of game became less so, and even cattle, attacked by disease, were fewer. R. Robinson commented in 1876:

> The Zulu have lost an enormous quantity of cattle within the last two years chiefly by disease, as the hides brought into Durban testify, & by the purchase of guns & ammunition – They are consequently anxious to replace them – & there is only one way in which it can be done – *by war*. Any one who knew the Zulu country (say) 20 years ago, with its magnificent herds of cattle would hardly believe how few they have now.[12]

RHINO HUNTING Rhino were hunted, though not sought after as much as elephant or buffalo. That said, thousands of rhino horns were shipped out of Durban over the years and by the 1890s the white rhino was nearly extinct, a few being confined to the junction of the Mfolozi rivers and the surrounding area. This illustration shows Baldwin killing a rhino cow. The calf, 'squealing most lustily', was attacked by dogs and captured. It was killed by hyena during the night. BALDWIN, *AFRICAN HUNTING*, 1863

Hunting parties

In the generation after the pioneer hunter-traders, which included men like Farewell, Fynn, Cane and Ogle at Port Natal, most of the white hunters who ventured to Zululand were amateurs. The hunters of the 1850s were healthy young men in their twenties out for a bit of adventure and, hopefully, some profit, though there is little evidence that vast fortunes were made. The comings and goings of these intrepid young men were often noted in the press as they hunted for two or three months and then did something else for the rest of the year. Few carried on this lifestyle for more than three or four years. It was something exciting to do before settling down.[13]

There were remarkably few professional hunters and even fewer aristocratic sportsmen. Even the one classic example of the latter, the Honourable William Henry Drummond, was not typical of the foxhunting British squire come to Africa to shoot Big Game. Another interesting feature of the white Zululand hunters was that they had mostly come from no further afield than Natal. Perhaps a false impression has been created with the publication of accounts of foreign visitors to the Zulu kingdom, but the fact remains that non-Natalian hunters tended to steer clear of Zululand, which had a reputation for being unhealthy.

Drummond was cutting about the difference in attitude between Natal-born whites and settlers like himself. Of one of the former he tartly commented, 'Yet such was his sloth and want of energy, qualities conspicuous in all African-born whites …'[14]

There were, however, one or two individuals who did approach hunting in a businesslike fashion. These included the ubiquitous George Cato, William Hartley and his partner Thomas Handley, and John Alfred White, known locally as Elephant White. Cato did venture into Zululand to hunt, but his main role in hunting was to act as an agent for various hunting parties. Elephant White, on the other hand, was very much involved in hunting expeditions, leading parties up into Zululand as well as employing his own African staff in hunting. William Baldwin was in one of Elephant White's hunting safaris, though he does not emphasise the point in his book *African hunting*.

In 1849 White had struck on the idea of navigating the entrance to Lake St Lucia.[15] Such ideas of using St Lucia as a harbour did, and have since, not come to anything. But it was White who was behind bringing a boat on a wagon up from Durban to the Black Mfolozi, where it was launched in January 1852. Whilst under attack by crocodile – targeting the hunters' dogs on board – the small craft made it safely to St Lucia, where, with a blue calico cloth sail, it was later employed in shooting hippo. One attacked it and damaged the vessel. In August of that year Cato was also employing a boat in the Umhlathuze Bay (Richards Bay).[16]

In the 1850s most hunting parties made for the Mfolozi junction, Lake St Lucia or the Phongola River west of the Lebombo Mountains. One group, comprising the Adams, Joubert and Hogg families (including the womenfolk) and W.H. Smith, hunted and traded in southern Zululand, making Ongoye forest their headquarters.[17]

Duration of hunting trips

A hunting trip or hunting-trading trip into Zululand was normally undertaken any time between March and November, outside the hottest of the Zululand fever-ridden summer months. Though such an expedition could not be described as leisurely, it was not an affair that could be undertaken in a rush, and it was not unusual for a trip to take three months or longer. Of course, men could be and were sent back to the Bay, as Durban was usual referred to, for additional supplies. One hunter observed that he began to think of returning home when the winter-flowering *Erythrina* was in blossom. Delays in travelling were frequent, especially when the hunter encountered the spring rains and the rivers dramatically and abruptly rose in flood.

The oxwagon

Captain Gardiner penned a nine-stanza verse entitled 'Waggon travelling in South Africa'. Two of the verses ran as follows;

> Resigned and patient you must be,
> For bumps and tossings you will meet;
> Sometimes you'll think yourself at sea,

> And oft be jerked from off your seat;
> And when you come to ford a river,
> The whole will creak, and gape, and quiver.

> Crack goes the whip – a passage breaks
> Through tangled boughs, and reeds, and grass;
> The sea-cow, scared, her haunt forsakes,
> And cranes shriek loudly as you pass,
> And loosened rocks in fragments strew
> The opening you have struggled through.[18]

The core of a hunting or a hunting-trading expedition was the oxwagon. This sturdy, slow-moving, unsprung vehicle was ideal for the rough terrain of Zululand. Its weight might mean that sand had to be dug out of drifts before a wagon could ford, but it also held the vehicle firmly on the ground. At about £150 plus the cost of a dozen salted oxen, wagons were not cheap.

As well as the canvas sail, along the side of the wagon were strapped the guns, often in covers of wild-dog or sometimes leopard skin.[19] So full of goods were the wagons that the hunter usually slept underneath or in a small canvas tent. Drummond recalled one miserable night when it rained and a stream of water came into his tiny tent. He scooped out two channels on either side in the forlorn hope that this would divert the flood.

The wagon ventured into territory without roads, and once the track ended much time had to be spent cutting overhanging tree branches to clear a way through the bush. Because of the threat of disease to the oxen and because the greater St Lucia area was a maze of vleis, swamps and lakes, it was the practice to leave the wagon in the hill country well away from the area. It was also common practice to send the wagon ahead north into the bushveld lying to the west of the Lebombo Mountains whilst the hunters first tried their luck at St Lucia Bay, following north when they had finished there. This meant that what was required for the camp had to be carried. And because of this the hunters' camp was a basic establishment, and indeed the roughest and toughest hunters did not even bother with a tent.

Staff

Even the lone white hunter on foot took with him some African staff to help in the adventure. These acted as porters and auxiliary hunters, the two functions sometimes divided and sometimes not, depending on the size of the party or the relationship between hunter and servant. From the accounts they appear to have been all men and mostly from Natal. Sometimes local people, including women, were hired as carriers and young boys as water carriers, but the hunting was done by the hunters' own men. There were also the gun carriers, who carried as well the ammunition. They had to keep up with the hunters during the chase.

'WILD FOWL SHOOTING AT THE PONGOLA' An interesting drawing from about the 1860s that well illustrates the thick bush that flanked stretches of the Phongola River, a favourite hunting groung. Birds were often shot in Zululand for food. Only in the closing decade of the nineteenth century was any attempt made to introduce a measure of protection for some game and for insectivorous birds.

LINDLEY, *AFTER OPHIR*, C. 1870

Baldwin speaks of a caravan of some 30 Africans carrying in a single line the prizes of the hunt back from Lake St Lucia to the wagon at the Black Mfolozi. On returning from a hunt in the bush it was the practice of the African staff to cut great slabs of meat off the killed animals and carry these back to camp as a 'jacket' over their shoulders.

The relationship between white hunter and African servant was important. Hunting was a dangerous business, and if the hunters – black and white – did not act as a team, they could all be in trouble. In particular it was important for the chief African or Khoi hunter to have a good working relationship with the white hunter, especially when, as in the case of Drummond and Leslie, upwards of 50 African hunters might be employed. In Leslie's case his senior hunter was a man called Untabine. Drummond's was Umdumela – 'my wise old companion'. Umdumela was an excellent hunter, but he was also prone to lecture the young Drummond on 'the sin and wickedness of not giving him higher wages'.[20]

Some Africans and Khoi were such good shots that they were retained mainly for hunting, and indeed some were left behind in Zululand after the white hunter had returned to Natal. These proxy hunters were not always popular with the local African people, no doubt because they considered themselves superior to their country cousins. According to Drummond, one such African hunter was living in Natal 'having retired upon his earnings'.[21]

THE WHITE HUNTERS

The mundane work of the African servant entailed carrying provisions from the wagon to the campsite, if the wagon was being left somewhere or being sent ahead; helping set up camp; cooking their own meals; gun carrying during a hunt; cutting up slaughtered game and carrying skins and hides, horns and meat back to camp; returning to elephant carcasses after the flesh had begun to rot and the tusks could be more easily cut out; and preparing skins and hides.

The hunter's camp and camp life

Another, and perhaps slightly better, epic poem of the tenacious Captain Gardiner in the 1830s records the hunters' camp:

> The lip moustached – the sallow face,
> Denote that haughty, thankless race,
> They'd sell their skin for brandy;
> E'en Erin's sons they far eclipse,
> In placing goblets to their lips,
> Whene'er they find them handy.
>
> A few I marked with strange attire,
> While crowding round a blazing fire,
> Some sea-cow fat devouring.
> Red caps and tattered frocks they wore,
> With brigantines besmeared and gore,
> Like border bandits lowering.
>
> In strange confusion, round them strewed,
> Muskets and powder-horns I view,
> With skins, and fat, and dogs, and game;
> For neither elephant nor buffalo
> They ever leave in peace to go,
> But fell with deadly aim.[22]

Hunters' camps were smelly places. The remains of the hunt lay about and attracted insects, giant cockroaches, equally impressive rats (and with them snakes), vultures and other, larger carnivores. Back in the 1830s Captain Gardiner lamented, 'My enemies, the rats, are here in greater force than ever; and although I purposely brought a stretcher with me, in the hope of raising my bed beyond their reach, one of them actually contrived to perch upon my head in the course of the night.'[23] Catherine Barter had four cats with her in her wagon when she went into Zululand with her brother, though two of them she gave away to a local chief who was having problems with mice.

William Drummond has left a vivid description of a hunters' camp in the Zululand wilderness:

> From these [tree] branches were suspended almost everything that could be thought of by the South African hunters – bandoliers, powder-flasks made of buffalo-horn, hunting-knives in sheaths made of a buffalo's tail, hunting charms, coats – mostly old red regimental ones, or military great-coats – blankets of many colours, native dresses of wild cat or antelope skins, calabashes of all sizes, containing buffalo or rhinoceros fat to be taken home to the owner's wives, and sundry other articles of native manufacture or use, not to mention the number of bright gun-barrels which were placed against the bank, or hung by loops of hide from the branches above, or the dozens of assagais and sticks that accompanied them. At night this was lighted up by a number of great fires in front of the main camp, while every one of the little bee-hive erections had its own fire before the entrance, round each of which were grouped a number of natives employed in telling hunting stories, or in chanting hunting songs, in the intervals of leisure afforded by their principal occupation of eating the meat roasting on sticks at every fire.[24]

The camp environment meant that hunters themselves were not inclined to wash very much. Besides there were good stories of those who had ventured into a river to bathe and who had not come out. William Humphreys recounted how on the way up to Zululand he had taken his clothes off and gone into a river for a swim. On emerging, he discovered that a leopard was sitting between his naked self and his neatly piled clothes. No, it was enough to brush off the ticks.

As well as the guns, there were bullet moulds, lead ladles, powder casks, shooting belts, boxes of percussion caps, bags of gunpowder, metal for making bullets and animal traps. The necessities of the camp were a few candles, some cooking utensils, some large clasp knives, a flint or steel for sharpening knives, and basic foodstuffs.

Liquor was consumed, but the problem of transporting the weight made this a limiting factor in camp life. The grog of choice was brandy, gin or rum, but at least one large camp in the 1850s had a problem with Charley Edmonstone, who took opium, drank laudanum, boasted of prizes he had not shot – 'I don't believe he knows whether he hits or misses' – and quarrelled much of the time.[25] But fights were rare, partly because many hunters were loners coming with a small number of African servants and partly because the life was so tough that once a basic meal had been taken, most were exhausted and went to sleep, to rise again very early the next morning.

Perhaps the most trouble in camp came from the nocturnal visitors. Lion were a great nuisance, attacking the cattle. One of Baldwin's oxen was so tormented one night when five lion molested the draught animals that it had to be shot the next morning. Leopard frequently took one of the hunters' dogs at night. Hyena stole what they could, including the skins hanging up to dry out on the branches of trees. And black rhinos had a

A NARROW ESCAPE AT THE MOUTH OF THE UMLALAZI RIVER, 1852 When shooting duck near the mouth of the Umlalazi River in January 1852, the hunter William Baldwin narrowly escaped being taken by a crocodile when wading across the river. Making it to the bank, he dropped his gun which sank to the bottom of the river and was never recovered.

BALDWIN, *AFRICAN HUNTING*, 1863

reputation for running into camp without warning and attacking the fire. That was unfortunate as it was the fire that kept the other predators at bay and it had to be kept alight all night by the watch on duty, if there was a watch.

Furniture was usually non-existent, perhaps a few packing cases. Some camps did not even have standard small 9–10 pound (4 kg) tents. Hunters were frequently soaked either from crossing rivers or from subtropical downpours. Getting a kettle to boil in the rain was a challenge. Some camps had a 'hartebeest house', which was essentially a lean-to made of branches and reeds. Mattresses were unknown, but woven mats could be comfortable enough when one got used to them.[26]

A few hunters brought books with them. Baldwin had Sponge's *Sporting tour*.[27] A surprising number also brought pen, ink and paper. Paper was a valuable commodity in early Natal and it is an interesting reflection of both the calibre of men and their attitude to the adventure they were on that they had a desire to put pen to paper. Of course, the humid climate did no good to paper or notebooks, and hunters were always trying to find a substitute – like tea mixed with gunpowder – for ink.

Occasionally when there was a group of hunters, they might amuse themselves with a rubber of whist or 'a little target practice and athletic feats, and finish up the evening with singing'. Wahlberg's camp celebrated New Year's Day in 1840 'with eating, drinking, dancing etc.' The African staff might sit aside at night and talk among themselves or the African hunters might also sing, though Baldwin was not, however, impressed by African singing. David Leslie commented that he preferred the Tsonga singing to that of the Zulu, but in general the sound of any singing human voice in the African bush seemed to have a soothing effect.

Not surprisingly in such a set-up, rumour and snippets of news were eagerly devoured. On 28 October 1850 one hunter in Zululand heard the news of 500 new settlers landing in Durban – the Byrne settlers. In October 1853 William Baldwin encountered a trader in the bush and the two of them had a 'jolly evening together, hearing all the news; among the rest, that England and France were positively at war with Russia' – the Crimean War.[28]

There was much work to be done in camp. Bullets had to be cast. Carcasses had to be skinned and the skins salted or treated with alum or arsenic soap. Guns had to be cleaned and oiled. Then there were the never-ending repairs. There were always things to be done to the wagon when it was in camp. On this manual labour hunters and servants would work alongside each other, the social strictures of Victorian society slackened in the bush.

The Zululand bush took its toll on the hunter's clothing, especially shoes or boots. After three months in camp he was frequently carving velskoens for himself out of hide. Some of the hunters must have looked like Robinson Crusoe as they walked along Durban's sandy West Street beside their wagon at the end of the adventure.

Supplies

The sort of personal supplies, as distinct from merchandise brought into Zululand by white hunters, varied, but there were basics nearly every wagon carried. These might include some of the following: mealies [maize], rice, potatoes, sugar, salt (for eating, curing and firing out of muzzle-loaders at hyena), coffee and brandy. The wholesome African beer – 'very good when not too thick' – could be obtained from the local population. To this list were frequently added tins of red herring, bags of biscuits (which soon went mouldy), paraffin and maybe some soap.[29] Pumpkin, cheese, chocolate, bread and jam were a luxury, but not unknown. Occasionally fruit might be found on a bush or tree. And Baldwin records: 'A honeybird met us, and called us vigorously. We followed, and he took us to a bees' nest, but owing to the incessant rains, there was but little honey in it. There was, however, a good deal of fun and excitement in following the little fellow.'[30]

There was, of course, the meat from the hunt. Delicacies mentioned in accounts are reedbuck liver, kudu marrow-bones, buffalo tongue, buffalo kidneys ('a great luxury'), eland steaks, a stew of buck and hippo meat seasoned with onions and pepper, hippo fat, gnu (wildebeest) tea, and, occasionally, if the hunter had the energy and inclination, a slowly cooked elephant's foot.

Wild fowl, such as duck, goose, dove, pigeon, bustard, korhaan, guinea fowl, quail, francolin and dikkop (now known as 'thick-knee') might well be on the menu. But even given these additions, poor or bad diet linked with or leading to disease as well as with exhaustion and prolonged exposure to the elements took its toll. When Baldwin returned to Durban in 1852, he weighed a mere 5 st. 11 lb (37 kg).

A pair of field glasses or a telescope was 'an immense assistance'. It was not unknown for supplies and especially gunpowder to be stolen from camp, but this was usually by the locals rather than the hunter's staff.

Hunting lore and the hunting bag

There was an etiquette to hunting that seems to have been generally upheld by these hardy hunters. Elephants when shot were often left in the bush and an ear cut to denote ownership, the tusks being removed later. Cutting off a tail also signified ownership. The first shot was usually given to the best shot in the party. The first to hit an animal gained that prize even if another dispatched the beast.

Then there were the practical actions that were taken, such as letting off shots to guide back a hunter who had not returned to camp by nightfall; the building of a huge bonfire when the camp was broken up, to dispose of refuse; and shooting some buck for the local population.

One of the problems when looking at these early hunters is to determine the extent of their bag. The temptation to exaggerate, especially when writing down an account for posterity, must have been very great. When one takes into consideration the additional African hunters these men employed, the figures cannot overall be so much exaggerated. Here are a few examples of the figures claimed by the nimrods of the Zululand wilderness:

DELEGORGUE: 8–9 months in 1842: 500 buffalo, 200 'wild boar' and small antelope, 60 eland, 43 elephant, 18 kudu, 4 rhino, 4 hippo, 2 waterbuck and 2 'quagga'.

COWIE: 1849: 86 elephant, but few large bulls.

CAPTAIN FADDY: 1849 (including Swaziland): 137 elephant, 42 buffalo, 39 eland, 17 rhino, 10 'net buck', 8 kudu, 7 'wild bore', 4 hartebeest, 1 lion, 1 hippo and 1 wolf (hyena).

BALDWIN: 1852 trip: 55 hippo and 1 elephant.

SHADWELL: 1853 (according to Baldwin): 150 hippo and 91 elephant.

HOGG: 1858: 95 elephant from a herd of 1 500–2 000.

DRUMMOND: late 1860s to early 1870s, in one day: 29 buffalo.

DUNN: There are claims of Dunn slaughtering thousands of buffalo, including one claim of more than 800 in three months. One specific claim by Dunn, in a three-month period: 203 hippo.

In William Baldwin's book *African hunting*, he names 20 species of animal that he killed in his five hunting trips into Zululand between 1852 and 1855 – 18 months in total in the field. In addition he names over ten other species, and some of these he may have shot. Baldwin also mentions 19 types of bird, though some of these have generic names such as bustard, goose and partridge and, as such, are difficult to identify. On the other hand, an unpublished hunter's diary for a 71-day hunting trip to Zululand in 1850 records 45 shooting occurrences. The number of animals noted as killed by at least five hunters was only 23 birds and 22 mammals; the mammals being 7 buck, 7 buffalo, 5 wild pig, 1 eland, 1 hippo and 1 hare. Recorded as having got away were 2 birds and 37 mammals: 16 buffalo, 9 buck, 5 elephant, 2 lion, 1 hyena and 1 wild pig.[31]

The hunters' dogs

Among the desiderata for which Shaka was prepared to trade ivory he listed the famous macassar oil, a seal, a likeness of George III – and also large dogs.[32] Perhaps the Zulu Napoleon got the hounds and they contributed to the distinctive dogs even today to be seen in Zululand and especially Maputaland. Certainly large dogs, deerhounds, mastiffs and the like were brought into Durban from abroad to hunt in Zululand, but these imports had a bad reputation with the local white hunters, who found that they succumbed quickly to disease. William Baldwin, who has quite a bit to say on the subject of dogs, talks of seven deerhound, purchased from Lord Fitzwilliam's keeper, in his 'outfit'. But these Scottish deerhounds all 'succumbed to the climate' sooner or later. In his book *Camp life and sport in South Africa*, published in 1878, Thomas Lucas comments:

> To assist the Zulus in the chase, large dogs of the lurcher breed are employed. They are held in leashes until required, and are very swift and staunch. Strange to say, English dogs will not live many months in Natal, but they are often imported for the purpose of crossing with the native dogs, especially the bull dog, which supplies the pluck so deficient in the native animal, and makes the latter most valuable for hunting purposes.[33]

William Drummond admired the 'Amaponda greyhound', describing it as follows: 'He was a fine-looking animal, approaching a staghound in height, but longer and more powerful both in the chest and hind-quarters, though in other points resembling a greyhound, all except his long ears, which stand erect like those of the wild dog (*Canis pictus seu venaticus*), gave him a most curious and wild-beast appearance.'[34]

Drummond claimed that dogs were not necessary for the hunting of large game, though he clearly did use them and even devoted a chapter in *The large game* to 'Hunting with dogs'. For

'ROVER: A NOBLE HOUND' Hunters loved their dogs, often more than the company of fellow human beings. Hunting accounts are full of the names of long-dead hounds which had performed noble service. Occasionally, as in this case with Vaughan Kirby's dog Rover, an illustration appeared in the hunting memoir.
KIRBY, *IN THE HAUNT OF WILD GAME*

the hunter's dog too often the price was death, and even Baldwin, who one suspects preferred his dogs' company to that of his fellow hunters, shot his hound Venture, who had become 'sulky' and would not follow him. And, of course, a hunter might shoot his own dog by accident. This happened to Drummond, and greatly distressed him. Usipingo had been a fine hunter, killing 37 buck in a six-week period. Of him Drummond wrote, 'I afterwards had faster dogs, and some with better noses, but I never had his equal in common sense.'

Then there were instances of dogs being killed when run over by one of the wagon wheels, but it was more likely for a dog to be killed by a wild animal.[35] Leopards in particular took a heavy toll on dogs. Robert Struthers's party lost five dogs to leopards in one night in April 1854. But there were other dangerous animals for the dog. Baldwin's Fly went missing and was presumed bitten by a snake, probably a mamba. David Leslie recalls an incident when an elephant trampled a dog to pieces. And no less than three of Drummond's dogs were taken by crocodile at the Phongola River. Baboons were another danger and, it was said, could decimate a pack of dogs in ten minutes. Drummond's 'great yellow dog' Leauw was killed by a gigantic warthog. This yellow hound may have been what was called a 'Boer-hound' or iGovu, so much beloved by Dingane.[36]

When the naturalist Robert Plant was wading over the entrance to Lake St Lucia to gain the eastern shore, his dogs had

'THE DEATH OF "LOUP"' Captain Lindley's dog Loup met his end as did many a hunter's hound – a tasty supper for a crocodile. LINDLEY, *AFTER OPHIR*, C. 1870

to swim the considerable distance. In his account Plant wrote in pencil in his little notebook:

> all went pleasant as any other water party need desire except that the poor dogs became exhausted before we reached the opposite bank and it was necessary to carry them through. I shall never forget the moanings of one poor brute as he struggled with his last strength. When making a last effort he clung around me with the energy of despair. It was an appeal not to be resisted and carry him I must. He was a brave dog as he afterwards proved in the face of many a buffalo but his courage had then entirely deserted him.[37]

Both bitches and dogs were used to hunt. It is hardly surprising that the hunters were often deeply attached to their hounds and mentioned their names in their accounts. Baldwin had dogs with names such as Crafty, Dusty, Fly, Hopeful, Hotspur, Juno, Laddie, Nettle, Ragman, Smoke ('my little pet') and Venture.[38] When 'alone among the Zulu', Catherine Barter had Stiggins to protect her. As well as Leauw, William Drummond's faithful companions included Old Shot and Usipingo.

The dogs were an integral part of the camp and camp life. Baldwin paints a lovely picture of a wet and miserable night spent under the wagon. At one end slept the African hunters

'curled up like dormice in their blankets, and generally sleeping through everything, and a host of wet and dirty, muddy and shivering, dreaming dogs on the top of us'. His 'best dog' was Ragman, a bulldog–greyhound cross, with 'a dash of pointer' – 'the best breed possible'. Ragman also had a powerful appetite, and would eat 'huge rashers' off a recently killed animal, 'when the sun is at the hottest, at which time very few dogs will feed, however hungry, saving us the trouble of carrying food for him'.[39] Hunting dogs were often great feeders and as a treat were sometimes given milk obtained from local African homesteads.

Dogs were good company and indispensable to the hunt, but they were also watchdogs for the camp, barking at any leopard, hyena or lion that ventured too near.

In the context of hunting in Zululand, horses were written about much less than dogs, probably because much hunting was done on foot. James Proudfoot had a horse called Blesbok. Baldwin had an old horse called Mouba ('sugar'). As was the South African practice, the creature was knee-haltered at night, which was a strap which kept the horse's head within a foot (30 cm) of its head. One night Mouba wandered off and amazingly survived for three months before being found, and still with the knee-halter attached.[40]

Death and disease

Accidents were, surprisingly, not too common. Wahlberg noted how a carbine had burst when hunting at Mfolozi in 1842, 'a great piece of loading chamber and tail-screw had vanished. Willem was wounded in the face, but only slightly, and burnt with the powder.'[41]

If hunters died, it was because of disease rather than because of camp accidents or because they were eaten by lion. William Baldwin, though, had a narrow escape when a crocodile nearly got him in the Umlalazi River in 1852: he was unscathed, though his gun went to the bottom of the river. Occasionally there were reports of a tragic mishap. In 1886, for instance, a Mr W. Brandon was accidentally shot dead when taking a loaded gun from his wagon.[42] Much more common was a hunter or even a hunting party being struck down by malaria.

The link between malaria and mosquitoes was not known to these early hunters. Indeed the link was only conclusively proved by Major, later Professor, Ronal Ross in India in 1897/98. A generation earlier in Zululand there was no shortage of references to 'clouds of mosquitoes' that were a terrible and uncomfortable nuisance. As one store owner commented, 'I was kept busy the whole night scraping my bare arms from shoulder downwards and arriving at hands with a roll of dead mosquitoes.'[43] There were some areas where mosquitoes were said to be very bad. Leslie commented that 'I believe, the birthplace of the mosquito-kind must have been upon the Usutu [River]'. The Nseleni, Mfolozi and Msunduzi rivers, and of course Lake St Lucia, all had a bad reputation as places where one might be 'eaten alive' by mosquitoes. It must be remembered that because of twentieth-century drainage systems and exotic afforestation, the greater St Lucia wetland is now a smaller area than it would have been in the 1850s.

Encamped at the northern end of Lake St Lucia where it links to the Mkhuze marshes, the hunter Robert Struthers commented in his journal on 24 January 1853:

> Mosquitoes are a dreadful pest here – it is very warm – but we have only the choice of being roasted & smoked in the tent or bitten all over – they will get under blankets in spite of every precaution – this seems a very unhealthy locality – although our tent is on an elevation the large flat of the Umkuzi & shores of the lake afford fruitful sources of miasma from the immense quantity of decomposing vegetable matter.

Attempts to burn cow dung had only limited effect unless the smoking pot was placed in a covered wagon, in which case one was overpowered by smoke and heat. And humid heat there was in Zululand. Baldwin, perhaps exaggerating, talks in December 1856 of 140 ºF (60 ºC) in full sun and 93 ºF (34 ºC) in the shade, with the shade temperature sometimes rising to 104 ºF (40 ºC).[44]

There was, however, a link made between 'the fatal miasma' swamp land and the disease. Lake St Lucia and the flats of Maputaland soon developed a bad reputation for the disease. Drummond commented that 'Nyala-shooting and fever are all but synonymous … I have never seen it [fever] south of the Bombo range.'[45]

There also developed a realisation that there was a time of the year when it was dangerous to health to remain in Zululand. In July 1855 the *Natal Mercury* stated that fever was very bad in Zululand, that the son of Mr Willey had died, and that the Zulus were suffering severely and several Africans in the service of white hunters had fallen victim. The paper also noted that it was very unusual for the winter season.[46] Yet there seems to have been a belief that the worst time of the year was not in January, February and March, when the disease was most virulent, but in spring and early summer. Drummond commented that by August the 'unhealthy season was rapidly coming on' and the white hunters were anxious to leave. And there was a belief that when the giant aloe and the coral tree (*Erythrina lysistemon*) flowered, it was time for the hunters to leave Zululand. This also would put the departure at late winter or early spring.[47]

In the late 1840s and early 1850s there was a series of disastrous hunting expeditions into Zululand, with at least 15 white hunters dying of fever, 7 dying in one party. That these hunting expeditions operated during the summer months was the height of folly, and the lesson seems to have been learnt in later years. William Baldwin deals with a disaster he was associated with in the following matter-of-fact way:

> On the 16th [March 1852] we started for Natal, and I can give from this date but a very poor account of anything more that occurred, as I must have had many days' insensibility myself. What I do recollect was that Arbuthnot and Monies joined the wagons again on the 20th, after two very hard days' elephant-hunting on foot, during which Arbuthnot killed one. Arbuthnot complained of being very ill, and threw himself down in the hut, from which he never rose, dying the following day of fever and ague. We made the best of our way to Natal to get advice for the rest of the sick, but on reaching our destination poor Price died also, within forty miles of the town. Monies stayed behind to bring out another wagon, having never had an hour's illness, when suddenly he took desperately ill, and died next day. McQueen reached Durban, where he died in a few days, though he never went into the unhealthy country at all; Purver, Hammond, and Etty, three elephant-hunters of White's party, also died in the Zulu country about the same time; Gibson, Edmonstone, Charley Edmonstone, and myself eventually, but not for nearly twelve months, got better again. We were all, I think, carried out of the wagons in Durban more dead than alive.[48]

Piet Hogg recounted 'one of the most horrible, and awfully thrilling, experiences which ever befell a human being'. In 1851 he and William Mayas were deputed by George Cato to take two Englishmen, two Scots and a Frenchman (named D'Elgasse) to draw charts of Zululand and to hunt. In early March they set off with a dozen African helpers, an oxwagon and one or two horses (the last later dying of horse sickness). Leaving their wagon on high ground, the party made its way on foot to the upper end of Lake St Lucia. Here, in early April 1851 disaster struck. All five visitors died of fever, the African helpers fled, as did Mayas. Hogg, who was attacked with fever too, recorded 'one day when the fever had somewhat abated, I experienced the horrible reality that I was alone amongst the dead!'

Hogg managed to drag himself away from the ghastly scene and, greatly weakened but clutching his rifle, set off south to the Tugela River and safety. 'I had no fear', he wrote, 'and a sense of perfect indifference to danger seemed to take possession of me.' Fortune at last smiled upon Hogg, for having trudged 80 miles (128 km):

> I saw a white man approaching on a pack-ox, and, though unaware of my presence in the neighbourhood, he was coming directly towards me; I sat quite still; when he saw me, he was much surprised at meeting a lonely white man in that part of

the country – and under such circumstances; We recognised each other, and, to my joy, he was one of my boy-hood's companions *Hendrick Strydom*; neither could speak for at first we were choked with tears.

Later Hogg returned to the site where five hunters had died. He found some human bones scattered around the place left by the hyenas and vultures. He collected them together and put them down a porcupine hole, in which mausoleum we trust they still repose.[49]

It was Hogg's belief that the five visitors died because they had persisted in using their own 'method of medical treatment, in preference to our more simple (*although, perhaps, more nauseating*) form'. This was no doubt true, though Hogg's obviously strong constitution must also have contributed to his survival.

There were, of course, other diseases apart from malaria that could be contracted, such as dysentery, smallpox and cholera. The references to having to brush large numbers of ticks off one's body at the end of a day probably meant that tick-bite fever must also have been common. But malaria seems to have been the primary killer. The ever-astute David Leslie commented: 'The great bugbear – the great deterrent – is the fever. Well, it is not pleasant, but one must remember that the many deaths we hear of are mostly of travellers who are exposed to all kinds of hardships – hunger, thirst, fatigue, wet, the burning sun of day, and the dews of heaven by night. They are half-dead before the fever comes.'[50] One had to be very fit to survive and be a successful hunter in the Zululand wilderness, not least because of the long distances one had to run in pursuit of one's prey.

The African population, of course, were not safe from malaria either, especially those who came into Zululand with white hunters or British officials and whose immune system might not have been so strong as the locals'. There is, however, little documentation on this, save for the occasional comment. It is not known how the Natal Africans fared when left behind in Zululand to hunt during the summer months for their white employers.[51]

Of course, it was not just the white hunters and the local population who were affected by malaria; later this was a major problem for the administrators, the police and the army. In the summer of 1890 Charles Saunders pleaded to be transferred from his eyrie on top of the Lebombo Mountains to Eshowe, where his wife and four children lived. 'It would be madness for any one to attempt to bring a wife & family down here,' he wrote. Though the mountaintop was free of malaria for most of the year, the surrounding lowland was fever-stricken. In the two months Saunders had been at the Ubombo magistracy, 'There has been a great deal of fever amongst the people who accompanied me here and one death – I myself have had a return of malaria fever contracted during the latter part of 1887 whilst proceeding to

Tongaland on Govt duty and have not been in the best of health ever since then.' Saunders had his own theory about malaria. In June 1891 he commented:

The grass is commencing to burn & as soon as it is all burnt in the low country travelling there will be attended with less risk of fever as when the rank vegetation of the summer is burnt off. I am of [the] opinion that the fires purify the air to a certain extent & destroy the forms of the disease which accumulate & are retained by the rank herbage that grows during the summer month remains until it is burnt off.[52]

Remedies

Once he was down with malaria, it was vital to get the sick man out of Zululand as fast as possible. Comments such as that made by William Cowie to George Cato in 1849 must have been all too common, 'Old Van Staden has shot a lot of Elephants but is lying sick at Umkosee, his wagon is in to fetch him.'[53] As for treatment, quinine was used when available, but once the hunter went down with a serious bout of malaria his decline and death was often very rapid. Quinine was taken in powder form, sometimes washed down with a shot of gin ('pure hollandse kanal') or brandy if available.[54]

The medicine chest could hold other substances that were employed: emetics such as a Victorian favourite, syrup of ipecac, laudanum, 'Dover's powder' and calomel (mercurous chloride). One recipe included one large teaspoon of mustard and hot water as an emetic, followed by a teaspoon of 'Stockholm tar'. This procedure was undertaken three times a day. In 1896 one colonial official in Maputaland was giving two of his African staff the following to counter fever, 'calomel in 5 grs is generally given and quinine 15 grs at intervals between the expected attacks. Port wine is given to keep up their strength. Tonight I am thankful to say everybody in camp is well.'[55] For bruises there was turpentine and oil; and, as mentioned previously, for sunburn, which was a serious problem, eland fat was regarded as effective.

Attack by human and animal

The remarkable thing about nineteenth-century Zululand is, outside the Anglo-Zulu War, how few whites were killed by Zulus. Even at the height of civil disturbance, a white person might quietly slip away unmolested. On one occasion, on a hot December day in 1856, Baldwin came across a scene of carnage, with decomposing bodies lying hither and yon across the bushveld. Then, to his fright, he met Cetshwayo and his entourage. But he need not have feared; beer was drunk, and the white hunters and the Zulu prince parted on the best of terms.[56]

Piet Hogg, though, had a story of a massive hunting party, costing £1 500, with some 400 hunters who left Durban in 1859 to hunt elephant in Mozambique and who were all killed there. How much of this is exaggeration is not known.

Death from wild animal attack was less frequent than from disease, though attacks did happen when out hunting, usually involving buffalo, lion, elephant or hippo.[57] In 1856 Wahlberg met his match in an old bull elephant who trampled him to death. But that was in what is now Botswana, not Zululand. William Drummond once received a knee wound from a charging buffalo and another time a warthog 'the size of a rhino calf' killed his dog Leauw and cut deep into the calf of Drummond's leg with a tusk. Drummond recorded, 'the blood flowed so freely as to give colour to a suspicion that some important artery was severed – a most unpleasant one when the means of stopping the hemorrhage [sic] are totally wanting'.

One of Drummond's African hunters died after a lion attacked him. Drummond and three helpers had carried the man on a litter 20 miles (32 km) to an African village but he died the next day.[58] On several occasions Drummond killed man-eating lions to help African villages. One such beast, an old male, he described as having 'hardly a tooth in his head … one of the largest and heaviest I ever saw'. Another example of a lion driven by circumstance into attacking humans was 'a large gaunt lioness, reduced by illness and starvation to a mere skeleton'. Drummond was quite firm that 'the lion of South and East Africa rarely goes out of its way to attack people'. And as for the leopard, he asserted, 'despite what Mr Layard has written to the contrary, man-eating leopards do not exist'.

Drummond's checklist of dangerous animals in Zululand was in 'different shades of danger', first the black rhino, then the lion, third the buffalo and finally the elephant.[59]

Profit and loss

Hunting could be a risky business, but it could also be a costly affair. There was the wagon, the oxen, the guns and ammunition, some trading goods, supplies and wages for the African staff. The staff might be paid in kind – in 1850 Piet Hogg promised his African staff a third of the price gained for the ivory. His bag, he claimed, was about 3 000 lb weight (1 359 kg). This being the case, the balance sheet for the hunting expedition might have looked something like this:

3 000 lb of ivory at about 5s. a pound:	£750
Payment to African staff:	£250
Expenses for the trip:	£237
Profit for the Zululand hunting trip:	£263

We do not know if Hogg did indeed pay his staff as promised or if the £263 profit was an individual profit or had to be shared out among the other white hunters. If the last was the case, then the profit can only have been about £65 a head.[60]

David Leslie's account for one trip, after paying his African staff, was 78 cattle for an outlay of £50 worth of goods. He reckoned he had 'about £120 over'.[61]

The prices paid for game products on the local Natal markets were, of course, not those reached on the London trading floors.

TABLE 7

PRICES OF WILD ANIMAL PRODUCTS SOLD IN NATAL IN 1846/47

ANIMAL PRODUCT	PRICE IN MARKET
Blesbok skins	4½d. each
Blue buck skins	4s. 6d. each
Buffalo hides	15s. to £1 7s. 3d. each
Bushpig (wild boar) skins	1s. 6d. each
Elephant tusks	3s. 6d. to 4s. per lb. Prices ranged depending on the size of the tusk; small tusks being as much as 8d. less per pound weight than large tusks.
Hartebeest skins	3s. 2d. each
Quagga (zebra) skins	1s. 6d. each
Rhino horns	5s. 5d. each
Tiger (leopard) skins	5s. 3d. to 9s. 4d. each
Wildebeest skins	10d. each
Zebra skins	1s. 10d. to 2s. 3d. each
Zebra hides	6s. to 7s. 1d. each

Table 7 gives a sample of prices paid in Natal for wild animal products in the mid-1840s.[62]

These profits mentioned were not princely sums. No doubt over a period of time a good hunter or a hunter turned hunting-expedition organiser might have enough to buy a farm. But even this, one expects, would have been in part paid for out of the profit from trading for Zulu cattle. There were no mansions built on Durban's Berea ridge from the profits of hunting in Zululand; those were the domains of the sugar barons.

Hunter's remorse

One has to dig deep to find evidence that any of these Victorian hunters felt much remorse for what they were doing. The modern attitude to animal welfare and indeed animal rights was in its infancy. Yet one should not forget that some of the modern societies for the prevention of cruelty to animals were Victorian foundations, as were various measures designed to outlaw cruelty to animals. The establishment of game reserves and the protection of wild animal species should not be divorced from this growing Victorian concern for animals.

There is little evidence to support any theory that most hunters set out to be cruel to animals, even if their methods resulted in cruelty. Such cruelty included leaving wounded beasts behind in order to catch up with the rest of the herds. When a Zululand female elephant was shot and collapsed squealing in pain, Drummond shouted to his hunters, 'Don't fire; it can't get away; its shoulder's broken; let's go after the others.'

Occasionally hunters might comment that they 'pitied the poor animal' they had shot. F.R.N. Findlay, having shot three reedbuck, noted, 'I greatly regretted the deed when done, especially as it had been the outcome of my bad humour.' Drummond talks of his pity for a wounded eland, with 'great beseeching eyes' and of his lack of an excuse for killing a leopard: 'I had not even its excuse of hunger and necessity.'[63]

But be all this as it may, there was certainly none of the modern sentimentality towards the natural kingdom, save in the sense of respect for a beast that had put up a determined – if unequal – struggle to evade death. Hunting was an accepted pastime, and in the case of Zululand a dangerous pastime, which made it so much more exciting.

What did exist with the more intelligent hunters was a realisation that the continued existence of big game in particular was threatened: they were experiencing the twilight of the hunting age in Zululand as far as elephant, buffalo and hippo were concerned. Drummond knew well that the extermination of game was approaching 'day by day, almost hour by hour'. Yet he then proceeds in 400 pages to chronicle dozens of accounts of his slaughter of the wildlife of Zululand. Despite this paradox,

Drummond did feel strongly for the future existence of the big game, especially of elephant. In his chapter on elephant hunting, he comments:

> I cannot leave this subject without adding my protest against the wanton and wasteful wholesale destruction of these animals that has now been going on for so many years. It is utterly impossible that it can last much longer, as any one who glances at the statistics of the export of ivory from the east coast must at once see. Slowly, but surely, this useful animal is being extirpated, merely for the purpose of supplying Europe with ivory ornaments and billiard-balls.[64]

'Boer filibusters and pot-hunters'

Though white settlement came to Zululand only from the late Edwardian era, there had been already whites settled in parts of western Zululand in the nineteenth century. The civil disruptions in Zululand in 1883 and 1884 had given Afrikaners the opportunity to ally with Prince Dinuzulu against Zibhebhu: the price of such co-operation was land. Thus a vast track of north-western Zululand, including the 3 000 hectare Ngome forest and much of the highveld grazing, had been alienated from the Zulu monarchy, and become the Boer-controlled New Republic. Then in the Emthonjaneni area there was a group of white farmers, mostly Afrikaners, who had also gained farms out of the conflict. The intervention of the British in 1886 blocked their incorporation into the New Republic as a form of protectorate. Nevertheless, they were permitted to retain the Emthonjaneni farms at a nominal quitrent in what was termed Proviso B.[65] So it was that much of western Zululand with its natural resources was alienated from the Zulu people. And in these areas there was little effort made to decelerate the destruction of game or forestland.

But the Boers were no more strangers to Zululand than they were to Swaziland. For years Boer hunters entered both regions to hunt in wintertime, when they sometimes brought their stock into the country. Swaziland suffered more from their hunting expeditions for the simple reason that the Transvaal government had joint control of the country with the British from 1890 and sole control from 1894. By the Edwardian era, it was stated quite bluntly, 'Swaziland as a hunting ground cannot compare with the countries east of the Lebombo.'[66]

In Zululand Boer hunters were mainly to be found in the west and the north. Not infrequently they encountered British hunters, and their meetings were sometimes acrimonious. Both Leslie and later Drummond had heated encounters with Boers over disputed hunting grounds. On occasion, Afrikaner and British did hunt together, especially when both came from Natal.[67]

Later, after official British intervention in Zululand, relationships did not improve and British officials were incensed when they received reports of Boers cutting timber, hunting without licences or even extracting from the local population hut taxes in the form of cash, tobacco, and skins of wildcat, monkey or leopard.[68] By 1894 the Zululand government was writing to the Transvaal government, at the latter's request, giving details of the Zululand game regulations.[69]

Boer poaching went on for years and it is impossible to estimate how much game was destroyed in this way. The British were, probably with reason, fairly certain that royal game was targeted. But they had a problem, as the following note written by Magistrate Newmann of Ingwavuma in 1892 illustrates:

> The men of the Z.P. [Zululand Police] who came across these Boers did not ascertain their names. I had merely ordered them to warn anyone they might meet, and they had a written notice signed by me, setting forth that it is illegal for anyone to hunt in Zululand without leave and stating the penalty for such offence. This paper the Boers took.

I did not think it well to tell the Nonqai [Zululand Police] to arrest white men. The only possible way to prevent the destruction of Royal game in Zululand by Boers would be for a detachment of Z.P. with a white officer to be stationed near this border during the winter.[70]

The police were, however, instructed to seize any Boer cattle found grazing on the Zululand side of the Mkhuze River.

There were, of course, Afrikaners who did apply for and were granted hunting licences in Zululand. Even so, there were times of crisis when the British authorities felt it injudicious to allow Boers into the region, such as in 1888 when application was made by the respectable Emmett family of Vryheid.[71]

When the Anglo-Boer War broke out, Magistrate Colenbrander wisely withdrew from his remote station at Ingwavuma into the Maputaland bush in advance of a large Boer commando. For a period the Boers were once again unmolested and allowed to hunt as they pleased in that part of Zululand and Maputaland.

List of some hunters in Zululand, 1840s–1870s[72]

Only the names of traders who are known to have hunted or traded in wildlife products have been included in this list.
* Denotes those who died (probably from malaria) in Zululand or on his immediate return to Natal
‡ Denotes those killed or mortally wounded by wild animals in Zululand

William Adams	Hans Delange	Piet Hogg	Henry Paxton
W.H. D'Alamaine	Johannes de Lange	Joubert family	Charles Phillips*
David Carnegy Arbuthnot*	Adulphe Delegorgue	Christian Krauss	Dirius Potgieter sen
Casper Badenhorst	D'Elgasse*	Koos Kruht	H.A. Pretorius
Louw Badenhorst jun.	David Divana‡	David Leslie	E.R. Price*
Louw Badenhorst sen.	Hon. William Henry Drummond	Dr H.J. Luke	James Proudfoot
William Charles Baldwin	Thomas Duff	– McGibson	William Purver*
Lieutenant Barnes	G.W. Duncan	William Hay McLean*	Septimus Sanderson
Charles Barter	John Dunn	David McQueen*	George Shadwell
Matthew Barr	Charles Waterton Edmonstone	Salomon Maritz	R.W. Shadwell
James Bell	Charles Edmonstone jun	William Mayas	W.H. Smith
Daniel Bezuidenhout	Hon. C. Ellis	William Mayoss	– Steel
Hans Bezuidenhout	Charles W. Etty*	Isaac Maxwell	Robert Briggs Struthers MD
James Brody	James Evans	Jan Meyer	Hendrick Strydom
George Cato	– Fletcher‡	J.H. Monies*	Johannes Strydom*
Henry Cato	Alexander Forbes	– Moreton	Henry Tafelt
John Clark	Dirk Fourie	Dr Morris	Cornelis van Rooyen
Lieutenant Clifton	Henry Frances	Christian Muller	Koos van Staden
Stephanus Combrink	– Gaisot	Gideon Nel	Marthinus Viljoen
William Cowie	– Gibson	J.J. Nel	– Walmsley
H. Dafel	Angus 'Jack' Grant	Willem Nel	John Alfred (Elephant) White
W.H. D'Alamaine	Frederick Hammond*	Isaac Niekerk	– Willey
Henning J. Davel	Captain Harris*	Henry Ogle	
Isaac Johannes Davel	William Humphreys	John Ogle	

REFERENCES

1 National Archives, London, FO 403/302, 7322, 15 August 1896, quoted in Carruthers, 'Game protection in the Transvaal, 1846–1926', p. 198.

2 Campbell Collections, Durban, Miller papers, Von Wissell 'Reminiscences', fol. 32. The great hunter Selous also often hunted elephant on foot. Baldwin usually hunted on foot but had a dilapidated horse called Bill that he sometimes rode, jumping off to shoot. Horses, however, on account of horse sickness, rarely lasted long in low-lying Zululand. See also Drummond, *The large game*, p. 356; and Leslie, *Among the Amatonga*, pp. 8–9.

3 KZNA, ZGH 757, 2244/1894 and ZGH 758, Z 460/1894; and Ward, *Records of big game*, 1896 and 1899 editions. Rowland Ward himself hunted in Zululand, see 1896 ed., p. 119.

4 Isaacs, *Travels and adventures*, 1, p. 184.

5 *Natal Mercury*, 18 October 1854.

6 *Natal Almanac and Register*, 1885, p. 96.

7 Ballard, 'The role of trade and hunter-traders', p. 9.

8 Ludlow, *Zululand and Cetewayo*, London, 1882, pp. 39–40, quoted in Kemp, 'Johan William Colenbrander', pp. 32–33.

9 See, for example, Baldwin, *African hunting*, pp. 5, 29–30, 45, 133.

10 Ballard, 'The role of trade and hunter-traders', pp. 8–9; and KZNA, SNA, 1/1/7, miscellaneous papers, 1/1857, 'Zululand traders: Claims for losses sustained by the Zulu disturbances in December 1856'.

11 Killie Campbell Collections, Cato papers, W. Cowie to G.C. Cato, 10 September 1849; and Spencer, *British settlers in Natal*, 6, p. 5.

12 KZNA, Robinson papers, A 354, 4, Robinson to Jameson, 13 September 1876.

13 See, for example, *Natal Times*, 10 December 1852 and 7 January 1853.

14 Drummond, *The large game*, p. 267.

15 *Natal Mercury*, 31 March 1853.

16 Baldwin, *African hunting*, pp. 12 and 19; and Campbell Collections, Durban, Cato papers, August 1852.

17 Spencer, *British settlers in Natal*, 1, p.11.

18 Gardiner, *Journey to the Zoolu country*, pp. 324–5.

19 Baldwin, *African hunting*, pp. 8 and 106; and Drummond, *The large game*, pp. 191, 231, 294 and 312.

20 Drummond, *The large game*, pp. xi–xii, 246.

21 Baldwin, *African hunting*, p. 135; (Barter), *Alone among the Zulus*, p. 123; Buckley, 'Geographical distribution of the larger mammals of South Africa', p. 278; Drummond, *The large game*, pp. 17–21, 38, 51, 70–1, 137, 149–50, 161, 164, 190, 226–7, 229–30, 238, 246, 252 267–8, 273, 276 and Chapter 7; Merrett and Butcher (eds.), *Struthers*, p. 38; *Natal Mercury*, 25 October 1854 and 11 July 1855; Van Jaarsveld, *Mtunzini*, p. 27; and Webb and Wright, *Stuart Archive*, 3, p. 226.

22 Gardiner, *Journey to the Zoolu country*, pp. 111–13.

23 Gardiner, *Journey to the Zoolu country*, p. 124; and Pridmore (ed.), *Humphreys*, 13 September 1851.

24 Drummond, *The large game*, p. 29.

25 Spencer, *British settlers in Natal*, 6, p. 19.

26 Baldwin, *African hunting*, pp. 64, 116, 121; and Drummond, *The large game*, pp. 152–5, 185, 192.

27 Baldwin, *African hunting*, p. 33.

28 Baldwin, *African hunting*, p. 51.

29 See, for example, KZNA, Morewood papers, anonymous hunting diary, 1850.

30 Baldwin, *African hunting*, pp. 53, 131.

31 KZNA, Kitbird collection, Piet Hogg papers, A 79, vol. 7, fol. 26; and Morewood papers, A 1273, anonymous hunting diary.

32 Spencer, *British settlers in Natal*, 6, p. 273.

33 Lucas, *Camp life and sport in South Africa*, p. 102.

34 Drummond, *The large game*, p. 319.

35 Killie Campbell Collections, Durban, Cato papers, 17 October 1852.

36 Drummond, *The large game*, pp. 238 and 336–38; Merrett and Butcher (eds.), *Struthers*, p. 49; and Leslie, *Among the Amatonga*, p. 14.

37 Robert Plant notebook, private ownership.

38 For Baldwin's comments on dogs in Zululand, see *African hunting*, pp. 4, 7, 24, 34, 36, 40, 44, 49–52, 60–62, 74, 101, 112–13, 115, 118, 125, 128, 140. See also illustrations opposite pages 107, 118, 119.

39 Baldwin, *African hunting*, pp. 7, 115.

40 Baldwin, *African hunting*, pp. 112–13.

41 Craig and Hummel (eds.), *Johan August Wahlberg*, p. 89.

42 KZNA, ZGH 697, newspaper cutting, 1886.

43 Baldwin, *African hunting*, pp. 11, 25, 134; Killie Campbell Collections, Durban, Miller papers, Von Wissell 'Reminiscences', fol. 21; Drummond, *The large game*, p. 298; and Merrett and Butcher (ed.), *Struthers*, p. 25.

44 Baldwin, *African hunting*, p. 135.

45 Drummond, *The large game*, p. 378.

46 *Natal Mercury*, 11 July 1855.

47 Drummond, *The large game*, p. 162.

48 Baldwin, *African hunting*, pp. 22–3.

49 For malaria-related deaths in Zululand, see Baldwin, *African hunting*, pp. 5, 22, 93; (Barter), *Alone among the Zulus*, pp. 11, 99–100; KZNA, Kitbird collection, Hogg papers, A 79, vol. 7, fols. 22, 23, 26; *Natal Mercury*, 6 September 1854; and Spencer, *British settlers in Natal*, 1, p. 60

50 Leslie, *Among the Amatonga*, p. 259.

51 KZNA, 1/UBO, 3/1/2, Report for the year 1892 (Turnbull), fols. 110–112; and ZA 27, Report on Tongaland, 1896, fols. 25–27.

52 KZNA, 1/UBO, 3/1/1, letterbooks, 17 December 1890, fols. 73–75 and 15 June 1891.

53 Campbell Collections, Durban, Cato papers, Cowie to Cato, 10 September 1849.

54 Gosnell, *Big Bend*, p.162.

55 KZNA, ZGH 793, Bosman to Clarke, 21 October 1896.

56 Baldwin, *African hunting*, pp. 136–7.

57 See, for example, Craig and Hummel (eds.), *Wahlberg*, p. 32; and KZNA, Hogg papers, 1854 and 1857.

58 Drummond, *The large game*, pp. 269, 276–7, 337.

59 Drummond, *The large game*, pp. 15, 130–1, 231–3, 239, 252–65, 273, 276.

60 KZNA, Kitbird collection, Hogg papers, fol. 20.

61 Leslie, *Among the Amatonga*, p. 31.

62 *Natal Witness*, 24 & 31 July 1846 and 17 December 1847.

63 Findlay, *Big game shooting*, pp. 203 and 224.

64 Drummond, *The large game*, pp. 220–1.

65 Laband, *Rope of Sand*, pp. 375–76.

66 KZNA, ZGH 708, Report on Tongaland, SNA 1033/1887, fols. 49–50; and *Swaziland, Tongaland and northern Zululand*, War Office, London, 1905, p. 9.

67 Drummond, *The large game*, pp. 267, 284, 294–5. See also Baldwin, *African hunting*, p. 93.

68 *Correspondence relating to certain native territories situated to the north-east of Zululand*, c-7780, p. 34.

69 KZNA, ZA 44, letter dated 9 February 1894 and ZGH 755, minute paper, Z 131/1894, 9 February 1894.

70 KZNA, 1/NGA, minute paper, ND 304/92, 13 July 1892.

71 KZNA, 1/NGA, minute paper, ND 31/1888, 31 March 1888.

72 Many of these individuals have entries in Shelagh O'Byrne Spencer's excellent series *British settlers in Natal: A bibliographical register.*

CHAPTER 4

White residents

A NATAL COASTAL FARM
Plantation farms were scattered along the north coastal subtropical belt of Natal. It was not uncommon for hunters and naturalists to stop over at such farms.
REV. G.H. MASON, *ZULULAND: A MISSION TOUR IN SOUTH AFRICA*, 1862

As well as the whites who visited the country there were white people who lived in late-Victorian Zululand permanently or for a long period. The Boers of Emthonjaneni have already been mentioned but the most famous white resident, and indeed the most prolific hunter in Zululand in the colonial and immediate pre-colonial period, was John Dunn.

John Dunn

In 1897 Charles Barter published *Natal and Zululand: A poem*. Among the many contemporary characters alluded to in this epic verse was the following reference to the greatest of the nineteenth-century Zululand hunters:

While far away, like English park,
Dotted with trees, with herbage green
A space of open ground was seen:
There, circled by lofty wall
We saw the military kraal
Where with John Dunn, the prince [Cetshwayo] of late
A mighty hunt did celebrate.[1]

John Dunn was the son of an eastern Cape 1820 English settler called Robert Newton Dunn, who had come to Port Natal in the mid-1830s. He acquired an estate called Sea View not far from the tiny village and witnessed the dramatic events when the Zulu razed the settlement and when the British and the Boers fought each other. He was killed in September 1847 when he fell from his horse, possibly after it had been surprised by elephants. John Dunn was then about 14 years old. His mother died four years later and Dunn was left to fend for himself. It was a hard existence at Port Natal, especially without parents. It is hardly surprising that he turned to transport riding and hunting in Zululand. In July 1854 the hunter William Baldwin was meant to meet up with Dunn – 'a friend of mine' – at the Phongola River, but Dunn had just been carried out of the area 'almost dead', presumably from malaria.[2]

Dunn was soon fluent in isiZulu. Befriended by Captain Joshua Walmsley, the British authorities' Zulu Border Agent at Nonoti, Dunn saw action at the battle of Ndondakusuka in 1856. Though he had fought against Cetshwayo in the Zulu civil war, the young white man impressed Mpande's son, and he was soon living as a headman in southern Zululand.

Southern Zululand was then sparsely populated, partly because of the civil war, but also because of the substantial numbers of large and dangerous game in the area. Dunn set about establishing a fiefdom for himself, gathering upwards of 6 000 followers around him and eventually marrying, as well as Catherine Pierce, 48 Zulu wives. He consolidated his position not only by advising Cetshwayo, especially after he became king in 1873, but also by importing arms into Zululand specifically for Cetshwayo's Usuthu followers. He also undertook what can only be described as an extermination policy against the big game of southern Zululand.

When the Anglo-Zulu War broke out, Dunn and some followers fled to Natal, and the 'White Chief' advised the British army on the drive into Zululand which culminated in the burning of his old master's capital at Ulundi on 4 July 1879. After this Dunn was rewarded by being granted one of the 13 chiefdoms into which Zululand was divided. Even when this scheme failed in 1883, Dunn, with a clan of about 30 000 Zulu and Tsonga, still managed to turn circumstances to his advantage. Until he died on 5 August 1895 Dunn effectively kept southern Zululand fairly quiet in difficult circumstances, under the discreet eye of a British resident and a handful of magistrates in what was termed the Zulu Reserve.

Emotions ran high over John Dunn: he was seen as a coward, an opportunist, a gunrunner, a traitor to his culture and a traitor to Cetshwayo. To this description some today might add a despoiler of the indigenous environment, be it fauna or flora. It may well be that at least some of these allegations are accurate. He was certainly tough and pragmatic, a man who lived in a twilight world between two cultures, never quite forsaking the company of Joe Cato and the like. He was always quiet and courteous on his visits to Durban; he was a man who paid his bills and who could mix without embarrassment with the men of stature in Natal.

As far as Dunn's activities in the hunting field were concerned, he appears to have run perhaps the largest hunting enterprise in the history of South Africa. He was said to employ several hundred Zulu hunters, trained by himself and many of them armed with rifles. Dunn's hunting appears to have had a dual purpose. The first was to clear southern Zululand of dangerous game to make the region safe for human settlement. Dr Ballard in his book on Dunn talks of the lion, buffalo, elephant, hyena and crocodile which were in the Ongoye region when Dunn arrived to live there in 1857. Africans had largely abandoned the area and travelled there only when well armed. The second purpose was mercantile: Dunn ran a commercial hunting outfit. He entertained and offered hunting to white visitors, especially British army officers, administrators and merchants.

Though many other hunters passed through southern Zululand and hunted there, John Dunn was permanently on the spot and, as such, was probably responsible for much of the decimation of the area's big game. One always has to be cautious of hunters' hunting claims, but Le Roux is probably correct when he wrote of Dunn being responsible for the destruction of several hundred elephant, over a thousand buffalo, and over a thousand hippopotamus. Certainly by the mid-1880s many species of large game were scarce in the reserve.[3]

The British military

From the conclusion of the Anglo-Zulu War in 1879 onwards there was a British military presence in at least southern Zululand. However, it must be said that this was not particularly large. Nonetheless, in the area around Eshowe, there were British soldiers only too eager to get in a little sport, and John Dunn was ever pleased to facilitate a day's shooting. In fairness, it is also true that the Victorian army officer was often equally desirous to be collecting plants or butterflies in the cause of science.

It was over the cutting of timber rather than shooting animals that the civil and military authorities tended to be at odds. The military was a great consumer of timber, and the OC was generally not enthusiastic about paying for licences, nor indeed overly concerned about where timber was obtained. The governor's intervention was required to emphasise the point that there were now conservation laws in force in Zululand.[4]

As far as hunting was concerned, individual British army officers had hunted in Zululand from at least as early as 1852 and probably earlier. By 1900 the governor, Hely-Hutchinson, had to issue strict instructions to Strathcona's Horse that 'the big game in Zululand is not to be shot or destroyed. There are still a few Rhinoceros, white & black, hippo, nyala, koodoo, impala, buffalo, & wildebeeste. The big game is strictly preserved. The white rhinoceros is a really extinct animal.'[5]

There is, however, no evidence that the military in Zuluand

TABLE 8

ZULULAND TRADING STORES IN 1902, WITH LOCATION AND DATE OF ESTABLISHMENT

DISTRICT OF ZULULAND	NUMBER OF TRADING STORES	DATES OF ESTABLISHMENT
Nquthu	9	1886 (4), 1888 (3), 1892, 1893
Nkandla	10	1886, 1887 (2), 1888, 1891, 1892, 1894, 1896, 1898 (2)
Eshowe	6	1880, 1883, 1884, 1894, 1895, 1899
Emthonjaneni	3	1892, 1895, 1896
Mahlabatini	7	1887 (2), 1889 (2), 1890 (3)
Ndwandwe	5	1886, 1890, 1891, 1893, 1894
Umlalazi	3	1881, 1882, 1889
Lower Umfolozi	2	1886, 1891
Hlabisa	4	1891, 1892, 1893, 1894
Ubombo	5	1895, 1897 (2), 1899, [1 with no date]
Ingwavuma	3	1897, 1899, 1902
Total number of stores	**57**	

during the Anglo-Boer War were in any way as destructive of the game as was the British irregular mounted unit in Swaziland know as Steinacher's Horse.[6]

Trading stores

A certain romance lingers around the old Zululand trading store, perhaps because one of them was the early home of one of the giants of South African literature, William Plomer. After the Anglo-Zulu War, trading stores supplanted the itinerant hunter-trader in his wagon with his beads, blankets and pick-handles. Like the mission stations, the trading store tended to be where most people lived. They were concentrated, therefore, in the south and the west of Zululand, as Table 8 illustrates. Only five of these stores pre-date 1886: those in the Eshowe and Umlalazi areas.[7]

In 1893 the popular writer of African adventure stories, Bertram Mitford, described the interior of a trading store on the border of Natal and Zululand:

A massive counter divides the interior, and against the further wall a row of shelves share their services with the beams overhead in holding the articles which constitute the stock-in-trade. And this is varied and abundant. Green blankets and Salampore … weigh down the shelves aforesaid. Old military surtouts and uniform coats hanging from pegs tempt those whose inclinations towards civilization may lie in the direction of sumptuary tawdriness, while striped shirts, and even moleskin trousers, find a fairly ready sale. Festoons of many-coloured beads and strings of brass buttons likewise tempt the eye of those gaudily disposed, while butcher knives and copper wire, rolls of tobacco and tins of snuff, coffee and sugar in canisters, tin-ware and three-legged cooking-pots, looking-glasses and accordions, a concertina or two, matches, candles and lanterns, together with other articles too varied for enumeration, are disposed around on shelves or pegs. The atmosphere of the place is dark and rather stuffy …[8]

The importance of 'this primitive temple of Mammon' in the saga of the destruction of wildlife might not seem apparent. There is, however, sufficient evidence to suggest that they were a factor. There were those store owners who were themselves energetic hunters. The most notable was Frank Green, who owned stores at the edge of Ongoye forest and at Umvutyini, both in the Umlalazi district. Further north in Maputaland was the colourful Field Cornet Ferreira who was not above collecting tax from the locals erroneously on behalf of the British government in the form of money, cattle or skins.[9] A man named Retcher ran a store there on the top of the Lebombo Mountains, where the Boers and the British vied for the hegemony of Chief Sambane's territory. Retcher also acted as the first game ranger for the newly proclaimed Pongola Game Reserve just to the west in Boer-controlled territory.[10]

The most famous stores in northern Zululand were owned by Messrs Wissell and Finetti: one at Ingwavuma and a second at Mtini. Ettore de Finetti was described by Wissell, or Von Wissell, as 'an irredentist Austrian of Italian descent' whose nickname was Pat O'Fenetti.[11] Their store was at Mtini, near the present Ndumo Game Reserve – where the Usuthu and Phongola rivers met to form the Maputa River – beside a large Natal mahogany tree, 'the worst place in Zululand for fever and horse-sickness'.[12] On the

'FARM IN THE TUGELA THORNS', 1860s Isolated from colonial Natal society, there existed a number of white farms either on the border of Zululand or actually within the region, as indeed there were white squatters in some of the southern Zululand forests. Life on these frontier farms was hard, but more than one hunter struck down by malaria had his life saved by the nursing given by a kindly farming family.

BATES, *ILLUSTRATED TRAVELS*

river they kept two large punts, each capable of carrying 20 people or four horses. Here, as in many Zululand stores, not only goods but also accommodation could be obtained. In the case of the Wissell and Finetti store, there was the added attraction of a young pet kudu called Bob, who was closely attached to Fenetti's pointer bitch Nelly. Sadly Bob was found dead one day having been stabbed. As Wissell remarked, 'Such generally is the way with pets, never a satisfactory ending.'

At some of the Zululand trading stores not only liquor but also gunpowder could be obtained. One trader in Ubombo asked and received permission to sell government gunpowder to the local African population, without a profit to himself, for he asserted it would bring custom to his store.[13]

Most trading stores in the game areas, not surprisingly, carried on a trade in wild-animal products. Wissell commented, 'Our principal lines were game-horns, fowls, hides, cattle and rubber, which we all disposed of in Delagoa.'[14] Later, when the authorities offered a bounty of 10s. for the head of a crocodile, Wissell set strychnine out in lumps of meat: 'The result was very satisfactory. Three days after the bait had been taken one would notice crocodiles floating in the water, the yellow bellies uppermost.' One month he killed 151 crocodile this way.

Wissell also took the famous hunter Selous to shoot nyala into the very thick Mahemane bush, with its cactus-like rhino thorn (*Euphorbia grandicornis*). 'Selous was very successful on that trip obtaining all the specimens he desired, for the British Museum,

Cape Museum as well as for himself.' Wissell added that Selous had not had time to shoot the 'Mhlengaan (the tiny Blue Livingstone antelope)', the only African buck Selous had not shot, and 'which is fairly plentiful in the bushes to the East of the Pongola'.

The Zululand trading-store owner was not beyond the unlicensed cutting of wood from the local forest or bush, but – more serious – some were not beyond either poaching royal game or trading in their products. In July 1897 the two owners of a store in Lower Umfolozi were tried and convicted of killing two white rhino. A search of the store and another they owned in Hlabisa, however, failed to reveal the skull and horns of the killed animals.[15]

Missionaries

Christian missionaries also played a role in the decimation of game, both direct and indirect, though they were perhaps less involved in this than were the store owners. The missionaries were scattered around Zululand, especially where there were concentrations of human settlement. In 1880 there were 17 mission stations.[16]

Missionaries frequently assisted white hunters that came into the territory, by providing accommodation or food to the traveller. The American Board Mission station at Esidumbeni near Groutville on the Natal side of the Tugela River border was a favourite stopping-off spot for both hunters and naturalists.[17] Missionaries also sometimes tended to a hunter who had gone down with malaria.

But missionaries too killed game, usually in response to the pleas of locals.[18] William Baldwin recounted visiting a mission station in October 1853 and finding that the missionary had gone off at the request of a chief 'to poison lions ninety or a hundred miles off'.[19] Catherine Barter described one method missionaries had of catching hyena:

At the Norwegian station they [hyena] were so numerous and troublesome that it was found necessary to devise some mode of destroying them, in order to preserve the sheep and goats. A small hut of wattle was erected in a convenient place, and the body of some dead animal was placed within it. A trap-door above the entrance was kept invitingly open, being held by a string fastened to the bait. The moment the hyæna entered and began to pull at the meat the door fell, and he found himself a prisoner.

During my stay the missionary caught several of these animals, and one morning two were found together in the trap. They were of different kinds. I conclude the larger one was *Hyæna cruenta*, the other one probably *H. villosa*, called by the Dutch 'Strand Wolf'. I was told that several of their relations stood outside the trap, after the two were caught, howling and making a terrible noise.[20]

Gun clubs

By the 1890s there were enough whites permanently in Zululand for rifle clubs to be formed. First came the Melmoth-based Nkandla Rifle Association, established in 1893, and this was followed by another in Eshowe in 1895. By 1899 the former rifle club had 20 members: 8 were store owners or assistants, 6 were policemen, 2 were prospectors, and the remaining 4 were the local magistrate, the clerk of the court, the district commissioner of mines and the local gaoler. The extent of the hunting carried on by these associations is not known.[21]

REFERENCES

1 Barter, *Stray memories – Natal and Zululand: A poem*, p. 46.

2 Baldwin, *African hunting*, p. 82.

3 For commentary on John Dunn see Ballard, *The transfrontiersman: The career of John Dunn in Natal and Zululand, 1834–1895*, pp. 330–353; *Dictionary of South African Biography*, 1, pp. 260–62; Le Roux, *Pioneers and sportsmen of South Africa*, p. 106; Lesley, *Among the Amatonga*, p. 21; Moodie (ed.), *John Dunn, Cetywayo and the three generals*, pp. 18, 29–30, 42; O'Byrne Spencer, *British settlers to Natal*, 5, pp. 174–77; Van Jaarsveld, *Mtunzini*, pp. 19–25; and Vincent, 'The history of Umfolozi Game Reserve', p. 32.

4 See, for example, KZNA, ZGH 774, minute paper, Z 116/1897, 17 February 1897. In Natal it was said that it was the British military who decimated the hartebeest population around Newcastle. See *Blue Book of Natal*, Newcastle magistrate report, GG 13, 1882.

5 KZNA, GH 1633, minute paper, RM C 138/00, 1 June 1900 and ZA 33, minute paper, CR 283, 31 May 1900.

6 Gosnell, *Big bend*, p. 39.

7 KZNA, GH 1562.

8 Mitford, *The gun-runner: A tale of Zululand*, p. 2.

9 KZNA, ZA 5, report, 1887, fol. 7.

10 *Correspondence relating to certain native territories situated to the north-east of Zululand*, c-7780, p. 34; and KZNA, ZGH 789, report, 26 May 1895 and ZGH 796, Foxon report, 1896.

11 Killie Campbell Collections, Miller papers, Von Wissell 'Reminiscences', 84 fols.

12 Gosnell, *Big bend*, pp. 161–62; and KZNA, ZA 31, minute paper, Z 680/96, includes a sketch map marking the site of the Wissell and Finetti store.

13 KZNA, 1/UBO, minute paper, UB 42/95, February 1895.

14 Killie Campbell Collections, Miller papers, Von Wissell 'Reminiscences', fols. 45–6.

15 KZNA, 1/MEL, minute paper, PB 313/1897, 24 July 1897 and 1/NGA, minute paper, ND 390/1892, 29 September 1892 & ND 181/1893, 20 June 1893.

16 KZNA, ZGH 715, 1880 Boundary Commission, p. 24.

17 *Hooker's Journal of Botany*, 4, 1852, pp. 257, 260.

18 KZNA, 1/MTB, minute paper, H 260/1901.

19 Baldwin, *African hunting*, p. 52.

20 (Barber), *Alone among the Zulus*, p. 174.

21 KZNA, ZA 32, confidential minute, R 23/99.

Soldiers of King Eyo

Soldier of Soso

CHAPTER 5

African society

In 1853 the *Nautical Magazine* carried the reminiscences of Charles Maclean, the supposed legendary 'John Ross', of his time in the land of the Zulu in the 1820s. In one of these articles Maclean recalled:

> Though the Zulu country abounds with game of almost every description, hunting forms no part of the native pursuits, either as a source of pleasure or profit. This can be accounted for by the aversion which the Zulu has for all animal food excepting that of oxen … The King occasionally indulges in hunting the elephant and the hyena, with which the country about Natal is much infested.[1]

But was that really the case? This question leads to another: To what extent did African society made use of indigenous plants and wild game and how did this affect the wildlife, bush and forest? Some white commentators in the nineteenth century were convinced that Africans were a destructive and negative force when it came to what today we term environmental matters. But this belief had racial undertones. Such comments were also often made out of ignorance of rural African society and of its ever-changing relationship with nature. Yet it is also too Rousseau-esque to talk of Zulu society living in harmony with nature or of there being a 'natural balance'. At the end of the day, Zulu society was little different from any other self-sufficient or partially self-sufficient rural agricultural society. Rather than a balance, there was a constant shifting, an ebb and flow, in the Zulu farmer's relationship with nature. If nature became too overwhelming, the farmer had to move – and there was the physical room for this to happen. Later, as boundaries were established and white authorities imposed ever-greater restrictions, this key element diminished and the relationship with the forces of nature changed. It was no longer so easy to move one's homestead in times of crisis, so life consequently became more difficult.

Nature was, of course, not always beneficent. Wild animals and locusts ate the Zulu farmer's crops and brought disease to his cattle, while some wild creatures, such as lions and snakes, more directly threatened human life. For the Zulu farmer as much as for the Victorian poet laureate, nature was 'red in tooth and claw', all too often seen as an enemy to be taken on, or at least kept at bay. The 'romance of the countryside' holds greater appeal for the twenty-first-century urban dweller than it might have held for the nineteenth-century farmer, black or white. Zululand may, in Dr Bryant's phrase, have been arcadia, but it was no utopia.

Names

This is not to deny that there was a great affinity between Zulu society and nature. The famous Victorian lady-traveller and botanical artist, Marianne North, recalled hearing Zulu women 'singing and imitating the calls of wild animals and birds'.[2] One only has to look at present-day Zulu surnames to see this Zulu affinity with nature. As Professor Turner has pointed out, there were Zulu clan names such as Ngwenya (crocodile), Ndlovu (elephant), Dube (zebra), Nduli (the river grass *Cyperus natalensis*) and Nala (the tree *Albizia forbesii*). Places were named after indigenous plants, too, such as Ingwavuma, after the Zulu name for the saffron tree (*Cassine transvaalensis*); Mkhuze, named after the lavender tree or umkhuze in isiZulu (*Heteropyxis natalensis*); Ubombo, named after the scented thorn (*Acacia nilotica*); and Hluhluwe, Zulu for monkey rope (*Dalbergia armata*). Rivers, mountains, homesteads and months of the year – uNhlaba (May), uNcwaba (August) and uMandulo (September) – also had nature-related names.

Similarly, Turner also lists such Zulu regimental names as im-Babazane (nettle), iHlaba (*Aloe* sp.), iHlabane (*Aloe* sp.), iKhwane (sedge sp.) and uTshani (grass).[3] Poland and Hammond-Tooke have highlighted the Zulu names frequently used to denote differently marked nguni cattle; most relate to birds, but some are names of creatures such as insects, snakes, and even the hyena and the eland. Thus a term used for a wild animal might be used to echo the hide coloration or pattern of cattle in a herd.[4]

'ZULU SOLDIERS OF KING PANDA'S ARMY' This famous drawing of King Mpande's warriors by George French Angas well illustrates the use that wild-animal products had in Zulu military regalia in the 1840s. Ostrich feathers, genet and monkey tails, leopard skin and otter skin all featured. ANGAS, *KAFIRS ILLUSTRATED*, 1849

TABLE 9

WILD ANIMAL NAMES IN ISIZULU

ENGLISH NAME	ISIZULU NAME
baboon	imfene
buffalo	inyathi
bushbuck	imbabala
chameleon	unwabu
cobra spp.	imfezi
crocodile	ingwenya
duiker	impundzi
blue duiker	iphiti
grey duiker	impunzi
red duiker	umsumpe/umkumbe
eland	impofu
elephant	indlovu
giraffe	indlulamithi
hippopotamus	imvubu nickname: ndindikuwela
hyena	impisi
silver-backed jackal	impungushe
black-backed jackal	ikhanka
kudu	bheka
leopard	ingwe
lion	ibhubesi
vervet monkey	inkawu
porcupine	ingungumbane
puff adder	ibululu
python	inhlwathi
reedbuck	umziki
black rhino	ubhejane
white rhino	umkhombe
steenbuck	iqhina
waterbuck	iphiva
wild dog	inja yehlathi
blue wildebeest	inkonkoni
bushpig	ingulube yehlathi
zebra	idube

As far as the big game was concerned, not surprisingly, these all had their individual names, some of which are contained in Table 9 above.

It is important to realise that these were not, and are not, obscure names unknown or rarely used. Samuelson observed how the children in Zulu society sat and taught each other 'the names of all the animals, trees, herbs and grasses'. There were also picturesque Zulu idioms taken from nature used in everyday discourse. Professor Koopman cites the morning mist lying over the rivers as *umlalamvubu* – 'what lies on the hippopotamus'.

Similarly, the hour of the day when 'the setting sun begins to cast shadows on the hillsides' was named *elezimpisi*, meaning 'the time of the hyena'.[5]

Ordinary hunting

There were various means by which the Zulu people acquired wildlife products. These included small-time hunting using domesticated dogs and spears, which could be undertaken at any time of year. Even after the introduction of guns into the territory in some numbers in the 1870s, this form of hunting for the pot continued. Hunting was done with a small shield (*ihawu*) and an assegai. The variety of these assegais is illustrated in Table 10.[6]

Hunting was frequently supplemented or indeed supplanted by the use of metal or rope snares and animal traps. Hunting pits (*igebe*) were also used, by both African and white hunters. These pits sometimes had stakes implanted in them on which the hapless animal became impaled. One pit was described as being 3 m deep and very narrow at the bottom. Bryant also lists a large cavern-like trap, a spring snare, a long tapering wicker-cage and various traps used by boys for obtaining wild animals and birds. Boys worked hard and competitively to develop skill in capturing birds.[7]

Then there were the large public hunting parties, or *inqina*, called by a headman. The battlefield tactic of the crescent formation was often employed and it is interesting to speculate in which usage it was developed first – the hunting field or the battlefield. A long fence, upwards of 400 m in length, might also be used to funnel animals. The weapons of the hunt were a bundle of assegais, the small hunting shield (*ihubelo*) and the knobkierie, a short wooden stick with a large knob at the end. How many of the hunting techniques were acquired from the San people it is difficult to tell. Bryant records the following:

> Elephants were frequently hunted with what was called an *iMpingo*. This was a tiny iron blade, no larger than one's thumb-nail, which, smeared with poison (probably learned from the Bushmen), was loosely inserted into a haft; which latter, after striking, soon fell away, leaving the blade embedded in the flesh. Such a poisoned blade, it was said, sufficed to kill an elephant within about six hours.[8]

One can only speculate on whether the legendary fires of sixteenth-century Maputaland had anything to do with hunting practices. Fire – started deliberately by hunters or caused by accident and leading to hunting – was a common enough phenomenon. In 1888 the Cape of Good Hope authorities banned forest hunts by African people on the ground that they 'invariably' led to forest fires. In 1903 Findlay suggested that in the Hluhluwe region Africans had 'fired the jungle' to drive game away from their homesteads, presumably because of the nagana threat.[9]

TABLE 10

ZULU ASSEGAI TYPES

ISIZULU NAME OF ASSEGAI	SIZE OF WEAPON		WEAPON USE
	LENGTH OF BLADE	WIDTH OF BLADE	
Iklwa	18″ [45.7 cm]	13/4″ [4.4 cm]	warfare
Untlekwane	12″ [30.5 cm]	11/4″ [3.2 cm]	stabbing
Isijula	7″ [17.8 cm]	11/4″ [3.2 cm]	hurling
Isipapa	7″ [17.8 cm]	3″ [7.6 cm]	hunting buffalo & big game
Ingcula	5″ [12.7 cm]	1″ [2.5 cm]	hunting & killing cattle
Indlodlela	2″ [5.1 cm]	'tiny blade'	–

The hunting culture

The Zulu and Tsonga killed wildlife for several reasons: for trade, food, clothing and regalia, remedies and rituals, cultural reasons, and to drive wildlife away from farmland.

The issue of trading in wildlife products is discussed later in this chapter. Suffice it to say that from 1790s the trade in wildlife products was considered an important aspect of state.

Closely connected with Zulu trading activity was the network of client peoples whom Shaka had defeated but not directly brought into the Zulu state, an 'informal empire' that included the Tsonga. In October 1903 James Stuart, the Zululand magistrate and collector of Zulu folklore, interviewed an old man, Bikwayo ka Noziwawa. Part of his testimony included the following:

> I used to go to Tongaland with my father – as mat-bearer … we used to go for genet skins for the warriors' dancing girdles; blue monkey skins for the strips worn at the side of the face; leopard and otter skins for the warriors' headbands; blue cloth to be worn by the king's isigodhlo; large red beads, and lion and leopard claws by chiefs; elephant tusks (for the king who would send them on to the Europeans); rhinoceros horns for making snuff boxes of the type carried in the ear lobe (for the amakosikazi); beads; calabashes, gourds, etc.; beer baskets, food baskets, ubusenga rings, ornamental sticks and knob-sticks, and many other articles – ostrich feathers, and umampabane beads worn by chiefs.
>
> We would go and demand these things. If people refused we would stab them. They had to pay tribute with these things in Zululand – that is, the nearer, small, low-country tribes.

A British colonial report on Maputaland, dated 1887, noted: 'Their [the Tsonga] tribute to the Zulus 50 years ago was paid in copper, ivory and catskins (leopard skins).' It also appears that in addition the Swazis and the Boers occasionally extracted leopard and monkey skins from the Tsonga.[10] Whether or not this implies that such commodities were scarce in the Zulu kingdom is a matter

for conjecture. This form of tribute was in addition to the ongoing barter trade. When David Leslie entered Maputaland in the 1870s he felt it worth his while lugging a 35-gallon (159 l) cask of rum with him as a sweetener for the Tsonga king.

The Tsonga were certainly fine hunters. In 1857, Robert Plant, on a fateful trip deep into Maputaland, made the following entry in pencil in his notebook: 'They [the Tsonga] combine the occupations of agriculturist and hunter. In the latter capacity they are very expert at attacking the elephants and other large animals with their assegais and by repeated wounds and shouting intimidate and finally kill him. Pit-falls we found in every direction.'[11]

According to Eugène Casalis, in the early 1860s, from Basutoland to Zululand came otter and leopard skins as well as ostrich feathers and the wings of cranes. In exchange the Zulu bartered cattle, hoes, blades for assegais, necklaces and copper rings. Whilst ostriches did occur in Zululand, as the nineteenth century progressed they became rarer, no doubt because of the demand for their feathers. These became expensive and on one occasion Elephant White (John Alfred White) exchanged four ostrich feathers for a goat. By 1893 the going rate in cash for sakabula (long-tailed widowbird) plumes varied from 10s. to 14s. each.[12]

Hunting and culture

As in many societies, the Zulu hunt was a form of ritual. It could mark a special event or a death – the 'washing of the spears'.[13] What was killed and what was done with the body of the dead animal could also be a matter for special rites. Lunguza, one of the informants of James Stuart, recalled the ceremony following the killing of a lion:

> Ordinary people could not put on decorations of leopard claws or lion whiskers. Dingane used to sit on leopard and lion skins. Any leopard or lion killed was carried by a body of men and taken to the king. The king would then jump over the animal. But if any man had lost his life in connection with the animal it would not be carried to the king but skinned on the spot.

THE RITUAL OF THE ZULU HUNTING DANCE is well captured by Angas in his *Kafirs illustrated*, 1849 (plate 14). Though game was not normally the stable diet of the people, the *inqina* was culturally important to the Zulu population. The large buck in this illustration is a reedbuck.

The king would give the great izinduna the skin to clean and make loin covers of it. It was not brought to the king.

In our district, if anyone was killed in a lion or leopard hunt, Jobe would be given permission to make loin covers out of the skin.

I remember seeing Dingane jumping over a leopard or lion. This was done, not in the isigodhlo, but in the cattle kraal. Dancing would accompany this. The king jumped only once. A beast would be killed and eaten along with the flesh of the leopard or lion. The cow meat must not be eaten alone. The leopard etc. would be skinned at Ndhlela's [Ndlela's] quarters. I do not know what became of the bladders. They were not worn, but kept by the izinyanga.[14]

There were hunting songs and chants, 'chanting wild songs, interrupted with long strings of the "strong names" of his ancestral spirits who had brought him through the danger'.[15]

That much hunting was regarded by the British authorities in the colonial era as poaching is undoubtedly true, though one can be sure that this was not quite how the African hunters viewed matters. In some respects the British left the chiefs to their own devices, within certain constraints. The restriction on both hunting and on cutting timber in forests was something which cannot but have brought home to Zulu communities the changed times in which they lived. Was the poaching of game, therefore, seen as a general ritual in itself – as an act of defiance – or was it just the universal poacher's 'thumbing his nose' at authority and getting something for nothing? Perhaps it was both, we cannot be sure; sadly poachers rarely leave diaries.

Hunting for food

The Zulu people were primarily cattle and agricultural people. Dr Bryant records: 'Meat is partaken of only as a luxury, not as an ordinary and indispensable article of food. Hunts are not frequent, occurring not more than half-a-dozen times within the year in any given locality; and when they do occur, it is only the favoured few who are blessed with a buck to bring home.'

The concept of game meat as a luxury is reinforced in the 1870s by William Drummond, who recounted African people on the Phongola River bringing him 'beer and Indian corn' in exchange for game meat.[16]

That said, one should not dismiss out of hand the notion that game and 'wild herbs' provided at times and in certain areas a significant proportion of the Zulus' diet, especially in the lower-lying regions where tsetse fly existed. Here, while cattle might be kept on the high ground in summer time and crops were certainly grown, game was often an important element in the staple diet. This was the case in much of Maputaland, where, according to Magistrate Stephens, prior to British annexation the African population 'relied on hunting as one of their chief helps to tide them over a bad season'.[17] But it was also the case that the African population ate game in those areas where people and game lived in close proximity. In expressing his concern about the possible boundaries of the proposed Umfolozi Game Reserve, the missionary Nils Astrup noted in 1894:

> There is a mountainous tract called Intabankulu, situated between the Uhlupekulu Mountain and Black Mfolozi in Entonjaneni [Emthonjaneni] Magistracy. There are at present 13 Kraals, and the region has been formerly more thickly populated. The people living there would suffer most heavily, if a possible intended 'hunting reserve' should be separated, so that its northern Border-line be drawn near to Intabankulu, because the inhabitants are prevented, by the Tse-tse fly following the big game, from having cattle, and they have consequently no other thing for life's support than corn *and Game*, (except a few goats).[18]

In times of crisis or drought normal supplies of food could be scarce. Baldwin in the 1850s and Hely-Hutchinson forty years later both make the same point concerning the reliance on indigenous fruits, berries, leaves and roots in times when food was scarce. The latter quotes 'a Natal colonist of long experience' who said the African population would never actually starve 'so long as there is rain enough for the wild salads and spinaches to grow'.[19] The fermenting of liquor out of the fruit or pulp of indigenous plants was widespread, be it from the lala palm or the Zulu plum.[20]

In the 1890s many requests to kill small game were granted out of season by the magistrates, though with the occasional caveat, 'Tell them [the chiefs] at the same time that no hunting parties known as "Inginas" will be allowed.'[21] By the new century, however, a sinister approach to these desperate pleas can be discerned at least in one instance, with the magistrate at Ubombo refusing hunting out of season because maize was in the local trading store to be bought. But only 85 Africans had taken out labour passes. The message was plain: work for the whites or starve. In fairness, though, this does not appear to have been the normal response of Zululand magistrates.[22]

Fishing was a feature of coastal and lagoon Zululand and Maputaland, and was no doubt an important dietary element in areas where cattle were not kept or were kept in small numbers.[23] An 1896 report on Maputaland written by Cuthbert Foxon made the following comment concerning fish and fishing: 'Fish are eaten throughout the country and are caught in basket shaped traps (Umono) made of thin sticks (much the same mode of making as eel traps) and with the hook and line – Perch and barbel appear to be plentiful in all the small "pools" about.'[24]

Hippo and crocodile were killed because they threatened the lives of those who fished.

Clothing and regalia

When the naturalist Adulphe Delegorgue visited Mpande in 1841, he described the Zulu king as looking 'beautiful, superb, magnificent, imposing'. Apart from the great shield, the purple silk, the tassels of red and green wool and the oxtails dyed red, there were monkey tails, otter fur, feathers of the purple-crested turaco and a kilt 'of strips of genet fur, 400 or 500 at least'. This was even grander than the attire worn by Shaka as described by Fynn some years earlier. In fact, with his long blue crane feather standing erect on the front of his otter-skin headband wreathed with scarlet features, Shaka no doubt looked more striking than Mpande.[25]

The Zulu state was not slow in exploiting its wild-animal resources, not only for internal consumption but also for trading purposes. Much emphasis has been laid on the early trading of the Zulu kings, especially with Delagoa Bay, as well as on the later trade conducted by white hunter-traders prior to the Anglo-Zulu War of 1879. But well into the colonial era, trade was still carried on by Zulus in skins and furs.[26]

This inevitably led to the phenomenon of professional specialist hunters (*iphisi*), such as leopard trappers. Some chiefs were said to hunt only for such royal regalia as crane feathers, genet fur and monkey fur. It was not a long step from this genre of hunting to mysticism and belief in the supernatural.[27] There was something awesome about the king and his courtiers in their full regalia, as indeed there was about the Zulu army in full battle dress. It was spectacular but it was also something to be feared.

Of Cetshwayo at the battle of Ndondakusuka in 1856, Laband states: 'He carried a dark-brown or black shield with a small white patch at the side, and wore (by some accounts) his black loincover of silver jackal and a buttock-cover of genet skin. His headdress was the band of otter skin with tassels of blue monkey skin and the tall crane feather of the uThulwana, possibly with a bunch of eagle feathers as well.' The opponent he defeated, Mbuyazi, had the misfortune just prior to the battle to have a gust of wind blow off his fine head plume of ostrich feathers in the presence of his commanders, something viewed as a bad omen.[28]

What wildlife products were worn? As with other matters relating to African society there was change over time, and the cinematic portrayal of a Zulu warrior in full regalia might be true for one period but not for the next. On the other hand, the black-and-white Victorian photograph perhaps goes to the other extreme and gives a drab impression of what was in fact a colourful ensemble. Bryant observes that 'the custom of skin garments might not have been a quite recent substitute among the Zulus for an earlier bark-cloth covering of a similar shape'.[29] If this was the case, then obviously the volume of wild animals killed for various products must have for a period increased in the nineteenth century from earlier times. Moreover, the importance of such products in the articles of tribute brought into Zululand may, at least in certain periods, be an indication of scarcity at home. The demands for military attire, especially cat skins (large and small), and bird feathers, as well as the fur of wild animals, such as baboon, bushbaby, meerkat, otter and weasel, must have at times been enormous. On the other hand, the influx of woollen and cotton blankets, gained through trade, would have relaxed the pressure on at least some species of buck, though probably less so on the demand for regalia items.[30]

Papini, apart from making the interesting comment that 'what was not eaten was not common attire either', well illustrates how there was a change with time concerning wild-animal products: fashions came and went, especially regarding what was the preserve of the elite; what had been reserved for royalty and the king's favourites might become more commonly worn later on; and what at one time it was taboo to kill, was not at another. This, in part, was probably influenced by supply and demand. Dr Bryant lists the Zulu royal game as elephant (for the tusks), honey badger (ratel), leopards (for the skin), lion and striped weasel (*inyengelezi*).[31]

Those animal skins, claws, tails and furs that were most commonly used as articles of clothing or military uniform in the mid-to-late nineteenth century included genet skins and tails, silverbacked jackal, leopard skins, lion claws, monkey, otter skins and what were sometimes described as 'wildcat' skins. The garments which incorporated such products included headbands (*umqhele*), cheek flaps or 'blinkers', girdles, kilts, loin covers and the like. Rhino horn or ivory was used for snuffboxes worn in the ear lobe and ivory was also used for various grooming implements and accessories. In addition, 'black finch', crane, eagle, turaco and ostrich feathers were used mainly as an indication of civil or military status. It has been estimated that in the youth regiments of the Zulu army each headpiece required 30 or 40 plumes apiece from the long-tailed widowbird.[32]

To protect these valued items of regalia there was the *isambo*:

This was a portion of the trunk of some soft-wooded tree, hollowed out so as to form a cylinder some three feet [1 m] long, closed at each end by a tight fitting cap (shaped while the wood was still wet and then allowed to dry hard) with a loop attached, by which the whole contrivance was tied, standing up, against the wall. In it were carefully laid out at full length the more-precious head-plumes of ostrich (*umBóngo*), blue-crane (*iMbangayiya*), or black finch (*umNyakanya*) feathers.[33]

Remedies and rituals

Papini has commented:

Something of the Zulu feeling about hunting may be reflected in the word for 'hunter' (*iphisi*) sharing the same root with 'hyena' (*impisi*), a beast abhorred as a witches' familiar. There are other clues in the language to how the wild was associated with the realm of supernatural evil: wild birds' tail-plumes *imigomba* worn as headdress, gave such an impression that *umgombane* meant not just 'fearsome person', but specifically 'witch or wizard'.[34]

There is nothing unique or extraordinary in this. Nor indeed is it a contradiction for nature to be made use of, but at the same time respected and even feared as a mystical force: the snake that enters the homestead and is left alone or the skin of the man-eating leopard left on the cattle kraal fence to rot are examples of that respect for nature. Similarly, there was the symbolism of the dismembering of the lion after its hunting, with various body parts being allocated to the main hunters involved in the kill, a practice extended sometimes to the field of human battle and misinterpreted by the British after the Battle of Isandhlwana in 1879.[35] The disembowelling of British soldiers was seen by whites as an act of savagery, whereas, in fact, it had a spiritual significance to the Zulus, who believed it liberated the soul.

As far as omens were concerned, nature played a significant role. Fynn cites some of the auspicious omens relating to war as elephants met by the Zulu army, a snake passing through the centre of an army, and eagles flying in a line. Conversely, the red duiker and a hadeda giving its distinctive cry on the approach of an army were bad omens.[36]

The inhabitants of Zululand and Maputaland made use of plant material for more than 'salads and herbs'. Indeed, vegetable material was more part of their basic everyday needs than were game products. African populations were reliant on saplings and thicket wood for the homestead, cattle-byres, kraal building, and firewood. The indigenous plants of the veld might be eaten, but they were usually also a supplement to the diet or a means of survival in times of hardship. The principal value of indigenous plants, though, was in the field of medicine dispensed by the traditional healers (*izinyanga*). It is very telling that when Robert Plant started collecting plants on the Makhathini Flats in the 1850s the locals assumed he was a doctor and brought him those who were ill, as well as sick cattle. Plant claimed that this embarrassing situation led to his Zulu name changing from Mequa to Melongu. In fact, Plant showed his ignorance of the region in this, for both are a corruption of the Sesotho and the isiZulu words for 'white person'.

THE HAMERKOP The hamerkop was left largely alone. It had the reputation of having an unpleasant taste and of bringing bad luck. Its large untidy nests were a frequent sight high up trees near water courses.
PARKER GILLMORE, *THE HUNTER'S ARCADIA*, 1886

It is said that King Mpande protected the forest of Ongoye because of the valuable medical plants it contained, though quite what 'protected' actually meant is unclear in this case.[37]

It is unfortunate that the 'father of Natal botany', John Medley Wood, did not go along with Maurice S. Evans's suggestion in the 1890s that the two of them write a book on the medical value of drugs used by the African population, which were extracted from indigenous plants – what today we would term ethnobotany. Unfortunately, Wood dismissed this proposal on the grounds that whatever value certain plants might have had, the 'system of administering them [was] wholly mixed up with Charlatanry and superstition'.[38]

It is true that wild animal products and indigenous plants were a key part of the production of medicines or *muthi*, and for charms and spells; and species such as the hamerkop bird (*uthekwane*) and the lesser bushbaby (*isinkwe*) fell victim as a consequence. Closely allied to this were the superstitions surrounding certain animals: the reincarnated warrior in the guise of the snake in the kraal and the protective influence of the white-faced owl (*umandubulu*). Then there were the wild creatures associated with rainmaking – the crocodile and the African python, 'not only the natural world's foremost embodiment of physical power and "togetherness undivided oneness", but seemingly the actual conduit of a supernatural "coolness" used by the rainmaker to bring rain'.[39]

Then there were the mystical creatures, such as the Esedowan (isidawana), a beast larger than a wolf with a great hole in its back, and the inyandezulu, a green grass snake, a metre or more in length, 'whose form kings and princes are said to assume after death'.[40]

Protecting farmland and homesteads

Several factors motivated the protection of farmland and of homesteads. In times of drought it was necessary to prevent wild herbivores, such as buck, hippo and bushpig, from eating pasture intended for cattle. Sometimes homesteaders wanted to prevent buck from spreading disease to domestic animals. Finally, carnivores that were a threat to the lives of humans and domestic animals had to be kept at bay or driven away. The point needs to be made, however, that the solution to protecting crops was also more often than not driving the game away. The creation of large noises at night to frighten away hippo and wildpig was not unusual.

In the Zulu kingdom small boys, too young to be herdboys, kept watch on the fields. These *izinkwebane*, sometimes in watch-huts, scared away the birds who came to harvest the African farmer's crop. Papini argues that when maize was introduced and dependency on sorghum decreased, so did the threat to the crop, giving these young boys more time to hunt birds, either for food or for their feathers. Birds were hunted with stones, throwing sticks or 'bird lime'. This 'lime' could come from various plants such as the sap from the giant-leaved fig (*Ficus lutea*) or the woody climber umbungwa (*Landolphia kirkii*), and was used by boys in Maputaland to entrap birds. If they were captured alive, there might also be the prospect of selling the birds to white people. Rose Monteiro, in her book *Delagoa Bay*, roundly condemns this practice and the cruelty involved, but there was a market for live birds and a price for a colourful sunbird or flycatcher could be extracted by these young boys.[41]

The threat to human life from wildlife was a real one, especially when lion were in a region. Dr Bryant relates how a Zulu sleeping hut might have a soak-away urinal so that the occupants had no need to leave their sleeping quarters at night and risk meeting wild beasts.[42] Nor were the low entrance to many huts and the thornbush barricades around homesteads and cattle kraals only for defence against surprise attack from humans. More frequent were the encounters with animal denizens of the night: the lion, leopard and hyena.

Restricting factors in game destruction

The king

When Captain Gardiner visited Dingane in the 1830s he showed the Zulu monarch a full-length portrait of the English king, George IV, one in his robes and another in naval uniform. 'But,' Gardiner recounted, '[Dingane] was evidently more gratified with the hunting scenes than with any [other] that had been shewn him.'[43]

The martial Zulu have been portrayed as being as likely to take to the warpath as the hunting trail, but the reality is, of course, more complex. The role of the Zulu was both positive and negative in the question of game protection and destruction. All in all the monarch's influence, at least until the declining years of Mpande, was probably more positive than negative, except for the hapless elephant that was regularly killed.

The Zulu kings were well aware of the social benefits to be derived from organising large hunts, and it is well established that certain areas and indeed certain species of game were reserved for the king. What is not certain is the exact time-scales of such embargoes.

It appears that at certain times some species received royal protection or were the hunting preserve of the king only. In March 1889 the British resident commissioner for Zululand wrote to the governor, Sir Arthur Havelock, concerning the introduction of game protection measures into the colony:

> since order has been restored, the subject has again been attended to, and I have now by circular letter to the Resident Magistrates directed them to take the necessary steps to ensure the preservation of Game in their respective Districts in terms of the law.
>
> I do not anticipate any difficulty in enforcing the law; the Zulus are already aware of its existence and they were accustomed to restrictions in the killing of certain descriptions of large game during the reigns of Mpande and Cetywayo. They would understand the explanation of the Magistrates that the intention of the law is to protect ordinary game during the breeding season.

Similarly in 1895 Magistrate Turnbull commented that Cetshwayo 'had a law promulgated with a view to the preservation of buffalo'.[44] In 1912 a magistrate upheld a conviction handed down by a chief against someone who, against 'Zulu law and custom', had killed a crocodile 'without permission from the authorities'.[45]

King Shaka (1818–1828) is reputed to have reserved as the royal hunting ground the Mbhekamuzi valley, a tributary of the Black Mfolozi some 24 km west of the modern Imfolozi Game Reserve. Shaka organised hunts in the Mfolozi junction area at iYembene, where the remains of hunting pits are said to be the legacy of his great victory hunt after his defeat of the Ndwandwe chief, Zwide. It is said that Shaka directed elephant hunts from the vantage point of Nqolothi.[46] Henry Francis Fynn recorded Shaka had confiscated six guns from a party of white hunters who had shot in his reserve elephant ground. The king commented: 'I have given the whites from the Imslatense [Umhlathuze] to the Umzimvoobo [Umzimvubu] to shoot in, which is surely large enough, but if they come and kill all my elephants, where shall I procure ivory to purchase things of them?'[47]

Cetshwayo on his way to meet Theophilus Shepstone in July 1873 organised a great hunt or *ihlambo* in the thorn country of the Umhlathuze valley. The *ihlambo* was a purification ritual following a death, in this case of King Mpande. It was the 'final ceremony connected with a king's obsequies, the *amabutho* had to wash their spears in blood to remove the evil influences that would have accumulated upon them during the time of mourning'.[48] It is said that the warriors formed a circle five miles (8 km) in diameter and closed in, killing large quantities of game.[49]

But ceremonial hunting was only one facet of the royal Zulu hunt. Hunting had been big business since the time of Shaka's predecessor, the great Mthethwa chief, Dingiswayo. He had from the mid-1790s traded with the European trading fort at Delagoa Bay. Zulu ivory and cattle were willingly exchanged for beads, blankets, brass, cloth, 'tiger-cat, and monkey skins'. One caravan of porters going north from Zululand to Delagoa Bay was 100 strong. Later, Shaka's desire for European medicines and remedies was such that it was claimed that he ordered out his regiments on great hunting expeditions to kill elephants for their ivory.[50] Whatever the reason, the centre of the ivory trade appears to have oscillated between Delagoa Bay and Port Natal. First it was Delagoa Bay, and then under Shaka both Delagoa Bay and Port Natal were involved. With Dingane it shifted back to Delagoa Bay again.

While the ivory trade brought material benefits to Dingiswayo and Shaka, the control of that trade, as Smith has pointed out, 'was a tool for the strengthening of the state'.[51] That being the case, it is little wonder that there was a royal monopoly on the trade, at least until white penetration some years later. Even then there was the semblance of the old order with permission having to be obtained from the king before hunting of big game could commence. In 1842 the Swedish naturalist Johan August Wahlberg visited King Mpande and, having pleased him with presents of red ribbons, beads and crane feathers, made a request to hunt:

> Since he [Mpande] appeared to be well-disposed towards me, I preferred my request for leave to hunt in the Umfolozi area; but he immediately interrupted me, saying that he himself desired to organize a hunt there, and that the game were scared away by gunfire etc.; but in the end he granted it to me for a month's time, though he was not prepared to let me stay longer.[52]

William Cowie told George Cato in September 1849 that he had had very great difficulty in getting permission either to trade or to hunt, and he had 'paid dear for it'. A year before Cowie had warned the establishment in Pietermaritzburg that there were parties in Zululand hunting without the king's permission and that they 'are likely to get into trouble with Panda'.[53]

On 31 August 1853 William Baldwin, the greatest of the self-publicising white hunters in Zululand, commented:

Likwázi, the prime minister before mentioned, came down to us – a fat, good-tempered, jovial fellow – made the peace, and eventually all was settled amicably; but our long-meditated route was peremptorily forbidden, and we were obliged to rest satisfied with the shooting Panda thought fit to give us in the Slatakula bush, where the old fellow knew well there were rarely any elephants worth shooting. He is a wily old savage.

The following May, Baldwin met two traders who were returning to Durban because Mpande had stopped all trading, allegedly because two of the king's senior captains had died from dysentery.[54]

On the other hand, some British hunters, like Elephant White, in the late 1840s and early 1850s, ingratiated themselves with Mpande to the extent that they seem to have done what they wished. But there was another side to the issue of getting permission to hunt or trade. According to Charles Edmonstone, it was wise for traders to make an arrangement with Mpande or they 'would be completely humbugged' by the chiefs.

Of course, the further from the centre of Zulu royal power, the less control there was, or rather the less constant control. Around St Lucia royal control over Africans' hunting 'royal game' seems to have been less than in the interior. It might be supposed, however, that the Tsonga, though a client people of the Zulu king, were free to hunt what and when they liked. A note in the *Natal Times* of December 1852 suggests this was not always the case: 'The refugees who have recently arrived at the Inanda are the remnant of the UmTsonga tribe, against which the late commando of Pande have been directed, on the plea of having allowed elephant hunting without first obtaining the King's sanction.'[55]

It was not only the Tsonga that did not always toe the Zulu line; hunting parties of Swazis might descend into what today is Zululand to hunt. Baldwin describes one such hunting party as 'immense'.[56]

There were certain animals that were considered African royal game or royal beasts. These included cheetah, crane, elephant, lion, leopard, lourie (turaco) and the python. Quite what that meant varied with time. What skin was reserved for royal use by one generation might well not be the exclusive sartorial domain of the next. One king might reserve permission to hunt buffalo to himself, but with his passing such a dictate would quietly fall away.

Then to complicate matters sometimes certain parts of a wild animal were reserved for royalty, but other parts were not. And here again practice could change with time. Various items from royal beasts could be worn only by the king, but the monarch could also permit their being worn by those in his favour, such as the *amazipho*, the choker of lion claws.[57]

According to Delegorgue, in the 1840s, the flesh of the elephant, like that of the white rhino, was not eaten: 'whoever violates this rule is an *om-phogazane* [*umfokazana*] (a worthless man). They prize only the fat and use it to anoint their skins before the dance; they also use it to soften their skin cloaks.'[58]

It has been pointed out that contrary to cinematic portrayals and modern usage, the leopard skin was not the material most commonly associated with royalty or chieftaincy. Mpande did not normally wear a leopard skin, Dingane used it only to sit on and Cetshwayo wore the skin only as a house coat.[59]

Other factors

Obvious factors such as areas that were regarded as sacred or protected by taboo or superstition helped to protect game. And there was the question of supply and demand. Then, how much could physically be carried needs to be put into the equation. It is all very well speaking of a caravan of 100 porters walking slowly to Delagoa Bay 175 years ago, but what they carried was a modest amount compared with what an articulated lorry might transport now in a single day.

As the nineteenth century progressed, the number of firearms in Zululand increased tremendously. In his 'Stray memories, Natal and Zululand: A poem', published in 1897, the larger-than-life Pietermaritzburg magistrate and former Zululand hunter, Charles Barter, recalls a Zulu hunt in which two men were shot by accident:

But other forms of death await
Those who these orgies celebrate;
The rifle in a Zulu's hand
Is like a blazing fire brand.
Danger it means for all around
Or death, without a warning sound.
For as the circle onward came
And clos'd upon the frighten'd game
Which, wildly seeking room for flight
Broke from the thicket into sight,
The lust of slaughter furious grew
Till all restraint it overthrew;
From either side the bullets sped,
And many an antelope fell dead.

The accidental wounding and even killing of hunters by other hunters in these great hunts was not unknown. In September 1853 Charles Edmonstone took part in one and accidentally shot a man in the foot, an error which cost him a 3s. cotton blanket in compensation.[60] Hunting could also lead to fighting, with people being injured, and the gathering of large numbers of armed men could cause tension between neighbouring chiefs. Indeed, the famous 'mock hunt' at the Mfolozi in 1856 was intended to be a military show-down, one which in the event fizzled out. Conversely, hunting was sometimes used to settle disputes, and Bryant says they could also be used for getting rid of people: 'They were termed *iNqina-mbumbulu* [inqinambumbulu] ('a-treacherous-hunt') or *iNqina yōZungu* ('a conspiracy hunt'), the only game intended to be killed on such occasions being those doomed individuals.'[61]

No doubt all the comments about people being killed and injured at large hunts were correct, and the shooting of beaters is not unknown elsewhere in the world. With the use of guns in these mass hunts, the carnage of wildlife was no doubt great. But this had not always been the case. The ever-observant young aristocrat William Drummond wrote of the five-year period (1867–1872) when he hunted in Zululand. He recorded a great hunt where some 800 people took part, killing mainly duiker and reedbuck. Marshall Clarke recorded a hunt in 1895 where there were between 200 and 250 beaters. Of another Zulu hunt, Drummond notes:

> upwards of five hundred men would form a circle driving the game inwards, while those who depended on the speed of their dogs would stand outside at such spots as their experience suggested would be chosen by the antelopes to break out at. The poor brutes had thus to undergo the chasing of scores of curs, and then to run the gauntlet of dozens of spears before they reached the place where the fast hounds were stationed, so that it was no wonder that many were caught; indeed, it was extra-ordinary how many escaped under all these disadvantages.[62]

The last phrase is interesting. These hunts were cultural events not gatherings for the procurement of food.

Warfare

The impact of warfare on wild creatures in Zululand is worthy of comment. That Zululand could be an unsettled place at times in the nineteenth century is clear. There was periodic internecine civil unrest, the most notable, after Shaka's revolution, being the struggle between Cetshwayo and his half-brother Mbuyazi at the end of 1856. The hunter William Baldwin was not far distant from the fighting and had to traverse the battle area less than a fortnight later. He noted, 'The whole air was tainted with dead bodies for the last twelve miles, which I walked against a head wind … I was never so glad of anything in my life as getting the Tugela between me and the dead.'[63]

There was also conflict between the Zulus and other African peoples, such as the Swazi. The explorer and botanist Captain Garden, collecting plants and hunting game between the Phongola and Usuthu rivers in 1852, wrote of seeing herds of buffalo up to a thousand strong and a herd of 30 elephant as well

as large numbers of Swazis 'fleeing in every direction' to escape the Zulu army.[64] And there was conflict, too, between the Zulus and whites, be they Boers or British.

On the one hand, sometimes because of war, people had to rely on game and natural vegetation for survival.[65] As will be seen later, it was also common practice to use forests as places of concealment and places of refuge for people and cattle during times of crisis.[66]

The iNqina in colonial times

A case can be made for the argument that by the 1890s the organisation of great hunts had became a form of social control. Of course, to an extent it had always been that: a community activity, enjoyed by all participants and given with the blessing of the king or chief. But by the 1890s such largesse rested with the British magistrates in Zululand. Surviving evidence would seem to suggest that the magistrates took this aspect of their duties seriously, even consulting the governor on the subject. Such tightening of official control over large hunts was also taking place in Natal.

The granting of permission to hold a great hunt, or indeed the direct decision of the magistrate that there should be a hunt, gave the British official an opportunity to lecture the chief on the importance of the game laws. A magistracy hunt could be for reasons of policy: to clear game from a road or from an area of dense population. It could also be as a symbolic opening of the hunting season, thus emphasising the existence of the closed season and of the game regulations. That most conscientious of magistrates, James Stuart, was not slow in lecturing the Nyawo chief Sambane on the game laws before granting permission for a lion hunt. The number of game to be killed was sometimes specified, often as few as two buck. And as the magistrate, district surgeon and a few African policemen could turn up, the likelihood was that the slaughter would not be great.[67]

The corollary of this official control of formal hunts was that there was an inevitable increase in the use of hunting snares and traps. Guns were an important element, but ammunition was precious, and unlicensed weapons, as many of them were, might be kept for emergencies, not for everyday sporting pursuits, which might draw the attention of the local magistrate, who was ever on the lookout for 'illegal arms finds'.[68]

Human population density

While the factors raised above both weighed for and against the survival of substantial quantities of wildlife in nineteenth-century Zululand, one of the key factors in favour of the survival of any quantity of game in Zululand was population density. It is true that game and cattle did sometimes graze over the same ground and that game 'abounded' near some kraals.[69] But the fact

TABLE 11

HUMAN POPULATION ESTIMATES IN ZULULAND, 1895

DISTRICT	AREA IN SQUARE KILOMETRES	ESTIMATED HUMAN POPULATION	POPULATION DENSITY PER SQUARE KILOMETRE
Eshowe	3 626	53 000	14.6
Nquthu [Enquthu]	1 554	22 000	14.2
Nkandla [Enkandla]	3 108	24 000	7.7
Emthonjaneni [Entonjaneni]	2 072	14 000	6.7
Ndwedwe [Endwedwe]	6 216	22 000	3.5
Lower Umfolozi	4 144	14 000	3.4
Ubombo [Obonjeni]	5 180	12 000	2.3
Hlabisa [KwaHlabisa]	6 475	15 000	2.3
Ingwavuma [Engwavuma]	1 730	24 000	14.0
Totals/averages	**34 105**	**200 000**	**5.9**

remained, generally speaking, that where an area was sparsely or only seasonally populated by humans – such as in parts of Maputaland – large game might be found, though because of the constant movement of game, even this could not be guaranteed.[70] In the early days of white hunters in Zululand, hunting groups might go for several days without seeing very much game.

The reasons why the game population might be sparse in certain areas at one time or another varied. It might have been because of human or cattle disease such as nagana or malaria. An irregular or scant water supply might be another factor. As mentioned above, warfare could be a cause. John Dunn noted of the Ongoye region where he settled after the Zulu civil war in 1857, that it was 'a part of the country totally uninhabited, and abounding in game'.[71] The presence of lion could also deter human habitation.

Some of the early maps of Zululand mark areas as 'uninhabited', such as that around the Ndumo region, though from archaeological evidence this was not always the case. A sketch map of the St Lucia wetland complex, drawn by William Cowie in June–July in 1848, is particularly interesting. Specific locations of African homesteads are marked, as well as such comments as 'thickly populated & cultivated – sheep & goats, no cattle' (eastern shore) and 'many kraals' and 'open country – many cattle' (south of False Bay). It also contains such environmental information as 'large forest about 12 miles long' (western shore); 'Good reed flats about 15 miles long – marshy' (area where the Mkhuze River enters Lake St Lucia) and 'dense bush – large timber' (northern peninsula dividing Lake St Lucia and False Bay). It is therefore easy to see which areas were thickly populated and which sparsely populated.[72]

Estimated population densities in Zululand as a whole in 1895 – the year the game reserves were established – reveal that the game reserves were situated in the least densely inhabited

districts: that is, Lower Umfolozi, Hlabisa and Ubombo. This area totalled 6 100 mi.[2] (41 000 km[2]) and had a human population density of only 6.7 per mi.[2] (2.5 per km[2]). Table 11 illustrates the point. The fact that the population of neighbouring Swaziland cannot have been much above 63 000 is also significant given the fact that Swaziland was one of the 'escape valves' or corridors used by game.[73]

The Ingwavuma district was some 668 mi.[2] (1 730 km[2]) with a population density of 36 people per mi.[2] (14 per km[2]). But this statistical overview gives a false impression of the district, as the population was concentrated on the cooler heights of the Lebombo Mountains, while the hot, swampy flats to the east of the mountains were much less densely populated.

Table 12 presents a startling contrast between the population of the four 'big game districts' in 1895 and a hundred years later. This shows a quadrupling of the population, with a twelve-fold increase in Lower Umfolozi. Even allowing for boundary changes and the reliability of the early statistics, the figures clearly show

TABLE 12

CHANGES IN APPROXIMATE HUMAN POPULATION NUMBERS IN FOUR 'BIG GAME' DISTRICTS OVER A CENTURY

NAME OF DISTRICT	HUMAN POPULATION IN 1895	HUMAN POPULATION IN 1994
Lower Umfolozi	14 000	166 000
Hlabisa [KwaHlabisa]	15 000	89 000
Ubombo [Obonjeni]	12 000	53 000
Ingwavuma [Engwavuma]	24 000	63 000
Totals	**65 000**	**271 000**

how sparsely populated these districts were. A telling quotation is to be found in David Leslie's book published in 1875:

> In the afternoon I climbed a hill, and had the most splendid view I ever witnessed. I sat with my face towards Nodwengo [KwaNodwengu] (Panda's Palace) … To the left I saw the sea at a distance of at least 70 miles, and the country in that direction was actually black with bush everywhere I looked – all flat, except just at the sea, where it seemed to rise. The Zulu country must be very thinly populated, for the extent; as, from the hill, I saw at least fifty miles on every side, and on the seaward at least seventy, and, within my view, I don't think there were more than thirty kraals.[74]

The forestlands

The relationship between African people and the forests in Zululand was a mixture of exploitative use and reverence. There was the practice of burying chiefs and kings in forests that were sacred. Dingane and Cetshwayo both were laid to rest in or at the edge of forestland, the former at Hlathikhulu forest and the latter in Nkandla. The importance of this was recognised by the colonial authorities. When the 1906 Zulu insurrection was being crushed, Natal's governor gave specific instructions that a guard be mounted over Cetshwayo's grave in the forest to ensure that no British troops attempted to desecrate it.[75] And, as with certain wild animal products, it appears that at times certain species of tree, such as Cape teak (*Strychnos decussata*) and red ivory (*Berchemia zeyheri*), would be reserved for royal use, or at least certain products such as sticks could be carried only by persons of rank.

There were also reports of dead bodies being left in woods 'to be devoured by wild animals'. It is not surprising, therefore, that some woods were associated with death and were as such to be avoided, tales of invisible dogs and malevolent living dead adding to their mystique.[76] Conversely, there were circumstances under which people were attracted to the forests: they were frequently used as a place of refuge, or to hide cattle or conceal an army.[77] It was to Ngome forest that Cetshwayo fled after his defeat in 1879 at the hands of the British. In 1884, during the Zulu civil war, both sides used Qhudeni and Nkandla forests as strongholds, with Chief Usuthu's forces finally occupying both forest ranges, thus cutting off the British sub-commissioner at Nquthu. Later, in the 1887–1888 period, when there was renewed unrest, Dukuduku and Ngome forests were used as refuges.[78]

Interestingly, during the Anglo-Boer War, though the Boers looted the Qhudeni store, they 'showed a wholesome respect for the main bush, which could cover the movement of numbers of scouts, and be held against them by a handful'.[79] In 1906 a confidential British War Office manual recorded:

> A long period of peace and quiet living has caused these strongholds to be almost forgotten, and their intricacies are not familiar to the 'young warrior' of today as they were to his predecessor of the disturbed times when the details of good positions, favouring a stout resistance when hard pressed in their strongholds, were freely discussed by members of the same faction. In those days it was a duty to know all paths and springs in and about the stronghold, and so much was the stronghold a factor in the safety of the families that they learned to regard it with that jealousy that has already been referred to.[80]

The British were wrong, though. For the very year the manual appeared, the last stands of the insurgent Bhambatha and his followers were in neighbouring Nkandla and Qhudeni forests. Unlike the Boers, the British had no qualms about entering both forests in pursuit of the insurgents. It is an interesting comment on the generally cordial relationship that existed between the white woodcutters and the local African population, that it was one of the woodcutters, Elias Titlestad, who went into Qhudeni forest alone following the death of Bhambatha. After two days he was able to persuade 284 insurgents to come out of the forest and surrender.[81]

African society made ready use of the forests, not merely as a source for 'herbs' and honey but more so for their timber, which was put to four main uses. First, there was the fuel which woodland provided. At one time, and up to perhaps the early 1870s, large quantities of charcoal must have been prepared for smelting iron.[82] Second, Zulu domestic furniture and utensils were made of wood, for example basket rims, cattle troughs, chairs, drum frames, food platters, milk pails, pillows, smoking pipes, snuff boxes, spoons and ladles, tools, and vessels. Third, weaponry construction, be it for knobkieries, fighting sticks, cudgels, or spears, required strong, though not necessarily hard, wood. Timber used for weapon construction included such species as Cape blackwood (*Maytenus peduncularis*), coast silver oak (*Brachylaena discolor*), cross-berry (*Grewia occidentalis*), Natal wild pear (*Dombeya cymosa*), silver raisin (*Grewia monticola*) and water iron-plum (*Drypetes arguta*).[83] And fourth, building homesteads and fences undoubtedly consumed a vast amount of timber. Nineteenth-century estimates of the number of saplings necessary to construct a single building vary from 100 to 1 000.[84] Table 13 points out the quantity of wattles or cut branches taken out legally from Qhudeni forest in three different years. In 1899 G.H. Davies, the resident forest ranger, commented lugubriously on the cutting of saplings: 'The mature trees in Qhudeni forest have a small chance of being replaced.'[85]

TABLE 13

BUILDINGS AND KRAALS ERECTED BY AFRICANS FROM TIMBER TAKEN FREE OF CHARGE FROM QHUDENI FOREST

YEAR	NO. OF BUILDINGS	NO. OF KRAALS	VALUE OF TIMBER
1896	461	173	£304
1897	526	97	£268
1900	200	n/a	n/a

Meanwhile, agricultural expansion ate away at the forest margins. In 1938 Deneys Reitz, writing of Zululand, observed, 'The African knows the value of forest soil.' This was true, and the clearing of land at the edges of forests was common practice. The new resident magistrate at Ingwavuma reported the following to his superior in Eshowe in September 1895:

I informed Sambana [Sambane] I had just taken a walk into the forest close by and going in had found considerable portions of it had been destroyed by burning (caba) [ukusha]. Sambana [Sambane] laid a good deal of stress on the benefit arising from such a practice as this of burning trees. He said some of the best crops were got in this way and he hoped the practice would be allowed to continue, especially as only the 'outskirts' of the forest were injured.[86]

As will be seen in a later chapter, the 'honeycombing' of forests for agricultural practices was to become a truly thorny issue between the British forest officials in Zululand and the local population.

Miscellaneous items made of wood products included ropes, made from bark; some items of clothing in earlier periods, also made from bark; and, at least in Maputaland, dug-out canoes made from hollowed-out trunks of trees – 'a most clumsy and slow craft'.[87]

To what extent all this denuded the forests and reduced what had been forest and woodland to savannah is a matter for debate. It is difficult not to conclude that a mixture of cattle grazing, erosion of forest edges for agriculture, homestead construction and fuel consumption had an impact on the forest environment. Some ecologists today, though, question the nineteenth-century thesis that the forests of South Africa have been dramatically reduced in size. But the historical evidence for colonial Natal would seem to contradict this, at least for that region. In Zululand, though, where white commercial forest exploitation was probably – outside Ngome forest – less disastrous, the rate of forest recession may have been slower.[88]

REFERENCES

1 Gray (ed.), [Charles Rawden Maclean], *The Natal papers of 'John Ross'*, p. 82.

2 North, *Recollections of a happy life*, 2 vols., p. 276.

3 Turner, 'The pervasive influence of plant names in Zulu onomastics', *Nomina Africana*, 14: 2, pp. 21–32.

4 Poland and Hammond-Tooke, *The abundant herds*, Chapter 2.

5 Bryant, *The Zulu people*, p. 365; Ellis, 'Game conservation in Zululand (1824–1947)', p. 4; Koopman, *Zulu names*, p. 262; and Samuelson, *Zululand, its traditions, legends, customs and folk lore*, p. 88.

6 Bryant, *The Zulu people*, p. 392; and Webb & Wright (eds.), *Stuart Archive*, vol. 2, pp. 223–4, 244 and vol. 3, pp. 291–2.

7 See for example, Baldwin, *African hunting*, p. 79; Bryant, *The Zulu people*, p. 688–91; KZNA, 1/MTB, minute paper A 2211/1896, 18 June 1896; Webb and Wright (eds.), *Stuart Archive*, vol. 1, pp. 275 and vol. 3, pp. 225; and (Barter), *Alone among the Zulus*, p. 122.

8 Bryant, *The Zulu people*, p. 686. For a full account of the ritual and practice of the inqina, see Bryant, *The Zulu people*, pp. 682–86.

9 Findlay, *Big game shooting and travel*, p. 199. See also McCracken, 'A history of indigenous timber use in South Africa', pp. 277–283; and Webb and Wright (eds), *Stuart Archive*, vol. 1, p. 276 n. 10 and vol. 4, p. 314

10 KZNA, ZGH 704, 7 February 1887 & ZGH 789, Saunders to resident commissioner, 8 July 1895; and Webb and Wright (eds.), *Stuart Archive*, vol. 1, pp. 63–4 and 68. See also *Correspondence concerning certain native territories situated to the north east of Zululand*, c-7780, p. 34; and KZNA, ZGH 704, report, 7 February 1887, fol. 3; and 'Report on Tsongaland', 8 July 1895, fol. 5.

11 Leslie, *Among the Zulus and Amatongas*, pp. 218–19; and Notebook of Robert Plant, 1857.

12 Baldwin, *African hunting*, p. 69; and KZNA, 749, minute paper NQ 25/1893, 10 January 1893.

13 Webb and Wright (eds.), *Stuart Archive*, vol. 1, p. 355.

14 Webb and Wright (eds.), *Stuart Archive*, vol. 1, p. 323.

15 Drummond, *The large game*, p. 245.

16 See Bryant, *The Zulu people*, p. 265; and Drummond, *The large game*, p. 233.

17 KZNA, 1/UBO, minute paper, 12 July 1896.

18 KZNA, 1/UBO, R 2732, 30 November 1894.

19 Kew Archive, South African letters, vol. 192, Hely-Hutchinson to Thiselton-Dyer, 27 October 1897; and Baldwin, *African hunting*, pp. 74 and 117. See also (Barter), *Alone among the Zulus*, p. 116; Bryant, *Zulu–English dictionary*, p. 440; KZNA, 1/ING, minute paper R 1881/1903, 1 August 1903; and Webb and Wright, *Stuart Archive*, vol. 2, p. 111, vol. 3, pp. 225 and 238, and vol. 4, p. 8; and Bryant, *The Zulu people*, p. 273 lists some of the 'wild herbs' eaten by Zulu people.

20 See, for example, KZNA, 1/UBO, report for 1892, fol. 109; and KZNA, ZGH 708, SNA 1033/87, 17 November 1887, fol. 20.

21 KZNA, 1/UBO, minute paper R 2354, 31 August 1896.

22 KZNA, 1/UBO, minute paper R 2093, 7 September 1903. But see also minute paper R 1178, 21 September 1906.

23 See, Hedges, 'Trade and politics', p. 54.

24 KZNA, ZGH 796, 1896, report on Tongaland. See also ZGH 789, report, 9 October 1895, fols. 3–4 and ZGH 793, Bosman to Clarke, 23 September 1896.

25 Delegorgue, *Travels in southern Africa*, vol. 1, p. 201; and Stuart and Malcolm, *The diary of Henry Francis Fynn*, p. 74.

26 For an example of this, see KZNA, 1/NGA, minute paper ND 385/1894, 4 December 1894.

27 See Papini, 'Some Zulu uses for the animal domains', pp. 188 and 192; and Webb and Wright (eds), *Stuart Archive*, vol. 4, pp. 8–9.

28 Leband, *Rope of sand*, pp.143–4. Had Mbuyazi won this civil war, the development of Zulu–British relationships could well have been very different. Writing to Downing Street in January 1857, Sir George Grey commented, 'the former of them ["Cetywayo"] heading all the troublesome young spirits in the country, especially those who were hostile to Europeans, the latter ["Umbulazi"] gathering about him the quietest and best disposed part of the nation'. See Cape Archives, Cape Town, GH 23/27, vol. 1, 17 January 1857, fols.4–8.

29 Bryant, *The Zulu people*, p. 139. See also Saunders, 'Report on Tongaland', c-5089, 1889, p. 48.

30 See Ballard, 'The role of trade and hunter-traders', p. 15; and Papini, 'Some Zulu uses for the animal domains', pp. 196 and 208.

31 Bryant, *The Zulu people*, p. 686 and Papini, 'Some Zulu uses for the animal domains', pp. 193–6, 201–2 and 207.

32 See Stuart and Malcolm (eds.), *The diary of Henry Francis Fynn*, pp. 14, 74, 89, 147–9, 151, 274; Papini, 'Rainbirds and power in the Zulu kingdom story', p. 10; Papini, 'Some Zulu uses for the animal domains', pp. 185–198; and Webb & Wright (eds.), *Stuart Archive*, vol. 1, pp. 63–4 and 355 and vol. 2, pp. 223–4, 243.

33 Bryant, *The Zulu people*, p. 146.

34 Papini, 'Some Zulu uses for the animal domains', p. 192.

35 Webb & Wright, *Stuart Archive*, vol. 3, p. 304; Adrian Greaves, *Isandlwana*, pp. 146–48; and Loch and Quantrill, *Zulu victory*, pp. 228–29. See also Stuart and Malcolm, *Diary of Henry Francis Fynn*, pp. 96–7, 317.

36 Stuart and Malcolm, *Diary of Henry Francis Fynn*, p. 317.

37 Pooley and Player, *KwaZulu/Natal wildlife destinations*, p. 107.

38 *The Agricultural Journal* [Natal], vol. 6, pp. 345–7; and McCracken, *A new history of Durban Botanic Gardens*, p. 106. Evans and Wood did co-operate on the first volume of *Natal Plants*, six volumes of which were published between 1898 and 1912.

39 Papini, 'Some Zulu uses for the animal domains', p. 194; and Berglund, *Zulu thought-patterns and symbolism*, pp. 55–56, 60–61.

40 Bryant, *The Zulu people*, p. 353.

41 Ellis, 'Game conservation in Zululand', p. 5; Monteiro, *Delagoa Bay*, pp. 51–53 and 161; Papini, 'Rainbirds and power in the Zulu kingdom story', pp. 8–9; and KZNA, Cedara Agricultural College papers, 735/1901, extract from letter, 8 April 1901.

42 Bryant, *The Zulu people*, p. 203.

43 Gardiner, *Journey to the Zoolu country*, pp. 120–121.

44 KZNA, 1/MTB, minute paper R 239/95, 12 October 1895; and KZNA, ZA 42, 13 March 1889, fol. 148.

45 *Zululand Times*, 19 and 23 August 1912.

46 Webb and Wright (eds.), *Stuart Archive*, vol. 3, pp. 291–92; Pooley and Player, *KwaZulu/Natal wildlife destinations*, p. 124; and Vincent, 'The history of Umfolozi Game Reserve', pp. 11–12. It is said that Johannes de Lange once slaughtered a large herd of elephant in this valley.

47 Stuart and Malcolm, *The diary of Henry Francis Fynn*, p. 256.

48 Leband, *Rope of sand*, p. 167.

49 Ellis, 'Game conservation in Zululand (1824-1947)', p.9.

50 Ballard, 'The role of trade and hunter-traders', p. 4, Stuart and Malcolm (eds.), *The diary of Henry Francis Fynn*, pp. 131–2; and Leslie, *Among the Zulus and Amatongas*, p. 255.

51 Smith, 'The trade of Delagoa Bay as a factor in Nguni politics, 1750–1835', pp. 171–189. See also Stuart & Malcolm (eds), *The diary of Henry Francis Fynn*, p. 10.

52 Craig and Hummel (eds.), *Wahlberg*, p. 88.

53 Campbell Collections, Cato papers, Cowie to Cato, 10 September 1849; and KZNA, SGO III/1/2, Cowie to Moodie, 26 July 1848. See also reference in 1850 to a shooting party being turned back on Mpande's orders, KZNA, Morewood papers, A 1273, hunting diary, 8 October 1850.

54 Baldwin, *African hunting*, pp. 39, 67. See also (Barter), *Alone among the Zulus*, p. 34; and Struthers, *Hunting journal*, p. 35.

55 *Natal Times*, 24 December 1852.

56 Baldwin, *African hunting*, p. 128.

57 An interesting discussion on this subject is contained in Papini, 'Some Zulu uses for the animal domains', pp. 193–97.

58 Delegorgue, *Travels in southern Africa*, 1, 286.

59 See Papini, 'Some Zulu uses for the animal domains', p. 193 with reference to S. Kloppers, 'The art of Zulu-speakers in northern Natal-Zululand', Ph.D. thesis, University of the Witwatersrand, 1995, p. 198. See also Webb and Wright (eds.), *Stuart Archive*, vol. 1, pp. 46, 323.

60 See Barter, *Stray memories*, pp. 47–8; Baldwin, *African hunting*, p. 45; KZNA, 1/MEL, minute paper PB 356/1893, 24 August 1894 and 1/MTB, minute paper H 149/1896, 14 April 1896; and Webb and Wright (eds.), *Stuart Archive*, vol. 4, pp. 130–1.

61 Bryant, *The Zulu people*, p. 687; Leband, *Rope of sand*, pp. 140–1; and Webb and Wright (eds.), *Stuart Archive*, vol. 3, p. 238.

62 Drummond, *The large game*, p. 320; KZNA, 1/EPI, 3/1/1/1/1, no. 14, 24 November 1887, fol. 70; and KZNA, ZA 46, diary, 30 August 1895.

63 Baldwin, *African hunting*, pp. 134–7.

64 KZNA, Garden papers; and Gosnell, *Big Bend*, p. 4.

65 Webb and Wright (eds.), *Stuart Archive*, vol. 4, p. 1.

66 See, for example, KZNA, 1/ESH, 3/2/5, 1904 telegram.

67 See, for example, KZNA, 1/EPI, letter book, 13 March 1900, fol. 137; 1/ING, minute papers R 1970/1892, 30 August 1892 and R 2094/1893, 13 September 1893; 1/MEL, minute paper PB 14/1894; and KZNA, ZGH 789, 29 September 1895, fol. 2–3. See also Natal Circular number 25/1892, 31 October 1892.

68 KZNA, 1/MBT, minute paper A 2211/1896, 18 June 1896.

69 See, for example, KZNA, ZA 46, diary, 10 August 1895.

70 References to areas of Zululand being uninhabited or very sparsely inhabited include: Baldwin, *African hunting*, pp. 69, 128; Campbell Collections, Miller papers, Von Wissell t/s, fol. 41; *Correspondence relating to certain boundary questions in Zululand*, c-6684; Gardiner, *Journey to the Zoolu country*, p. 198; Leslie, *Among the Zulus and Amatongas*, pp. 198, 258–9; *Records of Natal*, vol. 5, p. 186; KZNA, Morewood papers, A 1273, Anonymous diary, 19 November 1850 and ZA 19, 1891, fols. 29–30, ZA 27, R 4451/96, fols. 14–15 and Report, fol. 24; and Mrs Wilkinson, *A lady's life and travels in Zululand*, p. 186.

71 Moodie, *John Dunn, Cetywayo and the three generals*, p. 14.

72 KZNA, SGO, III/1/2, W. Cowie to D. Moodie, containing a map of St Lucia region by W. Cowie, June and July 1848. See also KZNA, ZGH 697, Captain G.E. Grover, 'Sketch map of Zulu Land', 1878.

73 Gosnell, *Big Bend*, p. 32; and KZNA, ZGH 769, Zululand Blue Book (MS) 1895, fol. 116–17. Head counts in colonial Zululand were done using the hut-tax as a basis. In the 1904 census, which gave the population of Zululand as 210 253, the calculation was on a three and eleven-thirty-sixth persons-per-hut basis.

74 Leslie, *Among the Zulus and Amatongas*, p. 27.

75 Bryant, *The Zulu people*, p. 720; KZNA, GH 1562, 29 April 1906; and Webb and Wright (eds.), *Stuart Archive*, vol. 4, p. 124.

76 See for example, Bryant, *Olden times in Zululand and Natal*, pp. 159–60; and Gardiner, *Journey to the Zoolu country*, p. 188.

77 For cattle being put into the forestlands in time of crisis, see, for example, KZNA, ZGH 685, minute paper 154, 7 August 1883.

78 McCracken, 'Qudeni', pp. 77–78; KZNA, ZGH 702, memorandum, 3 February 1887, ZGH 686, minute paper, 7 September 1883, ZGH 685, minute paper, no. 147, 31 July 1883; and *Zululand, Further correspondence …*, c-5522, p. 67.

79 G.H. Davies, 'Forests in war', *Agricultural Journal*, 10 May 1901.

80 *South Africa: Military report on Zululand*, pp. 17, 20–22.

81 Bosman, *The Natal rebellion of 1906*, pp. 56–9, 106.

82 See Bryant, *The Zulu people*, p. 388, and Holden, *The past and future of the kaffir races*, p. 241.

83 As well as Bryant, a good source for information on traditional uses of wood products is Pooley, *Trees of Natal*.

84 McCracken, 'The indigenous forests of colonial Natal and Zululand', p. 24.

85 *Agricultural Journal*, 22 December 1899.

86 KZNA, ZGH 789, minute paper R 229/95, 29 September 1895, fol. 3–4.

87 KZNA, ZGH 793, Bosman to Clarke, 31 August 1896.

88 See Jeff Guy, *The destruction of the Zulu kingdom*, pp. 4–5 and 'Ecological factors in the rise of Shaka and the Zulu kingdom', in Marks and Atmore, *Economy and society in pre-industrial South Africa*, pp. 102–19; and McCracken, 'Dependence, destruction and development', pp. 277–83.

CHAPTER 6

Guns and roads

Two additional factors that significantly influenced the decline in the big game of Zululand were firearms, giving the means of destruction, and roads, giving access and facilitating logistical support.

It seems obvious that the arrival of firearms would hasten the decline of game populations – so obvious, that this factor in the equation must be treated with caution. Though from the time of Dingane guns came into Zululand in increasing numbers, traditional hunting with spears, dogs and traps has continued in Zululand to this day. Dingane and later Cetshwayo recognised the potential of firearms. They were useful tools for hunting and they were important for wielding political power. Indeed, Dingane recognised that it was as important to keep guns out of the hands of potential rivals as it was to have them oneself. His successor, Mpande, was not beyond demanding guns in return for short-term hunting rights given to white hunters. Similarly, Mpande had ivory stocks – four or five huts packed with ivory – which he was quite willing to trade for guns. In 1846 it was reported that Fieldcommandant Jacobus Potgieter had been told by Mpande that he had 400 muskets, and that the king had shown Potgieter his ammunition house which contained 30 or 40 barrels of gunpowder and between 4 and 5 'loads of lead'.[1]

By the late 1860s and early 1870s guns were coming into Zululand in larger quantities, and, in particular, there was an increase in the number of African-owned firearms. This was mainly due to three factors: the inflow of cash earned by Zulus on the diamond fields; John Dunn's activities; and the growing tension in the region. By the early 1870s a resident or semi-resident African population, often from Natal, who hunted for whites living south of the Tugela River, was already well established in Zululand. In fact, as early as the 1830s, Captain Gardiner commented on this phenomenon of African hunters being employed by whites from Port Natal.

By the time of Cetshwayo's coronation in 1873 it was estimated that the new Zulu king could count on nearly 600 riflemen, excluding John Dunn's armed hunters.[2] It was later claimed that in 1875 or 1876 all who attended a military *ibutho* had to possess a gun, and certainly the number of guns in the kingdom increased considerably.[3] It would be naïve to suppose that these guns were not also turned on the large game of Zululand, or at least to the extent that the ammunition supplies allowed.[4]

Types of firearms

In the early days guns could be traded for ivory with the elephant hunters who entered Zululand. The problem for Zulu people, however, was two-fold. First, the weapons obtained were usually primitive, unreliable and often ineffective in killing larger game. Much has been made of the breech-loading rifles that came into Zululand. But the reality was that by far the largest number of the guns in Zululand, even into the twentieth century, were muzzle-loading tower muskets, the *isithunqisa*, rather than the infinitely more deadly breech-loaders, the *ingebe*.

The muzzle-loader was effective only at short range and then only if the shot hit certain parts of the body of the larger game. Some of the older-type rifles were not much better. William Drummond makes much of this point, observing that 'seldom a single ball kills these large animals'. He also noted that some old bull buffalo would take 30 bullets before succumbing. One black rhino took 10 hits with a 6 lb weight shot fired from a large-bore elephant gun. Drummond recalled how on one occasion his friend David Leslie had killed an elephant with a single shot, but on another occasion it had taken 35 or 37 bullets to bring an animal down. It is not surprising, then, that for days on end the hunter in the 1860s, or even the 1870s, might go without managing to kill an animal, though they often wounded game.[5]

Not only were there velocity, range and accuracy problems with the muzzle-loaders, but as the following comment from a Zululand hunter in 1850 illustrates, they were slow to load:

I went out in the morning to shoot some pidgeons [*sic*]. I returned with 5 could have shot more but I saw a fine Buck a short distance off. I drew the charge of small shot out of the Gun and put in a Ball which I had hard work to get down & by the time I was ready he had bolted – so I returned.[6]

The second problem facing the Zulu population in relation to firearms was that of obtaining a regular supply of gunpowder and shot. This matter is discussed later in this chapter.

Despite these problems, the advantage for the African population was that the antiquated tower musket was fairly cheap, even with the extortionate profit made when it was first brought in by traders. In 1860 such a weapon might cost a mere half-crown. The price did rise, but never much above 10s. a weapon. Initially this musket could be exchanged for ten cattle, which in turn might be sold in Durban for £50, an exorbitant profit. Later the price declined to one musket for one ox, and in the early 1870s the price was back to a half-crown.[7]

After the Battle of Gingindlovu in April 1879 the British army recovered 435 guns from the battlefield; 425 were muskets, 5 were Martini-Henry rifles, 4 were double-barrelled fowling pieces, and 1 was a revolver.[8] From the 1880s British authorities were quite prepared to allow the African population to possess these tower muskets legally, but were reluctant to permit them to upgrade to more modern weaponry.[9] The motivation that wild pig or buck were eating crops and had to be controlled was readily accepted by the local magistrate.[10] Of course, the person who owned the gun in the eyes of the authorities, and the person who actually used it, were not necessarily the same.[11]

The white hunters

The white hunters and travellers who entered Zululand generally had more sophisticated weaponry. In the early days, though, breech-loaders were rare. The long-barrelled elephant gun could be effective, but it was heavy and cumbersome, especially when having to be carried over any distance. Nonetheless, elephant guns were imported into Durban from the Cape and were used in Zululand; they were still being imported into Durban even in the 1870s.[12] Adulphe Delegorgue boasted in 1841 of his 'great 600 calibre rifled elephant gun'. Other forms of muzzle-loaders were tried with varying degrees of success. In 1839 Wahlberg made much of his sawn-off double-barrelled gun, even though one of its barrels burst.[13]

Later, Burrow, Snider, Terry and Westley Richards rifles were sometimes used by the select few and the Martini-Henry was much prized. Rifle cartridges were, however, expensive at about 15s. a hundred. Many hunters also brought with them a shotgun. There were a few revolvers in circulation, .380, .450 and .455, mostly amongst the white population. More common for many white hunters were the serviceable 45s. muskets imported by Charles Bales. His pricing policy was to 'take the net cost with guns, add the 10/6 per barrel & double that is my selling price'.[14]

In 1894 H.A. Bryden summed up the development of armoury and its impact on the game of South Africa:

In the days of matchlocks, and even of flint guns and smooth bores, the destruction proceeded, of course, much more slowly than at present. But with the introduction of percussion caps a great change came quickly in the annual bill of slaughter. Improvements in rifling and precision rapidly followed, and finally came the modern breech-loader to complete the work of destruction.[15]

In the case of Zululand this statement needs to be modified, of course, as the more modern weapons were introduced more slowly into the region. Even when they arrived they were not always as effective as possible since the hot humid climate, especially of eastern Zululand and Maputaland, created far from ideal conditions to keep and preserve firearms in good working order. And whilst there were reports of coloured and Sotho gunsmiths in Zululand at various times, these were not numerous and hardly likely to be seeing to the maintenance of much else but weapons of warfare.[16] While guns undoubtedly contributed to the destruction of much game, it is understandable why traditional methods of hunting with dogs and spears, and with traps, have lived on.

Regulations

From as early as the 1830s the British traders at Port Natal had tried in one way or another to regulate the supply of guns and gunpowder to the Zulus. With the British occupation of Natal in the 1840s the colonial authorities decided that measures had to be enforced to restrict the trade. Subsequently a general regulation imposed a large £50 fine for illegal sales of gunpowder to Africans.[17] After the Anglo-Zulu War there was a strict clampdown on the importation of arms and ammunition into Zululand. Then, under Proclamation 2 of 1887, all guns, cartridges, pistols, lock stocks, barrels and percussion caps imported into Zululand had to be registered by a magistrate. Under Proclamation 7 an import duty was imposed of £1 for each gun, 5s. for each pistol and 6d. for every pound of gunpowder.

Border checks were frequently carried out and wagons searched by Captain Joshua Walmsley, the border agent, and his detachment of police.[18] In 1886, £75 was placed on the 1887 annual Zululand estimates for 'searching wagons', with the attached comment:

It has been found necessary to exercise the greatest vigilance to prevent the introduction of spirits, arms and ammunition from Delagoa Bay through Central Zululand into the [southern Zulu] Reserve and from thence probably into Natal.[19]

In 1896 tariffs for hunters coming into Zululand were more reasonable: 1s. for each firearm; 3d. for each pound weight of gunpowder; and 3d. each for every 100 or fewer loaded cartridges, empty cartridges or percussion caps. One was, however, in very

THE HAZARDS OF BOATING ON ST LUCIA, 1852   In 1852 Alfred 'Elephant' White organised a hunting expedition into Zululand. On top of one oxwagon was placed a boat. After much hardship, this eventually reached and was launched at the Black Mfolozi River. Despite attack from crocodile, which destroyed oars and rudder in their attempt to reach the dogs on board, the small craft finally reached Lake St Lucia, where it was then attacked by a hippo. Surviving this, the little vessel was fitted with a blue calico sail and proved useful in hunting hippo on the lake.   BALDWIN, *AFRICAN HUNTING,* 1863

real danger of forfeiting both gun and ammunition if they were not declared and then later discovered.[20]

As for the guns which were already in Zululand or were imported legally or otherwise, when the British finally took control of the whole of Zululand they attempted to extend the system of licensing firearms that had existed in the African Reserve in southern Zululand. They were, however, nervous about disarming the population, so for many years the British were well aware that there were unlicensed guns among the African population. It was never the 'opportune time' to call in these illegally held arms. There was argument on this issue, with the magistrates sometimes advising disarmament, not so much because of a feared insurrection but because they argued that if the African population was not disarmed, it would be 'hopeless to expect to preserve what little royal game still survives in the country'. Conversely, Resident Commissioner Osborn argued that he feared disarming the population would result in disturbances.[21]

But by 1895/96, with the imminent handover of Zululand from imperial to colonial control, matters were taken in hand. A circular dated 15 January 1895 instructed magistrates to start registering firearms in the possession of African people. It was not until October 1896 that the resident commissioner in Eshowe could report to the governor that 'the registration of guns in the possession of Zulus has been completed'. Once this had been achieved, the policy became one of issuing as few new permits as possible to the African population; there could be exceptions, though. Cuthbert Foxon wrote in support of one chief who had no gun and who wanted a double-barrelled muzzle-loader: 'I beg

TABLE 14

THE NUMBER OF LICENSED FIREARMS IN ZULULAND IN 1896

TYPE OF FIREARM	NUMBER	PROPORTION OF TOTAL
Muzzle-loading musket	2 915	84
Martini-Henry rifle and carbine	318	9
Double-barrelled breech- and muzzle-loading	144	4
Other types of guns	48	1
Westley Richards rifle	30	1
Snider rifle	29	1
Total number of guns	**3 484**	**100%**

to recommend his application as there are 26 guns in the hands of the people of his tribe, and it therefore places the Chief in a derogatory position when hunting with them to be carrying assegais, and he is a good loyal man.'[22] And conversely, in 1896 the Ubombo magistrate refused to issue a man called Ngwanane with a licence for rifle ammunition on the ground that he lived in the newly established Pongola–Mkuze Game Reserve.[23] The total of 3 434 firearms registered in Zululand in 1896 is summarised in Table 14, and well illustrates the point of the number of antiquated firearms to be found among the Zulu population.[24]

Information on guns in individual areas is relatively hard to come by but some information has survived, at least relating to legally held firearms. In the Ubombo region in 1894 there were 119 Africans listed by name who owned guns and wished to retain them, though the following year the number of registered guns was given as 565. In 1897 in Lower Umfolozi there were 288 guns 'known to exist in this District'. In 1905 Sigananda's Cube people in the Nkandla area had 68 licensed firearms including a Brown Bess carbine, a Snider rifle, a Lee-Enfield, 5 Martini Henry rifles and 60 muzzle-loaders, of which 3 were double-barrelled.[25]

Gunpowder

The major drawback in using firearms in nineteenth-century Zululand was the difficulty in obtaining gunpowder and shot. The British authorities were anxious about the supply of firearms to the Zulu and measures were taken to limit and control the importation of not only guns but also gunpowder into Zululand. Natal Ordinance No. 3 of 1848 restricted any importation, including by hunters, to 10 lb weight (4.53 kg) of gunpowder per wagon when they crossed the Tugela. Further regulations in this regard followed in 1852, 1862 and 1887.

Some people looked elsewhere for supplies. In 1852 the *Natal Witness*, remarking on a decrease in the supply of ivory coming into Natal, observed that the unsettled state of the region must be a cause, and 'the restrictions on the sale of gunpowder have also contributed to this result. Delagoa Bay will possibly prove a rival in this matter.'[26] Eighteen months later the paper was back on the issue again, commenting that the Portuguese at Delagoa Bay were 'prepared to supply gunpowder and take as much ivory as [they] can get'.[27]

In 1855 and 1856 this issue of the Portuguese importing arms into Delagoa Bay came to a head, involving the Colonial Office in London. The Portuguese were keen to win British favour in the hope they would stop Mpande from attacking the fort at Delagoa Bay as successfully done by Dingane in 1833. Wishing in the circumstances to gain some concession in return, the British ambassador in Lisbon raised the issue of the sale of gunpowder at the Portuguese enclave. He reported the Portuguese attitude as being that the sale of gunpowder at Lourenço Marques was inconsiderable and that the Africans only used it for elephant shooting and for their festivals, and not for warfare. It was stated that between 1851 and the end of 1855, only 9 952 lb (4 508 kg) of gunpowder passed through the custom house at that seaport.[28] This figure may, of course, have been more, as the Portuguese knew the British were opposed to the trade.

Not surprisingly, the governor-general of Mozambique was opposed to any restrictions being placed on the sale of gunpowder as it would 'greatly affect the general commerce' of the settlement. He stated that when the Africans 'sell an Elephant tooth they always bargain for a certain number of charges of Powder to employ in a fresh hunt'. Besides, the Portuguese were at Delagoa Bay by grace and favour. They had no wish to alienate the local population. As the *Natal Witness* commented: 'The Portuguese have not, and so far as we are aware, do not pretend to have, any claim of domain at Delagoa Bay. They have, indeed, a trading factory there, with a few dozen negro soldiers, who exert no authority beyond the walls of their fort.'[29]

Despite the Portuguese desire to gain British support in restraining Mpande, there is no evidence that the sale of about a ton of gunpowder to the African population of the region diminished.[30] It should be noted that the charge for an elephant gun was about four drams (14 g) of powder. The slaughter of elephant in Mozambique must have been extensive. The practice certainly did not stop in 1856. In 1858 William Hogg sent two of his men to Delagoa Bay with £3 to buy powder. As late as 1883, there were still such accusations being made in Natal, with the issue made worse by the fact that the Portuguese were selling gunpowder cheaper in Lourenço Marques than in Durban.[31]

By the 1870s the 'African trade gunpowder' in the region was an inferior commodity 'which contains under 70 per

Saltpetre'.[32] This poor quality would have affected velocity. But be this as it may, large quantities of gunpowder were coming into Zululand by the back door. It was estimated that John Dunn imported into Zululand from Delagoa Bay, as well as thousands of guns, about 10 000 barrels of gunpowder in the five years preceding the Anglo-Zulu War. The arming of the northern Tsonga by the Portuguese to help fight the Shangaan in 1894 also cannot have helped the lot of game in south-east Africa.

Yet while British colonial restrictions drove part of the trade underground, they also drove many weapons out of use. The official desire to regulate the sale of gunpowder could mean several days' walk to Melmoth or Eshowe for some Africans who held gun licences, for sales outlets were restricted. And when wild pig, monkeys or baboons were destroying the mealie fields, such a delay in obtaining a half-pound weight of powder was a serious matter. By 1905 it was reported that 'there are large numbers of obsolete firearms in the country, principally tower muskets, but practically no powder'.[33]

Shot

If gunpowder was in short supply, ammunition was even scarcer. For the older guns shot could be and was made *in situ*. Part of the paraphernalia of the white hunter in Zululand, along with the gun-covers and iron ramrods, was moulds for doing this. The weight of shot varied, but William Drummond mentions using shot varying from ten-to-the-pound weight to the larger six-to-the-pound.[34] Some 15 years earlier Robert Plant commented, 'In travelling here [in Zululand] it is necessary to be well armed on account of the numerous large animals which abound – and guns of less calibre than six to the pound are next to useless. These, with the necessary ammunition, form a very heavy load.'[35] For elephant, a larger bore had to be used and with it a heavier shot, anything from a 4 oz to a hefty 8 oz shot (125–250 g), though elephant were hunted with anything from a six-to-the-pound shot.

Then there was the question of the hardness of the ball. Ideally, it was of the correct firmness when the teeth made just a slight indentation in the bullet. Lead was the main component, but if large game was being pursued then a harder medal had to be added. This might be tin or pewter, in a proportion of four parts lead to one part hardening agent. Quicksilver was occasionally added to the cocktail. Iron did not prove satisfactory, as the shot tended to fly too high, and when it hit its mark it would drill a hole through the bone of larger animals rather than smash the bone and disable the creature.[36]

As the hunting trip continued and even surplus of hardening material to make shot had been exhausted, the camp's canteens, tin mugs and the like were melted down. In the last resort, hard tallow fat found about the intestines of buffalo and waterbuck was mixed with molten lead and the cast immersed in cold water.[37] There was one advantage of making your own bullets. When there was a dispute over who had killed a beast, the matter could be resolved by cutting out the ball, which could then be identified as coming from a specific mould.

Gun-running

Apart from approved British channels there were, of course, other sources of munitions for the Zulu nation. First there were the gun smugglers. In 1846 the Natal colonial secretary informed the governor at the Cape of 'the prevalent belief that the Zoolahs have been largely supplied with them [firearms and gunpowder] by traders and elephant hunters'. From various statements collected at the time it would appear that this was true. One trader's wagon on the trip up to Zululand was said to contain 240 picks, 800 or 900 lb of iron, 2 bags of salt, 200 lb of lead, 1 barrel containing 50 lb of gunpowder and 6 muskets commonly called 'halflaayer' and 'braviaan bouten'. This load was imported into Zululand by the Irish settler Daniel Toohey. He had been in Natal since 1835 and by the late 1840s was living and trading at the Tugela River.[38]

By the very nature of this trade, little is known of it, save that money was to be made of the exercise. It is possible that Nathaniel Isaacs, the early Port Natal adventurer, may have been involved in gun-running, and rumour had it that Durban department store magnate and mayor Benjamin Greenacre had traded guns with Africans when young, though there appears to be no evidence of this. Indeed, a stanza relating to Greenacre might suggest the opposite:

Why I'm poor's not far to seek,
In the 'brain line' I am weak:
Tho' honesty itself.
I've never had the brains
To trespass down gun-running lanes,
So haven't got the pelf.[39]

Be this as it may, there were those who did carry on an illicit trade in firearms. Johan Colenbrander was mixed up in the trade, as was colourful Johnny Mullins, a colonial Irishman who ran guns across the Tugela River for Cetshwayo in wagons with false bottoms.[40]

As has been seen in an earlier chapter, from the Zululand side of the border John Dunn made no secret of his activities of importing arms into Zululand. In the 1870s Sam Beningfield's sons, Frank and Reuben, were closely associated with selling guns to Dunn, first direct to Zululand and later, when the British tightened up on the firearms regulations, through Delagoa Bay. Though Dunn's bringing Cetshwayo about 15 000 muskets and some 380 breech-loaders from Delagoa Bay might not technically

'CROSSING THE UMVELOOSI', 1880 This poignant pencil sketch of an oxwagon crossing the Mfolozi River comes from Captain Ludlow's *Zululand and Cetewayo* (1882). Many wagons were left in this area, where the oxen were safer from disease, while the hunters travelled on foot to the lower-lying hunting grounds around Lake St Lucia. Nonetheless, there were many varying dangers near the Mfolozi drift, from lion to snakes and mosquitoes.

be termed gun-running when Zululand was an independent kingdom, it was certainly a mechanism for getting round British restrictions. In October 1878 Sir Bartle Frere, the British high commissioner in South Africa, reported to London that the firm of Beningfield and Son were undoubtedly the major suppliers of firearms to the Zulus.[41] Yet, one can exaggerate the number of firearms in Zululand. During the Anglo-Zulu War it was estimated by the British that the Zulu had 8 000 firearms.[42]

In April 1910 the *Zululand Times* claimed, possibly with some accuracy: 'In the seventies [1870s], a bit of gun running was done across the Tugela, but the greatest number with accessories, were carried by Tongas, in bundles of firewood, from North Coast ports.'

Roads

The existence or non-existence of roads affected the distribution of game and, of course, the ease with which hunting parties could approach them. Early maps of Zululand usually give a false impression, for the 'roads' that are marked were often little more than bridle paths. But even where there were dirt roads, these did not facilitate swift transport. Though the affable Colonel Hime, later prime minister of Natal, quipped that 'the sun is our best road-maker', that assistance was soon undone by the torrential downpours of the subtropical summer.

Heavy wagons were used to traverse Zululand dirt roads. Indeed, these remarkable vehicles could survive on or off roads where a sprung vehicle would not have lasted long. But even

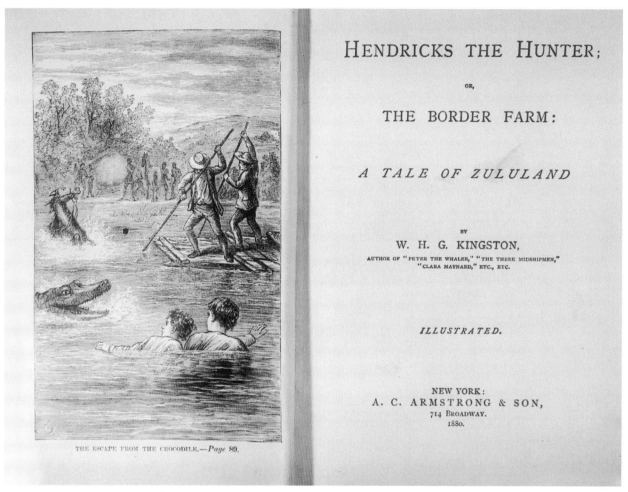

HENDRICKS THE HUNTER;

OR,

THE BORDER FARM:

A TALE OF ZULULAND

BY

W. H. G. KINGSTON,

AUTHOR OF "PETER THE WHALER," "THE THREE MIDSHIPMEN,"
"CLARA MAYNARD," ETC., ETC.

ILLUSTRATED.

NEW YORK:
A. C. ARMSTRONG & SON,
714 BROADWAY.
1880.

THE ESCAPE FROM THE CROCODILE.—*Page* 89.

TITLE PAGE OF W.H.G. KINGSTON'S HENDRICKS THE HUNTER; OR, THE BORDER FARM: A TALE OF ZULULAND Published in New York in 1879 with an 1880 imprint. This gripping yarn is excellent in all but its illustrations, which have the Africans looking like Amerindians, the white colonists like American settlers and the crocodiles like alligators.

wagons had their drawbacks. It was not for nothing that Lord Chelmsford had said, 'Ox-wagon transport is enough to destroy the reputations of a number of commanders.'[43]

There were vast areas of Zululand where horses would not survive long, therefore oxen had to be used for transport, and even they were susceptible to disease. They were very slow moving. As Denis, a character in the contemporary adventure story *Hendricks the hunter: A tale of Zululand*, observes, 'A man who travels in this country must have a vast amount of patience. He must not value time as you do in the old country.'[44]

The British military in the 1879 Anglo-Zulu War improved a few roads in southern Zululand to facilitate the movement of supplies, but by the late 1880s there was only really one 'main road' in Zululand. In fact, it formed something of a transit route between Natal and the gold diggings in the eastern Transvaal

(Mpumalanga). This ran from the lower Tugela drift up to Eshowe, round near St Paul's mission station, crossing the Mfolozi not far from Ulundi, and then running due north over the Mkhuze and Phongola rivers well west of the Lebombo Mountains. In the south an inland road from Natal that entered Zululand via Helpmekaar and Rorke's Drift joined this road. None of these roads ran through the principal game areas, which were to the east.

Zululand's roads were not in the best condition. In 1886 it was reported that 'the main wagon Roads in and through this district are in a very bad condition and in parts almost impassable: especially is this the case in regard to the road leading from Rorke's Drift to Central Zululand'. The volume of traffic on this main inland road varied. In 1886, 615 wagons moved through Rorke's Drift in the Nquthu district, 302 entering Natal from

GUNS AND ROADS

Zululand and 313 leaving Natal and entering Zululand. Five hundred of the wagons were destined for Zululand or the adjacent Boer New Republic. The remaining 115 wagons were en route for the Transvaal gold fields or Swaziland. In the first seven months of 1887, 1 084 wagons passed over Rorke's Drift, and 737 were on their way to or returning from the eastern Transvaal gold fields.[45]

The only road into Swaziland from the south – Rathbone's Natal Road – was 'in reality little more than a bush track'. In Maputaland as late as 1887 there were no roads beyond the track from Zululand that terminated at the Mkhuze River.[46] The remaining roads in Zululand led to the various magistrates' posts and to a few mission stations. Several of these roads between the magistracies, unfortunately for the wild animals and their protectors, did pass through game areas, such as Umdhletshe and just east of the Mkhuze Poort.

There were one or two old hunter-trader routes, such as the coast road in southern Zululand that ran from the Tugela up to the Umlalazi and the Umhlathuze rivers, before joining the inland road. These hunters' ways were, however, little more than tracks, as were later routes in Maputaland that bore appropriate names such as 'Saunders' wagon track' and 'Pierce's wagon track'. Indeed, in 1896 Bosman, writing from the Maputaland–Mozambique border to Marshall Clarke, commented that 'The big wagon is here, bush has to be cleared for a wagon track. No vehicle has been in this part of the country before.' Much time was spent in discussing expanding, altering and improving the Zululand road system, but the truth was that it remained primitive well into the twentieth century.[47]

Journey times varied greatly. Rivers would be in flood, and drifts often had to be cleared of sand – a dangerous exercise given the large number of crocodiles in the rivers of Zululand. The growth-rate of plants in Zululand was such that it did not take long for vegetation to sprout in a road and for overhanging branches to impede or prevent progress. An outbreak of war or cattle disease could all but stop road transport in Zululand and then it was not long before nature reclaimed her own. One military report in 1905 commented that many of the roads in Maputaland 'are now so overgrown as to be almost indistinguishable'. All this assisted the game to survive and multiply.

Travel time could vary greatly, but in the 1850s one might expect to take at least eight days to walk from Durban to Lake St Lucia, and sometimes this journey took two weeks. Another eight days would bring one to the Phongola River, as long as one avoided the wetlands of St Lucia and the Mkhuze swamp. That journey was difficult and slow, the length of the wetland system taking upwards of three days to traverse. In 1853 a friend of Joe Cato's wrote of his journey around Richards Bay: 'After a weeks toil through mud, swamp, and every other difficulty, we have got from one side of the Bay to the other, and now we are famined for the present …' In the heat of the December 1856 William Baldwin walked from the Msunduzi River south to the Tugela, some 88 km in 16½ hours, 'the greatest walking feat I ever performed'.

Further north, in the 1890s, an oxwagon might take eight days to lumber from the magistracy at Ubombo, on the top of the Lebombo Mountains, down the steep incline and then north along the track on the lower east side of the range before ascending the hill again to the magistrate's seat at Ingwavuma. On the other hand, an African runner could complete this same journey in a day. Generally speaking, 25 to 30 km a day was very good going in an oxwagon in Zululand. In 1896 it took one official ten days to journey from Eshowe to Cuthbert Foxon's station at Pelandala's kraal in northern Maputaland.[48]

Hunting was in part limited to what an oxwagon could carry, which was certainly not as much as a modern lorry. Furthermore, much hunting was done without the assistance of vehicle or draft animal, especially around St Lucia and in Maputaland. This by necessity limited the hunter's bag.

Later, when transport riders came into their own, and regular trips were undertaken to supply the Zululand stores and the settlements of the eastern Transvaal, the roads were to spell the death knell for much game. When the transport riders' oxen began to die, the wild animals were blamed for transmitting disease. The authorities therefore lifted restrictions relating to the killing of game in the vicinity of a major road. The result was a slaughter of game along these trade routes and, for the first time in Zululand, the consequent isolation of herds of wild animals away from these thoroughfares.

REFERENCES

1 For an interesting article on the subject see J.J. Guy, 'A note on firearms in the Zulu kingdom with special reference to the Anglo-Zulu War, 1879', *Journal of African History*, 12: 4, pp. 557–70. See also, Eldridge, *Records of Natal: Government House Despatches, vol. 1, 1845–1846*, pp. 396–404; Killie Campbell Collections, papers of B.A. Bell, uncatalogued, fols. 6–7; Baldwin, *African hunting*, p. 88.

2 Moodie (ed.), *John Dunn, Cetywayo and the three generals*, p. 42.

3 *Zululand Times*, 8 April 1910.

4 This phenomenon of firearms being rapidly introduced among a rural population is by no means unique. In eighteenth-century Ireland, French muskets distributed among the peasants of Munster in the hope that revolution might be incited led not to speedy revolt but to the decimation of the surviving herds of deer in the region.

5 Drummond, *The large game*, pp. 23, 37–38, 40–41, 56, 71, 83, 125–26, 220. Wahlberg noted in 1842 how it took six shots, four at point-blank range, to kill a white rhino at the Mfolozi. See Craig and Hummel (eds), *Wahlberg*, p. 91.

6 KZNA, Morewood papers, A 1273, hunting journal (anonymous), Saturday 27 October 1850.

7 Ballard, 'The role of trade and hunter-traders', pp. 14–16; Guy, 'A note on firearms', p. 560; and Saunders, *Report on Tongaland*, c-5089, p. 47.

8 National Army Museum, London, Lord Chelmsford papers, Return of firearms captured at Gingindlovu, referenced in Knight, *The anatomy of the Zulu army*, p. 169 and 185 n.

9 KZNA, minute paper, ND 182/04, 11 March 1904.

10 See, for example, KZNA, 1/NGA, minute paper, R 1323/1890.

11 KZNA, 1/NGA, minute paper, ND 341/99, 25 August 1899.

12 CTA, CO 3980, memorials, 5: 163, 19 March 1835.

13 Craig and Hummel (eds.), *Wahlberg*, pp. 22, 37–38; and Webb (trans.), *Adulphe Delegorgue's Travels*, 1, p. 164.

14 KZNA, AGO, unregistered correspondence and papers, 1853–1871, file marked 'Gun Running', Bates to Steel, 24 June 1871.

15 Bryden, 'The extermination of great game in South Africa', pp. 538–39.

16 Guy, 'A note on firearms', p. 560.

17 Owen, *The diary of the Reverend Francis Owen*, p. 65; Pridmore (ed.), *Humphreys*, p. 12; and Smith, 'The trade of Delagoa Bay', pp. 188–89.

18 See, for example, Baldwin, *African hunting*, p. 5; KZNA, 1/EPI, minute paper, R 1444/1893, 24 June 1893; and Spencer, *British settlers to Natal*, 5, pp. 63–4.

19 KZNA, ZGH 700, Estimates for 1887, 13 October 1886.

20 KZNA, ZGH 769, New licence system, 1 December 1896; and KZNA, 1/EPI, minute paper, LU 114/1893.

21 See, for example, KZNA, 1/UBO, minute paper, UB 249/1891, 23 October 1891; and KZNA, ZGH 825, Hely-Hutchinson to Colonial Secretary, 5 March 1894, fols. 200–201.

22 KZNA, 1/EPI, letter book, 24 April 1900. This was a modest request. In the early 1870s Drummond observed that all the great chiefs possessed 'a capital breech-loader'.

23 KZNA, ZGH 796, R 1825/1896, 14 May 1896.

24 KZNA, 1/NGA, minute paper, ND 136/1899, 28 March 1899; ZGH 772, 22 October 1896; ZA 27, 1896, fol. 24; and 1/ING, minute paper, ND 341/1899, 25 August 1899. Even a hundred years later it was possible occasionally to come across one of the old muskets in rural Zululand.

25 KZNA, 1/UBO, 'Report of arms … Ubombo, for the year ending December 31, 1895', 3/1/3; UB 94/1894, minute paper; 1/EPI, letter book, May 1897, fol. 316; and 1/NKA, minute paper, list of firearms, 1905.

26 *Natal Witness*, 30 January 1852

27 Killie Campbell Collections, Captain Garden's diary, 2, fol. 241; and *Natal Witness*, 30 June 1854.

28 Leslie, *Among the Zulus and the Amatongas*, p. 15.

29 *Natal Witness*, 10 May 1850.

30 *Natal Witness*, 30 June 1854; and CTA, GH 23/26, no. 5 of 1855, fols. 68–69 and no. 42 of 1856, fol. 373; GH 1/251, no. 124 of 1856, fols. 53–60; and GH 1/254, 1856, fols. 38–47.

31 KZNA, CSO 2557, confidential minute papers, C 56/1883. See also, *Natal Mercury*, 20 January and 10 February 1863.

32 Guy, 'A note on firearms', p. 560 n.

33 KZNA, 1/ING, minute paper, IN 125/1902, 15 February 1902; and *Swaziland, Tongaland and northern Zululand*, War Office, p. 87.

34 Drummond, *The large game*, pp. 71, 254, 408–9.

35 Robert Plant notebook, private ownership.

36 Baldwin, *African hunting*, p. 12. For the inventory of the celebrated hunter R. Gordon Cumming elsewhere in South Africa, see Cumming, *Hunting adventures in South Africa*, p. 20.

37 Drummond, *The large game*, pp. 111–17.

38 See Eldridge (ed.), *Records of Natal: Government House despatches, vol. 1, 1845–1846*, pp. 393–404; and Spencer, 'Early Irish settlers in Natal, 1824–1862', p. 192.

39 Spencer, *British settlers to Natal*, 7, p. 231. See also *Graham's Town Journal*, 8 November 1836, quoted in Spencer, *British settlers to Natal*, 4, p. 41; Knight, *The anatomy of the Zulu army*, p. 167; and *Military report on Zululand*, War Office. Guns were sold further north quite legally by Durban merchants. See KZNA, AGO, 254A, R.W. Dickinson, 8 May 1872.

40 Kemp, 'Johan William Colenbrander', pp. 168, 171–2; and Jackson, 'The capture of Johnny Mullins', pp. 200–202.

41 Ballard, 'The role of trade and hunter-traders', pp. 14–16; Guy, 'A note on firearms in the Zulu kingdom', p. 560; Public Record Office, London, CO 879, 17/208, no. 4; and Spencer, *British settlers in Natal*, p. 267. The British, however, were not always convinced about claims of illicit gun trading. See KZNA, ZA 34, minute paper, 911/1905.

42 Guy, 'A note on firearms', p. 560; and Public Record Office, London, CO 179/135, no. 3389.

43 Bennett, *Eyewitness in Zululand*, p. 40.

44 Kingston, *Hendricks the hunter*, p. 63.

45 KZNA, ZGH 708, Return of wagon traffic, 1885–1887.

46 *Swaziland, Tongaland and northern Zululand*, War Office, 1905, pp. 25, 27; and KZNA, ZGH 704, Robert Grantham, 'Report on Amatongaland', 11 January 1887, fol. 2.

47 See for example Curson, 'Preservation of game in South Africa', 1924, p. 414; KZNA, ZGH 715, Boundary Commission report, roads, p. 16; 1/UBO, letter book, 3 October 1893, fol. 77; and minute paper UB 65/90, 8 December 1890; and ZA 27, report, 1896, fol. 27, ZGH 698, no. 23/1886, 16 July 1886; and ZGH 793, 21 October 1896.

48 For examples of travel times see Baldwin, *African hunting*, pp. 92–93, 135; Leslie, *Among the Zulus and Amatongas*, p. 243; *Natal Almanac*, 1899, pp. 650–57; KZNA, 1/UBO, 3/2/2, 14 October 1896; and LU 286/1893, Itinerary of governor's tour of Zululand; ZA 27, minute paper, R 4451/96; and ZGH 697, 14 January 1886 and 789, 1 June 1895.

A ROAD IN ZULULAND Roads and guns posed the greatest threat to the Zululand wilderness. Fortunately roads were few and far between. All were dirt, mainly sandy tracks, and some little more than bridle paths. Roads meant oxwagon transport, which in turn meant tsetse fly and disease, with the shooting of game along roadsides being permitted by the authorities.

(PHOTO P.A. McCRACKEN)

SECTION III

Conservation

DURBAN Durban in the 1840s was little more than a village. A romantic memory lingers over the settlement as it then was, with its sandy streets, low flea-infested thatched houses, oxwagons and piles of ivory sitting along the wharf waiting for shipment. Not far distant on the Berea there was danger indeed with buffalo, leopard, python and elephant in the thick forest that covered the ridge.
ANGAS, *KAFIRS ILLUSTRATED*, 1847

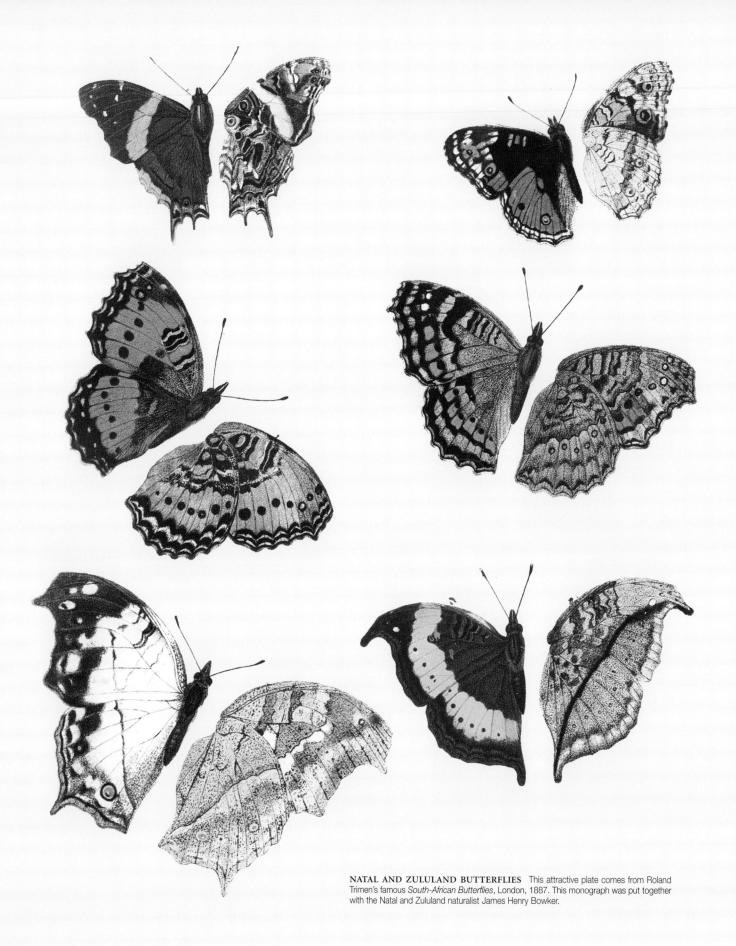

NATAL AND ZULULAND BUTTERFLIES This attractive plate comes from Roland Trimen's famous *South-African Butterflies*, London, 1887. This monograph was put together with the Natal and Zululand naturalist James Henry Bowker.

CHAPTER 7

The Zululand wilderness revealed

(Left to right) **WHITEBELLIED SUNBIRDS** Sunbirds were very popular among nineteenth-century naturalists. Zululand offered no fewer than a dozen species.
GORGEOUS BUSH SHRIKE   The elusive gorgeous bush shrike was and is common enough in Zululand if one is prepared to enter the thickest bush.
PRIRIT AND CHINSPOT BATIS Batises from both sides of the subcontinent, the pririt from the dry west and the chinspot from the subtropical east. The distinctive 'three-blind-mice' call of the chinspot batis was a familiar sound to the hunter and trader visiting Zululand.
E.L. LAYARD, *THE BIRDS OF SOUTH AFRICA*, 1867

By the Edwardian era, colonial government bacteriologists, geologists and meteorologists were taking an interest in Zululand, though often their progress was slow and fraught with problems. The local jailer took the daily meteorological readings at Hlabisa but when he went off on leave no one bothered to continue the readings.[1] An early reference to the intervention of the Natal veterinary service in Zululand appears in 1903 when a veterinary surgeon was sent to the Ndumo area to investigate the deaths of 20 hippo at Nyamithi and Umbumbi pans. The vet, Dr Fyrth, concluded: 'In my opinion death was due to vegetable poisoning, as owing to the drought, the usual food of the animals was scarce & they were eating anything to be found. I noticed a large amount of poisonous solanaceous plant (*Datura*

straonium) growing in the neighbourhood & this no doubt was the cause of death.'[2]

It would, however, be many a long year before vets were employed full-time to oversee the welfare of a wild animal in Zululand. By the Edwardian era in Britain, the Cape or even in Natal, the general public's awareness of the Zululand environment firmly rested on what they saw in botanic gardens, zoos and museums, as well as what they read in the published accounts of earlier hunters and naturalists. Even the curiosities of natural history so beloved by the Victorians in the great European exhibitions helped with this process. In the London Exhibition of 1862, for instance, the 'Necklace of Ornamental Beetles (Elytræ) from the Amatouga Country', George Cato's exhibit of 'Papyrus from St Lucia Bay' and the Reverend Mr Schreuder's 'Ufozwe wood (excellent for cabinet work)' helped reveal the secrets of the Zululand wilderness to the outside world.

Hunters' accounts

It is ironic that the word of Zululand's treasure house of natural resources was spread in part by the white hunters who did so much to destroy the region's fauna. There were pieces in newspapers and articles in journals, but in particular there were several accounts of hunting trips that appeared prior to British military intervention in the region.[3]

On 11 January 1862, ten years to the month after he first began hunting in Zululand, William Charles Baldwin of Lytham, near Leylands in Lancashire, signed a contract for a hunting reminiscence with the London publisher Richard Bentley. In 1881 Bentley also published Frederick Courteney Selous's classic volume, *A hunter's wandering in Africa*. Baldwin's book covered his hunting experiences between 1852 and 1860, the first part dealing with Zululand and the latter four chapters with his experiences in the interior of southern Africa, as far north as the Victoria Falls. Initially entitled *Ten years sporting in southern Africa*, the volume appeared in 1863 under the title *African hunting and adventure, from Natal to the Zambesi including Lake Ngami, the Kalahari desert, etc. from 1852 to 1860*.[4] A French edition appeared in Paris in 1868 under the title *Du Natal au Zambèse, 1851–1866. Récits de chasses*.

The first five chapters of Baldwin's book contained accounts of five hunting trips to Zululand between 1852 and 1855:

1. To St Lucia: January to March 1852
2. To 'Zulu country':   July to October 1853
3. To Maputaland: April to August 1854
4. To 'Zulu country':   April to June 1855
5. To 'Zulu country':   October to December 1855

Baldwin was a close associate of John Alfred White (Elephant White) and belonged to his hunting syndicate. Yet as publicity for the volume spread through Natal and abroad, it was Baldwin's reputation that was established, not wholly deservedly, as one of the great white hunters of Africa. The book did, however, also establish in the public mind that Zululand was a hunter's paradise. One reviewer, however, made no bones about the content of the volume:

> … except as a wholesale record of the butchery of sundry elephants, giraffes, hippopotami and other unfortunate Mammalia, he might as well have been travelling in the moon. Of the geography, natural history, or ethnology of the regions he has visited he tells us nothing; indeed he seems to take for granted that every cockney who reads his book knows as much about Southern Africa as he does himself.[5]

There is some truth in this catty comment. Baldwin's book is not in the same league as W.H. Drummond's *The large game and natural history of south and south-east Africa*, which was published in Edinburgh in 1875 by Edmonston and Douglas.

The Honourable Henry William Drummond was the second son of the 9th Viscount Strathallan, who through inheritance became the 15th Earl of Perth. In 1867 the 22-year-old Scottish aristocrat began hunting in Zululand and Maputaland, and continued to do so until 1872. His book, written from journals, diverted from the norm of a chronological account of hunting adventures to chapterisation centred on animal species. The result is that Drummond has, in effect, edited his own journals, and in so doing given more thought to his memoir than is usual in such cases. The weakness of the book is Edward Hodges's illustrations, which seem to have been an amalgam of Drummond's own sketches and drawings taken from specimens in the Natural History Museum in London.[6] Though in fairness to the book, there are some reasonably good larger plates.

In the Anglo-Zulu War Drummond acted as Lord Chelmsford's civilian intelligence officer and was for a while special war correspondent for the *Natal Witness*. Riding Percy, the grey, which the French Prince Imperial had tried to mount when he was killed, Drummond was among the first to leap the thorn fence into Cetshwayo's royal homestead at the Battle of Ulundi on 4 July 1879. Though the horse returned, Drummond was not seen alive again, his body being later found amongst the burnt remains of the Zulu capital. Many lamented the death of the personable aristocrat who had adopted Natal as his home, not least his sweetheart, Maggie Macleroy.[7]

Drummond's original diaries have never been traced. He did, however, save for posterity the Zululand notes of his friend David Leslie. And following Leslie's premature death it was Drummond who, the same year his own monograph was published, had edited and privately printed in Glasgow Leslie's notes and some letters under the title *Among the Zulus and Amatongas*, another book which was to contribute to the wider world's knowledge of the Zululand wilderness.

The outbreak of the Anglo-Zulu War and the subsequent trials and tribulations of the British army did more than anything previous to draw public attention in Britain to the existence of the Zulu kingdom. Britain's prime minister summed up the new wonderment nicely when he remarked, 'A very remarkable people the Zulus, they defeat our generals, they convert our bishops, they have settled the fate of a great European dynasty.'[8]

The British Victorian army officer was often not averse to relieving the boredom and drudgery of colonial soldiering by painting and sketching, hunting, or collecting specimens of natural history. A case in point was Lieutenant Henry Harford, whose fine collection of Zululand butterflies is in the Durban

Natural Science Museum.[9] The basements of many British and Irish museums contain many such treasures from the age of the gentleman-naturalist-soldier. A local soldier-naturalist was the eccentric Colonel J.H. 'Butterfly' Bowker, formerly of the Cape Frontier Mounted Police. He not only supplied Kew Gardens with plants but also provided the Kew Museum with assegai spears and stone implements from the 'Umbolvu river near St Lucia'. Marianne North recounted that on one occasion 'Colonel Butterfly' caused great offence to the Empress Eugénie when he showed her a photograph of himself holding a large butterfly net in front of the grave of her son, the Prince Imperial.[10]

But the Anglo-Zulu War also attracted novelists, and in late 1879 the popular American story-writer W.H.G. Kingston wrote *Hendricks the Hunter or, The border farm: A tale of Zululand*. It was published by A.C. Armstrong and Son of New York and appeared in late 1879 with an 1880 publication date. It was a ripping yarn, but containing much that was factually accurate, and whilst the illustrations were 'American' rather than South African, as a publicity agent for the Zululand wilderness the popular book could not have done a better job.

Naturalists' accounts

From the 1830s onwards there was a trickle of naturalists venturing into Zululand. Some of these, like Andrew Smith and Johan August Wahlberg, left letters or accounts that subsequently have been published.[11] Wahlberg's periodic travelling companion, the 'dapper and flamboyant' Frenchman Adulphe Delegorgue, did, however, publish an account of his southern African experiences in Paris in 1847. This was under the title *Voyage dans l'Afrique australe notamment dans le territoire de Natal dans celui des Cafres Amazoulous et Makatisses et jusqu'au tropique du Capricorne, durant les années 1838, 1839, 1840, 1841, 1842, 1843 & 1844, avec dessins et cartes par M. Adulphe Delegorgue (de Douai)*. This two-volume epic includes useful material on Zululand, but only in recent years has the work been translated and published in English.[12]

An imposing volume, the coloured plates of which are frequently reproduced, is George French Angas's *The Kafirs illustrated in a series of drawings taken among the Amazulu, Amaponda and Amakosa tribes; also portraits of the Hottentot, Malay, Fingo and other races inhabiting southern Africa: together with sketches of landscape scenery in Zulu country, Natal and the Cape Colony*. This folio was published in 1849 by J. Hogarth in London. Whilst there is text, the purpose of the volume is clearly the lavish illustrations. There is, however, an intriguing reference to Angas's now-lost journal made in Natal and Zululand. Be that as it may, like *Hendricks the hunter*, little could do more to publicise Zululand than the publication of this superb folio volume.[13]

GEORGE FRENCH ANGAS We owe much to George French Angas for his magnificent pictures of Zulu life in the late 1840s. He was born in Newcastle-upon-Tyne in 1822 and came to South Africa in 1847 having spent some time in Australia. In 1849 his *Kafirs illustrated in a series of drawings taken among the Amazulu, Amaponda and Amakosa tribes; also portraits of the Hottentot, Malay, Fingo and other races inhabiting southern Africa: together with sketches of landscape scenery in the Zulu country, Natal and the Cape Colony* was published in London along with a text drawn from a now lost diary. Angas died in London in 1886. ANGAS, *KAFIRS ILLUSTRATED*, 1847

One of the plates in Angas's volume is of a family of nyala buck. As mentioned in Chapter 1, Angas's contribution to science in the Zululand context was the scientific discovery of this attractive antelope in 1847, in the 'low undulating hill, scattered mimosa bush' country north of St Lucia Bay. Angas's sketches and notes were taxonomically written up for the Zoological Society of London by Dr Gray and the buck named in 1849 *Tragelaphus angasii* in honour of Angas's father. It was not until July 1851, however, that the Natal hunter James Proudfoot exhibited at a meeting of the Zoological Society of London specimens of both sexes of nyala which he had shot himself.[14]

The botanists

Published works such as those of Angas and Baldwin helped establish in the public mind, especially in Britain, the fact that Zululand had remaining populations of big game that had been decimated and even exterminated in many other parts of the subcontinent. But these revelations were enhanced by particular

MARK McKEN Plant hunters in Zululand in the 1850s and 1860s had to be rough and tough. The best of these was the fiery, hard-drinking Scottish curator of the Durban Botanic Gardens. Mark McKen had worked on the Bath Botanic Gardens in Jamaica before emigrating to Natal, where he managed a sugar plantation and served two terms as a curator. He was fluent in isiZulu, short-tempered and an excellent plant collector, who regularly supplied Kew Gardens with plants new to science, some of which were named *mckenii* after him.   DURBAN BOTANIC GARDENS

studies and visits undertaken by scientists from specific disciplines. Two of these – one in the 1850s and another in the 1890s – illustrate the point.

In the second half of the nineteenth century the major group of scientists to venture to Zululand were the botanists. The missionaries had already occasionally taken an interest in the flora of their new and wild parish, Miss M.C. Owen and the Irish lay preacher Wallace Hewetson being the earliest.[15]

The Byrne settlers brought with them the first professional resident botanist to the region. This was the fiery Scot Mark McKen (1823–1872), who had worked at Bath Botanic Gardens in Jamaica and who was the robust curator of Durban Botanic Gardens (1851–1853 and 1860–1872). In the early 1860s McKen and William Tyrer Gerrard collected over much of what is today KwaZulu-Natal, including Zululand. McKen, a fluent isiZulu speaker, was one of the great plant hunters of nineteenth-century Africa, matched only later by his brother-in-law, the great taxonomist and plant hunter, John Medley Wood (1827–1915).[16]

South-east Africa did not have a particularly good reputation among foreign scientists, which meant that locals largely had the field to themselves. One Natal magistrate, Captain Albert Allison, dryly observed in 1892 that foreign botanists 'have not an unnatural dislike to take the plunge amongst savage life, that is in localities where possibly instead of collecting, they might be collected'.[17]

Wood himself once admitted that there were areas where he would not venture to collect plants unless he had a police escort. Nonetheless, no scientist was ever killed by the Zulus while collecting there, though, as will be seen shortly, at least one scientist feared for his life during a civil war in Zululand.

Medley Wood was curator and then director of Durban Botanic Gardens from 1882 to 1913, and director of the Natal Colonial Herbarium from 1886 to 1915. During his tenure as curator, often assisted by the ubiquitous John Dunn, Medley Wood collected plants in Zululand in 1887, 1888, 1889 and 1895. He is particularly famous for his six-volume *Natal Plants*, published between 1899 and 1912, as well as for his discovery of the unique specimen of the cycad named after him, *Encephalartos woodii*. It is little wonder that the director of Kew wrote to Hely-Hutchinson, the governor of Natal and of Zululand, 'I am very glad that you think so well of Medley Wood. I regard him as a credit to the Colony.'[18]

Wood recorded his discovery of the cycad on a steep south-facing slope at the edge of Ongoye forest in southern Zululand in 1895 as follows:

> In the year 1895 I was on a botanical collecting trip with wagon and oxen in Zululand, and having reached a spot where the country was very rough, I stayed for several days botanising in the vicinity, and in so doing found a solitary clump of Encephalartos, consisting of four stems, the tallest of which was 18 feet high, with proportionate girth of stem, and with a few offsets at the base; the stems were all male, and not another plant of the species could be found in the vicinity, though we found a number of plants of E. brachyphyllus, of which we took away a number of specimens.[19]

TABLE 15

ZULULAND PLANTS LISTED BY MEDLEY WOOD, 1894 AND 1908

	1894	1908
Total number of genera	79	201
Number of named species	58	286
Number of unnamed species	21	20
Total number of species (named & unnamed)	79	306

In 1894 and again in 1908 Wood published lists of the scientifically known plants of Natal and Zululand. The Zululand plants are summarised in Table 15. This well illustrates the extent of the scientific discovery of the flora of Zululand in the late colonial era.[20]

Though professional botanists such as McKen, Gerrard and Wood and amateurs such as Dr Stanger, Dr Sutherland and John Sanderson have left well-deserved reputations as pioneers of KwaZulu-Natal botany, the father of Zululand botany was a very different character.

Robert Plant

Like McKen, Robert Plant was one of the British Byrne settlers to Natal in 1850. He arrived with his wife Dolly and their three children and had been a nurseryman in England. He was probably the R. Plant who compiled *The New Gardener's Dictionary*, published in London in 1849. Between July 1854 and August 1856 he was curator of the Durban Botanic Gardens. But try as he did, he was not terribly happy there, on one occasion observing: 'I find so quiet a life irksome. Remaining stationary so long is too nearly the existence of an oyster to meet my erratic taste.'[21]

Plant's real passion was collecting natural history specimens. This earlier career had given him contacts in London with the Chelsea Physic Garden, William Wilson Saunders and the Horticultural Society, Kew Gardens, the great nursery firm of Veitch, and especially with some of the prominent gentlemen amateur botanists such as Samuel Stevens of Bloomsbury Square. It is even possible that Saunders was responsible for Robert Plant going to Natal and Plant's collector brother sailing for Latin America. Certainly, Saunders and Stevens received consignments of natural history specimens from Robert Plant, which they kept or sold on, remitting a proportion of the profit back to the collector.

Like many Victorian scientists Robert Plant was a polymath, whose interests extended to insects and shells. This might today be dismissed as a lack of scientific precision, but it gave the nineteenth-century scientist a more global insight than possessed by many a modern scientist. Not that this prevented Plant from having his enthusiasms. In 1855 he gushed to Stevens, 'And now for the insects, my especial favourites too.' A few months later he complained, 'On the whole, plants are not so satisfactory as other things and yet entail much more trouble.' To Sir William Hooker at Kew he even asserted, 'Insects are more portable and, permit me to add, more profitable.'[22]

A consignment often netted £35 and on one occasion Plant received a draft for £100. But cash was needed with a growing family and the expenses of collecting were high. A wagon cost £150 to buy or 15s. a day to hire.

Though Plant made a trip to Mauritius and the Seychelles in 1853, it was to Zululand that he was drawn again and again. Even when unable to leave the botanic gardens or when he was farming at Vaal Hoek, near Tongaat, north of Durban, he sent his trained African staff into Zululand to collect in the same way the hunters sent their men up to Zululand to hunt. Once Robert Plant reported: '[The man] I sent to St Lucia last year has never returned – probably died of coast fever. He was one of my best hands and I regret his absence very much.'

But despite all his talk of insects and profits, Robert Plant was essentially a plantsman and when Kew suggested he undertake

A NATURALIST'S ZULULAND NOTEBOOK, 1850s Robert Plant's notebooks contain delightful drawings that he made of beetles, birds and plants. Though remembered as a plant hunter, Plant was also fascinated by insects and supplied a London natural history dealer with a regular supply. In 1857 Robert Plant indiscreetly told the director of Kew Gardens that 'insects are more portable and, permit me to add, more profitable'. MRS JOAN READ

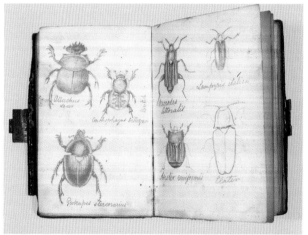

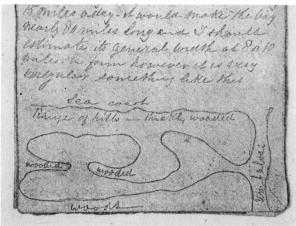

THE TRAVELLER'S TALE As well as sketches, Robert Plant used a pencil to record in his notebooks accounts of his adventures in Zululand. The map at the bottom of the page is his sketch of Lake St Lucia. MRS JOAN READ

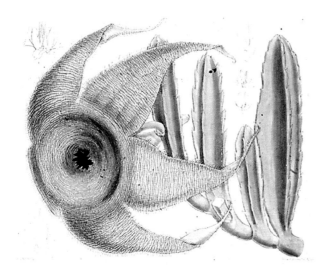

STAPELIA GIGANTEA Though the largest flowering and best-known plant of the family Stapeliae, this plant, which was discovered in Zululand in the early 1850s by Robert Plant, was slow to gain recognition. When Robert Plant died in 1858 his widow sent it to the Durban Botanic Gardens. After two years there it finally flowered and two years later, in 1862, the curator Mark McKen sent a specimen to Kew Gardens in England. Curiously, it was to be another 15 years before it was described by N.E. Brown.
CURTIS'S BOTANICAL MAGAZINE, t7068 (1889)

that which had not been attempted before – a flora of Natal – he was not slow to respond: 'I am so wedded to this beautiful colony that nothing would give me greater pleasure than to assist in making its richness known … I beg to place myself unconditionally at your disposal for the purpose named.'

From the first, Robert Plant had been drawn to Zululand. Just over a year after his arrival in Natal he set off on his first epic journey there. It was to prove an adventure. He crossed the Tugela and started collecting in southern Zululand, reaching the forest of Ongoye, which he loved. He pressed on and probably got as far as St Lucia. Then things went wrong. He never managed to meet up with the wagon he had sent ahead. Some of his cattle began to die. Worse, turning inland, he ran straight into civil unrest. Perhaps panicking at the sight of Mpande's warriors, Plant jettisoned most of his precious collection and hurried back to Natal.

The abortive trip did produce one benefit for science. In 1852 *Hooker's Journal of Botany* published Plant's account of his adventure. It was not only the first botanical account of Zululand but also the first botanical paper by a Natal resident in any scientific journal. In fact, the paper contained much also on the wildlife and countryside he passed through.[23] It was a life he relished. A year later, writing to Dolly from the Seychelles, he remarked, 'Decidedly I am altogether unfit for further communication with what is called civilised life. I am becoming a savage.'

When Plant gave up the curatorship of the botanic gardens, his mind increasingly turned to Zululand, to which he seems to have returned several times. Finally on 21 January 1858 he left Dolly, their five children and the attractive farm at Vaal Hoek, and with four African assistants set off up the road towards Zululand. Crossing the Tugela the party stopped briefly at Ongoye forest before pressing north to the Mfolozi River, where there were hundreds of 'ducks, cormorants and other water fowl'. Here they left the wagon and waded across the river near its mouth, which was so wide that the dogs had to be carried. Of the St Lucia complex Plant recorded:

> The margin, in most places, is fringed with tall reeds, in some places a mile in width and the number of hippopotami is astonishing. The water is tidal though the inflow does not seem to be much. A pair of rose coloured flamingoes, alarmed by our approach, rose out of the reeds as we gained the opposite shore and hundreds of ducks, cormorants and other water fowl are found all along its banks.

Moving along the eastern shore of Lake St Lucia, Plant was thrilled by the vast number of shells in the coastal forest. Moving north into the land of the Tsonga, he remarked on the reed huts laid out around a large tree 'like an English village'. Through the bush they pressed on and after four or five days emerged into more open elephant territory. Two of the Africans remained here to hunt whilst the rest move on in search of orchids. They crossed the Pongola and moved across a land teeming with game – wildebeest, zebra, buffalo, nyala, waterbuck, baboon, elephant and rhino.

How far north the party continued we do not know; certainly, they ventured into what is today Mozambique. Locals were recruited to carry the ever-increasing collection of plants, made greater when they discovered a wood festooned with orchids. Finally, they turned for home. Then the trouble began.

The recruited labour refused to continue to help and neither payment nor threats would set matters right. One by one they melted away into the bush. This meant that Plant and his own men had to move the plants in relays. Then Plant went down with malaria and was laid low for three days. Progress now was slow as the small group made its way down to the fresher air of the Maputaland coast. A sore knee also made Plant's walking painful and slow. Matters were not helped by the excessive heat.

The party was in sight of St Lucia when the malaria returned to Plant. They made it to Mkhumbi's kraal where Plant collapsed. For three days he suffered in the stifling heat of a hut, before he was carried out and placed under an acacia tree. Here he lay for a further nine days and nights. And it was here at dawn on what was probably 15 March 1858 that the great plant hunter died: South Africa's first martyr of botany.[24]

They buried him at the African homestead overlooking St Lucia. The stone-covered grave became a landmark and 'a beacon of

SIR JOSEPH HOOKER Most of the plants collected by botanists in Zululand ended up either in the Durban Botanic Gardens or were sent from there to the Royal Botanic Gardens at Kew outside London. From the 1840s until 1905 Kew Gardens was controlled by the Hooker dynasty. Sir Joseph Hooker was director from 1865 until 1885 when many Zululand plants new to science were described in the Kew Herbarium.   SOUTH AFRICAN NATIONAL BIODIVERSITY INSTITUTE, PRETORIA

warning to those who, for the love of science, gain or curiosity, attempt imprudently to traverse that fatal country'. The African staff collected their master's belongings, his gun and the little notebook with its pencilled jottings, and what plants there were, and set off for Vaal Hoek and Dolly. The last entry in Robert Plant's notebook was a prayer that he might be spared to return home to the farm. Six years before Plant himself had written prophetically of the St Lucia area: 'Elephants seem in great plenty all over this district, as we frequently saw herds of them. There are few inhabitants of this part, which argues little for its healthiness.'

When the news of her husband's death reached her, Dolly Plant wrote to Kew Gardens offering to send them any dried specimens she could find around the house. The living plants were sent to Durban Botanic Gardens. It was only in 1862 that one of these was forwarded by Mark McKen to Kew and a further 15 years before it was scientifically described by N.E. Brown as *Stapelia gigantea*, the greatest of the Stapeliae. Robert Plant also discovered the attractive *Streptocarpus saundersii*, which he originally sent to William Wilson Saunders.[25] Robert Plant is remembered in another stapelia, *S. plantii*, in the orange-flowered *Gloriosa plantii* and in the fern *Lastrea plantii*. Plant's flora of

'BUTTERFLY' BOWKER'S ANNOTATED BUTTERFLY BOOK This copy of Roland Trimen's *Rhopalocera Africæ Australis: A catalogue of South African butterflies (1862-1866)* was presented by the author to the eccentric Natal naturalist Colonel James Henry Bowker, popularly referred to as 'Butterfly' Bowker. The much-annotated volume is interspersed with sheets on which Bowker has glued butterfly wings. Bowker collected plants and insects in Zululand but gave great offence to the Empress Eugénie when he presented the photograph of himself at the site where the Prince Imperial was killed showing him holding a large butterfly net.   DON AFRICANA LIBRARY, DURBAN

TABLE 16

LIST OF TREE LANDMARKS ON AN 1885 ZULULAND BOUNDARY MAP
BETWEEN THE UMLALAZI AND UMHLATUZE RIVERS

AFRICAN/COMMON NAME OF TREE ON MAP	NO. OF SPECIES MARKED	PRESENT ENGLISH NAME	SCIENTIFIC NAME
bangamlota	1	tasselberry	*Antidesma venosum*
dumgamise	1	Natal ebony	*Euclea natalensis*
Ficus sp.	6	–	[Species unspecified]
impafa [umphafa]	1	buffalo thorn	*Ziziphus mucronata*
umdoni	2	waterberry	*Syzygium cordatum*
mkamanzi	2	ankle thorn	*Acacia robusta*
mkambi	1	paperbark thorn	*Acacia sieberiana*
nsinsi [umsinsi]	3	coast coral tree	*Erythrina caffra*
insizi [umsinsi]	2	common coral tree	*Erythrina lysistemon*
munga	5	sweet thorn	*Acacia karoo*
nqawe [umnqawe]	1	scented thorn	*Acacia nilotica*
umganu	4	marula	*Sclerocarya birrea*
umgugada [umgugudo]	1	Transvaal saffron	*Cassine transvaalensis*
umhlahle	1	coastal golden-leaf	*Bridelia micrantha*
umhlonhlo	1	common tree euphorbia	*Euphorbia ingens*
umkhamba	6	paperbark thorn	*Acacia sieberiana*
umqabaqaba	1	broadleaved coral tree	*Erythrina latissima*
umqokolo	2	Natal apricot or possibly glossy sourberry or caper bush or Kei apple	*Dovyalis caffra*
umqoqo	1	cats whiskers	*Clerondendrum gladrum*
umtolo	1	common hook thorn	*Acacia caffra*

Natal botany never appeared and it would be over 40 years before a flora specifically of the region began to appear in print.

A postscript to this sad tale can be added. Dolly continued to farm Vaal Hoek for a number of years. At the International Exhibition in London in 1862 an example of the tea she grew at Vaal Hoek won a special award. Later she moved to Durban, dying 50 years later at the age of 93.

Botanical map

In 1885 an attempt was made to define various Zululand boundaries, in particular that of John Dunn. One sketch-map in particular is of interest to the historian of the Zululand wilderness. This traces a boundary from a hill named iHombane, just beside the main wagon road up to Eshowe. The boundary map runs for some 30 km from this road to the Umlalazi River, then north-east round the western end of the Ongoye mountain range and on to the Umhlathuze River. What is interesting about this pen-and-ink map is that 43 of the 80 landmarks are trees. This includes 20 different species of tree. Table 16 lists these 1885 tree landmarks on what must be the first Zululand botanical map.[26]

The birders

Many species of bird were recognised and named in Zulu society. Some white hunters and travellers were also familiar with certain of the species found in Zululand. Perhaps top of their list was the vulture. Henry Francis Fynn recounted visiting the macabre site where the bodies of King Shaka's victims were dumped. 'It was truly a Golgotha swarming with hundreds of vultures.'[27] A generation later, William Drummond noted seeing at one Zululand waterhole Namaqua dove, turtle dove, an eagle owl, francolin, nightjars, parakeets and crowned plover. The honeyguide was a source of curiosity to travellers as was the ground hornbill. The latter was said to be good eating, though rather tough. Also eaten were the dikkop, dove, duck, francolin, goose, guinea fowl and korhaan.

The large raptors could hardly fail to be noticed. Baldwin recalled shooting a martial eagle:

While staying at the kraal I killed the finest specimen of the eagle tribe I ever saw, and regretted much that I had no arsenical soap to preserve the skin. I saw a great commotion among a troop of guinea fowls across the [Black Mfolozi] river, and presently this fellow rose, so gorged that he could only just rise, feathered to the toes with beautiful black and white plumage, and talons fearful to look upon.[28]

As far as the scientific discovery of the region's avifauna is concerned, in the 1830s Andrew Smith described a number of bird species the type-specimens of which came from what is today KwaZulu-Natal. These included:

african broadbill (scientifically discovered in 1839)
yellow-bellied bulbul (1834)
lazy cisticola (1843)
buff-spotted flufftail (1839)
square-tailed drongo (1834)
Natal francolin (1834)
grey go-away bird (lourie) (1833)
mangrove kingfisher (1834)
Natal nightjar (1845)
wattled plover (1839)
Natal robin (1840)
olive sunbird (1840)
yellow warbler (1847)

Delegorgue scientifically discovered the bronze-naped or Delegorgue's pigeon in 1847. Other collectors of bird specimens in south-east Africa were at various times C.F.F. Krauss and another German zoologist, Dr Wilhelm Peters (1815–1883). Peters discovered the African crake in Mozambique in 1854. He also discovered and named a number of fish species common to Zululand and Mozambique.[29] Johan August Wahlberg made six trips into Zululand between 1839 and 1844. The birds he recorded included the Egyptian vulture, the fish eagle, a species of weaver, a 'partridge', a bush shrike and a rock thrush. He collected two species of barbet new to science on the Umlalazi: the white-eared barbet and the golden-rumped tinker-barbet.[30]

The London naturalist and trader in 'curiosities of natural history', Samuel Stevens, who did so much for Robert Plant, also encouraged other naturalists in Natal to send him specimens of the avifauna of Natal and Zululand. These included Thomas Ayres and the reclusive William Gueinzius. That quantities of bird skins were coming from Natal and Zululand to London is evident from the series of articles by John Henry Gurney on birds of Natal that appeared in *The Ibis* between 1860 and 1863.[31] It was not, however, until the Woodward brothers arrived on the birding scene that the true extent of the birdlife of Natal, and especially Zululand, was revealed to the world.

THE WHITEBACKED VULTURE Large numbers of vultures would often congregate near a hunter's encampment where carcasses were hung up on trees and intestines thrown into the nearby bush. Such unhealthy, smelly and morbid camps were paradise for the vulture and hyena. PARKER GILLMORE, *THE HUNTER'S ARCADIA*, 1886

British colonial officials and, in particular, compilers of reports and commissions frequently mentioned game and birdlife. This was especially true in the 1880s and 1890s of those reports relating to Maputaland. Here on and around the rivers and pans birdlife flourished, though unfortunately for precise analysis, names given for these are usually of genera rather than species.[32]

The report of the Zululand boundary commission of 1880 recorded:

There are endless varieties of birds from the enormous black vulture to the small and beautiful humming bird. Quail of a small description abound throughout Zululand. Partridges are not so plentiful; while the brown pheasant was rarely seen. In some parts, especially in the bush on the banks of the Black Umfolozi River, Guinea fowl are plentiful. A small slate-coloured dove may be found throughout the country. And large flocks near old camps or in the thorn districts. The black finch, with a tail quite out of proportion to the size of its body, was frequently met with; the tail feathers of this bird are highly prized by the Zulus and Swazis for head ornaments. Koran, Paauw, and plover, are also common. Many of the large snake-killing buzzards, with enormous red bills, were seen near the Black Umfolozi.[33]

The hunters occasionally commented upon the birds they encountered. William Baldwin mainly wrote of game birds he had shot. These included quail, korhaan, 'blue heron' and 'ducks, widgeon, geese, waterrails, cranes and divers'. He thought the dikkop 'the daintiest bird in Africa'.[34]

Drummond believed the Zululand ostrich was 'being rapidly exterminated'. He talks of the spur-winged geese often to be seen feeding in the maize (mealie) fields during the early morning, sometimes not less than 20 m away from the village fence. He comments on vultures, the different species of korhaan or 'pauw', the Namaqua dove, crowned plovers, francolin, the 'great owl' (*Bubo* sp.), the 'rhinoceros bird' and of parrots and turtle doves feeding off sycamore figs on the western side of the Phongola Poort. He threw stones at the honeyguides that he said were 'not a pleasant accompaniment to the hunter', as they warned the game that humans were present. Drummond also talks of the song of 'one of the commonest bush-birds' that hunters imitated to tell the hunting party to take cover.[35]

It is to Drummond's credit that the second appendix in his book is devoted to naming 36 varieties and species of bird, giving English, Zulu and scientific names.

Robert and John Woodward

South-east Africa's greatest birders in the late Victorian period were the red-headed bachelors and Anglican missionaries Robert Blake Woodward and his slightly younger brother John Deverell Stewart Woodward. Both had been born in Bathford, England, and immigrated to Natal about 1872. They also appear some time in their younger years to have visited America, about which they published a book entitled *Wandering in America*.

For a number of years the brothers worked as missionaries in Natal at St Luke's Mission Station near Harding, and later they were associated with the American Board for Foreign Missions at Adam's Mission Station near Amanzimtoti.[36] They also appear to have farmed or at least kept a smallholding in the Ifafa area on the Natal south coast.

Having some private capital made them freer agents than many of their counterparts, and they soon were drawn into the general study of Natal's natural history. Out of this grew their fascination with the birdlife of the region. Frequently their homestead was more of a menagerie than a centre for missionary endeavour. Injured or captured birds and animals lived there and were no doubt treated with assiduous attention. The brothers were not mean with their knowledge and were eager to share the information they gathered, be it with the local bird expert, G.

Hutchinson, or with the 'industrious and prolific' Richard Bowdler Sharpe (1847–1909) of the Natural History Museum in London. They also corresponded with local colonial employees, on one occasion concerning the 'depravities' of ticks.[37]

At first the brothers did not confine themselves to birds, but collected any curiosity of nature that came their way. They published on natural history subjects in magazines and in the local press. By 1894 the brothers were well enough established with the Natural History section of the British Museum in London to be requested by Sharpe to undertake a collecting trip for bird specimens. They used this linkage as a means to apply to take their guns into Zululand free of duty.[38]

In Zululand they felt that the greatest treasures in the bird kingdom might be found. Here too they had the convenience of being able occasionally to escape camping beside their large spring cart and experience the relative comfort of a mission station. By July 1894 the brothers were on the banks of the Tugela River. What they recorded as having seen in the ensuing fourteen months is summarised in Table 17.

The adventurers were careful to keep within the various regulations then in force in Zululand. The magistrates granted their requests, though the resident magistrate for Lower Umfolozi was not slow to point out to the brothers:

> With regard to your wish to proceed to the mouth of the Umfolozi, I must draw your attention to the fact that No 2 Game Reserve is at the 'Mapelane Hill' and in the Lagoons & forest surrounding it, I am therefore to request that you will not shoot bird or game in that locality. There is no objection to your shooting in the Umbonambi.[39]

The following year, 1896, the Woodwards were back collecting in Zululand. Marshall Clarke, the British resident commissioner of Zululand, in his diary entry for 7 March 1896 recorded:

> Arrived Mbegamuzi at 11.30 (2½ hrs) and halted until 2 pm. At this point we met the Woodward brothers who are employed in shooting birds for the British Museum – They were in route for the Bombo [Lebombo Mountains].[40]

That July saw the brothers in the Mkhuze area.[41] They had come down here from the highlands to the west. They recorded, 'Hearing that the Umkuzi was better wooded and a good place for birds, we took a two days' journey across country to the Umkuzi "Poort". On the way through the thorn country they encountered a jackal trotting along 'looking uncommonly like a

WOODWARDS' BARBET R.B. and J.D.S. Woodward were two Christian missionary brothers with a keen interest in the birdlife of Natal and Zululand. They birded extensively in Zululand in the 1890s, sending specimens to the British Museum and publishing accounts of their trips in *The Ibis*. This fine illustration of the Woodwards' barbet or the green barbet, *Stactolaema woodwardi*, which the brothers found in Zululand's Ongoye forest, appeared in *The Ibis* and was the frontispiece in their book *Natal Birds*, which was published in 1899.

TABLE 17

BIRDING TRIP UNDERTAKEN IN ZULULAND BY R.B. AND J.D.S. WOODWARD, 14 JULY 1894 TO EARLY SEPTEMBER 1895

NB: Where there is some doubt regarding identification, the most likely name is given in square brackets after the Woodwards' entry. Latin names are those given by the Woodwards.

DATE	AREA	BIRDS SEEN BY WOODWARDS	WOODWARDS' NOTES
July 1894	Crossed the Tugela River into Zululand		Had a spring cart large enough to sleep in, a pair of horses (later oxen substituted), an African helper, guns & ammunition.
	Inyoni flats	*Cinnyris gutturalis* (Honey-suckers) [scarlet-chested sunbird]	Black & scarlet breasts
	John Dunn's house	Ground hornbill [paauw (bustard)]	Largest & best game bird in SA.
	Mthunzini region	*Limnocorax niger* (waterhen) [black crake]	–
		Catriscus apicalis (reed-bird) [broad-tailed warbler]	Warbles cheerfully, as it runs up & down stalks.
		Pied kingfisher	Common
		Cinnyris verreauxi [eastern olive-sunbird]	Scarlet side tufts, otherwise sombre plumage. New to the Woodwards.
		Barbatula bilineata (yellow & black barbet)	A little bird. New to Woodwards. [golden-rumped tinkerbird]
		Halcyon orientalis (crab-eater) [brown-hooded kingfisher]	Confined to coastlands. Very common.
		Smilorhis leucotis (black & white barbet) [white-eared barbet]	Small. Similar in plumage to the common *Halcyon albiventris*, but different notes.
		Cringer flaviventris (yellow breasted bulbul) [yellow-breasted bulbul or greenbul]	Chattering. Very common.
August – c. October 1894	Ongoye forest		Built a hut & 'remained for some time'.
		Hadedas ibis	Great roosting place near encampment. 'Used to be more common in Natal.'
		Purple-crested turaco or lourie	Scarce. Killed by Zulus for their red feathers for headdresses.
		Poeocephalus robustus (Levaillant's parrot) [Cape parrot]	'Flocks fly screaming overhead.'
		Green or Woodwards' barbet (a new barbet)	Thicker parts of woods and feeds on berries.
		Pogonorhynchus torquatus (red-crowned barbet) [red-fronted tinker-barbet]	Common but shy; small; sings in heat of day; ventriloquous; known as the 'Little Tinker'.
		Pogonorhynchus torquatus (red-fronted barbet) [black-collared barbet]	Handsome bird, very familiar in bush country.
			Ride to the low country for two days.
		Halcyon orientalis (kingfisher) [brown-headed kingfisher]	New to the Woodward brothers.
			Back to forest camp.
		Lamprocolius phoenicopterus (green starling) [Cape glossy starling]	Common & pretty; glossy plumage; bright orange eyes; large flocks; eggs bluish; lively and cheerful habit; 'one of the most striking of SA birds'.
		Lamprocolius melanogaster [black-bellied glossy starling]	Smaller than previous sp.; distinctly blue; confined more to bushes.
		Red-winged starling	Rocks & kranzes; very noisy; very fond of rock-plum.
		Asio capensis (swamp owl) [marsh owl]	–
		Strix flammea (white owl) [barn owl]	Common
		Narina trogan	Abundant in Ngoya
October 1894	Road to Eshowe		Added disselboom to spring cart and replaced the 2 horses with 4 large oxen. Also secured a driver and forelooper (leader)
		Gorgeous bush shrike	Scarlet throat makes it very conspicuous in thickets; cheerful song 'kong kong, koit' one of pleasantest of the spring sounds.
October – December 1894	Umhlathuze valley near St Paul's mission	Namaqua dove	Generally in pairs around African homesteads or on road sides. New to Woodwards.
		Bee-eaters *Merops bullockoides* & *M. pusillus* [white-front bee-eater and little bee-eater]	Very common here – especially partial to hot sheltered valleys.
		Sunbirds: malachite, scarlet-breasted & black	
		Cuckoos: emerald, redchested & golden [Dideric cuckoo]	
		Widowbirds: red-collared & long-tailed (isakabula)	Often fall victim to the sticks of the boys, who are fond of decorating themselves with its feathers.
		(Eastern) paradise whydah	New to Woodwards.
		Common waxbills	Rooibeks
		Pin-tailed whydah	Nest in small tree in open land, very loosely made, of grass, lined with fowl's feathers, 6 small white eggs.
		Cape canary	Common
		Crithagra ictera (Mealie-bird) [yellow-fronted canary]	Abounds everywhere; mealie-gardens.
		Red-throated wryneck	In open park-like areas on these highlands. This bird flies from tree to tree, making a harsh chattering cry, which has sometimes been mistaken for that of a Hawk … up the trunks of trees … the tail is composed of ordinary soft feathers … plumage reminds one of the Nightjar; it has red-brown eyes.
		Yellow-throated longclaw	Common everywhere. It is naturally very tame: boys knock over numbers of them with their sticks, and grass-fires are apt to destroy their nests.
		Orange-throated longclaw	The finest of our larks
		Pied crow	Frequents the vicinity of our outspans … the constant companion of the vulture.
		Black-coloured or violet-backed starling	The cornland crow
		Plum-coloured or violet-backed starling	Glossy thrush … violet colour with snow-white belly.
January 1895	Road to Mfolozi via Melmoth		

DATE	AREA	BIRDS SEEN BY WOODWARDS	WOODWARDS' NOTES
January – February 1895	Valley and tributaries of the White Mfolozi River.		'In this district we found a number of birds that we had not seen elsewhere'.
		Guinea fowl	Favourite resort at junction of White Mfolozi and Tegwen.
		Rollers, hornbills & go-away birds or grey louries	Much frequented … in the beautiful park-like glades.
		Lilac-breasted roller	'a splendid bird' … not very common … shy.
		Giant or Verreaux's eagle owl	Largest of our owls … wings 4 foot 6 inches … black eyes.
		Pearl-spotted owl or owlet	Only 7 inches … does not hoot or screech.
		Poecephalus fuscicapillus [brownheaded parrot]	Small green parrot … southern limit of species.
		Kingfishers & 'crabeaters'	Plentiful
		Halcyon cyanoleuca [woodland kingfisher]	Lovely blue plumage.
		Pygmy kingfisher	Plentiful … pretty little Natal crab-eaters … nest in side of an antbear's hole.
		Halcyon fuscicapilla [brown-headed kingfisher]	Common everywhere … it is very fond of crabs.
		Half-collared kingfisher	Flies rapidly up and down most of the rivers … lives off fish.
		Giant kingfisher	15 inches in length.
		Hamerkop	
Feb. 1895 (some weeks)	Umbegamusa (Mbhekamuzi) and Black Mfolozi River.		'were told [Umbegamusa] was a good place for birds … beautiful district … obtained less and fewer variety than at the Umhlatoosi [Umhlatuze] and on the White Umfolozi'.
		Oxpeckers	Numerous here.
		Guinea fowl	Abundant.
		Natal francolin	Bush francolin … 'Tuquali' … 13 inches [33 cm] … common in woods & thickets … pleasant evening call-note … around kraals & homesteads … Dr Livingstone noted 'the screaming of the francolin proclaims man to be near'.
		F. subtorquatus (common partridge) [coqui francolin]	Frequents the open-land … 10 inches [25.4 cm] … eggs pure white, laid in the long grass … very tame in winter season.
c. Mar. 1895	Highlands of Nongoma district via Ivuna store	*Otis afra* (korhaan) [southern black korhaan]	Here several.
c. April – May 1895	Church of England mission … no regular road beyond … lost way … district of 'Hlwati' in sight of Edukumbaan Mt.		Stopped for some time … saw few birds; but the abundance of flowers attracted a large number of butterflies, of which we obtained a nice collection.
	Makawe Hill … 7 miles off … extensive view of St Lucia …		Few days here … disagreeably cold north wind.
Early June 1895	Descended to flats		Outspanned under a spreading mimosa tree.
		Guinea fowl	Large flocks … shot a few, but without a pointer they are hard to get.
		Paauw [korhaan]	Common here in open grass … as many as 18 in a day.
		Kori bustard	The great bustard or paauw … can run at great speed.
		Korhaan	Listed as *Otis afra*, but probably blackbellied korhaan.
		Secretary bird	
27 June 1895	Began homeward journey via the coast route	Dikkop [thick-knee]	Probably spotted dikkop … large yellow eyes; 'good eating'.
Late June – late July 1895	Crossed Hluhluwe River at the high drift To junction of Hlabisa road near St Lucia coalfields To banks of Mfolozi River Outspanned near Norwegian mission station		Here we collected a good deal of wild cotton, which is useful for stuffing birds.
22 July 1895	Bare grassy hills		Not found many birds.
	To Umango small wood		
	To Umbonambi (near mouth of the Mfolozi River)		Sandy bush-covered hills … very pretty part of the coast.
		Hadeda ibis	Common here.
		Yellow-billed cuckoo [green coucal or malkoha]	Extraordinary cry, inhabits thick bush.
		White-eared barbet	High up trees.
		Green pigeon	Fat … plentiful.
		Narina trogon	
		Klaas's cuckoo	
		Great egret	3 foot [1 metre]
		(African) sacred ibis	
c. August 1895	To Umsineni River, near fine pyramid-shaped Umpomvu		
	To magistracy amongst low hills. Crossed Umlatusi River & on to Mr Green's store (7 or 8 km from Ngoye forest).		
	Ngoye forest		Tent in forest surrounded with wattle fence … Ngoye squirrel.
		Green or Woodwards' barbet	A favourite resort … in no part of Zululand have we seen so many.
		Trumpeter hornbill	Common here, as it is in most places … naturally half tame … cry of: he he he-he-he.
		Redbilled hornbill (*Tockus melanoleucus*)	We constantly saw parties of 5 or 6 dotted over the bare hills outside the forest … very useful in destroying snakes; fortunately it is one of the few birds protected by law … egg shell is very strong, of a dull white colour, and as large as that of a goose.
		Ground hornbill	
4 Sept 1895	Umlalazi on over 'ugly country' to Umbezan and on to the Tugela River, crossing 'over into the land of civilization again'.		

dog' and they shot a 3 m-long black mamba snake. In the days they spent in the Mhkuze area they recorded seeing the following bird species – what might be termed the first Mhkuze bird list:

• White-fronted bee-eaters in great numbers.
• *Laniarius quadricolor* [probably the gorgeous bush shrike], plentiful in the thickets here. Its cry during the pairing-season is very musical, and sounds exactly like 'Bob, bob, bob o'link' oft repeated.
• Zambesi Green Shrike (*Laniarius galaris*) [probably the olive bush shrike]. Here we first met … hops about the thick scrub and has a low chuckling note.
• Brown-headed parrot in most of the thorn north of the Umfolozi.
• Grey Plantain-eaters (*Schizorhis concolor*) [grey go-away-bird/lourie] in parties of two or three, are often met with climbing about the thorntrees, uttering their extraordinary cry like the long drawn-out mewing of a cat.
• Lesser honeyguide was generally solicitous for us to follow it in quest of honey. It has a peculiar chattering cry which it emits when it wants to lead a person to a bees' nest, and when followed flies on from tree to tree in advance.
• Red Ground-Cuckoo (*Centropus senegalensis*) [Burchell's coucal] common everywhere. It keeps to the low scrub and is fond of old mealie-gardens. It seems never to fly high … During the summer its cry is constantly heard, especially in damp weather. Its voice resembles the letter *o* repeated many times, beginning at a high key and falling low.
• African black duck flying up and down this river [Mhkuze]. The young birds seem to remain with their parents for a considerable time; we have seldom seen more than two old ducks together, but have killed as many as five half-grown birds with one charge.
• Blue Lourie (*Corythaix porphyroe*) [purple-crested turaco/lourie] feeds on wild figs and berries and keeps mostly to the tops of the trees.
• Guinea-fowl are plentiful; we found them very good eating, not unlike turkey.

On their return to Natal after these epic trips, the brothers were clearly excited at what they had achieved. They dispatched 66 bird specimens to Sharpe at the British Museum and sold the museum a further twenty. They now put pen to paper and in 1897 and again in 1898 papers appeared in *The Ibis* relating to the birds of Zululand.[42] But the Woodward brothers had a more ambitious plan. They would do something never attempted before, a book on the birds of the region.

The problem with their idea of a book was that they needed cash to pay for its publication. In September 1897 the brothers wrote to the local press asking for the names of those who would be prepared to buy such a volume when it was published. They said that they wanted to produce a small handbook of some 150 pages that would sell at about 3s. 6d. so that it would be accessible to the general reader. This clearly did not elicit sufficient response so in December 1897 they wrote to Harry Binns, the prime minister of the then self-governing Natal, and asked for a small government publication subsidy:

> Our idea is to bring out a small handbook containing about 250 pages to sell at not more than 5/-. This though scientifically correct would be written in popular style so as to be useful to anyone commencing the study of this subject. Such a book would be especially suitable to put into the hands of Colonial boys, and if made attractive would induce them to study the works of God in Nature instead of wasting so much of their time in harmful literature.

They went on to say that 3s. 6d. would be their recommended selling price. They also pointed out that the only South African bird book, *Layard's Birds of South Africa*, edited by Dr Sharpe of the British Museum, was published many years before and sold at £3 a copy. They enclosed an offprint from *The Ibis* concerning their collection of bird specimens in Zululand.

But the ministry of education was not interested and on 6 January 1898 sent the brothers a polite rejection letter. The under-secretary did, however, say that 'if the book you refer to is issued and proves to be one which would be useful as a handbook in Government schools, then the Government would, no doubt, favourably consider the question of purchasing a number of copies for use in the schools'. Hely-Hutchinson, the governor, had not been too far off the mark when he confided to Sir William Thiselton-Dyer in 1896 that 'the Natal Government … are rather backward in promoting the advance of science – between you and me'.[43]

Despite such disappointments, the brothers pressed on with their project and in 1899 their 215-page *Natal Birds* appeared, printed by P. Davis and Sons of Pietermaritzburg. *Natal Birds* listed 386 species found in Natal and Zululand and reproduced the attractive J.G Keulemans lithograph of two Woodwards' barbets which originally appeared in *The Ibis* in 1897. Today copies of the book fetch over R3 000 (£250) a copy.

What became of the brothers is uncertain. One report had it that John Woodward drowned in the flooded Tugela River on returning to Natal from a birding trip to Zululand. The successes of the Woodward brothers included the identification, for the first time south of the Zambezi, of the eastern (yellowspotted) nicator, *Nicator gularis*. The brothers were remembered in the names of two birds: Woodwards' batis (*Batis fratrum*) and what is today called the green barbet but which for many years was named Woodwards' barbet (*Stactolaema woodwardi*). This Zululand barbet was thought to be a separate species from *S. olivacea*, which is found in East Africa. Both were named by the great ornithologist Captain George Ernest Shelley, the nephew of the famous poet. The East African barbet was described by Shelley in 1880 and the Ongoye specimen in 1895. Today both populations carry the earlier scientific name *S. olivacea*.

Zoos

The 1850s saw the Colony of Natal and its Zululand hinterland as a source for zoological gardens in Europe. Indeed Natal and Natalia became the toast of Dublin when the city's Royal Zoological Gardens of Ireland acquired the first of what was to become its famous lion breeding stock in May 1855. Thanks to a grant from the Irish administration they paid £285 for the pair of lions. Two other young lions 'in perfect health' had been sold in Natal a few years earlier for £15 for the pair.[44]

The greatest of the nineteenth-century animal traders was the larger-than-life Hamburg-born Charles Jamrach (1815–1891), who physically resembled one of the era's most earnest and famous proponents of science, Prince Albert. Jamrach's warehouse, which was like a zoo in its own right, was on the notorious Ratcliffe Highway facing the grand entrance to the London Docks. It was here that many an unfortunate Zululand creature of the wilderness found itself immured. One visitor in 1861 was shown a room in this zoological Aladdin's Cave in which there were 6 000 parakeets. Jamrach bought animals from sailors and used agents across the globe to obtain specimens for zoos, pet shops and private collectors. Many stories were associated with this interesting character, such as the day he single-handedly wrestled to the ground one of his tigresses, which had escaped from his menagerie and attacked a nine-year-old boy.[45]

William Barter, a future chairman of the Natal Bank, was one of these animal-trader agents with whom Jamrach had to deal. Others, such as Burton Stather and John Parks, were also connected with the trade, as were several Zululand hunters, such as James Proudfoot, who supplied firms that traded in wild animals, such as Messrs Henderson and Smerdon, and Adler and Escombe.[46] Occasionally references appeared in the Natal press to animals at Durban docks destined for Europe's zoos. In 1869 the *Natal Mercury* recorded:

> On Tuesday morning a trader might have been seen walking into town [Durban] from the Vley, accompanied by the inevitable touter and followed by a young quagga [zebra] and four or five young wildebeeste which appear to be very tame and followed their owner in a docile and tractable manner.

These animals were purchased by Messrs Adler and Escombe and will be forwarded to one or other of the Zoological gardens in England or on the continent.[47]

Occasionally advertisements appeared in the Natal press seeking live wild animals for export. One was placed by the Cape Town firm of C.M. Villet and Son, who were seedsmen, florists and 'collectors of natural curiosities'. The advertisement ran as follows:

> A constant supply of WILD ANIMALS, for which good remunerating prices will be given, on their delivery in Cape Town – Animals of the rarer sort will be preferred, particularly Male lions and tigers [leopards], Blue wildebeast, hartebeast, Eland, Geems Bock, Ostriches, Quaggas, Rhinoceros, giraffes, etc, etc. Apply to VILLET and Son, Long-street.[48]

Figure 4 illustrates well the fluctuation in numbers of wild animals exported out of Durban harbour between 1854 and 1888. Numbers were generally not great except in certain years, which coincided probably with specific orders. Between 1854 and 1898, 2 682 wild creatures, which had a value of £8 783, were shipped out of Port Natal. Not all these animals came from Zululand – some were from Natal and others from the interior – but a fair number must have come from the nearest source of surviving wild game, Zululand.

In the years 1854 to 1856 the following were exported: 17 lion, 10 leopard, 2 hyena, 2 wild pig, 2 zebra, 1 eland and 1 jackal. Values of animals exported varied but were generally in the region of: £40 for an eland; £20 for a hyena; £15 for a wild pig or a zebra; and £5 for a jackal or a hartebeest. Lion usually varied in value from £15 to £67 each, and leopard from £10 to £21 each. In 1888, 244 tortoises were shipped out of Durban valued at a total of £10. These figures were the animals' price in Natal. Of course, if these creatures survived their onward journey, Mr Jamrach's asking price was considerably more than this.

FIGURE 4

EXPORT OF LIVE ANIMALS FROM DURBAN (1854-87)

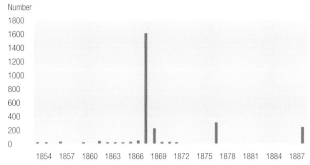

The mortality rate in getting the captured animals out of the bush to Durban was very high. Drummond wrote of his taking a white rhino calf after his mother had been shot. The small creature did not live, but it is preserved for posterity in a coloured illustration on the title page of Drummond's *The large game*. Drummond also recounts a narrow escape he had when he tried to steal a lion cub from under the nose of its mother:

> … seizing it [the cub] with both hands; but I had counted without my host; the little beast snarled and bit and tore at my bare arms in such a fashion that I was glad to fling it away, and scuttle up the tree again as fast as I could out of the way of the enraged mother, who was coming down at full gallop, her tail carried out straight behind, and looking the very personification of fury. She rushed right against the tree in her blind hurry, and then reared up, glaring at me and roared terribly …[49]

If the animal was brought out of the bush still alive, then there was the further trauma of the sea passage and the incarceration in Jamrach's warehouse, prior to the final journey to the new caged home. The overall mortality rate must have been very high.

Museums

It is not surprising, given the Victorian gentleman's general interest in the natural environment, that specimens of natural history should sometimes find their way from Zululand to museums and the exhibits of learned societies. In 1875, for example, the lower canines of a hippo from Lake St Lucia, shot by the Honourable C. Ellis, were exhibited by the Zoological Society of London. The outer curve of the teeth measured 30 in. (76.2 cm) and were supposed to be the largest ever obtained.[50]

By the 1890s Zululand magistrates were receiving occasional requests for permission to hunt for specimens for museums. Some of these came from the Durban, Pietermaritzburg or Cape Town museums, but some were from foreign museums such as Kristiana Museum in Finland and the Stavanger Museum in Norway. Collectors for the Natural History section of the British Museum were also shooting in Zululand. The advantage of using local colonists to hunt and collect, as the British Museum did, was that there were no running costs, only payment for specimens received, making it much cheaper than sending out a professional collector.[51]

Requests were mainly for specimens of royal game. Permission was usually granted for the shooting of single specimens of these, though not, after 1895, in the game reserves. Later, local museums were not averse to exchanging surplus Zululand specimens with other museums. This was especially so with the Natal Government Museum in Pietermaritzburg.[52]

In 1903 the Natal government took over control of the museum in Pietermaritzburg from the Natal Society. One of the first things the new management committee did was to appoint Dr E. Warren from University College, London. Warren was to remain as director of the Natal Museum until 1935, during which time he was to become a zealous campaigner for wildlife protection in Zululand.[53]

No sooner had Warren arrived in Natal than he was on his way to Zululand. The circumstances were peculiar if not extraordinary. The Zululand Delimitation Commission was touring Zululand in 1903 collecting evidence for its report which would partition Zululand into areas of white and African farming. The Natal Government Museum, with the permission of the commission, which included Charles Saunders, sent a Durban taxidermist called F. Teschner to travel with the commission and collect and prepare specimens for it.

In June 1903 Warren himself and a member of the museum's committee crossed the Tugela and visited the commission's camp, which was then at Hlabisa. Their purpose was to increase the interest of Saunders in the museum, to see how Teschner was faring and to instruct him on how to preserve the lower forms of vertebrates, as well as to make a preliminary survey of the fauna of eastern Zululand. Part of Warren's report of this visit ran:

> During the visit hunts were organised for the sole purpose of providing specimens for the Museum … it is undoubtedly an unique opportunity for obtaining specimens of the rarer species of the larger mammals and birds. All the members of the Camp are taking a great interest in the Museum, and have promised to obtain specimens of both reptiles and fishes … Mr Saunders recommends that Mr Teschner should be allowed to accompany the Commission into Tongaland in order that a greater variety of species may be obtained … Mr Barnup and the Director have made considerable collections of the fauna of Zululand including numerous species of mollusca, lepidoptera, coleoptera, arachnida, crustacea, peripatidae etc. and some of the species will undoubtedly prove to be new to Science.

Tescher finally returned to Natal from Zululand in September 1903. His tally included 81 mammal skins, 25 of which were to be mounted and the others used for exchange with other museums. The skins listed included:

Blue buck (1); Bushbuck (4); Wild cat (3); Chacma [baboon] (2); Cheetah (1); Duiker (2); Feline genetta [genet] (2); Hippopotamus (3 skins and one complete skeleton); River hog (3) [bushpig]; Hyaena (1); Black-backed jackal (2); Klipspringer (2); Livingstone's antelope [suni] (2) ; White-tailed mongoose (1); Nyala (4); Pallah [impala] (1); Redbuck [probably a red duiker] (4); Reedbuck (6); Red rhebuck (4); Black rhinoceros (3 skins & 1 skeleton); Serval (1); Steenbuck (13); Vervet monkey (3); Waterbuck (8); Blue wildebeest (4); Burchell's zebra (1).

Another list includes such species as wild dog, porcupine, white-faced monkey (samango monkey), hornbill, long-eared owl and snake. In addition, there were some 25 birdskins, but most of these were duplicates of the museum's holdings, with the exception of the yellow-billed hornbill. Warren commented, 'Bird-life appears to be scarce in Zululand.'[54]

A further expedition went out from the Natal Government Museum to Zululand in 1905–6. This was undertaken by Fred Toppin. He collected small mammals, insects, birds, reptiles and fish. Charles Saunders recommended the Eshowe area for being particularly good for insects, including butterflies.

Toppin eventually made his base at Kosi Bay. Here he collected indigenous African medicines and had many adventures. These included being injured when he was washed off a rock by the sea, and chasing, with varying degrees of success, a 2 m-long green mamba, an elephant shrew, an antbear ('they are fairly plentiful here') and a spoonbill. He also went after turtle eggs and crocodile eggs. On 9 November 1905 he wrote: 'Kosi Bay is really a good place. I have got some grand fish, all different to what I got on the trawlers, and in Durban.' The cost of this expedition was not low. By March the bill, excluding Toppin's salary, stood at £226, including £89 for wages; £61 for wagon hire; £36 for tents, tools, boat, traps, cartridges, cooking utensils and small apparatus; £14 for railway fares and cartage; £14 for a camera, and £12 for personal expenses. It was an indication of the value the museum placed on the treasures of the Zululand wilderness.[55]

News of the area's store of natural treasures continued to attract museum specialists. One of the most adventurous expeditions was conducted by the Pretoria Museum in 1914, mainly on the Portuguese side of Maputaland. Elephant White would have shaken his head at the sight. The party consisted of eight white men and between 180 and 190 loads of equipment and personal effects. These included 12 bags of mealiemeal, six bags of salt, two bags of rice, one bag of potatoes, four tents with accessories, eight chairs, two tables, 12 cases of rabbits, 14 guns and ammunition, as well as gin and whiskey. In addition, there were 50 African porters obtained from the prison in Lourenço Marques. Whilst fewer mammals were obtained than on Warren's expedition of 1903, the party did get an adult male elephant – it was quite a nightmare:

> The skin is very thick, in some places quite 3 inches and everywhere full of bloodvessels especially on the trunk … the most striking sight was offered by the head. This was partly skinned, and one mass of blood. Still the eyes had not lost their brightness and stared at one with the most cunning expression …

At 11 we try to turn the animal, but the combined efforts of about 40 men, are not sufficient to impart the slightest motion. We now order the boys to remove one frontleg and shoulderblade and one hindleg, after this the belly is opened to remove the interior. A huge stream of water pours out from the stomach and an astonishing mass of intestines protrude. In a short time the sandy soil is converted into a stinking pool of half digested food …

To my astonishment, I find no intestinal worms. Ticks were present in great numbers, they ran about in all directions, and every moment we find them on our dress, and several times we are too late and they have already stuck to our bodies … Now all the flesh was cut off from the vertebrae, the ribs were cut off, the remaining legs skinned as far as possible and at last at three o'clock we were able to turn the animal. Now the work was lighter and at four the skin was off. The whole process had taken exactly 14 hours. A good open space had been made in the meantime and the two parts of the skin were brought there. This was not easy. There were 40 men, but we could not lift the large piece; so by combined efforts the skin was dragged out of the dirt. There was just time to salt it before dark. The one piece took about one full bag of salt, the other piece which was partly beamed took only 1/4 bag.[56]

REFERENCES

1 KZNA, 1/ESH, minute papers E 36/1905 and E 93/1905; 1/ING, minute papers IN 654/1902 and 17 November 1904; and 1/MBT, minute papers 22 August 1902 and H 249/1903.

2 KZNA, 1/ING, minute paper R 2576, 27 October 1903.

3 Some of the published accounts of early white hunters in Zululand do not fall into this category as they have been edited and published only in recent years. This is not to say that they may not have been intended for publication. The journal of Robert Briggs Struthers, who hunted in Zululand between 1852 and 1856, is a case in point. Written up in a neat hand in a handsome volume, this account was clearly taken from notebooks kept in the field, probably with an eye for publication. Sadly original notebooks no longer appear to exist. See Merrett & Butcher (eds.), *Robert Briggs Struthers: Hunting journal, 1852–1856, in the Zulu kingdom and the Tsonga regions.*

4 British Library, London, Additional MS 46617, Bentley papers, LVIII, 11 January 1862.

5 *Natal Mercury,* 7 April and 13 November 1863. See A.L. Harington's essay on Baldwin in *Dictionary of South African Biography,* 3, pp. 42–43.

6 Natural History Museum, London, Zoological Department letters, vol. C–D, Drummond papers, DF 200/2 fols. 238–40.

7 Duminy, *The Royal Hotel,* p. 53; Lock & Quartrill, *Zulu victory,* pp. 47–8, 136–40, 160, 171, 184 and 306; and *Natal Witness,* 27 February 1879.

8 Raymond, *Disraeli,* p. 347.

9 *Sunday Tribune,* 17 May 1998.

10 North, *Recollections of a happy life,* 2, p. 274.

11 See Kirby (ed.), *Andrew Smith and Natal;* and Craig and Hummel (eds.), *Wahlberg.*

12 This valuable source has been translated by Mrs Fleur Webb and re-published in English by the University of Natal Press, 1990 and 1997.

13 See A. Gordon-Brown's entry on Angas in *Dictionary of South African Biography*, 2, pp.10–11. See also Natural History Museum, London, Zoology Department, donations, April 1848 to September 1873.

14 *Proceedings of the Zoological Society*, 4, 1848, p. 89 and 1850, pp. 144 and 199.

15 Gunn & Codd, *Botanical exploration of southern Africa*, pp. 187–8 and 268–9; and Harvey, *Genera of South African plants*, p. 419.

16 Herbarium specimens of nineteenth-century plants collected in what is now called KwaZulu-Natal are to be found in the Kew Herbarium, London; Natal Herbarium, Durban; the National Botanic Gardens of Ireland, Glasnevin; the National Botanical Institute, Pretoria; the Natural History Museum, London; and the herbarium of Trinity College Dublin, Ireland. See, for example, 1 600 specimens collected by William Gerrard in Zululand *c.* 1865 in *The history of the collections in the Natural History Departments of the British Museum*, 1, p. 97.

17 Kew Gardens Archive, South African letters, vol. 189, Allison to Kew, 16 May 1892. For an account of plant hunting in nineteenth-century Natal and Zululand see McCracken and McCracken, *Natal the garden colony: Victorian Natal and the Royal Botanic Gardens, Kew*.

18 See McCracken, *A new history of Durban Botanic Gardens*; and KZNA, Sir John Robinson paper, Dyer to Hely-Hutchinson, 7 May 1895.

19 *Gardeners' Chronicle*, 25 April 1908. Three of these original stems can be seen today in the Durban Botanic Gardens. On 27 May 1916 the remaining stems of Wood's cycad were hauled out of Ongoye forest by mules under the direction of the local forester and Medley Wood's successor as curator of Durban Botanic Gardens, James Wylie. See Forestry Department Archive, Eshowe, FD 3, PN 3.

20 Table extrapolated from J. Medley Wood, *Preliminary catalogue of indigenous Natal plants*; and 'Revised list of the flora of Natal', *Transactions of the South African Philosophical Society*, 18: 2, pp.121–280.

21 Plant papers, Plant to Stevens, 16 April 1855.

22 Plant papers, Plant to Stevens, 12 March and 27 November 1855; and Kew Archive, South African letters, 191, Plant to Hooker, 15 April 1857. Plant also supplied insects to the British Museum.

23 R.W. Plant, 'Notice of an excursion in the Zulu country', *Hooker's Journal of Botany*, 4, pp. 257–65; and note on R.W. Plant, *Hooker's Journal of Botany*, 4, pp. 222–3.

24 For an obituary, see *Natal Mercury*, 15 April 1858.

25 See *Curtis's Botanical Magazine*, 1861, t5251 and 1889, t7068. Robert Plant's son Robert was to become a famous superintendent of African schools and author of a book entitled *The Zulu in three tenses*.

26 KZNA, ZGH 694, 1885.

27 Stuart and Malcolm, *Fynn*, p. 78.

28 See Baldwin, *African hunting*, pp. 9, 27, 53, 70–71, 73–4, 79, 82–3, 85, 93, 109, 114, 118, 127 and 131; (Barter), *Alone among the Zulus*, p. 145; and Drummond, *The large game*, p. 91.

29 Skelton, *Freshwater fishes of southern Africa*, pp. 3–5.

30 Craig and Hummel (eds.), *Johan August Wahlberg*, pp. 31–2, 90 and 93–5.

31 See, for example, *The Ibis*, 1859, pp. 234–51; 1860, pp. 203–221; 1861, pp. 128–36; 1862, pp. 25–39 and pp. 149–58; 1863, pp. 320–32; 1864, pp. 346–61; 1865, pp. 263–76; 1868, pp. 40–52 and 460–71; and 1873, pp. 254–59.

32 See, for example, KZNA, ZA 27, 1896, Report on Tongaland, fol. 24; ZGH 704, 7 February 1887, fol. 3; ZGH 708, 17 November 1887, fols. 17, 24, 49; and ZGH 796, 1896, Report on Maputaland.

33 KZNA, ZA 19, 1880; and *Report of the Zululand Boundary Commission*, pp. 25–6.

34 Baldwin, *African hunting*, pp. 9, 30, 51, 79.

35 Drummond, *The large game*, pp. 13, 18, 59, 79, 92-98, 126, 139–40, 156, 205, 247, 280, 336, 343, 407–12, 419.

36 See B.J.T. Leverton's entry on the Woodward brothers in the *Dictionary of South African Biography*, 4, pp. 795–6.

37 Stearn, *The Natural History Museum at South Kensington*, pp. 174–8. See also, for example, Natural History Museum, London, Zoology Department, donations, October 1873 to October 1882; and KZNA, AGR 527, Claude Fuller to Messrs Woodward Bros, 21 November 1899.

38 KZNA, ZGH 757, Z 418/1894, 19 May 1894.

39 KZNA, 1/ESH, letter book, 26 July 1895, fol. 455. See also 1/EPI, letter book, Silvertson to RM, 5 August 1895; and 1/ESH, letter book, 6 February 1896.

40 KZNA, ZA 46, Resident Commissioner diary, 1895–96.

41 *The Ibis*, 1898, pp. 221–3.

42 *The Ibis*, 1897, pp. 400–422 and 495–517; and 1898, pp. 216–28 and 517–25.

43 *Natal Witness*, 29 September 1897; and KZNA, CSO 1542, 9073/1897, 22 December 1897. For Hely-Hutchinson's comments to Thiselton-Dyer see Kew Gardens Archive, South African letters, 190, 13 July 1896.

44 V. Ball, 'Observation on lion-breeding in the gardens of the Royal Zoological Society of Ireland', *Transactions of the Royal Irish Academy*, 28, August 1886, pp. 725–9 and 748–49; *Freeman's Journal*, 2 May 1855; and *Natal Witness*, 17 December 1847. Natal and Natalia had a total of 10 cubs, Natalia dying in September 1859 whilst nursing the last of her three litters. Natal fathered a further 32 cubs with lionesses called Old Girl (12 cubs) and Anonyma (20 cubs). Natal died in the Dublin Zoo on 11 January 1864, aged about 12 years old. His skeleton is in the museum of Trinity College, Dublin.

45 Buckland, *Curiosities of natural history*, 1866, 2, pp. 96–9; *The Times*, 6 and 9 September 1891; and *The Strand Magazine*, 1, 1891, pp. 429–36.

46 Brooks, Natal, p. 123; Hattersley, *More annals of Natal*, p. 126; Ingram, *Colony of Natal*, p. 247; *The [Durban] Mayor's minute*, 1910, p. 220; *Natal Mercury*, 20 March 1869; *Natal Star*, 28 May 1856; Spencer, *British settlers in Natal, 1824–1857*, 2, p. 13; and Von Wissell, 'Reminiscences of trading days in Natal and Zululand', Campbell Collections, Miller papers, file 204, fol. 71.

47 *Natal Mercury*, 23 February 1869. See also *Times of Natal*, 17 March and 21 August 1869.

48 *Natal Witness*, 26 February 1856; and Gunn and Codd, *Botanical exploration of southern Africa*, pp. 362–3.

49 Drummond, *The large game*, title page & pp. 20, 117–20, 279. See also, National Botanical Institute, Pretoria, 'Maputa expedition', fol. 34.

50 *Abstracts of proceedings, Zoological Society of London*, 1 January 1875.

51 Findlay, *Big game shooting*, p. 229; Natural History Museum, London, DF 232/6, O. Timms, fols. 241–2; KZNA, 1/EPI, minute paper R 2007/1893, R 1254/1894, 21 May 1894 and R 2571/1894; 1/MEL, minute paper R 2637, 14 November 1893; 1/UBO, minute paper R 1118, 10 May 1893; KZNA, ZGH 694, minute paper 6069/1890, 23 October 1890; ZGH 733, minute paper 158/1896, 4 December 1890; ZGH 759, minute paper R 1626/1894; ZHG 764, letter from E.B. Parkinson, 12 June 1895; ZGH 777, minute paper R 1683, 30 June 1897; and ZGH 835, letters, W.E. Peachey to Morton Green, 11 March 1897 and W.E. Peachey to F.R.N. Findlay, 5 July 1897.

52 Natural History Museum, London, DF 216/4, Donations, Vertebrate Section, 1916–1923, December 1918, Dr Warren.

53 A critical commentary on Dr Warren is contained in Brooks, S.J., 'Playing the game', master's dissertation, Queen's University, Ontario, 1990.

54 KZNA, Natal Government Museum papers, administration 1902–13 and collecting specimens, 1889–1903, documents dated 30 June and 25 September 1903.

55 For Toppin's expedition, see KZNA, NGM, Toppin to Warren, 20 October 1905; 9 and 12 November 1905; 24 December 1905; 1 and 12 January 1906; and 2 February 1906. See also Saunders to Cooper, 8 May 1905. There is a cryptic note at the end of Saunders's letter which reads, 'Thanks for what you say about my late mother's flower studies. I hope what has been done will meet the case without friction.' Some of Katharine Saunders's flower paintings are still housed in the Natal Museum, Pietermaritzburg.

56 National Botanical Institute, Report on the Maputa expedition, fols. 12–13.

CHAPTER **8**

Back from the brink: rules and regulations

The British victory in the Anglo-Zulu War of 1879 heralded a period of uncertainty and disruption in Zululand. The territory was divided into 13 fiefdoms loosely linked to the British authorities in the Colony of Natal south of the Tugela. It was a recipe for disaster and civil unrest was not slow in coming. Seven long years followed before the inevitable happened and Zululand was formally annexed, becoming a British colony in its own right but with the governor of Natal also serving as governor of Zululand.

As elsewhere across the globe, and indeed as elsewhere in South Africa, nature conservation 'followed the flag'. In 1900, for example, five weeks before the formal annexation of the Transvaal Republic in 1900, with the Anglo-Boer War still raging, the British were issuing instructions on game preservation.[1] This was reminiscent of the way the British had behaved 23 years earlier in 1877, when they had previously annexed the Transvaal Republic and set about enforcing the protection of the region's indigenous forests.

In Zululand in 1887 it was not long before rules and regulations were being drawn up by the resident commissioner in Eshowe.[2] In this exercise Melmoth Osborn was helped by Zululand Proclamation II of 1887, which made all Natal ordinances operative in the Colony of Zululand. This included the 1853 Ordinance No. 4 which was aimed at protecting bush. As will be seen, regulations relating to the protection of the great indigenous forests of Zululand were the first environmental protection measures to be enforced by the British authorities.

Proclamation II was also invoked to introduce into Zululand the existing Natal game regulations. Writing to Governor Havelock in March 1889, Osborn reported:

> Shortly after the proclamation of Zululand as a British possession in 1887, the Resident Magistrates in the different Districts directed their attention to the provisions of the Natal Law No. 23 of 1884 which provides for the preservation of Game and availed themselves of opportunities to bring the law

into operation as far as practicable. Owing however to the occurrence of the disturbances last year it was not possible to carry out the provisions of the law, but since order has been restored, the subject has again been attended to, and I have now by circular letter to the Resident Magistrates directed them to take the necessary steps to ensure the preservation of Game in their respective Districts in terms of the law.[3]

There can be little surprise that the British tried to protect some of the fauna and flora of Zululand. As mentioned earlier, members of that late Victorian generation of British administrators were often particularly interested in 'nature study'. They collected butterflies and birds' eggs, and they corresponded with learned scientific societies and public institutions such as Kew Gardens, the British Museum and the Royal Geographical Society.

In the case of big game, it was recognised that Zululand still contained specimens of game already extinct in Natal and the Cape. As early as May 1888, the governor was writing on the subject,[4] and by 1890 Zululand had largely adopted Natal's second game Act, which dated from 1884.[5]

The Natal regulations from 1893 were more specifically adapted for Zululand conditions. The downgrading from royal game status to closed-season protection of such species as buffalo, kudu, zebra and southern reedbuck reflected the growing concern with the disease nagana.[6] Table 18 sets out the Zululand measures passed in 1890, 1893, 1897 and 1906 relating to the protection of mammals. Minor amendments to the Zululand game regulations were made in 1892 and 1893. The shuffling of species from one category of protection to another was no doubt confusing for magistrates and hunters alike, but it reflects which animals officialdom considered to be becoming scarcer or which species needed to be reduced in numbers because of the on-going human and cattle health scares from the mid-1890s. At the same time measures were taken to protect various bird species.[7]

The first three proclamations of 1890, 1893 and 1897 were

TABLE 18

ZULULAND GAME LEGISLATION (MAMMALS), 1890–1906

Note: Figures in square brackets indicate the maximum number of specimens of a species which might be shot by a person in a year.

ANIMAL	ZULULAND PROCLAM-ATION NO. 3 (1890)	ZULULAND PROCLAM-ATION NO. 5 (1893)	ZULULAND PROCLAM-ATION NO. 2 (1897)	NATAL ACT NO. 8 (1906)
Blesbok	Royal game	Royal game	Royal game	Royal game
Buffalo	Royal game	Closed season	Closed season [4]	Male: royal game. Female: royal game: special category, no hunting permitted
Bushbuck	Closed season	Closed season	Closed season	Male: closed season. Female: royal game
Deer [probably Java or Mauritian]	Not listed	Not listed	Not listed	Royal game
Blue duiker	Closed season	Closed season	Closed season	Closed season
Red duiker	Not listed	Not listed	Closed season	Closed season
Duiker	Closed season	Closed season	Closed season	Closed season
Eland	Royal game	Royal game	Royal game	Male: royal game. Female: royal game: special category, no hunting permitted
Elephant	Royal game: special category, no hunting permitted	Royal game: special category, no hunting permitted	Royal game: special category, no hunting permitted	Royal game: special category, no hunting permitted
Grysbok	Not listed	Not listed	Not listed	Closed season
Hares	Closed season	Closed season	Closed season	Closed season
Hartebeest	Royal game	Royal game	Royal game	Royal game
Hippopotamus	Royal game	Royal game	Royal game [2]	Royal game [1]
Impala	Royal game	Royal game	Royal game	Royal game [2]
Klipspringer	Royal game	Royal game	Closed season	Closed season
Kudu	Royal game	Closed season	Closed season [4]	Male: royal game [1]. Female: royal game: special category, no hunting permitted
Nyala	Royal game	Royal game	Royal game	Royal game [2]
Oribi	Closed season	Royal game	Royal game	Royal game
Piva	Royal game	Royal game	Not listed	Not listed
Quagga/zebra	Royal game	Closed season	Royal game	Not listed
Rabbit	Closed season	Closed season	Closed season	Not listed
Southern reedbuck	Royal game	Closed season	Closed season	Royal game
Mountain reedbuck	Not listed	Not listed	Not listed	Royal game
Grey rhebuck	Closed season	Closed season	Closed season	Closed season
Black rhino	Royal game	Closed season	Royal game [2]	Royal game [1]
White rhino	Royal game	Closed season	Royal game: special category, no hunting permitted	Royal game, special category, no hunting permitted
Roan	Royal game	Royal game	Royal game	Royal game: special category, no hunting permitted
Steenbuck	Closed season	Closed season	Closed season	Royal game
Suni	Not listed	Not listed	Closed season	Closed season
Springbuck	Royal game	Royal game	Royal game	Royal game: special category, no hunting permitted
Waterbuck	Royal game	Closed season NB: 1895–97 classified as royal game	Closed season [4]	Royal game [2]
Black wildebeest	Royal game	Closed season	Closed season [4]	Not listed
Blue wildebeest	Royal game	Closed season	Closed season [4]	Closed season

introduced while Zululand was a colony in its own right. The 1906 Act was the product of the self-governing Natal parliament, which by then had control of Zululand. Fines of upwards of £10 were laid down for contravention of the regulations: killing an elephant, for example, carried a fine between £50 and £100. Licence fees could be expensive, especially for the shooting of royal game, a £10 payment being required for a permit to shoot hippo or black rhino. Restrictions on the number of head of game permitted to be killed were also made by the issuing magistrate. The protection regulations created four main categories or schedules of game:

1. Game that enjoyed no protection at all

There were some animals that were never to be protected in the colonial era, either because they were considered to be common or because they were regarded as vermin. The list was a long one which included all species of reptile, fish, and insect; all carnivores, primates and rodents; and bats. To this list was added aardvark, bushpig, pangolin, warthog, and various bird species, mainly non-insectivorous. Those animals that were regarded as vermin included baboon, civet, crocodile, hyena, jackal, leopard, lion, monkey, snakes, warthog and wild dog.

2. Game which was protected from hunting during a closed season

This included most types of buck, rabbit and hare and, extraordinarily, for a brief period in the 1890s, black rhino and white rhino. The dates of the closed season varied according to schedule and often altered with a new proclamation.

3. Royal game, which could only be hunted with a permit issued by the governor

As the table shows, the species regarded as royal game changed with the years, with the exception of those species always on the list of royal game: blesbok, eland, hartebeest, hippo, impala, nyala, as well as roan antelope and springbok, the latter two probably not then existing in Zululand.

4. Special category game, also referred to as royal game

These animals could not be hunted. They included at one time or another female buffalo, female eland, female kudu, elephant, black rhino and white rhino.

There were occasional bungles when animals were placed in the wrong schedules, the worst being when rhino were excluded as royal game.[8] Occasionally extra clauses were added to a permit. In 1895 Hely-Hutchinson wrote to the resident commissioner in Zululand:

It has occurred to me that in granting applications for the destruction of game in Zululand … a condition might justly be made, to the effect, that any good specimens of horns or heads which are procured should be preserved and handed over to you at Eshowe. These could be mounted and either sent to Maritzburg for decoration of the hall at Government House, or kept by you for ornament at the Residency, Eshowe … We may be within measurable distance of the total destruction of game in Zululand and before that takes place I think we should have specimens for the two houses.[9]

TABLE 19

PROTECTION OF GAME BIRDS

	ZULULAND PROCLAMATION NO. 3 (1890)	ZULULAND PROCLAMATION NO. 5 (1893)	ZULULAND PROCLAMATION NO. 2 (1897)	NATAL ACT NO. 8 (1906)
Crane	Closed season	Closed season	Not listed	Royal game
Dikkop	Not listed	Not listed	Not listed	Closed season
Wild duck	Closed season	Closed season	Closed season	
Guinea fowl	Closed season	Closed season	Closed season	Closed season
Ground hornbill	Royal game	Royal game	Royal game	Not listed
Korhaan	Closed season	Closed season	Closed season	Royal game
Ostrich	Royal game	Royal game	Royal game	Royal game
Partridge [probably francolin, quail sp.]	Closed season	Closed season	Closed season	Closed season
Paauw [bustard sp.]	Closed season	Closed season	Closed season	Royal game
Pheasant [francolin sp.]	Closed season	Closed season	Closed season	Closed season
Secretary bird	Royal game	Royal game	Royal game	Royal game

Protection of bird life

It was not just mammals in Zululand that were listed for protection, or a degree of protection. Regulations relating to the protection of wildlife in Zululand also included the protection of certain species of bird life. There were essentially two categories of protected birds: game birds and some insectivorous birds.

Between 1890 and 1897 a number of proclamations were issued to protect the game birds of Zululand. These included three species of the royal game (ground hornbill, ostrich and secretary bird) that could be shot only with official permission, as well as species, listed in Table 19, that had a closed hunting season.

In 1906, under a Natal Act, the dikkop was added to the list of game birds that had a closed season and wild duck was dropped from the list. In 1906 the cranes became royal game and, amazingly, the ground hornbill and secretary bird ceased to be royal game, though both species regained protected status as insectivorous birds in 1910, thus giving a four-year open hunting season for these noble birds. Wild ducks regained a measure of protection in 1910.

The second category of birds to be protected was those that were regarded as beneficial to agriculture, the insectivorous birds. When Zululand became a province of Natal in 1897, the Natal Act No. 33 of 1896 was extended to the region. This offered a degree of protection to one variety of bird and to five species of insectivorous birds. As illustrated in Table 20, Proclamation 22 of 1905 extended protection to 8 varieties and 43 species. Under Proclamation 56 of 1910 the list was expanded considerably to 38 varieties, 7 species and to all shrikes, except the energetic fiscal shrike.

Two points need to be made concerning these proclamations for the protection of bird life. The first is that some species were not protected, such as bulbuls, larks (except between 1905 and 1910), owls, raptors (except the secretary bird), sea birds and weavers. Second, there is little evidence to suggest that much was done to enforce these protective measures, though hopefully knowledge of their very existence might have restrained some from killing, injuring or capturing these birds or from destroying their eggs.

The forest regulations and organisation

As mentioned, Zululand Proclamation 2 of 1887 gave magistrates the same powers to protect bush in Zululand as existed in Natal. In fact, in the Reserved Territory of southern Zululand, which the British held under protected status from 1882 to 1887, initial attempts to preserve the indigenous forests had already begun. This was as well, for it was in the southern forests that commercial exploitation had been under way by white sawyers for at least a decade. The decimation of some of Natal's forests had forced woodcutters to look to the forests of the Drakensberg mountains and across the Tugela River to the mistbelt forests of

Zululand, especially that on the Qhudeni ridge. It was claimed, probably correctly, that the 'white chief' John Dunn had heavily worked Qhudeni forest.[10] In 1883 the British introduced a licence system for timber cut by whites as well as for resident Africans who wished to sell the wood. In the Nquthu Reserve these included the following forest tariffs:[11]

£1 per load of 40 poles
£1 per load of laths or wattles taken out of the reserve
2s. per disselboom
2s. 6d. per load of wattles used in the reserve
10s. per bundle of wood

In the period January 1884 to May 1886, 42 individuals in the reserve took out a total of 110 licences or permits and paid a total of £127 in fees. Elsewhere the norm for commercial sawyers was a straightforward £1 per month per saw – cutting what they liked, where they liked. No species of tree was explicitly protected even with a specific high tariff. The figure of 10s. for taking bundles of wood was high, even excepting that for every bundle taken, maybe up to 50 were quietly extracted from the forest without the sub-commissioner's knowledge. Before 1900, on average a mere 16 per cent of timber extracted from Qhudeni provided cash revenue. It is doubtful whether the revenue from other Zululand forests was proportionately higher.

The reality was that in most of the Zululand forests these measures were not enforced in these early years of British control. For a number of years after annexation in 1887, Qhudeni was the only Zululand forest where sawyers were licensed, even after the issuing of Zululand Proclamation 5 of June 1889 which set out a list of tariffs. These included £1 per saw per month, with varying amounts for loads of laths, poles and wattles. Disselbooms were 4s. each to cut and no species of tree was singled out for protection.

This state of affairs came to the attention of Colonel, later Sir Frederick, Cardew, who for a while was acting resident commissioner for Zululand. Cardew was one of those Victorian soldier administrators who was interested in botany to the extent that a volume of *Curtis's Botanical Magazine* was dedicated to him by Kew Gardens. Later, when governor of the colony of Sierra Leone, Cardew and the governor of Lagos, Sir Alfred Moloney, did much to support the network of botanic stations in West Africa.[12]

In Zululand Cardew soon realised that although the Natal forest regulations were in theory applicable to Zululand, they were not being enforced. In February 1890, the Cape forester H.G. Fourcade completed his impressive *Report on the Natal forests*. The *Natal Mercury* welcomed it with the comment that anyone who ignored forestry was 'crassly ignorant or densely stupid'. Natal went on to appoint a German forester as conservator of forests.[13]

TABLE 20

BIRDS PROTECTED AS 'INSECTIVOROUS AND OTHER WILD BIRDS'

• Protected species of bird (forbidden to kill, catch, shoot, and injure birds or destroy bird eggs)

•• Species protected in 1896 and therefore automatically protected in 1905

	NATAL ACT NO. 33 (1896)	NATAL PROCLAMATION NO. 22 (1905)	NATAL PROCLAMATION NO. 56 (1910)
Heron (all species)			•
Egret (all species)			•
Bittern (all species)			•
Mudlark [hammerkop]		•	•
White stork	•		
Stork (all species)	•	••	•
Sacred ibis			•
Hadeda ibis			•
Flamingo (all species)			•
Wild duck (all species)			•
Geese (all species)			•
Teal (all species)			•
Secretary bird			•
Gallinule (all species)			•
Plover (all species)			•
Lapwing (all species)			•
Small locust-bird [redwing pratincole]	•	••	•
Large locust-bird [probably the blackwing pratincole]	•	••	•
Cuckoo (all species)		•	•
Coucal (all species)			•
Nightjar (all species)		•	•
Swift (all species)			•
Narina trogon		•	•
Kingfisher (all species)		•	•
Bee-eater (all species)		•	•
Roller (all species)			•
Hoopoe		•	•
Ground hornbill			•
Barbet (all species)			•
Honeyguide			•
Woodpecker		•	•
Broadbilled flycatcher [African broadbill]		•	
Lark		•	
Swallow (all species)	•	••	•
Black cuckooshrike		•	
Grey cuckooshrike		•	
Drongo (large and small)		•	•
Black woodshrike [black flycatcher]		•	
Grey cuckooshrike		•	
Hartlaub's cuckooshrike [black cuckooshrike]		•	
Blackheaded oriole		•	
Oriole (all species)			•
Tit (all species)			•
Black & white titmouse [southern black tit]		•	
Jardine's babbling thrush [arrow-marked babbler]		•	
South African thrush [groundscraper thrush]		•	
Natal thrush [spotted or ground thrush]		•	
Thrush (all species)			•
Natal mocking bird [chorister robin]		•	
Natal chat thrush [Natal robin or red-capped robin-chat]		•	
Cape chat thrush [Cape robin]		•	
Warbler (all species)			•
Durban woodshrike [garden warbler]		•	
Bar-throated warbler [bar-throated apalis]		•	
Short-tailed bush warbler [long-billed crombec]		•	
Brown-throated bush warbler [burnt-necked eremomela]		•	
Green-backed bush warbler [probably a green-backed bleating warbler]			
Grey-backed bush warbler or tailor bird [grey-backed camaroptera]		•	
Fawny-headed bush warbler [neddicky]		•	
Common fantail warbler [zitting or fantailed cisticola]		•	
Smith's fantail warbler [lazy cisticola]		•	
Natal fantail warbler [croaking cisticola]		•	
Spotted flycatcher		•	
Blue-grey flycatcher		•	
White-flanked flycatcher [chinspot batis]		•	
Paradise flycatcher		•	
Flycatcher (all species)			•
Wagtail	•	••	
Wagtail (all species)			•
Longclaw (all species)			•
Fiscal shrike		•	
Black-backed shrike [red-backed shrike]		•	
Shrike (all species except fiscal)		•	
Lesser puff-back [black-backed puffback]		•	
Large puff-backed bushshrike [southern boubou]		•	
Red-winged bush shrike [black-crowned tchagra]		•	
Olivaceous bush shrike [gorgeous bush shrike]			
Orange-breasted bush shrike		•	
Large grey-headed bush shrike [grey-headed bush shrike]		•	
Helmet shrike [white or white-crested helmet shrike]		•	
Wattled starling			•
Tickbird (red-beaked rhino or buffalo bird) [red-billed oxpecker]	•	••	
Sugarbird (all species)			•
Sunbird		•	•
White eye		•	•
Bush weaver bird [forest weaver]		•	
Waxbill (all species)			•
Canary (all species)			•

Fourcade was keen to extend his report to include Zululand and in March 1890 suggested that he be allowed to pay a short visit to some of the area's principal forests. But Cardew was not going to start a process the authorities might not be able to control: 'Mr Fourcade has nothing to do with Zululand, the government of which is quite separate – I really, however, see no substantial reason why we should detain Mr Fourcade in Natal unless his evidence will be required during the L.C. [Legislative Council] discussion.'[14]

But though Cardew sent Fourcade packing, he did not forget the Zululand forests and set out to write his own report on them. The Cardew report was duly transmitted to London in March 1891 and appeared as a British parliamentary paper the following month under the title *Report on the forests of Zululand*. Though only 25 pages long, it contained a brief description of the main Zululand forests as well as details of proposed forest regulations.[15] Clearly alarm bells began ringing in Downing Street. The colonial secretary, Lord Knutsford, whilst stating that the report was likely to be of 'much use', warned that care should be taken in any forest legislation not to impose restraints on the African population 'which they would feel to be irksome and unnecessary'.[16]

While Cardew did not disobey this advice, he was not slow in instructing a magistrate who was handing out free permits to cut wood to 'please put a stop to it at once'. Cardew distinguished between cutting wood, which required a permit, and collecting firewood, which did not. In June 1891 he wrote to the magistrate at Ubombo: 'No wood should be allowed to be cut within 30 yards of the edge of the forest … I shall feel obliged therefore by your carefully explaining to them [the African population] as opportunities occur, the necessity for the proper conservation of the forests, not only in their own interests but in that of their descendants.' He went on to say that Africans should be subject to as little inconvenience and restraint as possible and as was consistent in effecting the protection of the forests.[17] The following month Cardew informed the resident magistrate that Africans were 'not to cut down trees to make clearances in such bush without the permission of the Resident Magistrate'.[18]

However, when Cardew moved on to greater things, the new resident commissioner, if not as knowledgeable about trees, was perhaps more in tune with the local population. This is not to say that nothing more was done. Forest regulations were introduced in 1894 and amended the following year, when Zululand forests were also protected from mining operations. Thus, at the time the game reserves were being set up, consideration was also being given to the conservation of the indigenous forests of Zululand.[19]

The 1894/95 regulations referred to those forests which were on Crown land and which fell under the resident commissioner and the resident magistrates. This meant most mist-belt and 'high'

forests and some of the coastal woodland. The African population was to be issued with free permits to cut and collect wood for domestic use. Significantly, for the first time individual tree species were singled out for a special cutting tariff. The favoured axle wood umzimbeet (*Millettia grandis*) was 10d. per cubic foot, stinkwood (*Ocotea bullata*) was 8d. per cubic foot and all other species listed 6d. per cubic foot. Though provision was made for the eviction of squatters, there is no evidence that this was ever done. The director of Kew Gardens in London was of no doubt that things in Zululand were moving 'in the right direction'.[20]

The handing over of Zululand to Natal in 1897 meant that for the first time, specialised foresters were introduced into the region. In 1898 Zululand was allocated one forest ranger (based at Qhudeni forest), two forest supervisors and 11 forest guards. As in the past, the Zululand police was also used on occasion. Colonel Cardew had had a lot of time for this force: 'The Zululand Police are a very highly disciplined body, and can hardly be surpassed as soldiers, and these very qualities will make them the more efficient as a constabulary force for police and detective duties when required.'[21]

The magistrates and police appear to have enforced the forest regulations with some vigour. One report has survived of two wagons carrying some 80 bundles of wattles and 12 of tambotie poles being pursued across two magisterial districts, catching them before they crossed the border into Natal. As with the game laws, the conviction rate for those caught was very high. In Hlabisa between 1899 and 1901, 80 people were charged under the forest regulations; only 4 were acquitted.[22] Fines varied. In 1883, for cutting wood without a licence in Qhudeni forest, James Harper was fined £2 and ordered to leave the area. Umswahli was fined three sacks of mealies or four sacks if the authorities had to collect them themselves. Another local was fined £1 for cutting poles without a licence.[23]

The next major development was the re-establishment of the Natal forestry department in 1902 with the eminent botanist T.R. Sim in control. This was done after the Cape forester J. Storr Lister wrote a 13-page report on the forests of Natal and Zululand.[24] The new dispensation comprised 22 forest stations of which 5 were in Zululand (Qhudeni, Nkandla, Ongoye, Empangeni and Somkhele). It is interesting to note that the Ongoye posting was considered necessary because the railway now ran nearby. A district forest officer was placed at Eshowe. In 1903 the Natal government gained control of Ngome forest, which had been for many years in the former Transvaal Republic. A forester and five forest guards were put into Ngome to try to control the excessive exploitation that had previously taken place there.[25]

The year 1903 also saw, largely at T.R. Sim's initiative, a new forest proclamation for Natal and Zululand. This was a much tougher measure than anything that had gone before and included the right of the authorities to evict Africans from forestland. It is doubtful, though, if the imperial authorities, as distinct from the colonial government in Pietermaritzburg, would have gone so far in imposing a strict forest law on Zululand.

Fifty-two species of tree were identified as fellable only after a licence had been granted; each tree to be felled had to be individually stamped by a forester. However, it was not the grumbles of the white sawyers that worried the authorities, but the complaints of the African population. In 1904 the Zululand Delimitation Commission expressed sympathy for the Africans who had complained 'bitterly, and we think with reason, about the [forest] regulations and the manner in which they have been enforced'. This resentment had been building up over several years. The result was a government circular in 1904 that modified the 1903 forest proclamation. Sim protested vigorously that the circular was 'unsatisfactory from a forest point of view'.[26]

The economic depression in Natal following the Bambatha insurrection led in 1907 to Sim being made redundant and forestry affairs passing to the control of E.R. Sawyer, the head of Cedara Agricultural College outside Pietermaritzburg. Forest income was about £2 000. However, the bulk of the £12 000 annual expenditure on forestry was not expended on the indigenous forests but rather on nurseries for exotic plantations, which were being planted especially in coastal Zululand, and on nurseries for raising fruit trees. Indeed, the indigenous forests were fast become white elephants.

When the Union of South Africa was created in 1910, the indigenous forests of Natal and Zululand passed under the control of central government in Pretoria, unlike the game reserves which remained the provincial responsibility. Indigenous forests in Zululand continued to be demarcated and were patrolled but the emphasis was now on the exotic plantations.

REFERENCES

1   For the 1900 measures, see Carruthers, 'Game protection in the Transvaal', p. 239. For a good concise overview of game conservation in Zululand, see Ellis, 'Game conservation in Zululand, 1824–1947'. A version of this honours dissertation is to be found under the title 'Game conservation in Zululand 1824–1947', *Natalia*, nos. 23–24, December 1993/94, pp. 27–44.

2   Game protection in Natal dates from only Law 10 of 1866. See Ellis, 'Game conservation in Zululand, 1824–1847', p. 1.

3   KZNA: ZA 42, 15 March 1889, fol. 148.

4   KZNA: ZGH 720, Z212/1889.

5   Natal Law No. 23 of 1884.

6   KZNA, ZGH 755, R 287/1894, British colonial secretary to Hely-Hutchinson, 2 February 1894.

7   KZNA, ZL Proclamations: 3 (1890), 4 (1892), 2 and 5 (1893), 2 (1897); and Natal Act No. 8 (1906). See also Vaughan-Kirby, 'Game and game preservation in Zululand', pp. 377–9.

8   ZL Proclamation 4 of 1892, KZNA: ZA 13, R 2838, 12 December 1892 and ZGH 749, Z 122/1893, 26 January 1893. For details of the various schedules, see Ellis, 'Game conservation in Zululand, 1824–1947', Chapter 3.

9   KZNA, ZGH 766, R 1985/95, 4 September 1895.

10 R. Burton, *Report of an inspection of certain forests in Natal and Zululand*, p. 5; F. Cardew, *Report on the forests of Zululand*, p. 5; and Storr Lister, *Report on forestry in Natal and Zululand*, p. 10. Dunn appears to have been restrained by Cetshwayo from exploiting Ngoye forest near which both the king and Dunn lived. It is, however, doubtful whether this restraint lasted long after the king moved his kraal to Ulundi. See Pooley and Player, *KwaZulu-Natal*, p. 107.

11 Killie Campbell Collections, University of KwaZulu-Natal, Nquthu Zulu Native Reserve, licence book, 1884–86; and KZNA, ZA 38, Zulu Native Reserve, 25 March 1883.

12 See McCracken, *Gardens of empire*, pp. 90 and 197. In 1887 Moloney published a book entitled *Sketch of forestry of West Africa*.

13 McCracken, 'The indigenous forests of colonial Natal and Zululand', pp. 31–2. Between 1891 and 1893 Natal had its own forestry department. When it was closed, forest matters were returned to the Surveyor General's Office, where forest matters had been dealt with prior to the establishment of the department.

14 KZNA, CSO 1252, minute paper 1506/1890.

15 F. Cardew, *Report on the forests of Zululand*, Colonial Reports, No. 2, Zululand, c-6270-1. For a draft of this report and various pieces of correspondence, see KZNA, ZA 12, R 1285/1891; ZA 43, letter book, report, 16 February 1891, fols. 50–91 and 114–15; and ZGH 833, letter book, fols. 228, 231.

16 KZNA, ZGH 739, minute paper, Z 423/91, 23 April 1891.

17 KZNA, 1/UBO, minute paper, UB 175/1891, 26 June 1891,

18 KZNA, ZGH 736, report of Resident Commissioner, February 1891, fol. 4; 1/MEL, minute paper R 1965/91, 26 June 1891; and NGA, 241, 20 July 1891.

19 Zululand Proclamation XI, 1894. Zululand Proclamation 7 of 1894 prohibited mining in Zululand forests. See KZNA, ZGH 764, minute paper Z 390/95 and ZGH 765, nos. 42/95, 13 July 1895.

20 KZNA, Sir John Robinson papers, A 354/3/32, Dyer to Hely-Hutchinson, 7 May 1895.

21 For the role of the Zululand Police in protecting the Zululand forests, see, for example, KZNA, 1/EPI, letter book, 30 September 1894, fol. 124 and 1/NGA, minute paper, ZP NA 75/1892, 29 September 1892.

22 KZNA, 1/MTB, 3/2/2, return of crimes, 1899–1901 and 1/NGA, minute paper, ND 5480/1896. It can be argued that the enforcement of the forest regulations in Zululand was not as rigorous as elsewhere. For instance, in the Transkei region of the Cape Colony between 1890 and 1897, there were no fewer than 3 638 prosecutions under the Cape's strict forest laws.

23 Killie Campbell Collections, UKZN, Nguthu Zulu Reserve, minute book, July 1883 and January 1884. See also KZNA, SGO, minute paper, 393/1899

24 Storr Lister's tour of Natal and Zululand forests was made at the suggestion of Claude Fuller, the Natal government entomologist. See *Agricultural Journal*, 4: 11, 2 August 1901, pp. 350–51.

25 KZNA, 1/MTU, report, DB/300/03, 27 May 1903; and *Agricultural Journal*, 27 May 1904.

26 *Agricultural Journal*, 28 April 1905, *Report … delineation commission*, pp. 39, 45, Natal Proclamation 58 (1903), Zululand Circular 7 (1904), and KZNA, GH 1562, minute paper R 1079/1904.

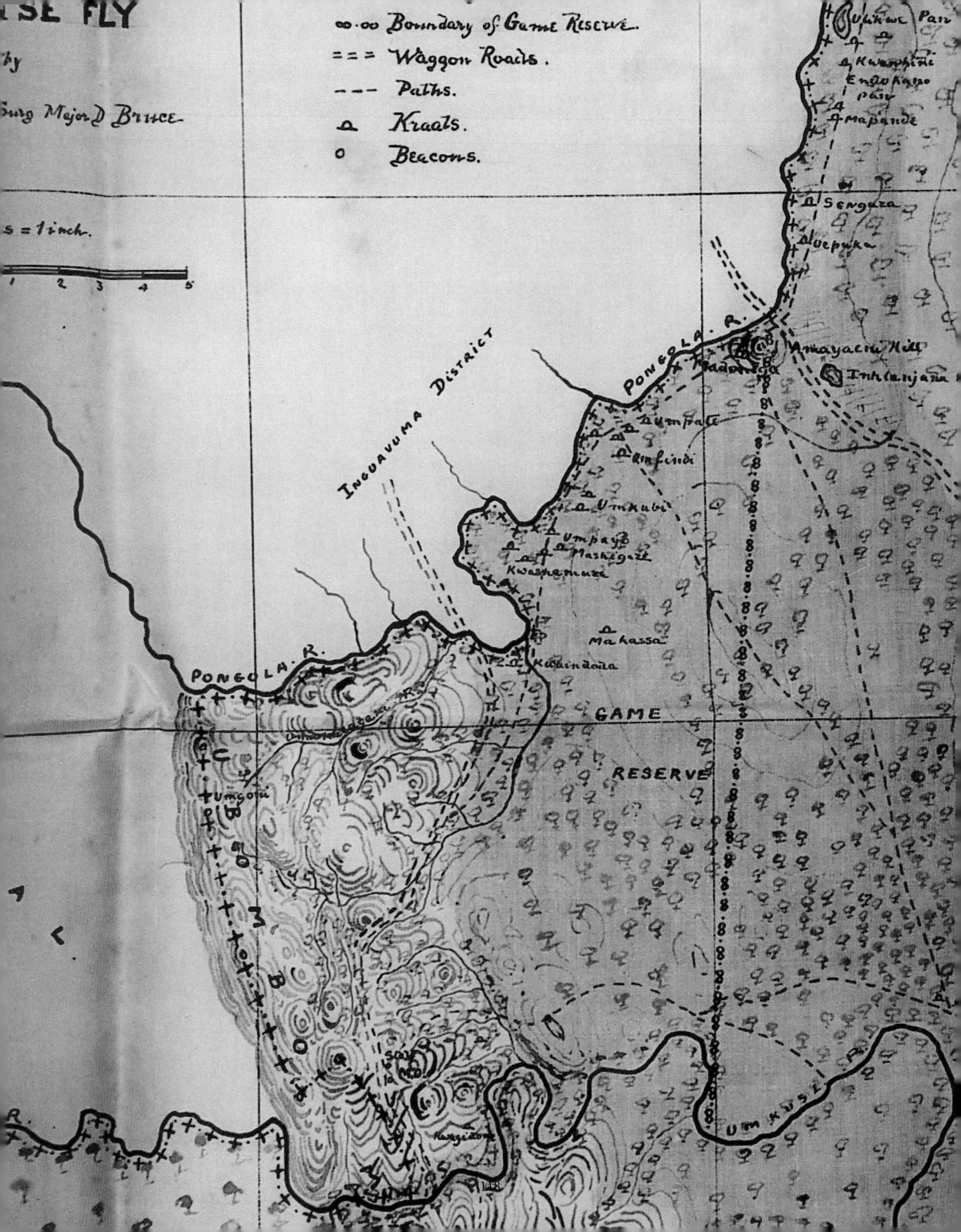

SE FLY
Surg Major D Bruce
Boundary of Game Reserve
Waggon Roads.
Paths.
Kraals.
Beacons.
s = 1 inch.
1
2
3
4
5
INGUAVUMA DISTRICT
PONGOLA R.
PONGOLA R.
Sengaza
Mapande
Amayacin Hill
Umfindi
Umkubi
Mashigeze
Kwasipemuze
Makassa
GAME
RESERVE
UMKUSE R

CHAPTER 9

The game reserves

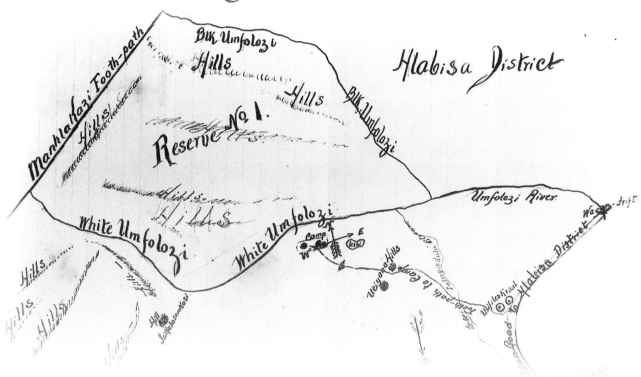

SKETCH MAP OF THE UMFOLOZI GAME RESERVE, JULY 1895   Only a few months after its proclamation Sigurd Silvertson, the first game ranger, drew this sketch map of the Umfolozi area for the local magistrate. Note the position of the ranger's camp, just south of the White Mfolozi River.   KWAZULU-NATAL ARCHIVES (1/EPI, 3/2/3)

Foundation

Tradition has it that an old-time hunter called C.D. Guise was the initial driving force behind the establishment of the Zululand game reserves. Certainly Guise wrote to the Zululand government on 19 February 1895 requesting three things. First, that the white rhino be added to the list of royal game. Second, that 'leave to shoot Royal Game should be very exceptional, to shoot the White Rhino absolutely prohibited'. The third request ran as follows:

> That the particular range of country in Zululand which embraces the habitat of the White Rhinoceros should be beaconed off as a game preserve, & no shooting or destruction

of game be allowed therein. The extent and limits I have no doubt can be ascertained from parties who have hunted there.[1]

Governor Hely-Hutchinson's response on this was a note to the resident commissioner, Marshall Clarke: 'I think there is merit in what Mr Guise says. What is your view?'

Clarke's view suggests that he was well aware of the plight of the white rhino and that steps were being taken for its protection. Magistrates had been instructed not to issue any licences to shoot rhino. A proclamation was being framed to add the rhino to the list of royal game. Finally the resident commissioners noted: 'I have before me all the papers connected with the proposed establishment of game preserves, and the question is receiving my consideration.'

MAP OF THE PONGOLA-MKUZE GAME RESERVE   In 1896 Sergeant-Major D. Bruce drew a map of the Ubombo district showing the distribution of the feared tsetse fly. This detail of that map marks the Pongola-Mkuze Game Reserve that existed from 1895 to 1897. Note that there are African homesteads in the northern section of the reserve and that the reserve is crossed by several bridle paths.   KWAZULU-NATAL ARCHIVES (ZGH VOL. 771)

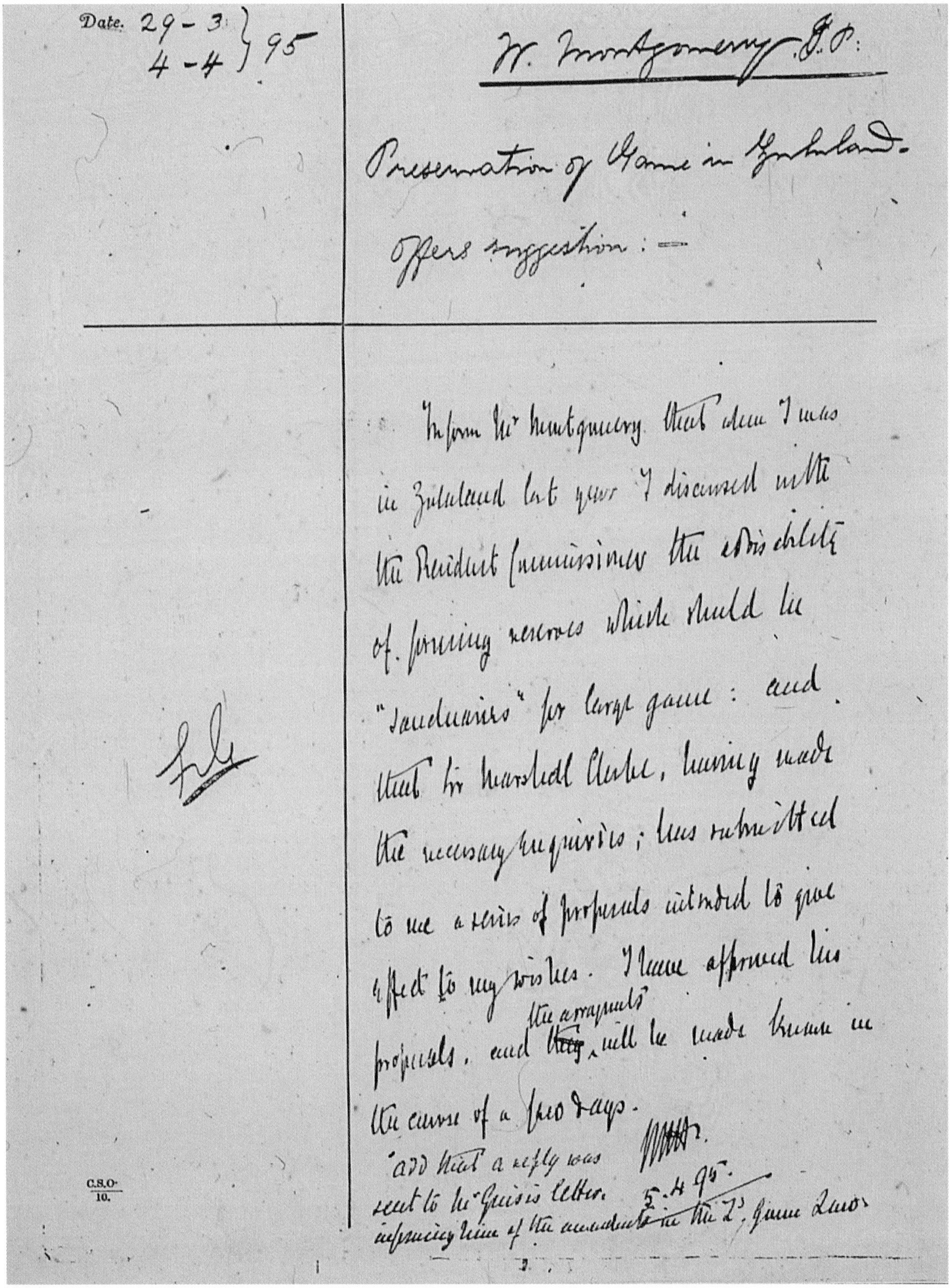

Date. 29-3 } 95
4-4 }

W. Montgomery J.P.:

Preservation of Game in Zululand.

Offers suggestion:—

Inform Mr Montgomery that when I was in Zululand last year I discussed with the Resident Commissioner the advisability of forming reserves which should be "sanctuaries" for large game: and that Mr Marshall Clarke, having made the necessary enquiries, has submitted to me a series of proposals intended to give effect to my wishes. I have approved his proposals, and ~~they~~ the arrangements will be made known in the course of a few days.

WHH.

Add that a reply was sent to the Guisi's letter. 5.4.95.
informing him of the amendments in the Z. Game Laws

File

C.S.O.
10.

ESTABLISHING THE GAME RESERVES A memorandum relating to the establishment of game reserves in Zululand, initialled by the British colonial governor of Zululand, Sir Walter Hely-Hutchinson. KWAZULU-NATAL ARCHIVES

Clarke's memo was written less than a week after Guise had written his letter. It is unlikely that Clarke started work and had got so far in that short period. More likely is that this notion was already in the public domain and that the resident commissioner had been working on the issue for some time. Indeed, Vaughan-Kirby puts the credit for the founding of the game reserves at the feet of the able resident commissioner of Zululand.

We know that Sir Walter Hely-Hutchinson, who was governor of both Natal and the separate Colony of Zululand, had an interest in natural history and did much for botanical enterprise when he served as a governor in the West Indies. He was in Zululand in 1894 and discussed the setting up of game reserves with Clarke.

Excitement around the issue of game preservation was stirred up by a number of factors. As early as 1891 there had been talk of establishing a nature reserve in the Drakensberg mountains to protect the remaining eland that lived there. The matter was even discussed in the Natal parliament. George Sutton proposed to the Legislative Assembly that the Giant's Castle region should be declared a game reserve. He was not successful.[2]

By 1894, Natal politicians found that their neighbour, the Transvaal Republic, had beaten them to it with the establishment of the Pongola Game Reserve. This was situated along a tongue of land between Swaziland and northern Zululand. Then public concern in Natal was aroused in August 1894, when the *Times of Natal* reported that a renowned hunter named C.R. Varndell had shot a white rhino in Zululand and had received £300 for the hide from the well-known British naturalist Rowland Ward. Official enquiries were instigated and the embarrassing fact was discovered that the local magistrate, Arthur Shepstone, had indeed granted permission for a white rhino bull to be shot for the '*purposes of a Museum*'. This was not the only white rhino Varndell had shot, for Ward's records note this nimrod also bagged a female white rhino in Zululand with a horn 29 3/4 in. (75.56 cm) in length.

According to F.C. Selous, Varndell's white rhino bull skin and skeleton were bought by Carl Jeppe and ended up in the Natural History Museum in Pretoria. Selous claimed a further six white rhino were shot in Zululand in 1894. It is little wonder a stir was created. In November 1894, the month before Guise wrote his letter to the secretary for Zululand, a letter in *The Field* from C.L. Leatham of Zululand confirmed the rhino killings.[3] What did not come out at that time, but was freely admitted by Magistrate Foxon in 1909, was that Foxon himself had also shot a white rhino in 1894 and sold it to Rowland Ward.[4]

Marshall Clarke submitted to Hely-Hutchinson a series of proposals concerning the establishment of game reserves in Zululand, which were subsequently approved. That there was pressure from men such as Guise and the magistrates D.W. Montgomery and Hugh Carbutt is clear. In March 1895 Montgomery quoted to the governor a letter he had received from Carbutt:

> … in the matter of preserving big game in Zululand. It would be a thousand pities I think if the district referred to was thrown open to Dutch 'pot hunters' and others, it is not as if a reserve had to be *made* here; it is ready made to our hands, and all we have to do is to preserve things in *status quo*: the doing so involves no trouble and no expense worth consideration.[5]

The truth of the matter was that it was clear to sober observers and in particular to the magistrates on the ground, that large mammals would need more than legislation to ensure their survival. A protected physical environment was required. Such had been the case in India where the forest reserves – the precursors of the modern game reserves – had existed for several decades. Ironically, in southern Africa it was in a non-British state that the concept was first adopted, though the Transvaal Republic owed much to the British annexation of 1877 to 1881 for its embryonic forest conservation policy.

The Pongola Game Reserve had been set up adjacent to Zululand on 13 June 1894, with the Dutch H.F. van Oordt as game warden. This long and thin reserve of seven 'farms', some 7.24 km by 32 km, contained some game, including hippo and lion. But only four months after the Zululand game reserves had been established, Van Oordt stated that the Zululand reserves had an abundance of game compared to what was in his reserve.

This Pongola reserve was strategically positioned as a natural thoroughfare for game. This was before the rinderpest and, if Stevenson-Hamilton is to be believed, Van Oordt's own hunting exploits. It was politically strategic, too, for the Boers. But the British annexation of Tongaland in April 1895 stymied not only the Transvaal's territorial ambitions but also the likelihood of a game reserve stretching on the western side of the Lebombo Mountains from the Phongola to the Mkhuze rivers. This area had once been one of the rich hunting grounds in the 1850s.[6]

On 8 April 1895, before the necessary regulations had been approved, Marshall Clarke was instructing his magistrates to prevent the hunting of game in what would be the new game reserves. By 18 April sketch maps of the proposed game reserves had been drawn, initially from a not very accurate general map sent by Hely-Hutchinson.[7] Finally, the Zululand Government Notice No. 12, dated 26 April 1895 and gazetted on 30 April 1895, proclaimed the first Zululand game reserves in which no game was to be killed. At least for the time being the Zululand wilderness was safe.

TABLE 21

ZULULAND GAME RESERVES, 1895 AND 1897

RESERVE NUMBER	DATE	NAME OF RESERVE [MAGISTRACY]	AREA SITUATED
1	1895–7	Cape St Lucia: (Mfolozi mouth)	'The range of hills and lagoons bounded on the north and west by the Umfolozi River, and on the east by the Indian Ocean.' [Included Mapalana area]
3	Post-1897	Lower Umfolozi	[It had been here in 1884 that Commander Moore of HMS *Goshawk* had erected a signboard which read 'British Territory'.]
2	1895–7	Umfolozi Junction	'The country between the Black and White Umfolozi Rivers from the junction of the rivers to the Mandhlagazi footpath'
4	Post-1897	Lower Umfolozi	[Note: Confusion is caused by the fact that magistrates in Lower Umfolozi consistently referred to the Umfolozi Junction Game Reserve as Reserve No. 1]
3	1895–7	Hluhluwe Valley	'A Straight line from the highest point of the Zangofe Ridge to the Mpanzakazi Hill, from thence to the present site of the kraals of Umdindwane, Mantingana, Saziwayo, and Umswazi; from the latter kraal to the nearest point of the Umzinene Stream; thence to the Mehlwana Hill, south of the Hluhluwe River; thence to the Mtolo Hill; from thence in a direct line with the same hill to the Hluhluwe River; and from there to the highest point of the Zangofe Hill.'
2	Post-1897	Hlabisa	
4	1895–7:	Umdletshe	[Generally low veld] 'The Umdhletshe Preserve bounded on the south by the Ingweni Stream, from its source near the Dukumbane Hill, to a point near the Ntambane Hill; from thence in a direct line with the Bumbene Store to the Mungwane Stream; thence up the course of that stream to its source; thence on to the Bombo Range and along its watershed to the Umsundusi River; thence up the course of that river to its source; thence in a straight line to the Bombolo Hills, and thence in a straight line to the source of the Ingweni Stream near the Dukumbane Hill.'
1	Post-1897	Hlabisa	
5	1895–7	Pongola–Mkuze	[North of the present Mkhuze Game Reserve.] 'The country between the Pongola and Umkusi Rivers and Bombo mountains, bounded on the east by a line from where the Pongola makes its sharp northern bend to where the Umkusi is joined by the Umhlohlela Stream.'
	Abolished in 1897	Ubombo	

These new game reserves are detailed in Table 21.

Hely-Hutchinson was keen that some effort should be made to keep a check on the game reserves. The local chiefs had been told to keep an eye open. It was also decided in June 1895 to appoint two game conservators 'for the purpose of supervising the Game Reserves that have recently been defined in Zululand, and generally to ensure a strict observation of the game laws'.

The timing of the establishment of the Zululand game reserves is significant. Hely-Hutchinson was well aware that the self-government or responsible government granted to the white population of Natal in 1893 would sooner rather than later mean the abolition of the Colony of Zululand and the incorporation of Zululand into Natal. Who knew what John Robinson's Natal government would do in Zululand with a governor whose power would then be restricted? If the game was to be preserved, Hely-Hutchinson had to secure reserves, or 'preserves', before the takeover. The British Tongaland Protectorate, proclaimed on 30 May 1895, and the annexation of adjacent Ingwavuma to the Colony of Zululand, would also have a significant impact on the

future of game conservation in southern Africa. Tongaland, or Maputaland as it came to be called, was to become one of the last bastions of game in south-east Africa as well as acting as 'game corridor' north into the wilds of southern Mozambique.

A letter, drafted by the governor himself, was duly dispatched to the editor of British journal *The Field* and on 6 July 1895 a piece duly appeared recording, 'Reserves have recently been established [in Zululand] within which no shooting is allowed. Were it not for these measures, large game would soon become extinct in Zululand.'[8]

Writing from Downing Street in London on 22 July 1895 the British colonial secretary Joseph Chamberlain informed Hely-Hutchinson: 'I have the honour to acknowledge the receipt of your despatch No. 49 of the 15th ultimo, and to express my approval of the steps which, with your sanction, Sir Marshall Clarke has taken for the preservation of game in Zululand.'[9]

The areas selected for conservation were those where wild animals were abundant. Even contemporaries called them natural game reserves. The Umfolozi–Hluhluwe complex was the haunt of large game even when the area had more people living there. Similarly the Lake St Lucia region had attracted hunters for decades, as had the Makhathini Flats and that bush area west of the Lebombo Mountains where in the 1850s Catherine Barter had bravely ventured to save her brother's life as he lay prostrate with malaria.

Hluhluwe was said to be 'the true home' of the buffalo and the 'very commonly met' black rhino. Umfolozi in 1898 was described as being 'mainly thorn Country with "Ntombote" in parts, and the large fig tree known as "Mkiwane" is to be found along the banks of the streams. The ground is very fertile.' In 1897 the magistrate listed the principal species of big game as:

- Kudu
- Waterbuck
- Blue wildebeest
- White and black rhino
- Warthog
- Zebra
- Buffalo
- The usual small game found in a Thorn country.[10]

Wild dog were abundant, but they were regarded as vermin.

At the turn of the century there were said to be about 15 white rhino in Umfolozi. When a white rhino carcass was found in 1903 in Maputa, the game ranger 'reports having seen six white rhino last month, and thinks there are still more'. The horn of the dead animal was 27$\frac{1}{2}$ in. (69.85 cm) in length. Twenty years after the reserve was proclaimed, Vaughan-Kirby gave their number as being 'between thirty and forty animals actually resident in the Reserve, as well as a useful number of calves'.[11]

Another reason why the game reserves where situated where they were was that people were thin on the ground; this vitally important issue of human density is discussed in Chapter 5. Marshall Clarke asserted in his annual report for 1895 that the game reserves were established in 'certain uninhabited parts' of Zululand.[12] In the case of at least one of these, Pongola–Mkuze, this is certainly incorrect. And in his April 1895 circular to magistrates, Clarke noted that no Africans 'at present living in any of these areas [future game reserves] are to be required to remove their huts, without the permission of the Resident Commissioner first obtained, and will have the right to kill or drive away game grazing with their cattle …' Clarke goes on to say that no African hunting parties were to be allowed in these areas and that chiefs would have to report all shooting parties (presumably white) coming into the reserved areas.[13]

One of the 'problems' in the Transvaal Republic's nearby Pongola Game Reserve was that the area was in part inhabited by those who owed allegiance to a chief called Sambane. As with the Pongola–Mkuze and Umdhletshe reserves, a resident population would inevitably be accused of poaching, though that is not the term they would have used.

That people had previously inhabited the Mfolozi valley region is obvious, though in what numbers is unclear. According to Vincent, the area was finally evacuated about 1882. In his 1897 report, the resident magistrate observed of the Umfolozi Game Reserve: 'The soil is very good. At one time the Mtetwa people lived both in and around this Reserve. The reason for their leaving was the advent of "Nagana" or the Tsetse fly which destroyed their cattle.' Umfolozi certainly had a bad reputation for 'being very deadly'. Nevertheless, it is doubtful whether the vicinity was ever completely uninhabited. If it had been, the early game conservators would not have complained about the poaching.

One can probably go no further than to say that the game reserves were at that time sparsely inhabited, inhabited only in part, or uninhabited on a permanent basis. But the point needs to be emphasised that in the whole Lower Umfolozi magisterial district, with its miles upon miles of thorn country, it was estimated in 1892 that there was a settled population of no more than 20 000 Africans and 16 white people. In the winter months came the white hunters as well as the transport riders on their way to and from Swaziland.[14]

A third factor determining the situation of the early game reserves, or at least most of them, was that they were remote and, though unfenced and largely unguarded, difficult to access. As late as 1916 Hluhluwe, the 'pick of the bunch', was the only Zululand game reserve 'into which wheeled transport [could] be taken, without encountering almost insuperable obstacles'. This clearly was a restrictive factor in white hunters extracting game products for commercial purposes.

Finally, with the passage of time, these game reserves became oases for much persecuted game, something confirmed by that redoubtable Ulsterman Vaughan-Kirby – 'Maqaqamba' – who observed animals making their way to the reserves and relative safety. On one occasion he comments that a 'fair troop' of wildebeest and of zebra, not previously represented in Hluhluwe, had 'taken up abode in this safe retreat'.[15]

Relative safety, though, was about all that was offered, since these reserves were not scientifically managed. There was no scientific staff present; indeed, the game conservators visited only occasionally and had to camp there when they did, as there was no infrastructure. There was no breeding programme, no habitat management, and certainly no thought of bringing tourists into the reserves. Most hunting parties had their licences inspected, and there was a rudimentary monitoring of the game. The concept was a simple one: what game was there, and that chose to remain in this unfenced region, was as far as possible to be protected from white sportsmen and African poachers. And that was how it was to remain for many decades.

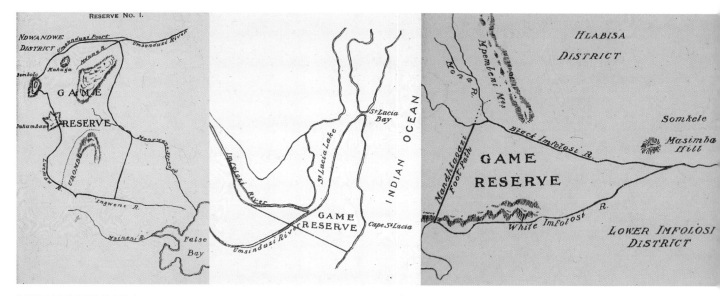

FOUR MAPS DELINEATING THE RE-PROCLAIMED ZULULAND GAME RESERVES IN 1897 Sketch maps of the four Zululand game reserves, Umfolozi, Hluhluwe, St Lucia and Umdhletshe. These were reproduced for colonial officials and published in the official *Natal Government Gazette* (27 April 1897) as well as in a confidential War Office manual for the British armed forces.

Further north, Vaughan-Kirby did have a rudimentary idea that it was desirable to go further. Writing to the Natural History Museum in London in November 1900, he observed of the Sabi–Crocodile rivers region:

> Eland, Roan antelope and ostriches used to be plentiful and though now extinct young specimens could be caught elsewhere & placed in the preserve with every prospect of thriving. The rare impala and Lichtenstein's Hartebeeste should also be introduced ... Part of the district lies within easy reach of a good railway [at Komati Poort] and of a good sea-port [Lourenço Marques]. Thus facilitating the introduction of new species from other parts and the exportation of live specimens for zoological collections, gardens, Parks etc ... Expenses which must be incurred may largely be met, as for instance by the sale of live specimens as above mentioned.[16]

The 1897 changes

In 1897 the British government in London finally agreed that the Colony of Zululand should be handed over to the self-governing colony of Natal. Zululand was to become a province of Natal. A commission was to deliberate on which areas of Zululand would be opened up for white commercial agriculture and which would be retained by the indigenous African population. The advent of the Anglo-Boer War delayed matters, giving a respite to both the African population and the game. It would be in 1905 that the delimitation commission report would be finalised and decisions taken regarding white settlement.

Prior to the handover of Zululand to Natal, London created a greater Zululand. First, it formally annexed to Britain the British protectorate of Tongaland (22 November 1897). Then on 24 December Britain transferred Tongaland to the Colony of Zululand. Finally, to complete the legal process, on 29 December 1897, the Colony of Zululand was annexed to the Colony of Natal.

Before the greater Zululand had been created the British decided that certain changes needed to be made to the existing system of game reserves. Under the provisions of Zululand Proclamation 2 of 1897 and Government Notice (Zululand) 16 of 1897 (27 April 1897), the following reserves were re-designated:

RESERVE 1: Umdletshe (previously No. 4) – shooting £10 per month.

RESERVE 2: Hluhluwe (previously No. 3) – shooting £10 per month.

RESERVE 3: St Lucia (previously No. 1) – no shooting permitted.

RESERVE 4: Umfolozi (previously No. 2) – no shooting permitted.

Charles Saunders, then acting resident commissioner of Zululand, in a letter dated 4 March 1897, starkly spelt out the reason for this reorganisation to Hely-Hutchinson:

> As it appears advisable to make a large reduction in the Big Game in Zululand in consequence of [the] spread of Tse-tse

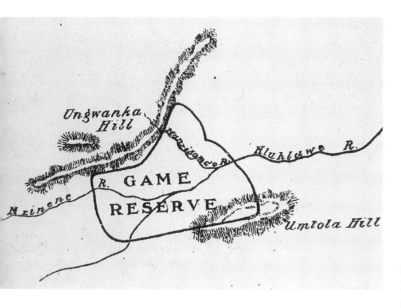

Fly with [the] considerable increase there has been in the large Game during the last few years, I beg to submit the following recommendations on the subject.

1. That the Reserve in the Ubombo District which lies between the Umkuzi and Pongola Rivers be done away with. The Main Road to Ingwavuma and that from Ubombo to the Amatongaland Protectorate pass through this Reserve, and, on account of the increase of Game "Fly" has become so numerous that every animal passing through there is affected and this renders the transport of supplies to those Districts almost impracticable.

2. That no shooting be allowed in the two reserves in Lower Umfolozi viz:- that at the junction of the two Umfolozi's and the one on the South of St Lucia Lake near the Coast. These Reserves are remotely situated from any main Roads and no danger is incurred by allowing game to increase there.

3. That whilst the two Reserves in Hlabisa District, each of which is near a main road, be maintained, shooting be allowed in these under the following conditions – preference being given to people who shoot for Museums: That each person shooting be required to take out a special licence for which a charge of Ten Guineas will be made per month or less period, and that the number of large game to be killed under such licence be limited to four head of each of the following species, viz:- Buffalo, water-Buck, Wildebeeste, Quagga, and Koodoo.

4. That a special licence be required in order to kill either the black Rhinoceros or Sea-cow, the charge for which should be two guineas and that no person be granted a licence to kill more than two of either of the above species during the shooting season in any year, and that no permission be given to kill Elephant or White Rhinoceros.

5. That a proportion – one in four – of the heads or horns of animals killed in the Reserves be handed to Government.

6. That Water-buck or Piva be deleted from schedule "D", Proclamation 5 – 1893. Wherever the Waterbuck is to be found, so far as my experience goes, the Tse-tse Fly abounds. Waterbuck have increased enormously of late years and there seems to me no necessity to include them in the Schedule of Royal Game.

Saunders's proposals were approved by Hely-Hutchinson on 11 March 1897 and the Pongola–Mkuze Game Reserve was abolished after an existence of only two years. Another factor leading to its demise may well have been the fact that part of this reserve at the eastern foot of the Lebombo Mountains was inhabited. Major Bruce's 1896 map marks nine named African homesteads within the demarcated reserve.[17]

That the Umdletshe Game Reserve survived the 1897 reorganisation is remarkable given the growing prejudice against big game. When the Umdletshe reserve (number 1) was finally abolished in 1907 the reason given was that it was crossed by the wagon road from the Somkhele railhead to Ubombo and Ingwavuma. The presence of tsetse fly in the reserve was considered a threat to draught animals.

Evidence exists that some of the expensive hunting licences provided for under the 1897 regulations were indeed purchased. The non-shooting policy in reserves 3 and 4 was, however, enforced as far as was feasible, not least because it was felt that shooting in the reserves would only drive game out of the reserves. And besides, much of the game, such as leopard and lion, which hunters wished to pursue were in 1897 said still to be 'numerous' in the Ubombo district.[18]

A short-lived Hlabisa Game Reserve (number 5) existed from 1905 to 1907, the year when the Umdhletshe reserve was also abolished. The Hlabisa reserve included land from the present-day Hluhluwe–Imfolozi Corridor down to the shores of Lake St Lucia. It was delineated as follows:

From the source of the Hluhluwe River, in a straight line to the highest point of the Mtolo Hill; thence in a straight line to the highest point of the Mteku Hill; thence in a straight line to the source of the Munywana Stream; thence along that stream to where it enters St Lucia Lake; thence along the Western shore of that lake to where the Inyalazi River flows into the lake; thence along the Inyalazi River to where the new Main Road from Somkele Station to Hlabisa Magistracy crosses that River; thence in a straight line to the junction of the Black and White Umfolozi Rivers; thence up the Black Umfolozi River to where the Mona River flows into it; thence in a straight line to the source of the Hluhluwe River.

With three designated game areas in Hlabisa, more than half the magisterial division was taken up with game reserves.[19]

The year 1907 also saw the extension of the Umfolozi reserve boundary to accommodate white rhino whose territory was outside the existing reserve.

From the junction of the White and Black Umfolozi Rivers, down the Umfolozi to where the Imvamanzi Stream joins it, thence along the Imvamanzi Stream to its source, thence in a straight line to the highest point of the Sangoyana Hill, thence in a straight line to where the Mandhlakazi footpath crosses the White Umfolozi River, thence along the Mandhlakazi footpath to where it crosses the Black Umfolozi River, and thence along the Black Umfolozi River to its junction with the White Umfolozi River.

The much-talked-of Giant's Castle was finally gazetted as a game reserve in 1907, though it had first been set aside as a reserve in 1903 and declared a 'demarcated forest' in 1905.[20] The Mkuze Game Reserve dates from as late as 1912 and was south of the location of the old Pongola–Mkuze reserve.[21]

And so we can see that between 1895 and 1912 game reserves occupied, at one time or another, all the land from the White Mfolozi in a crescent shape to the Phongola River, encompassing the plain to the west of Lake St Lucia and the hill country beyond that. This 'crescent of game' continued through the Swaziland lowveld on the west of the Lebombo Mountains and, to the east of the range, Maputaland and southern Mozambique, tracking round to the lowveld of Mpumalanga.

Table 22 illustrates the erratic existence of the Zululand game reserves.[22]

REFERENCES

1   KZNA, ZGH 762, 19 February 1895; Ellis, B. 'Game conservation in Zululand, 1824–1947', p. 32; and Pooley and Player, *KwaZulu/Natal wildlife destinations*, p. 17.

2   Barnes, *Giant's Castle*, Chapter 2.

3   Rowland Ward (ed.), *Great and small game of Africa*, p. 58; and Ward, *Records of big game*, p. 289.

4   KZNA, Natal Museum papers, Foxon to Arnold W. Cooper, 8 June 1909.

5   KZNA, ZGH 763, 29 March 1895; and ZGH 759, R 1886/1894. See also Gush, *Mkhuze*, p. 13; Pooley and Player, *KwaZulu/Natal wildlife destinations*, p. 17; and Vaughan-Kirby, 'Game and game preservation in Zululand', p. 380.

6   There had been talk of setting up game reserves in the Transvaal since the late 1880s. The Pongola reserve was the first, established by proclamation in June 1894, followed by the Sabi reserve in March 1898. For the Transvaal game reserves, see Carruthers, 'Dissecting the myth: Paul Kruger and the Kruger National Park', *Journal of Southern African Studies*, 20: 2, June 1994, pp. 263–83; Carruthers, 'Game protection in the Transvaal, 1846 to 1926', pp. 186–7; and Carruthers, 'The Pongola game reserve: an eco-political study', pp. 1–16.

7   KZNA, ZA 44, no. 21; ZGH 763, 268/1895; and NGA ND 154/1895.

8   *The Field: The country gentleman's newspaper*, 6 July 1895. For a discussion of wild game in Natal and Zululand, see also *The Field*, 27 and 31 July 1895.

9   KZNA: ZGH 765, minute paper, R 1845/1895.

10 KZNA: 1/EPI, letter book, report for 1897, fol. 346.

11 KZNA: 1/EPI, letter book, report of the RM for the year 1897, fol. 346 and 26 December 1898, fols. 414–5; 1/MTB, minute paper M 56/1903, 24 January 1903; and Vaughan-Kirby, 'Game and game preservation', p. 383.

12 *Colonial Reports: Annual. No. 169. Zululand*, p. 11.

13 KZNA, NGA 3/2/4, ND 154/1895, 8 April 1895.

14 KZNA, 1/EPI 3/1/1/1/3, 1891 annual report, fols. 1–3.

15 Vaughan-Kirby, 'Game and game preservation in Zululand', pp. 382–3.

16 Natural History Museum, London, DF 232/6, 2109, 13 November 1900.

17 See map drawn by Major D. Bruce, KZNA, ZGH vol. 771, 12 June 1896. See also Vaughan-Kirby, 'Game and game preservation in Zululand', p. 381.

18 KZNA, 1/NGA 3/2/5, ND 449/1897; and ZGH 835, W.E. Peachey to Morton Green, 30 March 1897.

19 See Natal Government Notice no. 93 of 1905; Curson, 'Preservation of game in South Africa', p. 412; and Vincent, 'The history of Umfolozi Game Reserve', p. 13.

20 Natal Government Notices 322 and 356 of 1907. See also Barnes, *Giant's Castle*, Chapter 2; *The Agricultural Journal and Mining Record*, 16 October 1903; and Natal Government Notice 356/1907.

21 Vaughan-Kirby, 'Game and game preservation in Zululand', p. 384.

22 Zululand Government No. 12 of 1895 (26 April 1895) and 16 of 1897 (22 April 1897); Natal Proclamation 2 of 1897; and Natal Government No. 93 of 1905 (3 February 1905). It should be noted that Umfolozi Game Reserve was subsequently de-proclaimed from 1932 to 1939 and again from 1945 to 1947.

TABLE 22

ZULULAND GAME RESERVES, 1894–1930

| • | : | years reserve was in existence | Procl. | : | year reserve was proclaimed |
| Boundary | : | year of boundary change | Deprocl. | : | year reserve was de-proclaimed |

	CAPE ST LUCIA	UMFOLOZI	HLUHLUWE	UMDLETSHE	HLABISA	PONGOLA-MKUZE	MKUZE	NDUMO	PONGOLA (TVL)
1894									Procl.
1895	Procl.	Procl.	Procl.	Procl.		Procl.			•
1896	•	•	•	•		•			•
1897	•	•	•	•		Deprocl.			•
1898	•	•	•	•					•
1899	•	•	•	•					•
1900	•	•	•	•					•
1901	•	•	•	•					•
1902	•	•	•	•					•
1903	•	•	•	•					•
1904	•	•	•	•					•
1905	•	•	•	•	Procl.				•
1906	•	•	•	•	•				•
1907	•	Boundary	•	Deprocl.	Deprocl.				•
1908	•	•	•						•
1909	•	•	•						•
1910	•	•	•						•
1911	•	•	•						•
1912	•	•	Boundary				Procl.		•
1913	•	•	•				•		•
1914	•	•	•				•		•
1915	•	•	•				•		•
1916	•	•	•				•		•
1917	•	•	•				•		•
1918	•	•	•				•		•
1919	•	•	•				•		•
1920	•	Boundary Deprocl.	•				•		•
1921	•		•				•		Deprocl.
1922	•		•				•		
1923	•		•				•		
1924	•		•				•	Procl.	
1925	•		•				•	•	
1926	•		•				•	•	
1927	•		•				•	•	
1928	Deprocl.		•				•	•	
1929			•				•	•	
1930		Procl.	•				•	•	

CHAPTER 10

Running the conservation system

The game reserves

The early game rangers

On 2 May 1895 William Windham, the secretary for Zululand, dispatched the following minute to the magistrate of the Entonjaneni District:

> As a number of applications for permission to shoot in Zululand are now being received, the Resident Commissioner considers it necessary that a special Constable should be appointed to supervise the Game Reserves in your District and to see that it is strictly respected. His Honour accordingly requests that you will engage the services of a suitable officer at once to carry out that duty.
>
> You will clearly give him to understand that his employment is temporary and may be terminated at any time without notice. His remuneration should be fixed at the rate of ten pounds a month … whilst his head-quarters will be for the present at Entonjaneni, the officer appointed should understand that his services must be equally available for employment in other districts of Zululand.[1]

In fact, funding was made available for two white game conservators as well as for a number of African game constables, 'not to exceed 10 in a month'. The conservators were to be paid £10 a month plus £2 a month for travelling expenses. The game constables were to be paid 30s. if they were employed for a full month's work. Total expenditure for the four reserves and for the checking of hunting licences in Zululand was not to exceed £39 a month or £468 a year. The cost of maintaining the game conservators in the period of the Colony of Zululand is summarised in Table 23

The game constables appear to have been uniformed; certainly monies were allocated for clothing.[2] Tenure for all was tenuous.

TABLE 23

GAME RESERVE CONSERVATORS, 1896–98

YEAR	NUMBER OF SUPERVISORS	COST PER AREA
1896	2	Lower Umfolozi: £120
1897	1	Lower Umfolozi: £120
	1	Entonjaneni: £36
1898	1	Lower Umfolozi: £120
	1	Entonjaneni: £36
Total (£)		**£432**

W. Pettie was informed that his position as conservator of game preserves in Lower Umfolozi was 'temporary, provisionally, and subject to summary termination'.[3] When Sigurd Silvertson was appointed a game constable he was paid £10 a month and told he must provide and maintain his own horse. In the event of a horse's death from nagana while on government business, compensation was usually paid to the game constable or forest ranger. Silvertson was based at the Lower Umfolozi magistracy, but was informed that the government reserved the right 'of employing your services in any part of Zululand'. Less than four months later, Silvertson's services were dispensed with and he was instructed to fill out discharge vouchers in triplicate on receipt of wages owing to him.[4] Silvertson had with John Maxwell unsuccessfully tried to persuade the government to recognise their claim to the Mzingazi coalfield; the authorities retained the mineral rights for themselves.[5]

Disease was another risk. As will be seen below, two of the known African game rangers in this early period died, probably from malaria, while employed in protecting the game reserves. It

GAME MAP OF PART OF MPUMALANGA (EASTERN TRANSVAAL) C. 1905 This interesting map appears in Vaughan-Kirby's biography *In the haunt of wild game*. From an article Kirby wrote in 1916, we know he had a similar map for Zululand. Sadly, no trace of this can now be found.

appears as if the game reserves were in the charge of the white rangers only during the winter hunting season and that in summer it was the African rangers who were stationed there.[6] Whatever the arrangements, the fact is that the areas where game was concentrated remained unhealthy for humans right into the twentieth century.

Two things strike one about the general figures for forests and game reserves: firstly, forests received attention before game reserves; secondly, more manpower and expense were devoted to the forests than to the reserves. The amount spent on nature conservation in Zululand between 1891 and 1898 totalled £4 047, about £500 a year.[7]

Sadly, we do not know the names of many of the foresters and game rangers of this early period.[8] Those we do have include the following:

SIGURD SILVERTSON, appointed on 1 June 1895, was special constable for the purpose of supervising the game in the Lower Umfolozi District. He was dismissed on 23 September 1895. In May 1896 he was employed as a court constable and messenger, and recruited to superintend roads in Lower Umfolozi. Later Silvertson became assistant to the noted surveyor L.M. Altern, who was attached to the 1902–4 Zululand delimitation commission.

DAVID D. TWEEDIE (1 June 1895) was special constable to supervise game preserves. He was described as follows: 'steady and reliable; has a thorough knowledge of the Zulu language'.

FRANCIS EVANS (25 July 1895) was a forest ranger at Ingwavuma.

W.E. PETTIE (12 May 1896) was conservator of game preserves in Lower Umfolozi.

W.C. MILES was a forest ranger at Qhudeni forest.

W.H. MOORE (3 June 1896) replaced Francis Evans as forest ranger at Ingwavuma. Evans became quartermaster to the Zululand Police. Moore had been assistant to Surgeon Major Bruce as an interpreter.

G.H. DAVIES (23 June 1896) was a forest ranger at Qhudeni forest, and formerly Zululand Police constable, replacing W.C. Miles. Davies took a great interest in his forest and supplied John Medley Wood of the Colonial Herbarium in Durban with specimens of the forest flora.

F. O. ECKERSLEY (1 June 1897) became forest conservator on the resignation of W.H. Moore at Ingwavuma.

SAMUEL DUNN (23 November 1898) was supervisor of game reserves in Lower Umfolozi.

MPAMA KA KAMBI was game constable at Umfolozi Game Reserve. He died of fever and dysentery on 17 January 1900.

INYANDA was game constable at Cape St Lucia Game Reserve. He died apparently from fever on 16 May 1900.

MAPUTA was game supervisor *c.*1903 at Umfolozi Game Reserve, Mahlabatini section.

DLUDLA was game supervisor *c.*1903 at Umfolozi Game Reserve, Mahlabatini section.

MADHLANGA was game constable between 1901 and 1905 at Umfolozi Game Reserve.

The early game rangers did their job well according to the few accounts that have survived, but, of course, there were occasional problems. The fact that Umfolozi fell, as it still does, between two magisterial divisions – most in Lower Umfolozi and a small western part in Mahlabatini – was potential trouble. In March 1900 the game rangers were drawn into a spat between the two respective magistrates around this division when confusion was created over a message which may or may not have been sent by Foxon in Lower Umfolozi to his counterpart in Mahlabatini. Feathers were ruffled at the perceived sending of black game rangers to instruct a white magistrate. But behind the indignation was the thorny issue of who controlled the reserve. It seems to have been agreed that the preservation of game was

> a mutual good that we are mostly agreed upon and, surely in an uninhabited wild such as that in question, the matter of a few yards of boundary is one scarcely calling for discussion. I shall be delighted to accept your [Foxon's] invitation to meet in the Winter for the enlightenment of us both on the spot, but at the same time I do not intend to institute myself into a boundary commission unless instructed by government to do so … however as I have said before our object is not to raise any boundary contention or to increase the boundaries of the district, but simply to ensure proper supervision of state game reserves.[9]

More serious was an accusation against game conservator Madhlanga for insubordination, contempt, insolence, impertinence and so forth. There also appears to have been a scuffle. Magistrate Turnbull, who could be tough, was fairly philosophical about the matter. He suspected Madhlanga to 'suffer periodically' from the effects of 'over-smoking hemp' combined with draughts of sorghum beer. He did not recommend his dismissal 'as he [was] an old servant of the Government' but instead proposed Madhlanga's transfer to Melmoth or the neighbouring Mahlabatini division.[10]

The Zululand police

Other factors also made crucial contributions to nature conservation in this late colonial period. One, which has been discussed in an earlier chapter, was the role played by the magistrates, who were generally sympathetic to forest and game protection. In the

Transvaal Republic all commandants, field cornets and such officials were from 1894 *ex officio* government gamekeepers.[11] But in Zululand that had already been the case since 1887.

The second factor was the role of the police. Even after Zululand had been formally annexed, there was not a large British military presence in the new colony – sometimes well under 200 soldiers. A paramilitary force drawn mainly from the local Zulu population maintained law and order. This was not a large force, having in 1896 some 257 members to cover the whole of the territory:

- 1 commandant
- 5 inspectors
- 1 quartermaster
- 1 sergeant-major
- 10 sergeants
- 20 corporals
- 219 privates

There were only 11 chargers and 19 troopers' ponies. When armed, the Zululand Police carried Martini-Henry rifles and bayonets.[12] The magistrates made ready use of this force in their drive to protect the forests and game reserves as well as in anti-poaching exercises.

It is important to realise that without the activities of African policemen little game conservation, both in and outside the reserves and especially in remote Maputaland, could have been achieved. By 1905 this vast area of Maputaland had a white population of only 25, of whom 10 were policemen. Maputaland had a bad reputation among whites, not merely because of disease but also because of the heat. As one official wrote in 1896 of the 'phenomenal heat' of Maputaland: 'The reflection of the sun's rays from the white sand gave some of us sore eyes.'[13]

The locally employed men were important as they knew the area and the community. Nevertheless, where appointed, it was the game rangers or game constables on the ground that held the line in the defence of the reserves. The magistrate of Mahlabatini had no doubts about the desirability of such appointments. In 1899 he observed concerning the western section of the Umfolozi Game Reserve, 'I endeavour to watch the country referred to by means of police supervision but it is not satisfactory. It is necessary that men should be in the locality constantly to properly supervise it.'[14] But, of course, it was usual for the game rangers to be allocated a contingent of Zululand Police, and indeed when the reserves were established the Zululand Police was increased by 20 men to cater for this additional responsibility. It was this combination of game rangers and police which produced results. It also incidentally created a paramilitary ethos around the Zululand game reserves that was to be emphasised much later long after the old colonial dispensation had gone.

Missed opportunity

The Zululand government could have taken one further step that would have helped the cause of nature conservation as it entered this difficult period. They should have appointed a senior official in overall charge of the game reserves. The resident commissioner and his magistrates were generally sympathetic towards the game reserves but they had no shortage of other problems facing them. Underlying all was the fact that they controlled a subject people who might very well rise up at any time to try and regain lost freedoms, as indeed some did in 1906. Yet it was truly a missed opportunity that there was already somebody eminently qualified for the position, and who was angling for the job. Writing from Sabi in December 1895, Vaughan-Kirby stated:

> I am anxious to know whether it is the intention of the Government to appoint a Manager or Superintendent over the preserved area [in Zululand], who could also see to the stocking of the preserve with game from other parts of the Continent; and whether if it is so intended, and such manager is not already appointed, whether you would favourably consider my application for the post.[15]

A former hunter, an educated man, a fellow of the Royal Zoological Society and with 16 years' experience of living in the bush, Vaughan-Kirby would have been the ideal person to get the new reserves on their feet and to meet the onslaught that they were to face. Eventually, in 1912 Vaughan-Kirby was appointed game conservator for Zululand. But by then circumstances were very different.

Policing Umfolozi

Disappointingly little has survived concerning the early Zululand game reserves. This is not altogether surprising given the circumstances under which the game rangers laboured. The fullest details of their activities relate to the Umfolozi Game Reserve. This, one suspects, is because it received more attention than any of the other reserves.

In March 1895, before the gazetting of the game reserves in April, a patrol of the Zululand Police was scouting the junction of the White and Black Mfolozi to see if game was being destroyed. The patrol reported that they had seen no big game, but that wild dogs were plentiful. Two of these had been shot and a third had been wounded but had escaped. The local magistrate noted, 'These dogs cross the country in packs of from ten to twenty in number, and systematically hunt the game, quantities of which they kill.'[16] It was to be a recurring theme, for in the magistrates' minds, wild dogs were vermin that had to be destroyed.

By late April three African privates in the Zululand Police and two of the new game African constables were being sent to

CAPE HUNTING DOG (*Lycaon Pictus*).

WILD DOG Much maligned, the wild dog was regarded as vermin by the early conservationists and shot whenever possible. PARKER GILLMORE, *THE HUNTER'S ARCADIA*, 1886

communities adjacent to the new game reserves and in particular to the chiefs. Their task was to point out the boundaries of the unfenced reserves and to instruct that no game was to be hunted in these areas.[17]

Between 8 and 13 June Umfolozi's first game ranger, David Tweedie, visited the reserve and compiled his first report, commenting, 'owing to the inaccessible situation of this preserve it will not be very liable to invasion by European hunters and the greater part of the surrounding country being sparsely populated [by African people]'. He reported that there were only a few kraals at the extreme northerly end of the Mandhlagazi footpath, the non-river boundary of the game reserve. These he wanted to see 'brought into closer supervision'. Concluding, Tweedie commented that he had asked the locals about the destruction of wild dogs 'by poisoning or otherwise' but learnt that it was not the custom of wild dog 'to return to their prey after participation'.

Tweedie had four African policemen with him. A standing camp was established 'about three miles [4.8 km] from the junction of the Mfolozi Rivers'.

The resident magistrate at Melmoth, Arthur Shepstone, was

most pleased with Tweedie's work and dispatched him forthwith to inspect the other districts. Ever keen, Tweedie also decided to follow some white hunters who had left their wagon and were hunting on foot. But by now he was convinced that wild dog were the greatest enemy to the game, more so than hunters.[18]

Writing from 'Umfolozi Preserve, Nceleni' on 31 July 1895, Tweedie noted, obviously with disapproval, that in his absence the magistrate had issued 'numerous shooting licences'. But he went on to make the interesting observation that very few of the hunters in the district would shoot either the number or variety of game granted them, 'as in many cases they do not exist without the Preserve, and if so in such numbers as render their shooting too laborious an undertaking for most hunters'.[19]

While Tweedie was busily engaged, others were not idle either. The second game ranger, Sigurd Silvertson, also visited Umfolozi, arriving about 28 June 1895 with five policemen. Fortunately a sketch map has survived, the earliest of the game reserve. This clearly shows the camp, just south of the White Mfolozi near the Ueyana Hills, west of where the Intuyinkulu Stream enters the White Mfolozi. He also had a base at Palane.

Silvertson said it was 15 miles [24 km] from the wagon drift and 14 miles [22.4 km] south-west of 'Usifile's kraal'. Silvertson's posse was just too late to catch a white hunting party. Two waterbuck, a zebra and a reedbuck had been killed and in a nearby African 'trapper-hut' were Martini-Henry cartridge wrappers, some paper with writing on it and the cover of a cocoa tin. Silvertson took measures to secure the illegally hunted horns and skins which had been left by the two white hunters – tall with dark moustaches – at the kraal of Msongeziyane ka Mpanza's, which was situated at Mfolozi's drift. They turned out to be two unpleasant Natal brothers called Slatter, who ignored Constable Bohle's instructions not to load the horns, skins and a 'private box' into their wagon and defiantly set off back to Natal.

This piece of excitement passed and Silvertson set about regular daily patrols of the Umfolozi Game Reserve and surrounding neighbourhood, noting that in the reserve, they encountered neither Africans nor animal traps. But Constable Mandulo did find four iron traps at the Ueyane Hills, just south of the White Mfolozi. He kept a diary, which sadly cannot be traced. One legitimate hunter in the area, Robert Armstrong, came to Silvertson one day and showed him a female klipspringer which was royal game and which he had shot with a rifle at 200 yards, thinking it to be a rooibok. The skin was confiscated and the hapless Mr Armstrong told to report to the magistrate.

The bag of the hunting party of Armstrong and Wilkinson was reported as 'a number of small game', plus two male kudu [25 June], one female quagga [zebra] [30 June], a bull and a cow buffalo [3 July] and a male kudu [9 July]. One bag of Mr Parkinson's hunting party was listed as seven buck, two zebra, one wildebeest and one old buffalo, and a second of four buck, two wildebeest and one wild pig at Umfolozi and six buck, two monkeys and one kudu bull at the Mendu Hills. The shooting was 'supervised' by Silvertson, something that must have annoyed the sportsmen. But the news would soon get round that the carefree days of unrestricted hunting in Zululand were at an end, or so it must have seemed. Silvertson also noted the presence in the area of the Woodward brothers, the great Victorian birders of Natal and Zululand.

In early July 1895 the resident commissioner called by on his way to Ubombo. The two discussed how to kill the wild dog: 'These animals were in plenty at the White Mfolozi [south of the river] and also in the reserve.' Silvertson started looking into the 'haunts, habits and lairs of the Wild dogs'. He reported:

> Wild Dogs have not fixed places where they stay, but are always moving by day; (but) by night they never move, but sleep in shelter of big stones or in 'Dongas'. When the females of Wild Dogs [have] got young ones, they generally remain in 'Dongas' until their young ones are big enough to move about.

> I beg to suggest that poisoned meat should be left in the 'tracks' of these animals and where 'spoor' are seen en masse. I have noticed, when patrolling in the reserve, that 'spoors' of the animals are frequently seen in the 'Big-game-footpaths'.

Silvertson's enthusiasm and devotion to duty came at a price. By the second week of July Silvertson was unwell, preferring to stay at the Lutheran mission station at Patane/Mthethwa. Silvertson would have liked to move his camp from the White Mfolozi – 'it being rather warm' – to midway between there and Usifile's kraal at the wagon road.

Silvertson was given medicine for dysentery by the Reverend Peter Aage Rodseth.[20] When this ran out he wrote to Eshowe asking for more, only to be told that medicine was not sent in the post. Finally, the unfortunate Silvertson appealed to the magistrate to help him, adding, 'I regret to say that I feel very bad this morning.' It was probably Silvertson's illness that led to his dismissal a few weeks later.[21]

The African summer approached and the rangers withdrew, though occasional patrols were sent out from the magistrate's office. The following spring the rangers were back in camp, initiating regular patrols, especially of the Umfolozi Game Reserve. W.E. Pettie had replaced Silvertson. Pettie was as keen as his predecessor, perhaps a little more officious. White hunters were closely monitored, but an assault made on the wild dogs, with poison laid down, accounted for the death of several. Pettie observed that he had not told the local African population where the poisoned meat was as he had only put it where they 'have no right to be', though he added that if he put poison down where the locals 'are likely to go I will inform them'. Some wild dog were also shot, though one gets the impression that they were not an easy target for the rangers, no doubt because the wild dogs soon learnt to give them a wide berth. Pettie recounts seeing a pack killing a buck in the Mfolozi River on 14 July 1896. The following comment by magistrate Arthur Shepstone further reveals why the wild dog became such a target:

> It is the general opinion that the spread of NaKana [nagana] is due to the koodoo and Quagga [zebra] having extended [in range] to the localities mentioned, and that this is in a great measure caused by the great increase in the number of wild dogs and other carnivorous wild animals in the Game Reserves.[22]

Poaching by the African population also now became a focus of the rangers. The magistrate was soon converted to this way of thinking. He noted, 'I am satisfied that a large quantity of game is killed during the closed season' and added that the rangers should endeavour to discover the kraals in which the poachers lived. A lengthy investigation took place into the poaching of two buffalo.

Pettie seems to have been relentless in his pursuit of those responsible, but he had his task made very difficult as the locals would 'screen one another so well'. The threat that an informer's associates would *tagata* – bewitch – him was also a factor.

Several interesting facts came out of the interrogation of the suspected poachers. One was that clearly many Africans had unlicensed guns. Secondly, there seemed to have been doubt in the poachers' minds as to what was and was not royal game – were klipspringer and kudu royal game or not? This, of course, may have been a bluff to avoid punishment. Thirdly, it seems sometimes to have been the practice to build a makeshift hut when out hunting or poaching, to use as a base. On several occasions the game rangers destroyed such huts when out on their patrols. Finally, entering the bush for reasons other than hunting emerged from enquiries carried out by the game guard. A local called Ngqukumbane stated that he and two others went to the thorns to collect honey; on another occasion he went to the reserve 'to get herbs used to dress the Isidwabas with'.[23]

Life in camp for the game rangers was very basic. Pettie, who was delighted when the magistrate sent him up a newspaper to read, wrote in pencil, 'I have no ink, the little I received having dried in the bottle, will you kindly send me a little Foolscap paper.'

By the winter of 1898 things had changed with the onslaught of rinderpest. Patrols in the game reserves seem to have been fewer. Wild dogs were still being shot and traps and snares confiscated. But more hunting licences appear to have been issued – 26 in the Umfolozi area in July alone. Two police patrols of Umfolozi in August went to inspect

> the condition of the big Game … and to search for skeletons of animals supposed to have died from Rinderpest. The report made is that there is a scarcity of Koodoo and buffaloes. No skeletons were found. Waterbuck and Zebra were reported to be plentiful in the Reserve.[24]

By summer the magistrate had noted that the area between the two Mfolozi rivers had become unoccupied some years earlier when nagana or tsetse fly appeared. 'This is said to have made its appearance with large herds of game which came from the North.' He ended with the comment that were the big game to be totally destroyed, the area would be fit for occupation by Africans. Attitudes were beginning to change.

In 1899, when the locusts returned to Zululand, Umfolozi Game Reserve was said to be well stocked with waterbuck and zebra. Slowly the numbers of buffalo and kudu began to recover. It was not until July 1900 that the game constables reported the spoor of buffalo in 'many places as well as that of a few koodoo'. South of the White Mfolozi were large troops of zebra as well as the old enemy, the wild dog, one pack in 1900 being said to be 16 strong. Foxon said they were coming out on to the more open country 'where the small game is plentiful'. By 1901 a bounty had been set on the head of the wild dog, though in December the magistrate noted that 'strange to say not a single wild-dog skin or head has yet been brought to the magistracy by anyone whereon to claim the Government award of the one pound'. The magistrate was also at this time freely giving permission to shoot crocodile in the district.[25]

A new difficulty was facing Thomas Maxwell, the magistrate at Lower Umfolozi, with people encroaching onto the reserve. The magistrate said they were going into a very unhealthy area and he concluded 'that the object they have in mind is poaching'.[26]

St Lucia

A note on the Cape St Lucia Game Reserve can be added, for as the nineteenth century drew to an end Mr Foxon began to take an interest in this charming area of lakes, lagoons, pans, rivers and high bush-covered sand dunes. Hippos were numerous and complaints of their destruction of crops grown by nearby African farmers were not uncommon.

The old St Lucia Game Reserve was said to be fairly plentifully stocked with small game, some waterbuck and one old elephant: 'The Game Constable at No. 3 Reserve [St Lucia] reports [November 1899] that he personally saw the single elephant there, which would appear to be a bull of great age, its tusks having crossed in front.'[27]

This elephant took to raiding crops, eating mealies and pumpkin. It was said also to have blocked a footpath that was used from 'the Mpukanyane' by charging anyone who walked along the path.

On 25 January 1900 a vigilant game guard observed three boats land from a vessel offshore. They contained five white men and were clearly intent on some sport. The guard accosted the party and was told they were out of Delagoa Bay en route for Durban and had come ashore for wood. The guard remained as some wood and a barrel of water were collected, and the party departed.[28]

Changed times

That the reserves had succeeded in acting as a reservoir and refuge for game in Zululand is clear from the reports of the dramatic decline in game numbers elsewhere outside Maputaland. Few as the early game rangers were – black and white – they were obviously dedicated to their task and fearless in their dealings with both man and beast. That they made use of their rifles is evident: Samuel Dunn, for example, had in the first half of 1899 received 120 rounds of ammunition and then applied for a permit for a further 90 rounds.[29]

Even within the game reserves some game was becoming rare.

TABLE 24

ZULULAND FORESTS: EXPENDITURE AND MANPOWER, 1891–98

YEAR	NUMBER OF CONSERVATORS	NUMBER OF GUARDS	WAGES	OTHER EXPENDITURE
1891	0	7	£126	Clothing
1892	0	7	£126	• £20 horse allowance • clothing
1893	0	7	£126	• £20 horse allowance • clothing
1894	0	8	£144	• £20 horse allowance. NB From 1894 wages included £2 a month for travelling expenses
1895	1	8	£264	• £20 horse allowance • £27 7s. 9d. to purchase a horse
1896	3 (2?)	8	£504	• £250 forest upkeep • £800 for new plantation
1897	2	8	£384	• £200 for new plantation
1898 (½ year)	2	8	£384	• £200 for new plantation
Total (£)			**£2 058**	**£1 557**

In 1903 the game conservators in Hluhluwe were instructed that they could no longer shoot warthog for the pot as these animals had become very scarce there, and that only with the magistrate's permission could they shoot duiker and steenbok.[30]

The forests

Expenditure on protecting the forests for the period of the Colony of Zululand is summarised in Table 24.

The division among the magisterial district of the African forest conservators and forest guards is summarised in Table 25.

The most noted of the Zululand foresters in the colonial era was the former Natal sawmill manager, G.H. Davies. In 1892 he

TABLE 25

ZULULAND FOREST RANGERS, 1891–98

MAGISTERIAL DISTRICT	YEAR/S	STAFF
Eshowe	1891–1898	3 African rangers
Nkandla	1891–1893	
	1894–1898	2 African rangers
		3 African rangers
		1 white ranger
Emthonjaneni	1891–1898	2 African rangers
Ingwavuma	1896–1898	1 white ranger

had worked in Schöpflin's short-lived forestry department in Pietermaritzburg and was then part of the rump of that department when it was consumed by the Surveyor-General's Office. From 1898 to 1904 he was Zululand's forest ranger, based at the Qhudeni mist-belt forest, after which Davies was the district forest officer for Zululand at Eshowe. Later in his career he was chief forester for southern Natal.

Davies, like the other Zululand foresters, led a hard and difficult life. The sawyers he had to deal with were rough and tough, the African population could be resentful and suspicious, and later the neighbouring white farmers could be cantankerous. Equipment was scarce. Davies admitted in 1903: 'I do not even possess a pocket compass or any other appliance at this station.' The Qhudeni forest inventory consisted of:

> Revolver, five-foot [1.5 m] cross saw, two axes, one inkwell, a hundred-foot [30 m] tape measure, T.R. Sim's *Forest Flora*, picks, shovels, spades, two hatchets, a road pick, cash box, stamp hammer, sieve, office table, set of pigeon-holes, rulers, gunter's chain, rake, watering can, six towels, paintbrush and hoes.[31]

Accommodation was rudimentary. The forester, if single, might live at one of the trading stores; but there sometimes might lie temptations. As late as the 1920s one Zululand forester, on 10 shillings a week, said the roof of his house had 22 leaks in it and the office was full of bugs. His wife complained 'in the bitterest terms of her lot'. Leaking roofs did not help when the poor forester had to write his monthly report, in duplicate, for his superiors in Pietermaritzburg.

It was not easy for women and children, often left alone in their wood-and-iron homes for days on end as their husbands patrolled the forests. The worst posting was Maputa (or Maphutha), looking after the Mangusi bush, away in the middle of the Makhathini Flats, 10 km from Kosi Bay, in hot and humid Maputaland. In 1904 magistrate Stainbank pleaded with the civil commissioner in Eshowe to move the forest officer from Maputa up to the magistracy at Ingwavuma on the Lebombo Mountains. He reported that the forester's 'wife and family were never free from fever'. Not surprisingly, this posting carried the relatively high salary of £250 a year.[32]

Travel was equally difficult. The dirt road from Qhudeni forest to Nkandla forest crossed at least six drifts and some hills with very steep gradients. Then on arrival at one's destination, the work was difficult. It entailed such matters as assessing the standing stock and marking what could be cut by sawyers; keeping an eye on Africans and sawyers in the forest; collecting fees; arresting those cutting or gathering wood illegally (from 1894 forest officers had the powers of a police constable); patrolling the forest; liasing with the magistrates and the Zululand Police, who also helped sometimes with patrols; writing regular reports; and maintaining logging books. It is little wonder that, as the following 1900 report of the Natal Colonial Herbarium illustrates, Davies escaped from his cares by collecting plants:

> The largest contributor ... has been Mr G.H. Davies of Qudeni, Zululand, who sent about 40 different species, chiefly shrubs, or trees, the specimens sent have been excellently well prepared, and in sufficient quantity, but they often suffered considerably in transit through the post. Amongst them are several new species, some rare ones, and a few that are not yet fully determined. I should be very pleased to have a few more such valuable correspondents as Mr Davies in other parts of the Colony, and I may again repeat that parcels of specimens will pass free through post, provided printed direction labels are attached to the parcels.[33]

REFERENCES

1 KZNA, 1/MTB, minute paper, H 214/1895.

2 KZNA, CSO, 1658, 7200/1900. See also, KZNA, ZA 44, Zululand letter book, no. 3, 9 June 1895.

3 KZNA, ZGH 770, R 2255/1896.

4 KZNA, 1/EPI, letter book, 1 June 1895, fols. 431–2; 23 September 1895, fols. 481, 494.

5 See Cubbin, *History of Richards Bay*, p. 36

6 *Colonial Reports: number 169: Zululand, 1895,* c-7944, 1896, p. 11.

7 Statistic extrapolated from Zululand annual estimates and ZA 16, ZA 116 and ZGH 788.

8 For these early nature conservation employees, see KZNA, CSO 1658, 7200/1900; 1/EPI, letter-book, 18 January 1900, fol. 75; 1/EPI, letter book, 21 May 1900, fol. 230; 1/MEL, 3/2/6, H 308/1895; 1/ING 3/1/1, R 1156/1900, 3 June 1897; ZA 16 and 116; and ZGH 264, 470/1895, 7 June 1895; ZGH 749, R 362/1893; ZGH 760; ZGH 789, Foxon to Hill, 20 July 1895; ZGH 854, 1897 Zululand Blue Book (MS).

9 KZNA, 1/MBT, letter book, 26 March 1900, fols. 453–7.

10 KZNA, 1/EPI, letter book, 1905, fols. 411–12.

11 Carruthers, 'Game protection in the Transvaal', p. 163.

12 KZNA, ZA 24, Zululand Police; and ZGH 728, *The local land forces of the British colonies,* p. 49.

13 ZA 27, Mr Bosman's report on Tongaland, 1896, fol. 34.

14 KZNA, 1/MBT, 30 April 1899.

15 KZNA, ZGH 768, R 146/1896, Kirby to Secretary for Zululand, 31 December 1895.

16 KZNA, 1/EPI, letter book, 31 March 1895, fol. 168 and 10 April 1895, fol. 176.

17 KZNA, 1/EPI, letter book, 30 April 1895, fol. 182.

18 KZNA, 1/EPI, letter book, 30 June 1895, fol. 195; 1/ESH, letter book, 18 October 1895; 1/MEL, minute papers R 1310/1895, 15 June 1895; PB 389 C/1895, 15 August 1895; and R 1791/1895, 17 August 1895.

19 KZNA, 1/MEL, 3/2/6, PB 370 A1895, 31 July 1895.

20 Hale (ed.), *Norwegian missionaries in Natal and Zululand*, p. 164.

21 KZNA, 1/EPI, 3/2/3, 30 June; 4, 9, 10, 12, 16, 20 and 28 July; 5 and 12 August 1895.

22 KZNA, 1/MEL, minute paper R 3617/1896, 19 October 1896.

23 KZNA, 1/EPI, letter book, 15 September 1895, fols. 210–11 and undated letter 1896, fol. 703–4; report June 1896, fol. 714. See also minute papers LW 369/1896, 369/1896 and 937/1896.

24 KZNA, 1/EPI, letter book, 31 August 1898, fol. 387. See also 2 February 1898, fol. 257.

25 KZNA, 1/EPI, letter book, 22 August 1901 and report December 1901.

26 KZNA, 1/EPI, letter book, report for February 1899, fol. 2, report for December 1900, fols. 384, 31 July 1900, fol. 284, and minute paper R5 59/1899, 4 March 1899.

27 KZNA, 1/EPI, letter book, report November 1899, fols. 29–31 and report December 1899, fols. 160–61.

28 KZNA, 1/EPI, letter book, report January 1900, fols. 89–91.

29 KZNA, 1/EPI, letter book, July 1899, fol. 705.

30 KZNA, MTB, minute paper, R 2412, 29 October 1903.

31 Forest Archive, Eshowe, W 6020/618.

32 Forest Archive, Eshowe, D 2000/6/8, 31 March 1927; and KZNA, 1/ING, minute paper, R 1553/1904, 29 July 1904. See also *Swaziland, Tongaland and northern Zululand,* War Office, 1905, pp. 94–5.

33 J. Medley Wood, *Colonial Herbarium: Report for the year 1900*, p. 4.

BUSHBUCK

Common throughout Natal and Zululand in the nineteenth century, the elusive and attractive bushbuck was hunted by locals and white hunters for its meat.

W.L. SCLATER, *THE MAMMALS OF SOUTH AFRICA*, 1900–1901

Trouble in Arcadia

'A RIVER SCENE', 1854 This idyllic scene of crocodile, hippo, pelican and flamingo is not unusual even today at St Lucia or in parts of Maputaland, but 150 years ago the whole of eastern Zululand and Maputaland, not just confined to game reserves, was teaming with wildlife.
BALDWIN, *AFRICAN HUNTING*, 1863

ELAND   At 1.8 metres in height to the shoulder, the eland was remorselessly pursued by white hunters in Zululand. Many were the tales of the nobility of this animal when under attack, with stories of the tenacity of eland vainly trying to protect fellow herd members which had been shot, or of individual animals standing defiantly to face the enemy and certain death.

W.L. SCLATER, *THE MAMMALS OF SOUTH AFRICA*, 1900–1901

CHAPTER 11

Enforcing the game conservation laws

The permit system

In studying the surviving overall statistics of the number of shooting licences for royal game issued in Natal for the years 1894 to 1896 in Table 26, two things stand out. Firstly, hunting licences were issued for only seven types of buck and two categories of game bird. Secondly, a relatively small number of permits were issued over the three years: on average only about 200 a year were granted for the whole of the Colony of Natal. It is little wonder that Zululand was a magnet for the sportsman.[1]

Several of these Natal licences were issued to magistrates, such as T.G. Colenbrander (Lower Tugela) and F. Fynney (Umlazi). Oswald Fynney was later to be magistrate at Ubombo. Reg Gush rightly points out in his interesting history of Mkhuze Game Reserve that for years prior to its proclamation as a game reserve in 1912, Fynney unofficially protected this area, keeping a watchful eye over activities there.[2]

Unfortunately no overall statistics have survived for Zululand; what is certain is that the amount of poaching by both whites and Africans was considerable. We know, however, that in 1893 in Lower Umfolozi only 31 shooting permits were issued by the magistrate. The figure for 1895 was 25. The magistrate, Thomas Maxwell, however, had no illusions that 'in many instances the privilege was very much abused, game being wantonly destroyed'.[3]

The magistrates

In the Transvaal Republic all commandants, field cornets and such officials were from 1894 *ex officio* government gamekeepers.[4] But, as stated earlier, in Zululand that had been the case already since 1887. The Zululand magistrates were usually men who had come up through the ranks, either of the Zululand Police or as court interpreters and messengers, such as Alexander Turnbull.

One of the most noted Zululand magistrates was Cuthbert Colenso Cook Foxon, who had progressed from a magistrate's clerk and Zulu interpreter in several Zululand districts, through sub-inspector in the Zululand Police, to agent and then deputy commissioner of the short-lived British Tongaland Protectorate (June 1896 to December 1897). He served as magistrate of the new division of Maputa until 1899 when it was incorporated into Ingwavuma. Foxon then had stints as magistrate in Lower Umfolozi (1899–1901), Nkandla (1901–1905) and Mtunzini (1905–1924).[5]

Foxon was an important figure in the drive to save the remaining large game in Zululand and, as was the way of things with the early conservationists, a keen huntsman himself. He also had the requisite toughness and tenacity to allow himself to become unpopular if that was what was necessary to speed up the message that the preservation of game was important.[6]

TABLE 26

NUMBER OF PERMITS ISSUED TO SHOOT ROYAL GAME IN NATAL, 1894–1896

YEAR	ROOI REIBOK	REITBOK	HARTE-BEESTE	ORIBI	STEENBOK	SPRINGBOK	RED BOSCHBOK	KORHAAN	PAAUW	TOTAL
1894	6	16	16	2	0	0	0	28	10	78
1895	70	52	26	18	3	2	2	94	24	291
1896	90	48	21	10	9	8	0	72	30	258
Total	**136**	**116**	**63**	**30**	**12**	**10**	**2**	**194**	**64**	**627**

ZEBRAS IN DURBAN AWAITING SHIPMENT FOR EUROPE, 1851
Such snippets as this appearing in Durban's *Natal Star* on 28 May 1851 were not
uncommon for the readers of the Durban press.

These magistrates were powerful men, not least when it came
to deciding who would and would not be allowed to shoot. Their
rulings tended to be unpopularly down-to-earth and pragmatic.
In 1910 a contributor in the *Zululand Times* complained: 'The
man who wants a few days shooting as a change from office store,
is most likely to be refused a permit. But the man who shoots for
the pot to keep him in biltong right through the year … will get
a permit … There is no rule to go by except the personal good
will of the resident magistrate.'[7]

Perhaps the most influential magistrate in Zululand was from
a higher stratum in colonial society. Charles James Renault Saunders
was the son of James Renault and Katharine Saunders of Tongaat.
His father, known as 'the Tongaat slasher', was an outspoken
member of the Natal parliament. His 'clever little wife', as
Marianne North somewhat cattily described her, was an amateur
plant hunter and botanical artist of note. The lily *Haemanthus
katherinae* was named by Kew Gardens in her honour. Their son
Charles was put into the colonial service in Zululand.

Charles Saunders was magistrate at Eshowe from 1888 to 1896,
with the exception of an uncomfortable year, 1890–1891, in the
remote magistrate's outpost at Ubombo. Here, high up on the
top of the Lebombo Mountains, the magistracy and police post
overlooked the hot and unhealthy plains of Maputaland.[8]

Like his mother, he was interested in nature and collected
plants. The succulent shrub called the kudu lily, specimens of
which he sent to Kew Gardens, was scientifically named in his
honour, *Pachypodium saundersii*. Saunders also discovered the
attractive bulb, the Maputaland grass crinum, *Crinum acaule*. In
addition, he was a collector of birds' eggs and of insects.[9]

In 1887 Saunders contracted malaria while in Maputaland,
which affliction was to recur in later years. He became resident

commissioner and chief magistrate of Zululand, being appointed
on 25 November 1896. With the transfer of Zululand to Natal,
Saunders's title changed to chief magistrate and civil commissioner for Zululand, a position he held through the difficult years
1897 to 1908. Hely-Hutchinson, the governor from 1893 to 1901,
thought very highly of him.[10] In 1906 Saunders was knighted.

Saunders was very sympathetic to the plight of big game in
Zululand, but perhaps he was more pragmatic about the issue
than were Foxon and some of the other magistrates, who had a
tendency to be uncompromising, especially when dealing with
the African population.[11] Given the ethos of the age, none was
opposed in principle to hunting, but Saunders realised that it was
as dangerous to place on the African population any further
restrictions relating to hunting as it was to restrict them from
cutting timber in the forests. His more lenient approach comple-
mented the firmer magistrates' stance and provided balance, but
events would shift that balance.

No such reserve existed when it came to 'Dutch pot-hunters'.
The magistrates were as one. The general British–Boer animosity
of the 1880s and 1890s played itself out in the Zululand
wilderness as much as in the dingy, dusty streets of the gold
shanty towns of the old Transvaal. As far as the magistrates were
concerned, burghers' hunting had to be discouraged. The very
month Mr Guise suggested the establishment of the Zululand
game reserves, Marshall Clarke lectured Hely-Hutchinson on the
necessity of writing to the government of the South African
Republic informing them that hunters from there had to have
permits to bring guns and ammunition into Zululand and that
'anyone found trespassing on crown lands in pursuit of game
without the permission of the Magistrate of the District … [was]
liable to fine or imprisonment'.[12]

Government's caution

The magistrates' superiors in Pietermaritzburg and London were
pleased with the Zululand game regulations, but from the start
urged caution in their implementation among the African
population, especially at times of instability. Governor Havelock
probably struck the right note when in May 1888 he commented
to Melmoth Osborn, the resident commissioner in Zululand:

> I take this opportunity of drawing your attention to the subject
> of the preservation of all kinds of game in Zululand. The
> destruction of game to such an extent as to permanently reduce
> its amount, is much to be deprecated. Circumstances have hither-
> to rendered it inexpedient to enforce rigidly the provisions of
> the Law for the preservation of game, since that law came into
> force in Zululand. I would ask you to consider whether it
> would not be well to gradually bring the law into force.[13]

No. 58   **ZULULAND.**   R 2597/03

GAME PERMIT.

Permission is hereby granted to _Mangakulana. Chief Nqwawe._ to shoot the undermentioned species of Game in Zululand, under the provisions of the Proclamation No. II., 1897, dated 22nd April, 1897, within a period of _One Month_ commencing from the _4th November_ and expiring on the _4th December_. 190_3_.

No Game may be killed under this permit until it shall have been produced to the Resident Magistrates of the respective Districts in which it is intended to shoot, from whom any license required under the law must be obtained.

Description _Hippopotamus_

Number _One._

Eshowe, Zululand
30th October 1903

C M Saunders
~~Resident~~ Commissioner.

ZULULAND GAME SHOOTING LICENCE Game permits to shoot royal game such as rhino or buffalo were issued only sparingly and in the case of hippo usually because the animal was destroying a farmer's crops. This 1903 licence made out to Chief Mangakulana is signed by Charles Saunders, Zululand's civil commissioner and one of the region's pioneering conservationists. KWAZULU-NATAL ARCHIVES (1/ING 3/1/3, R2397/1903)

The drafting of a game regulation specifically for Zululand rang alarm bells in Downing Street. In May 1890 the British colonial secretary, Lord Knutsford, commenting on the 1890 game protection proclamation, cautioned Governor Mitchell: 'As at present advised I should be disposed to think that until Zululand has become more settled, the strict enforcement of this law might lead to serious friction. In the meantime it would be well that great care should be exercised with regard to putting it in operation, so as to avoid difficulties with the native population.'[14]

The message was passed down the line and Osborn instructed his magistrates to exercise the utmost care to avoid difficulties with the African population in putting into effect the provisions of the new game law.[15] Such rejoinders no doubt had some

impact, though probably not as much as London would have liked. Four years later Osborn's successor, Marshall Clarke, while instructing magistrates to organise the driving of game away from settled areas, told them to be chary of giving leave to shoot in areas which were 'uninhabited owing to scarcity of water or other causes or where the large game [did] not come into contact with cattle, the property of the inhabitants of Zululand or such as [were] employed in transport riding'.[16] There were limits.

Licences

Hunting permits were requested for three reasons: for recreation, for food and to protect the crops of African farmers. It was the practice to specify the species to be shot and give a limit to the

THE SECRETARY BIRD The secretary bird was one of the first birds to be officially protected by the colonial authorities. Its reputation as a good snaker was not exaggerated.
PARKER GILLMORE, *THE HUNTER'S ARCADIA*, 1886

amount of animals that could be killed. The licence was also usually valid only for one month. Nor were birds neglected when magistrates listed what could and could not be shot.[17]

Generally the Zululand magistrates were reluctant to issue licences to kill more than two or three types of a species. They also had no qualms about instructing an applicant to reduce the quantity of animals that he applied to shoot. The chief magistrate in Eshowe could and occasionally did lay down overall maximum quotas for any species. The hunting of royal game was frequently stopped altogether, either when new game laws were being considered, as in 1890 and 1905, or when, as in 1893, 1895 and 1900, there was a perceived threat to species of royal game.

Sport
In addition to the usual licence fee, recreational sportsmen had to pay fees for bringing firearms (1s. each), cartridges (3d. per 100) and gunpowder (3d. per pound weight) into Zululand. Before it became a British protectorate in May 1895, most of Maputaland remained open for unbridled hunting. The extent of the carnage perpetrated there in the years between the defeat of Zulu power and British occupation (1879–1895) is unknown but it must have been considerable.

Though hunting licences were not required in Maputaland in those years, to reach there the sportsmen had to travel either through Delagoa Bay or across Zululand. If the latter, the hunter could either pass through Zululand without hunting or, more likely, attempt to persuade or bully the local magistrate into issuing him with a hunting licence. A case in point was Lieutenant Firmstone, who from 1891 to 1893 passed through Zululand each winter on his way to shoot at the 'sea cow swamps of Matongaland'.[18]

Magistrates themselves were not averse to a bit of sport and Foxon used to hunt as he travelled round his district collecting hut taxes. But even he was restricted in 1890 by the suspension in shooting large game, which is just as well as his list of desiderata included rietbuck, impala, nyala, waterbuck, kudu, buffalo, hippo and rhinoceros.[19]

Local conditions sometimes influenced both what was permitted by the magistrate to be shot and where hunting could take place. The appearance of locusts on the Makhatini Flats led the magistrate in June 1896 to forbid hunting on the low country so the game would be preserved until the spring 'to provide a means of destroying young locusts'.[20]

Food

Every year there was a closed season for various categories of game that might not then be shot, thus allowing the species time to breed. Frequently, however, there were requests, usually from resident whites, to shoot for the pot during the closed season. At first these tended to be granted, though the prohibition on killing rietbuck was retained. Such requests came from magistrates themselves, as well as from missionaries and white travellers and the like. But when the rinderpest struck, it was said to be impossible to get any fresh cattle meat in some areas and inevitably there was then a clamour for venison.

This situation carried on for several years with some whites being granted licences out of season, which not surprisingly was resented by the African population.[21] By 1901 an attempt was made to stop this waiving of the rules for local whites. As Saunders said, Africans 'cannot be punished, with any reason, if Europeans are allowed to kill game out of season'. This was in reply to an outburst of indignation from magistrate Alexander Turnbull. He liked his red meat and, sitting on the top of the Lebombo Mountains, he was being forced to eat 'fowls and tinned-stuff'. 'One buck a fortnight, I do not think, will make any difference to the number of small game in the District,' fumed the bull-headed Turnbull. But Saunders was not to be moved and reminded the magistrate that he received a special allowance of £50 a year to be where he was, a sum not granted to other magistrates.[22] We can only imagine Turnbull's response to this comment.

But Turnbull won in the end, and the following year a special concession was granted to whites living in the Ubombo district. They were allowed to shoot in the closed season one duiker, one steenbuck or a bushbuck and a few guineafowl 'per week, for each *household*'. The strict understanding was that these animals had to be shot by whites themselves and not by Africans for whites.[23]

This is not to say that all applications from Africans to shoot game for food were refused. In times of great shortage African people were permitted to shoot for the pot out of season. And occasionally an African request to kill a hippo, one of the special category of royal game, for food was allowed. In 1903 a headman, Manqakulana kaNgwanase, offered the authorities £10 to be allowed to kill a hippo on Sankonto Pan in the Ingwavuma district. The civil commissioner in Eshowe noted that this request should be granted as the pan was not far from Bumbe, where hippo were dying at that time. No fee was charged.[24]

Crops

Wild animals destroying crops was always a difficult problem for the magistrates, who usually advised frightening away large game rather than destroying it. When a 'very vicious' black rhino was reported to be eating crops near Sipongo Hill in Hlabisa, Charles Saunders corrected the resident magistrate, 'if the animal is eating crops it must be of the White species, as the black lives entirely on thorns, & no permission can be granted to kill the former.' The suggestion that a policeman be sent with a shotgun to scare off the beast elicited this dry comment from Inspector Evans of the Zululand Police:

> I do not think that the proposal to send a white policeman to frighten it [the rhino] away with a shot gun would have much effect. With only a shot gun the fright I should say would be on the policeman's side. I should recommend that [a licence] be obtained to have it shot.[25]

Hippo were a constant subject of complaints by chiefs to magistrates and occasionally permission was given to shoot a troublesome animal. As the years went by, however, Saunders was less inclined to approve such action, repeating his advice that shots should be fired at night to scare away any trespassing hippo.[26]

On the other hand, things could be seen in a different light if it were a white person complaining about a problem animal. In 1891 when J. Schwaub requested permission to shoot rietbuck that were eating some crops he had planted, the acting resident commissioner, the ever-zealous Colonel Cardew, hesitated at recommending the request to shoot this prized species on the ground of the precedent it would set. His superior, however, would have none of this, and bluntly stated, 'Mr Schwaub must protect his crops. I decline to create a precedent by the leave asked.'[27] A generation later Charles Warren asserted that African pleas that hippo were a danger to their crops were 'raised as an excuse for sport of killing an animal and obtaining the value of the hide'.[28]

African attitudes to the game regulations

As mentioned in an earlier chapter, Zulu kings at various times appear to have imposed restrictions on the hunting of various species and on hunting in specific areas. What was introduced by the colonial regime was, however, much more restrictive in terms of size of territory protected and the number of wild animal species protected. There was also the added dimension of the introduction of a closed season for hunting a host of animals.[29] How did the indigenous population react to all this? The simple answer is: with a mixture of reluctant acceptance and annoyance.

Following the formal annexation of Zululand in 1887, the magistrates were quick to inform the chiefs of the change in the

political situation and that they were now 'British subjects'. In the report on one such meeting, it is interesting to note that the question of the imposition of restrictive game regulations was the second item discussed after that of the imposition of a 14s. hut tax. In reaction to what Arthur Shepstone said at one of these meetings, the chiefs of Lower Umfolozi made the following reasonable request: 'With regard to the Game Laws they asked if they would not be allowed to kill Hippopotami and Riet-buck when destructive to their crops, and I promised to represent the matter for your Honour's consideration.'[30] This was to be a regular complaint in the years to come.[31]

On 22 May 1894 a great meeting was convened at Nongoma between Marshall Clarke, the resident commissioner, and some 300 Usuthu and their leaders. The question of tribal boundaries south of the Black Mfolozi River was the principal reason for this indaba, but the resident commissioner, perhaps foolishly, chose to raise the issue of game protection: 'His Honour then expressed his wishes in regard to the protection of game in places not used for the grazing of cattle. The idea of protecting wild animals seems to cause some amusement during which the Usuthu began to move away ending by rushing away bodily uttering the cry "Usuthu" without having given a parting salute.'[32]

The unhappiness surrounding the game laws did not diminish with the years. Giving evidence to a 1907 commission, one chief strongly urged the right of Africans to kill game within their districts, especially in times of scarcity: 'These buck serve no special purpose. They [the Africans] had to supply labour to the Government and paid their taxes and considered they were entitled to profit by the game.'[33]

Punishments

Enforcement of the game laws was something that predated the establishment of game reserves. For despite the entreaties of Downing Street, the governor and even the resident commissioner on the ground at Eshowe, there is little evidence that the magistrates turned much of a blind eye to poaching. Melmoth Osborn was not slow in telling Governor Havelock:

I do not anticipate any difficulty in enforcing the [game] law; the Zulus are already aware of its existence and they were accustomed to restrictions in the killing of certain descriptions of large game during the reigns of Mpande and Cetywayo. They would understand the explanation of the Magistrates that the intention of the law is to protect ordinary game during the breeding seasons in order that they may increase and become more plentiful for use of the people during the proper seasons.[34]

He had a point, of course, although it was one thing getting such commands from one's king, and quite another to be receiving them from a short-tempered white magistrate.

On the other hand, tribal courts also handed out punishment for the illegal destruction of game. In 1895 when a group killed a rhino which came near a kraal, and cut its hide up into sjamboks, Regent Wombe fined the one who first stabbed the rhino £2 and 'the rest of the miscreants' £1 each. The defendants appealed to Alexander Turnbull, the local magistrate. He recognised that the minimum fine of £50 was out of the question and he was not inclined towards a prison term, 'as long sentences, I think, punish Governments, or the public, more than the offenders'. He thought a more appropriate fine would be £5 for the kraal owners but less for the lads who had helped their fathers. Concerning Wombe's actions, Turnbull makes the following observation: 'The game law can hardly be considered Native law; yet I understand some slight misapprehension may invest Wombe's mind, as Cetewayo had a law promulgated with a view to the preservation of buffalo.'[35]

The magistrates seem to have been keen to book those who transgressed the game regulations, and if something dramatic occurred, they tended to cause a stir. When a report came through that a wagon containing 32 kudu skins, 9 buffalo hides, 3 zebra skins and a single waterbuck skin had passed through the Ndwandwe district, the hue-and-cry went up.[36] Similarly, in 1903 when the carcass of a white rhino was found in Umfolozi Game Reserve, Saunders's questions elicited a full report from Maputa, one of the game rangers:

I am a game supervisor in Mahlabatine Dist. On Friday, 23rd Jany '03 I was patrolling the reserve in company with Dhludhla, another game supervisor. When near the Mantiyana [Mantiyane] Hill, my attention was attracted by a number of vultures circling over a certain spot. I proceeded thither and found the skeleton of a white rhinocerous. There were numerous footprints of hyaenas and vultures about, and the bones were picked comparatively clean. There is one bone missing – the hip bone of one of the hind legs. The bones were strewn about, and considerably gnawed by wild animals. I think it is a full grown animal by the length of the horn. It is impossible to say what killed it, and also to determine its sex. It is nearly three months since we patrolled that particular part, but on my last visit to the place we did not see any vultures, or notice any smell. I think it must have died since we last patrolled there.[37]

LUNCHEON AT JAMRACH'S Opposite the great entrance gate to the London docks was Charles Jamrach's trading warehouse. Here many an unfortunate beast from Zululand and elsewhere – lion, elephant, crocodile, monkey, parrot or whatever – would be confined having survived a long sea voyage, prior to being sold on to the zoological gardens of Britain and Europe. *THE STRAND MAGAZINE*, 1891

THE SPUR-WINGED GOOSE Great flocks of spur-winged geese could be found on the pans of Zululand. Hunters found them a convenient and readily-available meal.
PARKER GILLMORE, *THE HUNTER'S ARCADIA*, 1886

Saunders ordered that the skeleton of this rhino as well as the remains 'of the one killed in your District a short time ago' be sent to his office. Maputa was also sent all the way to Eshowe to be interviewed by the resident commissioner about what he had found. White rhino had become special. As for Maputa, he was told to go back and find the missing bone.

Some magistrates were more tenacious in pursuit of poachers than others. And certainly as time went on, the magistrates appear to have got tougher. In 1887 three people got off with a caution for killing a hippo in the Msunduzi River, on the grounds that as the game laws had so recently been extended to Zululand, judgment was 'framed accordingly'. By 1902 people were being arrested for 'wandering' in a game reserve.[38]

Whites were fined as well as African hunters for contravening the game laws. That said, there was usually little alternative for an African convicted of poaching when a hefty fine or some months' hard labour were the options. Fines handed out varied, but £5 or £2 seems to have been the norm, plus the confiscation of any firearm and the cancellation of a gun licence if held.[39] Shooting

royal game also led to a cancellation of any hunting permit. Those caught with skins in excess of the number allowed by the magistrate had those skins confiscated. Confiscated horns and skins were usually sold.

Some specific punishments meted out by the Ubombo magistrate in Maputaland in July 1903 included:[40]

- Killing a wildebeest: £10 fine or two months' hard labour plus confiscation of gun
- Killing a wildebeest: three months' hard labour
- Ten people convicted of killing a hippo: fines varying from £5 to £15 or between two and four months' hard labour plus three guns confiscated. Two African constables to be rewarded.[41]

Table 27 shows statistics of cases brought before the magistrate for contraventions of the game laws in Mahlabatini district, which included part of Umfolozi Game Reserve.[42] The conviction rate was 96%.

In the later colonial period one class of poacher that seems to have acted with impunity consisted of those in the Ndumo region, who crossed the Usuthu River from Mozambique to hunt the nyala. The locals were instructed to keep a watchful eye open for these hunters. Trooper Stewart stationed at the Ndumo police camp was active in trying to stop the killing of impala and nyala in this northern Maputaland region. When magistrate Stainbank, who advocated the appointment of two game wardens to counter the poaching menace, requested that Trooper Stewart state how many nyala and impala had been found dead or dying from the 'effects of violence' in the previous 12 months, the policeman noted:

Nyala   16
Impala   –

Two of these Nyala were killed by Tiger [leopard]. Those that were shot by permission are not included in this number. Of Impala none to my knowledge except those killed by the Wild Dog. I presume the magistrate means those that were illegally killed.[43]

Forced removals

A punishment handed out occasionally, but not contained in the Act, was the banishment of the culprit from one area to another. The first instance of this was as early as July 1887 when Melmoth Osborn suggested such a course of action to magistrate Arthur Shepstone after several hippo had been killed in the Lower Umfolozi division, 'to prevent further trespass on their part. This of course after you have dealt with the existing charges against them.' Seventeen years later the same practice was still being implemented when, after three nyala were killed in the Ingwavuma district, the guilty men were 'transferred to Kosi Lake'.[44]

In 1902 magistrate Griffin determined to make an example of Umbanda, 'head of his own kraal under the Chief Mavuso'. Eventually Umbanda admitted:

> One morning early I went out to cut some grass for thatching my hut and I took my gun with me. I went down towards the Lake St Lucia to the reeds on the banks. This was on the northern side as one looks from the Grace M.S. I saw two buffalo, a cow and a half grown calf, the calf had two horns this long (indicates a foot long). I stole up to them and as they were feeding I shot the calf dead with one shot. It was a bull calf. There were only the two, I saw no more. I then skinned the young buffalo alone, and got my children to help me carry the meat up.

For this Umbanda was fined £20 or imprisonment for six months. He went to prison. The farmer's old tower musket dated from his soldiering days for Cetshwayo: 'I used to hide the gun in the bush & not keep it at my kraal.' It was confiscated. More,

TABLE 27

OFFENCES UNDER THE GAME LAWS: MAHLABATINI

YEAR	NO. PERSONS CHARGED	NO. PERSONS CONVICTED	NO. PERSONS ACQUITTED
1899	4	4	0
1900	56	54	2
1901	42	40	2
Total	**102**	**98**	**4**

however, was to befall him, for Griffin determined to shift him, 'kraal and all to some place where he cannot kill more royal game'. Magistrate Armstrong at Ubombo agreed that on release Umbanda should be moved to a strip of country lying between Kosi Bay and the sea.[45]

Changed times

Outside the game reserves, there was cause for concern. Foxon's report dated 31 December 1900 made gloomy reading for anyone interested in nature conservation:

> I regret to say, however, the small game such as Reit buck, diker [duiker], steenbuck, and birds of all classes, which abounded over all parts, and particularly in close proximity to the magistracy, seem to have been entirely shot off or to have died from Rinderpest. The scarcity of game is most noticeable to any who lived in these parts about 3 or 4 years ago, especially on visiting the old hunting grounds, where one was sure to put up from four or five head of game and now not a single thing is to be found, but I trust by carefully watching, and refusing as many permits as possible, in the coming season to restore the game in some small way, up to its former number.[46]

Ten thousand kilometres away in London, published proceedings of the long-planned 'convention for the preservation of wild animals, birds, and fish in Africa' spoke loftily of the 'cause which is as noble as it is important'. The seven countries participating in the conference, which had concluded on 19 May 1900, signed what was in effect a declaration of intent, which included a prohibition on the hunting and killing of young elephant. Its pioneering significance has largely been ignored today as then, but for Natal and Zululand, who declined even to send a delegate, it did not seem terribly relevant to their immediate problems of nature conservation, particularly the diseases that haunted Zululand.[47]

As early as 1895 Charles Saunders was becoming gloomy about the very survival of big game in Zululand, given the looming threat of disease in the territory:

Secretary Bird

Anteater.

Feeding Apes

Owls

Hyæna Dogs

Blessbuck

Gnu

Hartebeest

Blue Gnu (Calf)

Zebra

Porcupine

I am very loath to do so, but I must say I am fast becoming a convert to the belief that fly or Nagana is entirely due to, and will only be found in districts frequented by game. I think it is quite possible the fly follows certain kinds of game and not all descriptions of it. I have hitherto done my best to persuade myself that the game had nothing to do with the disease, but when you come into this district [Ingwavuma] and see herds of cattle thriving in all the low country between the Usuthu and Pongola rivers, wherever there is no longer game, and again all through the low country from about fifteen miles [24 km] southwards of the Umkuzi River, whilst no cattle can live in the strip between, which is exactly similar country by all appearances, but still contains large herds of big game, it does seem conclusive proof that the game in some manner is the cause of the disease.

Not many years ago game was to be found in numbers in the low country between here and the Pongola River, and at that time no cattle would live there. Now that the game has been destroyed or driven away cattle thrive, and it is now as good a cattle district as can be found in Zululand.

It seems sad from a sportsman's point of view, and I must say I share this feeling to a very great extent but feel convinced if the country is to be inhabited the large game must be cleared from all the habitable parts.[48]

The impact of the early game protection measures in Zululand is difficult to determine, for enforcement varied from place to place as well as from one time to another depending on who was the local magistrate. As early as September 1890 the *Natal Mercury* was suggesting that the new laws regarding game were producing results:

I heard today of two koodoo being seen on the flats …[the] result of the Royal Games Act, or they would not have been so bold. I anticipate in a very few years (if the Game Law is strictly enforced) we shall see koodoo, quagga, waterbirds and possibly buffalo and rhinoceros about these plains, for they are only on the borders [of Zululand] now.

The increased supervision of hunting, the introduction of a closed hunting season, the total ban on hunting royal game in some seasons, such as in 1900, cannot but have eased the lot of the hard-pressed game in Zululand and prepared it in some degree – not least in building up numbers – for the onslaught of uncontrolled white shooting from 1919 onward.

The great success of the early conservation movement, however, was the game reserves. Though some were to be deproclaimed and hunting permitted in others, two truths remain: the concept of a reserve for game and the fact that there were areas where white and African agriculture was excluded. Dark days might follow in the early twentieth century, but an oasis for the future had been created.

REFERENCES

1 *Natal Government Gazette*, 1896, pp. 764–68.

2 Gush, *Mkhuze – The formative years*, p. 13.

3 KZNA, 1/EPI, letter book, report for 1895, fols. 591–2; and KZNA, ZA 30, minute paper R27/94, 16 June 1894.

4 Carruthers, 'Game protection in the Transvaal', p. 163.

5 Spencer, *British settlers in Natal*, 6, p. 190.

6 *Dictionary of South African Biography*, 5, pp. 276–7; *Natal Witness*, 15 December 1934; Spencer, *British settlers in Natal*, 6, p. 190; and Van Jaarsveld, *Mtunzini*, Chapter 6.

7 *Zululand Times*, 19 August 1910, quoted in Cubbin, 'An outline of game legislation in Natal 1866–1912', p. 43.

8 On the proposal to set up the remote outpost of empire see KZNA, ZA 42, Osborn to Sir C.B.H. Mitchell, 12 May 1890. See entry on Saunders in the *Dictionary of South African Biography*, 4, p. 535.

9 McCracken and McCracken, *Natal the garden colony*, pp. 40, 71, 74; and KZNA, NGM, Warren to A. Cooper, 17 June 1903.

10 KZNA, ZGH 827, fols. 165, 324.

11 KZNA, ZA 32, 1755/1899.

12 KZNA, ZA 44, Zululand letter book, no. 10, 9 February 1894.

13 KZNA, ZA 6, Despatch No. 117, 10 May 1888.

14 KZNA, ZGH 729, minute paper Z369/1890, 13 May 1890.

15 KZNA, ZGH 729, minute paper Z393/1890, 20 June 1890, and ZA 42, 20 June 1890, fol. 348.

16 ZGH 755, circular, 3 January 1894.

17 See, for example, KZNA, 1/EPI, letter book, 2 April 1890, and minute paper LU 133/1904, 25 March 1904; and 1/UBO, letter book, 9 August 1893, fol. 31, and minute paper ND 1929/07, 23 May 1907.

18 KZNA, 1/ESH, letter book, 11 April 1890, fol. 15; and ZGH 749, minute paper Z213/1893.

19 KZNA, 1/NGA, minute papers R784, 12 April 1890 and R823/1890, 18 April 1890.

20 KZNA, 1/UBO, letter book, 1 June 1896, fol. 434.

21 See for example KZNA, 1/EPI, letter books, 3 and 7 September 1899, fols. 442, 467 and 13 September 1900, fol. 313; minute paper R 1401/1900, 30 August 1900; 1/ING, minute papers ND 18/1897 and IN 75/1900; and 1/UBO, minute paper R 19/1892.

22 KZNA, 1/UBO, minute paper R 1721/1901.

23 KZNA, 1/UBO, minute paper VB 460/1902, 22 September 1902.

24 KZNA, 1/ING, minute paper R 2297/1903, 28 October 1903.

25 KZNA, 1/MTB, minute paper, 4 February 1902.

26 See, for example, KZNA, 1/ING minute papers R 587/1903 and R1173/1905.

27 KZNA, 1/MEL, minute paper R2 10/1891, 21 January 1891.

28 KZNA, Natal Museum papers, confidential letter, Warren to the provincial secretary, 19 November 1910.

'ANIMALS FROM SOUTH AFRICA FOR A EUROPEAN MENAGERIE', 1885 A page from the *South African Illustrated News* (13 June 1885) showing some of the animals transported annually from South Africa to zoos in Europe. Many of these were shipped out of Durban. The mortality rate of wild animals on the voyage must have been high.

29 The introduction of a closed season for hunting had been strongly supported in Natal by the Natal Game Protection Association, which pressed the colonial government to impress upon the African chiefs the existence of this restriction. See KZNA, S.N.A., minute paper SNA 621/1884, 4 September 1884.

30 KZNA, 1/EPI, 3/1/1/1/1, 13 August 1887, fols. 14–17, 22.

31 KZNA, 1/EPI, letter book, 15 December 1892, and report for December 1899, fols. 69–70.

32 KZNA, ZA 22, R 1334/94, 23 May 1894, fol. 9.

33 *Natal native affairs commission, 1906–1907: Evidence*, 26 May 1907, p. 1051.

34 KZNA, ZA 42, fol. 148.

35 KZNA, 1/MTB, minute paper, H 356/1895, 12 October 1895.

36 KZNA, NGA, minute paper, 4 December 1894.

37 KZNA, 1/MTB, minute paper M 56/1903, 24 January 1903.

38 See KZNA, 1/LUF, criminal record book, 1887 to 1889, 8 August 1887; KZNA, IRD, 2, IRD 829/1902.

39 See for example, KZNA, 1/UBO, minute paper CM 91/1896; letter book, 6 and 16 July 1896, fols. 475, 488, and minute paper R 4329, 10 December 1896.

40 KZNA, 1/UBO, criminal record book, 1903.

41 KZNA, 1/UBO, criminal record book, 1903.

42 KZNA, 1/MTB, 3/2/2, return of crimes and offences.

43 KZNA, 1/ING minute paper R 1813/1904.

44 See, KZNA, 1/EPI, minute paper MD 4/87, 30 July 1887 and 1/ING, minute paper IN 373/04, 15 September 1904.

45 KZNA, minute paper R 2459/1902, 9 September 1902.

46 KZNA, 1/EPI, letter book, 31 December 1900, fol. 404.

47 KZNA, GH 1034 and Public Record Office, London, FO 2/818. The seven signatories were the United Kingdom, Germany, France, Spain, Belgium, Italy and Portugal.

48 ZGH 789, Saunders to resident commissioner, 8 July 1895, fols. 4–5.

CHAPTER 12

Trouble in arcadia

THE TRANSPORT RIDERS A tough breed of men, as fluent in isiZulu as in English, the transport riders negotiated the primitive roads in Zululand, supplying the isolated trading stores and pushing north to the gold diggings around Pilgrim's Rest. KWAZULU-NATAL ARCHIVES (C 1031)

When the Colony of Natal acquired Zululand, four game reserves already existed, while other areas, most notably Maputaland, still had substantial quantities of large game and 'unspoilt' bush and indigenous forest. In addition, a raft of regulations was already in place to protect the forest, bush, bird life and animals of the new province. What was on paper was impressive, but no sooner were regulations and game reserves in place than there descended threats to the very future of the Zululand wilderness.

Disease

Disease among animals was not uncommon in nineteenth-century southern Africa, but in the closing years of the century, Zululand was particularly hard hit. In earlier decades there had been the scourge of lung sickness, of which there had been a serious outbreak in 1861, as well as horse sickness, tuberculosis and red-water fever. Such diseases, it was claimed, helped produce the environment where game and tsetse fly flourished and which resulted in 'their persistent foothold at the Mfolosi junction and in the Mhlatuze valley'. Writing in 1870, David Leslie spoke of the 'Unakane' or tsetse fly having spread in the Zulu country, 'driving out cattle from places where they had thriven from time immemorial'.[1] What his source was for this we do not know; nor do we know the source for his statement that for some years after Mpande came to power (post-1840) the country about the junction of the two Mfolozi rivers 'was thickly populated and full of cattle'. In searching for the first comment on tsetse fly, it has been pointed out that one reference to the fly must refer to about the 1840s.[2]

In the absence of more evidence, however, it is impossible to say when nagana appeared. Game and Zululand were synonymous. It is true that game filled a vacuum left by a reduction in cattle and the resulting bush encroachment. But the game was there before nagana and one has no reason to doubt that its numbers fluctuated greatly according to circumstances and conditions. That game had lived quite happily in the past in close proximity with cattle is possible. Speaking to Sir Marshall Clarke in 1895, Chief Nkamba pointed out that 'about his kraal there was none [nagana] nor had there ever been any – Game at one time of all descriptions abounded near his kraal, and although the cattle grazed over this same ground and mixed with it they suffered no ill effects'.[3]

There were, of course, different varieties of tsetse fly in southern Africa, and the famous 'sleeping sickness' was not the menace in Zululand that it was further north. Nor was Zululand noted, as was Matabeleland, for 'the perpetual bites of the swarming "Tse-tse" flies'.[4] It was the mosquitoes that tortured in Zululand.

But in the 1890s nagana combined with the effects of locust invasions and of a drought – not to mention the psychological scares of the Zulu defeat and gradual colonisation – to make Zululand a potential ecological and human disaster area. It was about the worst possible time to set about establishing game reserves and protecting fauna and forest. And yet if these protective measures had not been taken when they were, it is doubtful if much would have survived.

Nagana

Nagana is a wasting disease caused by a trypanosome parasite which kills domestic stock and which is also present among wild ungulates.[5] It is transmitted by the tsetse fly, *Glossina pallidipes*. Vaughan-Kirby claimed nagana was carried by buffalo, wildebeest, kudu, zebra and the like, as well as by hyena and bushpig.[6]

As already mentioned, nagana had been present in Zululand for many years. The early white hunters had therefore soon learnt to be wary of taking their oxen into the 'fly country' and

frequently left the wagons on high ground, proceeding to the lower areas on foot. The effects of nagana had been dramatic, forcing black farmers in some regions to move and restricting the areas of their activities in others. Hunting and driving away game helped somewhat, but the reality was that, when malaria was added to the equation, it was noticeable that some areas of Zululand were sparsely populated. Here the game thrived. As the astute magistrate John Knight observed in 1891, 'The tsetse may therefore be looked upon as a kind of "fingerpost" indicating to man how far he may go with his cattle, and no further.' He also prophetically warned that the 'fly' would be used by those who wanted the abolition of the game laws 'to gratify their own greed for sport'.[7]

Some locals believed nagana was picked up by cattle from the saliva of game, especially kudu and zebra, left on grass commonly grazed by both animals. White people argued as to whether the tsetse fly was to blame or whether the disease thrived in 'conditions peculiar to the presence of large game'. As Saunders's comments have shown, the authorities were increasingly suspicious of the tsetse fly which was ever associated with large game. Proclamation 5 of 1893 had among other things downgraded from royal game to closed-season game such 'suspect' animals as kudu, zebra, reedbuck, waterbuck and wildebeest in an attempt to reduce game numbers and thus 'check' the spread of nagana.[8] The following March the first official government-approved game drive was organised in central Zululand. This occurred after pressure from the ever-troublesome farmers of the Proviso B block of farms in the Emthonjaneni district in central Zululand, a legacy of the Boer–Dinuzulu alliance of the early 1880s.[9] A dangerous precedent had been set.

The role of the tsetse fly in the transmission of nagana

In 1894 the government got the magistrates to start organising large hunts in which the African population would drive away the big game from settled areas and from roads.[10] In December 1894 Surgeon Major David Bruce, with a travel allowance for himself and his wife, was seconded on full pay from the medical army staff to Natal government service. His task was to 'make a bacteriological investigation of the disease nagana in Zululand'.[11] Then, and again from 1896 to 1897, from his station on top of the Lebombo Mountains, Bruce studied the tsetse fly and its relationship with wild and domesticated animals. He worked in that area which had been the old Pongola–Mkuze Game Reserve. He was to be credited with finally establishing the role of the tsetse fly in the transmission of nagana from infected wild game to domestic animals. As J.A. Pringle points out in his pioneering book *The conservationists and the killers*, Bruce proved that *Typanosoma* was the cause of nagana; that wild animals provided the reservoir for this parasite; and that tsetse fly transmitted the parasite from infected to healthy animals.[12]

Bruce was a serving officer in the British Army Medical Service. His appointment had been made at the initiative of Hely-Hutchinson. Writing to Sir William Thiselton-Dyer in July 1896, Hely-Hutchinson confided:

> I cannot get them [the Natal government] to spend money on the locust fungus, even. I started the tsetse-fly enquiry as Governor of Zululand, off my own bat, and the whole cost is paid out of Zululand funds. I got rather snubbed by the C.O. [Colonial Office] when I first proposed it: and only managed it by getting the War Office to send out Bruce as a member of the Natal Garrison, and then by applying for his services to the General here.[13]

A young kudu, half tame, was purchased, and experiments were made with its blood. The plan was to capture other wild animals. But all this would take time and 'cost money'. A few months later Hely-Hutchinson was privately conceding to the director of Kew that even if contact between cattle could be avoided, 'I expect the game will be too much for us … It is a dismal prospect. Indiscriminate slaughter of cattle was one of the causes of the Matabili outbreak: and we shall have to be very careful.'[14]

Bruce's progress was slow and one suspects his temper was wearing thin. That summer (1896–1897) the tsetse fly came up the Lebombo Mountains so Bruce had to stop his work. The governor's comment was that it provided for Bruce 'to get a little much-needed change' in Pietermaritzburg. By now there was clearly animosity between the major and the local magistrate. An attempt to get the scientist to toe the line concerning a hunting permit for the animals he had to kill met with the following response from Bruce: 'This is to inform you that I do not consider that you have any authority to cancel this permit, and also that if you carry out your threat of arresting me on my non-compliance with your order, that you do so at your own peril.'[15]

All was not well in the remote mountain-top hamlet of Ubombo.

Game protection vs. cattle ranching

In May 1898, six months after Natal acquired Zululand, Harry Binns, the colony's prime minister, wrote a minute concerning game protection. The section on Zululand ran as follows:

> There are two reserves within which game is absolutely protected at present. There are two other reserves in which all shooting is prohibited except under special licence from the Government. In other parts of the Province [of Zululand] the killing of Game is allowed under ordinary licence from the magistrate of the Division. Elephant and white rhinoceri are absolutely protected from destruction, as are regards hippopotami and black rhinoceri special permits may be granted by the Governor to persons to shoot not more than two of each in any one year.

> But in view of the established fact that the fly follows the game, and that cattle cannot exist in the areas frequented by the fly, it becomes a question as to whether the Government will be justified in preserving the game at the cost of clearing the stock from those districts of Zululand where fly prevails.[16]

For some the solution seemed simple. Get rid of the big game and Zululand could be thrown open to cattle ranching once the Natal settlers got their hands on the territory.

Horse sickness, locusts and drought

But there was more. Horse sickness had been a problem in Zululand for many years, which is why oxen were the staple draught animals in the lower eastern parts of the territory. Not that this stopped the more daring taking horses into these unhealthy areas. Some believed that animals that had been

PLANT HUNTERS IN COLONIAL ZULULAND In 1895 John Medley Wood, the curator of the Durban Botanic Gardens, discovered a new, and as it turned out, unique cycad at the edge of Ongoye forest in southern Zululand. Only male stems were found. No other specimen of the *Encephalartos woodii* has ever been discovered. In this photograph Wood's deputy, James Wylie, prepares to move some of the stems. They first dragged them by oxen and then transported by rail to the Durban Botanic Gardens, where four of the original stems are still growing.
KWAZULU-NATAL HERBARIUM, DURBAN

affected and recovered or had been regularly dosed with arsenic would survive a return visit to the area. This was, however, often an expensive assumption and even the sensible Saunders lost horses which he had risked taking onto the Maputaland flats. What did seem to survive longer than most draught animals was the unfortunate donkey, which gradually spread in use, descendants of which can still be seen in the Maputaland region today.[17]

During 1894 and 1895 there was drought in Zululand and great hardship was experienced among many African communities. Matters were not helped by an influx of locusts in 1895 and 1896 and by many horses dying.[18] Locusts were certainly not new to Zululand. Zulu tradition had it that the locust first entered Zululand in 1829 as revenge sent by a chief whose territory the Zulus had invaded. Another story, possibly conflated with the first, was that Chief Mjaji sent the locust invasion in the time of Mpande, but withdrew the locusts after an appeal from an emissary. And certainly one traveller in Zululand in 1850 noted, 'A great number of Locusts flew over us in Clouds … John went out after buck but was obliged to return back on account of the locusts being so numerous.'

Angas has a plate in his famous book of a 'snowstorm' of locusts, which must be dated about September 1847. Now in 1895 they were back with a vengeance. Writing from Ekutandaneni on 11 September 1896, the young Norwegian missionary Nils Schaug commented: 'the country is swarming with locusts which eat up everything that is planted. Some days they come in such swarms that they darken the sun.'[19]

The officials were keen in the winter of 1896 to restrict hunting in the Ubombo district, especially on the flats, so there would be sufficient game in the ensuing spring 'to provide a means of destroying young locusts'.[20] The locusts returned in 1898 – and again in 1903 and 1906.

Drought also returned periodically over the next decade in varying degrees of severity. Hely-Hutchinson was worried about the suffering in Zululand and in 1896 corresponded with Sir William Thiselton-Dyer, the director of Kew Gardens in London, about the possible nutritious value of some indigenous plants in Zululand. Concerning the loss of Zulu cattle the depressed governor observed that all the Zulus' 'social arrangements depend on them'. A year later the governor was equally worried, especially about conditions in the Ubombo district where nagana, locust and drought had all taken their toll and where he feared 'that under such circumstances there must always be a large increase in infant mortality'. He granted leave to the African population 'to kill all the game they could', but in correspondence with Thiselton-Dyer added that 'the main source of their food supply appears to have been the seeds, fruits, leaves, and roots of the plants which grow wild in the bush'. Hely-Hutchinson was

interested in botany and indeed was one of the main proponents in advancing the interests of botanic stations in the West Indies when he was a governor there.[21]

So interested was Hely-Hutchinson that he had specimens collected of the indigenous plants being eaten for famine relief by the locals in the Ubombo district. The curator of Durban Botanic Gardens, John Medley Wood, identified these 'as far as has been possible'.[22] The 37 plants are listed in Table 28.

There had been nagana, horse sickness, locusts and drought, but worse was to come to Zululand.

Rinderpest

Neither nagana nor horse sickness, locust nor drought was, however, to have as devastating an impact on Zululand in the closing years of the nineteenth century as the arrival from the north of rinderpest. This disease not only decimated the Zulu national herd but also hit many species of game, especially the buffalo, kudu and eland. And this at the time the game reserves were being established. The disease had made its way down from north of the Zambezi River.

In March 1896 the authorities issued a cautionary warning about rinderpest and spelt out the symptoms of the disease. It ordered the destruction of infected cattle, the burial of carcasses and the isolation of infected herds.[23] Meanwhile in the Transvaal Republic most of the hunting legislation was abolished and ammunition was being handed out so 'the destitute could procure food when livestock died'.[24]

After Bond's Drift between Zululand and Natal was closed to cattle, a farmers' meeting was held at Melmoth on 29 October 1896. This was attended by 42 farmers from the Proviso B block of farms, and two magistrates. Items which dominated discussion were the rinderpest, the closure of the drift, and nagana. It was claimed that tsetse fly had not appeared in the region until the arrival of big game three years earlier. One of the resolutions carried read: 'That the Govt. be respectfully requested to allow the large game in the Entonjaneni District to be shot or destroyed without a licence – and that no game preserve be reserved in the Entonjaneni district.'

Marshall Clarke, who had so recently been in support of setting up the Zululand game reserves, was now defeatist in confiding to Hely-Hutchinson: 'As regards "Nagana" the farmers have made a strong point; before long in my opinion large game in Zululand will have to be destroyed in the interest of the inhabitants.'

The governor, however, was not to be panicked. He authorised hunts to drive large game away from the area, but on the suggested extermination of game, the most that this member of the Irish ascendancy class would concede was, 'If this measure

TABLE 28

PLANTS AND FRUITS USED AS FOOD BY THE AFRICAN POPULATION OF UBOMBO,
c. 1896–7, AND IDENTIFIED BY JOHN MEDLEY WOOD

PLANT	GIVEN ZULU NAME (1898)	REMARKS
Aloe cooperi	icena	The inside of the stalk is scooped out and cooked.
Strychnos gerrardi [possibly black monkey orange (*S. madagascariensis*)]	umkwapa	The inside of this fruit, without the seed, is roasted.
Sclerocarya caffra [marula]	umganu	The fruit of this tree is made into beer. Pulp also eaten in Natal.
Cucurbitaceae	isisimbi	The leaves are cooked as a spinach with other herbs. [Note: In fact, it was usually the tuber that was eaten.]
Leucas sp.	idedelanyati	Leaves used as a spinach.
Leucas glabrata	umhlonyana	Leaves used as a spinach.
Hypoxis filiformis	isinongwe	The roots of this plant are boiled and eaten.
Nymphaea nouchali syn. *N. stellata* [blue waterlily]	izibo	A water lily. The tube is boiled for a short time. Also eaten in Natal
Maerua nervosa syn. *Niebuhria nervosa*	matandana	The fruit of this plant is eaten.
Cephalandra	igegetyhana	Fruit eaten.
Scilla, probably *S. lanceaefolia* [*Ledebouria revoluta* – common or waxy-leaved *Ledebouria*]	floba	The bulb is cooked.
Douyalis caffra syn. *Aberia caffra* [Kei apple]	umqokolo	A thorny tree; fruit eaten.
Scientific name not given	mcavusana	A tree, the berries of which are eaten.
Commelina sp.	intangamana	A plant; leaves eaten.
Ophioglossum capense	isankuntshana	A small plant; leaves eaten.
Vangueria infausta [wild medlar]	iviyo	A small tree; fruit eaten. Also eaten in Natal by Africans and whites.
Strychnos [monkey apple]	umpela	The berries of tree eaten.
Lantana rugosa [bird's brandy]	uguguvama	A small plant, the berries of which are eaten.
Ximenia caffra [sourplum]	amatunduluka	A tree; the fruit eaten/seeds contain oil.
Cucurbitaceae	untshungu	A creeper; the leaves make a spinach.
Aizoon canariense	matsana	A small plant; leaves eaten.
Celosia trigyna	isihlaza	Leaves and flowers eaten.
Scientific name not given	umpema	The same, I think, as Lantana rugosa.
Sarcostemma viminale [melktou]	mabelebela	Stems and fruit eaten. Commonly eaten by African women and children in Natal.
Riocreuxia torulosa [candle-vine]	ugwapa	Small plant; leaves eaten
Cucumis sp.	isendelendtya	A creeper; fruit eaten.
Ophioglossum reticulatum	isankuntana	Small plant; leaves eaten.
Solanum nigrum [black nightshade]	ixabaxaba	Leaves eaten – also berries.
Sonchus oleraceus [thistle]	bis	No remarks given.
Argyrolobium marginatum	izintondo	A small plant – the roots eaten both cooked and uncooked.
Cucurbitaceae	utshwalabe-nyoni	A creeper – leaves eaten.
Chenopodium ambrosioides [sandworm plant]	ibigicana	A plant, leaves cooked and eaten.
Trichilia dregeana [forest mahogany]	umkuhlo	A large tree – fruit eaten. Seeds contain oil which is used occasionally by Africans in Natal.
Leguminous plant, indeterminable	ubukobe	A small plant, roots cooked and eaten.
Scientific name not given	umsobe	Berries of plant eaten.
Scientific name not given	makukutwana	A creeper – leaves eaten as spinach.
Ehretia rigida syn. *E. hottentotica* [puzzle bush]	umgxele	A tree, the berries of which are eaten.
Lycium acutifolium	umbilibili	A small plant – the leaves eaten.

'ON A SMALL SAND BANK STOOD THE TWO NOBLE KOODOO BULLS AT BAY'. An illustration from William Drummond's classic *The large game* (1875), showing a hunting scene on the Phongola River where it dissects the Lebombo Mountains and enters Maputaland. Large sycamore figs and smaller acacia trees line the river banks. Drummond's dogs are in the river after the kudu – not without risk as it was here. Drummond lost a dog to a crocodile. Drummond described Phongola Poort as 'one of the most beautiful and thoroughly characteristic African scenes that I ever saw'. This area is now covered by the Jozini Dam.

[hunts] proves insufficient I shall be prepared to take into consideration the desirability of taking further steps in the matter.'[25]

On 23 April 1897, a few days before the Zululand game reserves were 'reestablished', a complete ban was placed on all cattle moving from Zululand to Natal. By then the situation was serious. The magistrate of Lower Umfolozi was quite blunt:

> I would strongly urge that the big game be destroyed without delay when I venture to say it will be found that the fly will disappear with the big game at least within a few months of the destruction of the game. This would then open a large section of the country for occupation. Besides there is no doubt that coal is found therein and indications point to the preserve of other minerals.[26]

This would be a well-worn cry in the years to come and even, to some extent, to the present day. But fortunately not all magis-trates at the time felt that way, nor indeed did the authorities. In 1898 they were so disturbed by the decline in game in Zululand, including Maputaland, that a ban was placed that season on the killing of any royal game.[27] This was followed in March 1899 with a two-year ban on any hunting – by Africans or whites – of either kudu or buffalo. Within two years the replacement of nagana by rinderpest as the public-enemy disease had in the mind of the authorities changed the kudu from being villain to victim.

Between 1895 and 1904 rinderpest was to be found in Zululand at one time or another in varying degrees of ferocity, initially more so in Zululand proper than in Maputaland.[28] By 1902 a 16 km exclusion zone for cattle was being created along the Maputaland–Mozambique border.[29] But the disease toll got worse, for after the rinderpest came the tick-borne East Coast Fever which also attacked cattle. Charles Saunders thought that some 80 per cent of cattle in Zululand had died.[30] It is as well that the British had established the game reserves when they did.

Hely-Hutchinson now gave permission for Africans, but not whites, to kill all the game they could.

The decrease in the number of cattle in Zululand, the establishment of a new game reserve which covered much of the Hlabisa magisterial district and the new game law of 1905, all led to an increase in game numbers in the opening years of the twentieth century. But as game numbers increased there came a gradual increase in the number of cases of nagana, which had noticeably declined in the closing years of the old century and the opening years of the new, when the rinderpest had been at its worse. With the railhead reaching Somkhele in 1903 and the opening up from 1906 onwards of large tracts of Zululand to the white commercial farming of sugar cane and cattle, the prospect for game suddenly looked bleak again.

The reaction was not slow in coming. The abolition in 1907 of the Umdletshe Game Reserve and of the newly created Hlabisa Game Reserve was due to the misfortune of a wagon road crossing them, and the resultant death of transport riders' oxen. With such fly-attracting game as the 'wandering' kudu, wildebeest, waterbuck, buffalo and zebra, it is little wonder these reserves did not survive. By early 1907 a team was out destroying game along the main road which crossed the Hlabisa district.

There was a sliver of a silver lining for the Zululand wilderness in the sad story of the rinderpest outbreak. It was said that oxen, the draught animals used by sawyers, had by the end of 1898 become too scarce and expensive to make the timber trade pay. Thus for a while the indigenous forests benefited from a decline in timber extraction.[31]

REFERENCES

1   Leslie, *Among the Zulus and Amatongas*, pp. 183–7.

2   Ellis, 'Game conservation in Zululand', p. 8.

3   KZNA, ZA 46, Resident Commissioner's diary, 10 August 1895.

4   Royal Geographical Society, London: Selous to Mrs Bates, 10 November 1882.

5   For detailed accounts of the struggle against nagana see Pringle, *The conservationists and the killers*; and Minnaar, 'Nagana, big-game drives and the Zululand game reserves'.

6   Vaughan-Kirby, 'Game and game preservation in Zululand', p. 387.

7   KZNA: 1/MEL, minute paper PB 285/1891.

8   KZNA: ZGH 755, R 287/1894. Colonial Secretary to Governor, 2 February 1894. See also ZGH 43, letter book, report March 1891, fols. 201, 285–6.

9   Duminy and Guest, *Natal and Zululand*, pp. 214–15.

10 KZNA: ZGH 755, circular 3 January 1894 and 1/MEL, PB14/1894.

11 KZNA: ZGH 762, no. 50, Z 28/1895.

12 See Pringle, *The conservationists and the killers*, Chapter 9. Mrs Bruce accompanied her husband to this remote location on the top of the Lebombo Mountains.

13 Kew Archive, South African letters, vol.190, Hely-Hutchinson to Dyer, 13 July 1896. See also letters dated 8 and 23 September 1896, 15 March and 27 October 1897.

14 Kew Archive, South African letters, vol. 190, Hely-Hutchinson to Thiselton-Dyer, 8 September 1896; and KZNA: ZGH 823, Hely-Hutchinson to colonial secretary, 8 August 1896.

15 KZNA: 1/UBO, UB 165A/1897, 13 May 1897.

16 GH 1034, Minute No. 10, 13 May 1898.

17 KZNA, ZGH 789, Saunders to resident commissioner, 8 July 1895; and *Swaziland, Tongaland and Northern Zululand*, pp. 28, 87.

18 See Brooks, *Natal*, p. 142. In June 1895 Saunders reported that of the 38 horses, 21 had already died. See KZNA, ZGH 789, 1 and 3 June 1895.

19 See ZA 46, diary, entry 10 August 1895; Angas, *The kaffirs illustrated*, plate 22; and Hale (ed.), *Norwegian missionaries in Natal and Zululand*, p. 198. The anti-locust legislation introduced into the Natal parliament (Act Number 33 of 1895) in 1895 did not apply to Zululand.

20 KZNA, 1/UBO, letter book, 1 June 1896 and KZNA: ZGH 769, minute paper R 1790/1896, 2 May 1896.

21 McCracken, *Gardens of Empire*, Chapter 2.

22 Kew Archive, South African letters, 190, Hely-Hutchinson to Thiselton-Dyer, 8 September 1896 and 27 October 1897.

23 KZNA: 1/MEL, PB 206/1896, circular, 20 March 1896.

24 Carruthers, 'Dissecting the myth', p. 267 and 'Game protection in the Transvaal', p.167; and *Staats Courant*, 837, 4 June 1896.

25 KZNA, 1/MEL, minute papers PB 532/1896 and PB 556/1896. In fact, three hunts had already been held in October with the aim of driving away the game. A further hunt was organised in November 1896. See also Minnaar, 'Nagana, big-game drives and the Zululand game reserves (1890s–1950s)', pp. 13–14.

26 KZNA, 1/EPI, letter book, report for 1897, fol. 346

27 KZNA, 1/MEL, PB 181/99, circular 30 March 1899 and 1/MTB, letter book, 27 June 1898. See also, Campbell Collections, Miller papers, Von Wissell 'Reminiscences', fol. 15.

28 KZNA, ZGH 769, minute paper, 4 April 1896.

29 KZNA: 1/ING, minute paper R 590/02, 15 November 1902.

30 Curson, 'Preservation of game in South Africa', p. 410 n.

31 *Natal Blue Book for 1898*, BB15.

Debenham & Smith, Photo.   Walker & Boutall Ph.Sc

Sincerely yours

Magasamba

CHAPTER 13

Postscript: white settlers and white elephants

The Boers' New Republic, founded in 1884, sliced a large, rich portion of grazing land away from Zulu control. Yet the effect of this might have been exacerbated if circumstances had been different, and widespread white settlement to the rest of Zululand had come in the 1880s. As it was, a white farming community, the so-called Proviso B block, did exist in the Entonjaneni district. Had the whole territory been divided up into white farmland in the 1880s there can be little doubt that there would have been no game reserves and no big game in Zululand today.

The delay of a generation in the agrarian colonisation of Zululand proved, in the long run, to be the saving of the Zululand wilderness, preserving at least the isolated pockets that remain to this day. This delay was caused by a combination of factors including the abortive attempt to partition Zululand into fiefdoms in the 1880s; the period of direct colonial rule in the 1890s; and the five-year delay in permitting white commercial farming after Zululand was handed over to the white colonists of Natal, a delay aided by disruption caused by the fighting of the Anglo-Boer War (1899–1902).

Much has been made of the wanton slaughter of game in Zululand in the post-1910 or Union period, which was rightly denounced as being a short-sighted and crude response to the continuing threat of nagana;[1] but several facts have been ignored in this denunciation. First, large quantities of game must still have existed in Zululand given that more than 200 000 head of game, mainly wildebeest and zebra, were to be slaughtered in these years. Second, though game reserves came and went, and though in reality these were sometimes paper exercises, the notion that there were game reserves in Zululand, and that in some form they would remain, was established in the public mind. This was the legacy the Victorians left nature conservation in South Africa.

The core of the problem was that it was only at the eleventh hour that public opinion in South Africa began to take game conservation seriously. This was especially so in the Eastern Cape and Natal, both of which should have been at the forefront of the movement. But white South Africa was a frontier society with a frontier mentality. In many respects, in fact, when it came to game, there was no fundamental difference between the attitude of rural African and rural white society: hunting wild animals for sport or for the pot was legitimate; wild beasts could be a threat to crops and even to human life. Nature could be respected, but it was often feared. It was not a partner because it was too much of a threat. It had to be conquered.

Speaking to the British colonial secretary in London in 1905, Sir S.H. Whitbread remarked, 'Of course, in South Africa there is no effective public opinion to enforce and support such things as game laws.'[2] To an extent, that had been correct in the case of game preservation, certainly in Zululand, where if it had not been for the officials – governor, resident commissioner, magistrates and the early game rangers – little would have been saved. On the other hand, Natal was famous in the Victorian era for its amateur botanists and its 'plant craze'.[3]

For a brief time in the 1880s a Natal Game Protection Association existed with Sam Beningfield as president, but it did not make a great stir and did not survive long. In the Edwardian era, attitudes did begin to change, though the advocates of game preservation were still not great in number. Nor were they environmental conservationists in the modern sense of the word. Their object was simply to preserve the game, or at least to save as much as was possible given the advance of 'progress'. Their values were those of their society, though their botanical and zoological knowledge was, even with the advances of the succeeding century,

MAQAQAMBA Frederick Vaughan-Kirby was an Ulsterman who made the African bush his home, first as a hunter and later as a conservator of game. Less well-connected than some of his contemporaries, Kirby should have been appointed conservator of game in Zululand in the 1890s. The failure by the British authorities to make such an appointment did not help the cause of conservation in early twentieth-century Zululand. But Kirby's subsequent appointment to the post in 1912 gave the Zululand game reserves a champion in difficult times. *KIRBY, IN THE HAUNT OF WILD GAME*

CHANGED TIMES The advent of the railway and the motorcar in Zululand meant the oxwagon would soon be obsolete, even if the oxwagon could better negotiate what went for roads in the region.

probably greater than that of many modern educated visitors to a Zululand game reserve.

In the case of Natal, the most noted early twentieth-century advocate for the wild fauna of Zululand was the determined Dr Warren, director of the Natal Museum in Pietermaritzburg from 1903 to 1934. Ernest Warren, who for some ten years sent collectors into Zululand, believed that what was needed there was national parks.[4] In 1909 he was the driving force behind the formation of the Natal and Zululand Game Protection Association, which found an ally in the Transvaal Game Protection Association.[5] The name of Alfred Duchesne Millar of Durban also deserves honourable mention as a pioneer of game protection in the Edwardian era. Such naturalists replaced to some degree – but, it has to be said, not as effectively – the imperial administrators who had been the key element in establishing a nature conservation policy in Zululand.

As the early decades of the new century passed and the uncontrolled slaughter continued, there did emerge in Natal a public revulsion against such destruction simply to placate a handful of farmers whom the government should clearly never have settled where they did. Writing in 1924 Dr H.H. Curson commented, 'It is doubtful whether controversy so bitter as that shown in Zululand has been experienced anywhere else where the authorities have endeavoured to protect the fauna.'[6]

The hero of nature conservation in this dangerous period after the Union was that veteran of the Mpumalanga bush, Frederick Vaughan-Kirby, who used a motorbike to visit the game reserves, which must have made travelling easier over difficult terrain. Mfohloza, or Maqaqamba as he was alternatively known, was chief conservator of game in Zulu-land in August 1911.[7] Later Vaughan-Kirby was given a white assistant. And if living at the nearest telephone and cable station at Nongoma, miles away from the game reserves, was an inconvenience, Vaughan-Kirby and his small but dedicated African staff nonetheless did as well as any could, given their parsimonious budget and the political forces that were arrayed against them.

In 1928 Vaughan-Kirby retired and was succeeded by Roden Symons. He resigned in 1930 and was in turn succeeded by the legendary Captain Harold B. Potter.

White commercial farming

The famous Zululand Delimitation Commission, under the guiding hand of Charles Saunders, sat from August 1902, reporting in 1904. Zululand was divided up like a jigsaw into areas of Zulu settlement and white farming regions: one and a half million hectares and one million hectares respectively. Most of the indigenous forests were placed under the central Pretoria government while the game reserves fell under the provincial government in Pietermaritzburg. This saved the game reserves.[8]

Once the broad areas had been agreed upon by the Natal parliament, land commissions were then set up to determine the effective use of the white farming areas. Farm surveys also had to be undertaken. All this took time, so that different parts of Zululand were transferred to white ownership at different times. Farms in the Mthunzini district were allocated in 1906, those around Mtubatuba in 1911, and so on. Needless to say, the longer the delay, the longer any game remaining on those lands survived.[9] The decision to settle former First World War soldiers on 72 farms at Ntambanana, south of Umfolozi Game Reserve, proved a fateful and unfortunate one. Indeed, given the nature of the area and its ecological history, it was a foolish decision.

In 1903 Finlay accurately forecast:

Can you blame us who love the wild animals of our country if we have a secret hope that many a year may pass before Zululand … is apportioned out into farms, and that the advance of cruel civilisation in that little corner of the great African continent may be checked and retarded? For surely no sooner will the Colonist have established himself in the country than he will raise a cry against the conservation of game, even in defined areas; he will argue that, as long as buffalo, wildebeest, waterbuck, rhino, and other large animals are preserved, so long will tse-tse fly remain to kill his span of trek-oxen whenever he has to pass through the littoral regions on his way to or from Durban; the hippo, he says, must go, as it destroys his plantations of sugarcane and eats his crops. Thus the settler will prevail, and Zululand be devastated of her rare and beautiful wild animals.[10]

By 1912 generous bounty rewards – 'the first non-protective measures' – were being handed out for killing what the farmers considered vermin:[11]

- £1 each for any cheetah, jackal or wild dog
- 15s. for a leopard
- 10s. for a crocodile
- 5s. for a baboon
- 1s. for a mamba

Of these the mamba and the crocodile – 'these loathsome creatures' – were the most threatening to human life, with fatalities being reported in the Zululand press.[12] This hatred of the crocodile was not confined to British Zululand; in German West Africa a consistent campaign was under way to shoot as many crocodiles as possible.[13]

Unfortunately for the authorities – though fortunately for the wild creatures – this bounty scheme proved too costly and in 1914 it was suspended. The Nkandla magistrate grumbled that vermin were no longer being destroyed and that 'Baboons and monkeys prove very destructive to the crops. Guinea fowl too, should be classed as vermin, being very destructive to the young mealies.'[14]

It would be naive not to imagine that it was just the threat of nagana that motivated the persistent attacks on Zululand's game reserves. Greed also had its place. Reg Gush in his history of Mkhuze Game Reserve quotes a 1914 government official based at Ubombo writing of the new game reserve:

… this is ideal country for cattle, having the appearance of an English park … a few years ago it was heavily stocked with cattle, but it is now given up entirely to game. There are thousands and thousands of wildebeest roaming around this area, and a large number of game, vermin, carnivore and other wild beasts. It is a shocking waste of excellent country.[15]

The last Zululand elephant

In a sense the Zululand elephant has never died out, for a remnant of the original herds that roamed Maputaland, and no doubt further south and west, still exists in the 30 000 ha Tembe Elephant Park on the South African–Mozambique border. The virtual demise of the elephant population in most of Zululand was regretted by some. In 1903 one finds a rather pathetic plea from the Umfolozi magistrate who begged for an elephant in his district. In fact, little did he know that he already had one, well hidden away at the coast.[16]

The last elephant in the St Lucia/Hluhluwe–Umfolozi region was the one mentioned previously, which lived for many years unmolested in the Cape St Lucia Game Reserve, or Dukuduku Game Reserve as it was sometimes called. In 1916 this animal was shot by a local, for which crime he received six months' hard labour. According to Vaughan-Kirby, it was a month before the incident became known so the skin had deteriorated. With the help of a sugar farmer, Kirby collected up as much of the skeleton

TABLE 29

ZULULAND GAME DRIVES AND GAME SLAUGHTER PROGRAMMES

YEAR	AREA	APPROXIMATE NUMBER OF GAME KILLED
1910	Hlabisa and Ubombo districts	Wildebeest, plus 3 (black) rhino and 7 kudu
1910	Ubombo district	'1 lion, 7 black rhino and large number of wildebeest'
1915–16	Southern Zululand and public roads – certain game can be killed by transport riders and travellers	Unknown
1916	13 Special Shooting Areas (SSA) established, many bordering game reserves (Prov. Notices 74 & 103)	Unknown – scattered game, which made the problem of nagana worse
1917	Ubombo district	25 000 + wildebeest. Skins selling at 1s. 3d. per lb. No rhino, hippo or nyala to be shot
1919	Ingwavuma	Unknown, but large quantities of game destroyed
1920	Umfolozi area	c. 5 000 head of game
1927	Ntambanana	2 000 + zebra
1929–31	Umfolozi area Elsewhere	26 539 head of game 6 045 head of game
1934	'Last great ihlambo hunt'	
1943	All areas except Hluhluwe Game Reserve	138 529 head of game
1942–50	Umfolozi and Mkuze Game Reserves	70 332 head of game
1943–50	Mkuze reserve area	38 552 head of game, including 17 060 impala, 7 436 grey duiker, 6 726 wildebeest, 4 385 nyala, 434 red duiker, 80 suni & 2 black rhino

as possible. The tusks were stolen from where they had been placed for safe keeping by the police, but two African detectives traced them to an employee of the South African Railways at Somkhele. He was arrested and pleaded guilty to the theft.[17]

The game drives

The issuing of private hunting licences continued after the colonial era, and the nimrods of Zululand, such as George Higg or the perennial Frank Green, could be guaranteed some press coverage once they had bagged their hapless hippopotami.[18] The suppression of the 1906 African insurrection may in an indirect way have affected the killing of game in Zululand. The officer commanding troops in Zululand, Colonel Sir Duncan McKenzie, having imposed martial law, set about disarming the African population. But the resultant decline in firearms in the province was soon to be reversed by the authorities themselves, with the precise objective of killing as much game as possible.

With the return of nagana as a widespread problem in Zululand the authorities turned to the old and crude expedient of organising game hunts or drives. Sometimes these were carried out by professional hunters, often they were not. Gun-toting types from all over South Africa were drawn like sharks to

a bloody killing frenzy. It should be remembered that smaller drives had been organised in the colonial period so the concept was not new. What was new was the scale of the slaughter and the acceptance by the authorities that game would not be permitted to survive outside the designated game reserves. How successful these drives were in driving game away from commercial farming areas is a matter for conjecture. In 1911 one government official commented:

I may say I have been convinced that 'drives' of game are no use, as it returns to its old haunts in a short time. In a conversation with Mr Fynney, Magistrate, Ubombo, he told me that every horse and mule, with the exception of one horse, which had been used during the 'drive' recently held in his Division, had died of 'Nagana'.[19]

Table 29 illustrates the major game drives and game slaughter programmes in the twentieth century. It does not include some smaller game drives such as those in 1919 and 1920.

By 1929 gangs of professional hunters – one white hunter with 10 black hunters under him – were working as teams on the grim task. The veld was littered with the rotting carcasses of the carnage. These game drives did not, of course, kill off nagana, but

TABLE 30

NUMBER OF GAME DESTROYED IN 1929–30 EXTERMINATION CAMPAIGN

SPECIES	IN UMFOLOZI GAME RESERVE	NEAR UMFOLOZI GAME RESERVE	TOTAL
Zebra	69	15 130	15 199
Warthog	216	3 456	3 672
Duiker	10	2 987	2 997
Bushbuck	22	2 173	2 195
Wildebeest	26	664	690
Waterbuck	26	504	530
Reedbuck	0	390	390
Steenbuck	1	306	307
Kudu	2	286	288
Bushpig	0	129	129
Buffalo	5	120	125
Mountain reedbuck	0	12	12
Klipspringer	0	5	5
Total	**377**	**26 162**	**26 539**

merely scattered the game. They were a blood sacrifice to try to pacify the angry farmers. Nor did the game drives come cheap. At the end of the day, it would probably have been cheaper for the government to buy out the farmers. What the slaughter did achieve was to create a cowboy ethos in Zululand, which extended into the reserves themselves. 'A plausible excuse for the butchers', as Warren said.[20] Colonel Jack Vincent, the father of the Natal Parks Board, was correct when writing of the 1929 game drives that '… some of the men initially employed were of a type who quickly set up private rackets, in such activities as illegal selling of hides and skins, and later the illegal grazing of cattle in remote areas'.[21]

Table 30 further breaks down these 1929 figures as quoted by Vincent. It should be noted that these are official figures and that actual numbers were probably greater.[22]

Naturally, poaching got out of hand. Once the poachers' bags were taken into consideration, the total quantity of game slaughtered in Zululand must have far exceeded any official figures. As Game Guard Dikidiki Nsele, in charge of Mkuze Game Reserve in 1925, noted, 'Sir, we are being made fools of.'[23] This situation no game ranger, black or white, ever likes.

The fate of the reserves

Some game reserves survived the transition from colonial to Union government and in 1910 Cape St Lucia, Hluhluwe and Umfolozi were still in existence.

Permanently deproclaimed reserves

In 1907 the Umdletshe Game Reserve was abolished. This had been one of the original four reserves established in 1895 and, like Hlabisa, had run down to the St Lucia complex. Several factors weighed against Umdletshe, such as its proximity to a fairly dense area of African settlement and the fact that it was traversed by a wagon road. The economic depression that followed the serious Zulu insurrection in 1906 cannot have helped matters. All in all, it is no wonder that this reserve, of which we know very little, survived as long as it did.

Hlabisa Game Reserve was also deproclaimed in 1907,[24] having been established only in 1905. This demonstrates the uncertainty that surrounded the question of game reserves in this late colonial era. The Hlabisa reserve included the western shores of Lake St Lucia, now part of today's Greater St Lucia Wetland Park, but also stretched inland in a corridor all the way to the boundaries of Umfolozi. Even after abolition, it was not unusual, throughout the twentieth century, for wild animals occasionally to move between the two areas as they had always done.

These 'secret journeys' usually made over long distances by lone animals were not confined to this area of Zululand. Even in the early twenty-first century it was not unknown for a single hippo to cross the Tugela and turn up in the coastal town of Ballito, only 50 kilometres from Durban, for example. The most celebrated, extraordinary and poignant of these odysseys was made by a young female hippo, named Huberta by the press. She wandered from central Zululand, south through Durban, on down along the south coast of KwaZulu-Natal, across the Transkei to a farm near King William's Town. Here a farmer shot her dead.

A footnote needs to be added regarding the Pongola Game Reserve of the old Transvaal Republic. It was for a while around 1905 *de facto* run by the nearby Ingwavuma magistrate, though any criminal cases relating to the 'Cinderella reserve' were dealt with by the magistrate in Wakkerstroom. During the Anglo-Boer War, it had been abandoned, but with the new British dispensation in the Transvaal, it was reproclaimed on 21 April 1903. Nevertheless, Stevenson-Hamilton's heart was elsewhere and it is a pity that it was not incorporated into the Natal–Zululand game reserve network.

The Pongola reserve limped on for some years, sometimes without official supervision but with a small number of people, including for a while two of the reserve's former game guards, keeping an eye on things. But clearly years of neglect and especially poaching had taken their toll. The amount of game in the reserve seems to have fluctuated and no doubt the reserve continued to act both as buffer and as passageway between Zululand, Swaziland, and to a lesser extent, the Transvaal. At various times kudu, lion, waterbuck, wild dog and even a few

TABLE 31

ESTIMATE OF GAME IN UMFOLOZI GAME RESERVE IN 1952

SPECIES	ESTIMATED NUMBER
Bushbuck	v. numerous
Duiker	v. numerous
Bushpig	v. numerous
Baboon	Plentiful
Genet (rusty-spotted)	Plentiful
Hyena	Plentiful
Leopard	Plentiful
Serval	Plentiful
Vervet monkey	Plentiful
White rhino	± 500
Waterbuck	± 100
Kudu	± 50
Mountain reedbuck	± 50
Nyala	± 50
Reedbuck	± 50
Steenbuck	± 50
Impala	± 10
Black rhino	± 10
Buffalo	4
Klipspringer	Few
Wildebeest	0
Zebra	0

elephant were reported in the old reserve. Its end came in 1920 when the minister of lands asked the Transvaal provincial administration for the land. The wonder is that it had survived so long into the new dispensation.[25]

Resurrected reserves

Two reserves or sections of former game reserves which were deproclaimed in the anti-game hysteria of the 1920s were resurrected in the 1930s. In 1907 Umfolozi gained an additional 9 300 ha to the south of the reserve to accommodate those white rhino who wandered beyond the confines of the reserve south of the White Mfolozi.[26] In 1920, however, after intense pressure from the white farming lobby, first the 1907 additions and then the whole of the old Umfolozi Game Reserve were deproclaimed. In 1930 it was reproclaimed, but in 1932 administration of the

reserve was handed over by the province to the state's Department of Veterinary Services, in whose hands it stayed for 20 years.

To complicate the story further, more deproclamations took place between 1932 and 1939 and again from 1945 to 1947. This perhaps gives the wrong impression, as Umfolozi was never alienated for commercial farming, and the influence of the conservator of game in Zululand continued to be felt. Indeed, from 1932 to 1940 African game rangers were stationed in Umfolozi and even after that rangers were used to chase straying white rhino back into Umfolozi. Finally, in 1952 Umfolozi was handed over to the Natal Parks Board.[27] An estimate of the number of large game contained in the reserve when the Parks Board finally acquired Umfolozi is listed in Table 31.[28] The figures demonstrate both the decimation of some species in the extermination campaigns and the success in protecting the white rhino population, which appears to have increased ten-fold in 30 years.

In 1928 the old Cape St Lucia reserve was deproclaimed as sugar farms encroached along the lower Mfolozi River, the mouth of which was altered in 1956. In 1938, however, a portion was reproclaimed and today the Maphelana Nature Reserve is a remnant of the original 1895 Cape St Lucia reserve.

Scandalous as was the deproclamation of Umfolozi Game Reserve, the point has to be emphasised that in the intervening decade the reserve remained Crown land where the white rhino was protected. There is continuity in the history of Imfolozi Game Reserve as there is with Hluhluwe from its foundation in 1895 to the present day – the oldest surviving game reserves in Africa.

New reserves

An extraordinary situation prevailed in early twentieth-century Zululand. On the one hand, game was being wantonly destroyed by the authorities, who eagerly handed out free ammunition to any undesirable who turned up with a gun. On the other hand, game reserves were retained, were deproclaimed only to be reproclaimed again, and even brand-new game reserves were created. As one correspondent to the *Natal Mercury* wrote as early as 1910: 'There appears to be a total absence of any policy in dealing with the big game question in Zululand. At one moment the cry is "Exterminate"; at another "Preserve".'[29]

The first of the new reserves, proclaimed in 1912, was about 15 000 ha at Mkhuze, east of the Mkhuze Poort and south of the Mkhuze River. This was remote from large-scale white farming, but bordered on African farmland, and indeed contained within its boundaries a traditional burial ground. The reserve should not be confused with the earlier Pongola–Mkuze reserve, which was north of the river bordering the lower slopes of the Lebombo Mountains.

The rinderpest had devastated the area some years earlier. In 1903 the local magistrate, Oswald Fynney, recorded:

This [game] forms an important feature of the [Ubombo] District, and it is to be regretted that even at this distant time the various species which used to abound here have not recovered from the ravages of rinderpest. Some, including koodoo, waterbuck, buffalo, and reedbuck are practically extinct.

The strictest measures have therefore been adopted for the proper preservation of game, and, if contained, should result favourably in time.

Much of the credit for the new creation of Mkuze Game Reserve must go to Fynney, who like many of the late Victorian Zululand magistrates, had watched over his district's isolated paradise until its proclamation. As with the other Zululand game reserves, Mkuze was already a sanctuary for game before its establishment; in fact, Mkuze was probably the only area in the Ubombo district where buffalo were still to be found.

Vaughan-Kirby acknowledged the role of 'the magistrate at Ubombo, in whose Division it [was] situated, and whose "mufti" reserve [was] the name by which it was known'.[30] Ramshackle as Mkuze might have been at the time of its establishment, nonetheless it contained:

- black rhino – 'a large number'
- buffalo
- bushbuck
- crocodile – 'of large size haunt the river and its banks'
- nyala – 'numerous'
- kudu – 'quite a nice lot'
- impala – '30 or 40 head'
- reedbuck
- warthog
- wildebeest
- zebra
- 'plenty of small game'.[31]

In October 1942, before the last, intense shooting campaign, it was estimated that in Mkuze there were 2 500 impala, 1 600 wildebeest and 1 500 nyala.

The second post-Union game reserve to be created was on the border with Portuguese Mozambique. On 16 April 1924 some 10 000 ha at Ndumo, bordered by the Usuthu and Phongola rivers, was proclaimed a game reserve. This thinly populated area had for many decades been known as a wildlife sanctuary. The great hunter Frederick Selous had shot there and had described the Mahemane bush in the area as the thickest bush he had ever encountered.

Ndumo was regarded as the chief breeding ground for nyala and impala, though it was the resident hippo population that merited its initial protection. Deneys Reitz, who had visited Ndumo in 1921 and again in 1924, particularly advocated the protection of this forgotten corner of South Africa. Once Ndumo had been proclaimed he is reported to have said, 'I have now done my duty to God and the hippo.'[32]

In 1927, a year before the old Cape St Lucia Game Reserve was abolished (1927–1938), a bird sanctuary was declared in the St Lucia area, and in 1935 another reserve was proclaimed at Richards Bay in an area of wetland and lagoon which in previous years had been a favoured spot for hunting hippo.[33]

The defeat of the tsetse fly

A long line of scientists followed Major Bruce in the quest to solve the tsetse fly problem. Two of them were sent to Zululand in 1921 by the Union government's Department of Agriculture: R.H.T. 'Fly' Harris, the son of Admiral Harris, was sent to Umfolozi and Dr H.H. Curson to Ntambanana. Harris was to become famous for his invention (with S. Deakin and W. Foster) of the Harris flytrap, which was to capture millions of tsetse fly. Harris had soon become convinced that the tsetse fly found its food source by sight rather than by smell. The trap was a large V-shaped affair, usually suspended from poles or a tree branch.[34]

Like Dr Bruce, Harris could be sharp-tongued. He lived in isolation in Umfolozi for the next 20 years, apart from a time when he was transferred to Pretoria, a move brought about by the tension created in the quest to destroy the fly. Indeed, Curson was correct when he wrote of the bitterness that surrounded the issue of 'Game versus farmer'. General J.C.G. Kemp, while minister of agriculture in 1931, made his famous comment:[35]

The only solution to the problem is to eliminate the host of the fly, which can only be done by eliminating the game reserves. Hluhluwe and Mkuzi must be abolished. The white rhino can be preserved at Umfolozi, but the rest of the game there must be reduced when it becomes plentiful. Settlers and game cannot co-exist. One must give way to the other.

Clearly in Natal there were those who not only disagreed with such a crude assessment but also saw the struggle as being something deeper. There was an element of the old Boer–British hostility in the struggle, and statements like that of the old rebel General Kemp did not help matters.

And yet it is too simplistic to reduce the struggle to one of Afrikaner nationalism versus English Natal liberalism. True, the conservationists were led by many members of old white Natal families, in the newly formed branch of the Wildlife Society, the most notable being the redoubtable Dr George Campbell. But support to save the game of Zululand also came from the likes of Deneys Reitz; the American scientist Dr Herbert Lang; the legendary game ranger, Stevenson-Hamilton; Natal's provincial secretary, J.M.N.A. Hershensohnn, and his successor, A.E. Charter; and from Dr Gill of the South African Museum. Nor were all cabinet ministers hostile like Kemp. P.G.W. Grobler greatly valued the animal heritage of South Africa. Mention needs also to be made of the work done on the ground to protect Hluhluwe Game Reserve by Captain Harold Potter, who with his wife ruled over the reserve for 26 years and who was the first ranger in charge of Zululand to live permanently in a game reserve.

The Harris traps appeared to have some success, though one should not forget that the extensive shooting of game in Umfolozi and Mkuze and neighbouring land continued in the period 1942 to 1950.[36] This is not, however, to deny the benefit brought by the Harris traps. By 1938 some 20 000 were in use in Zululand.[37] There were those who argued that the decline in nagana cases was part of a natural cycle. Be that as it may, the final nail in the fly's coffin came with Dr John Henkel's discovery in the mid-1930s that the fly only bred in specific sites. Destroy the breeding sites and you destroyed the scourge of Zululand. It was, however, some time before his theory was tested.

When it was tested, the authorities had the benefit of a chemical developed by the American military during the Second World War, DDT (dichloro-diphenyl-trichloroethane). This was mixed with BHC (benzene hexachloride) and was sprayed from low-flying aircraft. In 1941 Mkuze Game Reserve passed from the control of the Zululand Game Reserves and Parks Board to the government's Veterinary Department. It was to remain in their control until as late as 1953. Between November 1945 and January 1946 aerial-spraying from Avro Anson aircraft commenced, something that cannot but have had a dramatic impact on the natural food chain of the reserve, not least on the insectivorous bird population. Harris flytraps were also used. As Dr Henkel had proposed 10 years earlier, the breeding sites of the tsetse fly were located and the area then sprayed. Spraying followed at Hluhluwe and Umfolozi in the period 1947–51.

The experiment worked. The discovery of a vaccine for nagana at the end of the 1940s was the other major development in the battle against the disease.[38]

The Natal Parks, Game & Fish Preservation Board

The Province of Natal was unique in having its own nature conservation body in the Natal Parks Board. Its predecessors were the Game Advisory Committee,[39] founded in 1928, and the Zululand Game Reserves and Parks Committee, founded in 1937 with William Power as chairman. In 1947 Dr Campbell,

supported by William Power and Douglas Mitchell, the administrator of Natal, was the driving force behind the formation of the Natal Parks, Game and Fish Preservation Board.[40] This body was established by Provincial Council ordinance with Power as chairman of the board and Colonel Jack Vincent as secretary. The veteran game ranger Captain H.B. Potter was chief conservator of Zululand, being succeeded by his son Peter in 1950.[41]

In 1910 white Natal had been the reluctant partner in the creation of the Union of South Africa. They had had no choice but to enter the new political entity, but for years there were rumblings of discontent from 'the last outpost of the British empire', grumblings made worse by the influx of Afrikaners to occupy jobs previously held by white Natalians. It is interesting that the Natal Parks Board should be a bastion of the old dispensation and in particular of that generation of English-speaking white South Africans who had defied aggressive Afrikaner nationalism and joined the Union Defence Force to fight alongside Britain against Nazism and fascism. The organisation of the board's field operatives along quasi-paramilitary lines is a reflection of this, as indeed was the serious armed campaign it launched against poachers. Other battles at government level still had to be fought, as the desire to turn most of the Zululand game reserves into African or white farmland had not died.

Pooley and Player tell the story of the resurrected Umfolozi Game Reserve:

> It was not until 1953 that the first Natal Parks Board ranger was appointed. The first permanent house in the reserve was only built in 1957 and occupied by Ian Player and his family. The first huts at Mpila camp were opened to the public in 1958. The camp superintendent was John Kinloch and the ranger in charge of the southern crownlands was Nick Steele. The senior game guard was Magqubu Ntombela.

The first white tourists had been allowed in the mid-1930s into Hluhluwe where in 1934, 20 rest huts were built, 24 years before accommodation was provided for the public at Umfolozi. But the numbers of visitors at Hluhluwe in those early days was always very small. The general opening up of the Zululand game reserves for visitors from the late 1940s and early 1950s was paralleled by an independence of spirit in the Natal Parks Board. This persisted and ironically made the transfer from the apartheid era to the democratic one easier than one might have supposed for what has become Ezemvelo KwaZulu-Natal Wildlife.

The saving of the white rhino from extinction – Operation Rhino – and the creation of the Hluhluwe–Imfolozi Park and of the Greater St Lucia Wetland Park were essentially acts of historical throwback based on modern ecological science and indeed a version of a grander scheme proposed by Dr Campbell in 1937.[42] The re-assimilation of the apartheid-era KwaZulu Department of Nature Conservation – which dated from 1982 and was run by the able Nick Steele – was another example of how things might change without the integrity of the institution being undermined.

There was also the setting aside of the Imfolozi wilderness area, an idea first suggested by Jim Feely and Ian Player. The concept of the wilderness experience was to be ably proselytised in the second half of the twentieth century by Dr Ian Player. This and Operation Rhino have perhaps done more than anything to bring international recognition of the Zululand game reserves.[43] The declaration in December 1999 of the Greater St Lucia Wetland Park as a UNESCO World Heritage Site has enforced that recognition.

However, one factor often forgotten in the saga of the struggle for the preservation of game in Zululand is that much of Zululand is difficult to farm in a commercial sense, and especially so given the capital and equipment available in the 1920s. Some of the soil was poor, the climate could be unhealthy, communications could be difficult and flash floods could destroy a lifetime's work. And on top of this came nagana and various other cattle diseases. Nor was sugar farming without its trials in early twentieth-century Zululand, not least the problem of transport and milling. It is little wonder that many a commercial farm failed and that today in northern Zululand game ranching has been seized as an interesting commercial option.

The Zululand game reserves have an ethos of their own. They are not a set of mini Kruger Parks. Indeed, for the undiscerning, the apparent scarcity of game in some of them on occasion may draw adverse comment. But this is to miss the point. Catherine Barter's wilderness of the 1850s is that of the modern Zululand reserves: large areas of natural bush, wandering game sometimes seen but often not, a kaleidoscope of colourful and unusual birds, dirt tracks, flitting butterflies, poignant sunsets and the haunting blue-grey dusk quickly giving way to the tantalising noises of the African night. There is a feeling of timelessness.

White elephants: the indigenous forests

The great indigenous forests in some ways fared better than did the game reserves, in that they were generally left to the quiet care of the Union government's Forestry Department. This body soon recognised that the future of commercial timber production lay with exotic plantations of eucalyptus and wattle. It would, however, be a long time before the political will forced an expansion which could rival the vast quantities of timber being annually imported into the country. Zululand had had a few exotic plantations in the pre-Union period, the most notable being at Port Durnford. The First World War and the shortage of imported timber threatened many indigenous forests in South Africa. The extent of forest destruction in these war years still requires proper investigation. Similarly, the African location system threatened some woodland; Colonel Deneys Reitz visited Maputaland in 1938 and afterwards commented: 'The old Natal administration thought so highly of it [Mongosi forest] that a special forester was stationed there to protect the timber. Today the Mongosi lies a blackened waste.'[44]

In Zululand the climate made exotic timber production a forester's dream and, as the twentieth century progressed, more and more land was alienated to timber farming, much of it by private companies. As for the indigenous forests, they were largely forgotten, certainly by the public. The Victorian plant craze still imbued only a select few, such as General Smuts and the botanists of the Botanical Research Institute in Pretoria. For a period the indigenous flora was an important part, at least for some, in the pantheon of Afrikaner nationalism.

A police report from Nkandla dated 1912 discussed the scarcity of game in the area but did make the distinction between game in forests and elsewhere, the forest game being less scarce, though adding 'even there, it is not too plentiful'. It is not surprising that the denizens of the forest and the forest krantz – the baboon, the bushbuck, the leopard and the birdlife – should have fared better than their counterparts in the game reserves. It's true there was no shortage of poachers, but the increasing isolation of Zululand's indigenous forests, especially after commercial sawing declined from the 1920s, saved more than the yellowwood and the ironwood.

So the great indigenous forests of Zululand were left to themselves, and indeed some began the slow process of recovery. Ironically, the people in charge were not always of the same calibre as their Victorian predecessors such as G.H. Davies. In 1934 B.R. Simmons, the inspector of forestry, was shocked when he found that the forester in charge of Qhudeni and Nkandla forests did not even know the names of the indigenous trees. These were changed times indeed.

REFERENCES

1 The saga of the destruction of game in Zululand and the ultimate victory of the conserva-tionists is ably told in J.A. Pringle's book, *The conservationists and the killers: The story of game protection and the Wildlife Society of Southern Africa*. Another good account of the destruction and the campaign against nagana is to be found in A. de V. Minnaar's article, 'Nagana, big-game drives and the Zululand game reserves (1890s–1950s)', *Contree*, pp. 12–21. Another good source is Beverley Ellis's honours dissertation, 'Game conservation in Zululand, 1824–1947'.

2 *Journal of the Society for the Preservation of the Fauna of the Empire*, 2, p. 16.

3 See McCracken and McCracken, *Natal the garden colony: Victorian Natal and the Royal Botanic Gardens, Kew*.

4 For an assessment of Warren, see Brooks, 'Playing the game: The struggle for wildlife protection in Zululand, 1910–1930'.

5 The year 1909 also saw the passing of a general act regulating the export of certain wild animal products.

6 Curson, 'Preservation of game in South Africa', p. 410.

7 Ellis, 'Game conservation in Zululand, 1824–1947', *Natalia*, p. 38.

8 During the commission's tour of Zululand in 1904 Saunders wrote to Charles Warren and suggested he join them at the Mfolozi junction and acquire some specimens for the Natal Museum, including a white rhino. A telegram a few days later withdrew the white rhino offer. See SAP, Natal Museum papers, minute paper, NGM 53/1904, 31 May 1904 and telegram dispatched 3 June 1904.

9 Harrison, *Memories of early Matubatuba and district*, p. 11; and Van Jaarsveld, *Mtunzini*, Chapter 5.

10 Findlay, *Big game shooting and travel in south-east Africa*, pp. 220–21.

11 Ellis, 'Game conservation in Zululand', pp. 41–2. In the maze of game-related ordinances and notices which ensued in the following decades, one is of particular interest. Natal Provincial Notice 221 allowed for an owner of a farm to have his property declared as a game reserve. Curson says few 'availed themselves of this privilege'.

12 *Zululand Times*, 8 March 1912.

13 Stuchtey, *Science across the European empires*, pp. 49–62.

14 KZNA, 1/NKA, Report for May 1914, fol. 4.

15 Gush, *Mkhuze*, p. 11.

16 KZNA, 1/EPI, minute paper, LU 760/1903.

17 Harrison, *Matubatuba*, p. 93; KZNA, AGO, 1/8/152, SAP, Pietermaritzburg CID, 'Killing of an elephant at Umfolozi'; and Vaughan-Kirby, 'Game and game preservation in Zululand', p. 384.

18 See, for example, *Zululand Times*, 23 May 1910.

19 KZNA, NAD, 'Preservation of Game, 1910–1928', 4 January 1911.

20 See Sanas *News*, 7: 2, p. 15.

21 Vincent, *Web of experience*, p. 209.

22 Vincent, 'The history of Umfolozi Game Reserve', p. 39.

23 Gush, *Mkhuze*, p. 17.

24 Natal Government Notice No. 192 of 1907.

25 Carruthers, 'The Pongola Game Reserve', pp. 1–16; and KZNA, 1/ING, minute paper R 1071/1905, 12 July 1905

26 Natal Government Notice No. 322 of 1907.

27 The best account of this complex period in Imfolozi's history is contained in Vincent, 'The history of Umfolozi Game Reserve', pp. 13–16.

28 Foster's figures contained in Vincent, 'The history of Umfolozi Game Reserve', p. 34.

29 Quoted in *Zululand Times*, 21 October 1910.

30 Vaughan-Kirby, 'Game and game preservation in Zululand', p. 381.

31 For an interesting report on Mkhuze written by Vaughan-Kirby in 1912, see Gush, *Mkhuze*, pp. 14–15, 25.

32 Pooley and Player, *KwaZulu/Natal wildlife destinations*, p. 229.

33 See Ellis, 'Game conservation in Zululand, 1824–1947', *Natalia*, p. 41 and Cubbin, *History of Richards Bay*, p. 42; and Provincial Ordinance No. 353 of 1935.

34 For details of the Harris fly trap see Minnaar, 'Nagana, big-game drives', pp. 18–19.

35 See *The Mercury*, 27 April 1995; and Pringle, *The conservationists and the killers*, p. 126.

36 Ellis, 'Game conservation in Zululand, 1824–1947', *Natalia*, p. 42.

37 Gush, *Mkhuze*, p. 23.

38 See Minnaar, 'Nagana, big-game drives', p. 20; and Pooley and Player, *KwaZulu/Natal wildlife destinations*, p. 125.

39 Ellis, 'Game conservation in Zululand, 1924–1947', *Natalia*, p. 40.

40 Natal Provincial Ordinance No. 35 of 1947.

41 Pooley and Player, *KwaZulu/Natal wildlife destinations*, pp. 21–24.

42 'The anti-nagana campaign in Zululand', Sanas *News*, 7: 2, p. 19. The creation of the Hluhluwe-Imfolozi Park was made possible in 1989 by the proclamation of the linking Corridor reserve.

43 See Ian Player, *Zululand Wilderness: Shadow and soul*; and Pooley and Player, *KwaZulu/Natal wildlife destinations*, pp. 22–23, 125. In particular Ian Player will be remembered for the Wilderness Leadership School, which he founded in 1957. The first wilderness trail took place on 19 March 1959.

44 Reitz, 'The forests of northern Zululand', p. 29.

BIBLIOGRAPHY

1. PRIMARY SOURCES

Arquivo Histórico Ultramarino, Lisbon, Portugal:
India Maço, 137

British Library, London:
Bentley papers

Cape Town Archives (CTA):
Government House papers

Department of Forestry and Water Affairs:
Papers relating to Zululand forests

KwaZulu-Natal Archives, Durban and Pietermaritzburg (KZNA):
Attorney General's Office papers (AGO)
Colonial Secretary's Office papers (CSO)
Government House papers (GH)
Kitbird collection: Piet Hogg papers
Magistrates papers for:
    Babanango (1/BGO); Empangeni [Lower Umfolozi] (1/EPI); Eshowe (1/ESH); Ingwavuma (1/ING); Mahlabatini (1/MBT); Melmoth [Ntonjaneni] (1/MEL); Mtubatuba [Hlabisa] (1/MTB); Mtunzini [Umlalazi] (1/MTU); Nkandla (1/NKA); Nongoma [Ndwandwe] (1/NGA); and Ubombo [Lebombo] (1/UBO)
Morewood papers: Anonymous diary of a trading expedition to Zululand, 1850
Natal Museum papers (uncatalogued)
Secretary for Native Affairs papers (SNA)
Surveyor-General's Office papers (SGO)
Robinson papers
Zululand Archives, Resident Commissioner and Chief Magistrate (ZA)
Zululand Blue Books (MS)
Zululand Government House (ZGH)

Killie Campbell Collections, University of KwaZulu-Natal, Durban:
Ablett papers
James Bell diary
Blenkinsopp papers
Durban Botanic Gardens papers
Dunn papers
Captain Garden papers
Cato papers (Cowie's letters)
Gnutu Zulu Reserve minute book
Miller papers (Von Wissell's 'Reminiscences of trading days in Northern Zululand, 1895–1919')
Pietermaritzburg Botanic Gardens papers
Robert Plant papers
Shepstone papers
W.H. Smith typescript

KwaZulu-Natal Herbarium, Durban:
Strey papers
Medley Wood papers and reports

Natural History Museum, Dublin:
Insects, 1878–1884
Purchases, 1866–1872
Register, 1838–1850, 1851–1872, 1873–1883, 1883–1894, 1895–1901, 1901–1906

Natural History Museum, London:
Donations, vertebrate section (DF 216)
Donations, zoology section, 1848–1873 and 1873–1882
Drummond papers (DF 200)
Kirby papers (DF 200 and 232)

Privately held papers:
Papers of Robert Plant, Mrs Joan Read, Pietermaritzburg

Public Record Office, London:
Admiralty papers
Colonial Office papers

Royal Botanical Gardens, Kew, London:
Inward (plant and seed) exchange books, 1848–1908
Miscellaneous reports: Natal Botanic Gardens, 1866–1909
Natal miscellaneous, 1862–1909
Plant list volumes, 1, Australia, New Zealand and Polynesia, 1845–1863
South African letters, 1865–1900

Royal Geographical Society, London:
Captain Allen Gardiner papers
Selous papers

South African National Biodiversity Institute, Pretoria:
Notes on South African botanists
Report on the Maputa expedition, 27 May to 5 July 1914 (Dr H.G. Breyer)

2. NEWSPAPERS AND PERIODICALS

Agricultural Journal (Natal)
Bothalia
Curtis's Botanical Magazine
The Field
Gardeners' Chronicle
Hooker's London Journal of Botany
The Ibis
Natal Almanac and Register
Natal Blue Book
Natal Colonist
Natal Government Gazette
Natal Herald
Natal Independent
Natal Mercury
Natal Times
Natal Witness
Proceedings of the Zoological Society, London
Royal Botanic Gardens, Kew: Bulletin of Miscellaneous Information
South African Journal of Science
Times of Natal
Zululand Times

3. OFFICIAL PUBLISHED REPORTS

Bruce, D., *Preliminary report of the tsetse fly disease or nagana in Zululand*, Ubombo, 1895.
— *Further report on the tsetse fly disease or nagana in Zululand*, Ubombo, 1896.
— *Appendix for further report on tsetse fly disease or nagana*, London, 1903.
Colonial Reports: Annual, No. 169. Zululand, London, 1896.
Correspondence and reports relative to the state of botanical enterprise in Natal, 1882, Pietermaritzburg, 1884.
Correspondence relating to certain native territories situated to the north-east of Zululand, c-7780, London, 1895.
Correspondence relating to the affairs of Zululand, c-8782, London, 1898.
Correspondence respecting certain boundary questions in Zululand, c-6684, London, 1892.
Fourcade, H.G., *Report on the Natal forests*, Pietermaritzburg, 1889.
Further correspondence respecting the affairs of Swaziland and Tongaland (in continuation of c-5089, June 1887), London, 1890.
Military report on Zululand. Prepared for the General Staff, War Office, London, 1906.
Precis of information concerning Swaziland, Tongaland, and North Zululand, confidential, War Office, London, 1905.
Report by the joint imperial and colonial commissioners Zululand lands delineation commission, 1902–1904, Pietermaritzburg, 1905.
Report of the Zululand boundary commission and annexures, London, 1880.
Report on the forests of Zululand (Colonel F. Cardew), c-6270, London, 1891.
Report on Tsongaland, 8 July 1895.
Swaziland, Tongaland and northern Zululand, War Office, London, 1905.
Saunders, Charles, *Report on Tongaland*, c-5089, Pietermaritzburg 1889.
Zululand, Further correspondence respecting the affairs of Zululand and adjacent territories (in continuation of c-5522, August 1888), London, 1890.
Zululand lands delimitation commission, 1902–1904: Reports by the joint imperial and colonial commissioners, E166, Pietermaritzburg, 1905.

4. CONTEMPORARY WORKS

A short guide to legislation for the protection and welfare of animals and birds in South Africa, with particular reference to the Cape Province, Cape Town, n. d., c. 1935.

Abstracts of Proceedings, Zoological Society of London, London, 1875.

Aitken, R.D. and Gale, G.W., *Botanical survey of Natal and Zululand*, Botanical Survey of South Africa Memoir no. 2, Pretoria, 1921.

Angas, G.F., *The kafirs illustrated in a series of drawings taken among the Amazulu, Amaponda, and Amakosa tribes; also, portraits of the Hottentot, Malay, Fingo, and other races inhabiting Southern Africa: together with stretches of land-scape scenery in the Zulu country, Natal, and the Cape Colony*, London, 1849, repr. Cape Town, 1974.

Annual returns of progress (Natural History section of the British Museum), 1882 to 1890 and 1891 to 1895.

Baldwin, W.C., *African hunting and adventure from Natal to the Zambesi, including Lake Ngami, the Kalahari Desert, etc. from 1852 to 1860*, London, 1863, (repr. Bulawayo, 1981).
— *Du Natal au Zambèze, 1851–1866. Récits de chasses*, Paris, 1868.

Ball, V., 'Observations on lion-breeding in the Gardens of the Royal Society of Ireland', *Transactions of the Royal Irish Academy*, 28, (Science), August 1886, pp. 724–49.

Barter, C., *Stray memories of Natal and Zululand: A poem*, Pietermaritzburg, 1897.

(Barter, C.), *Alone among the Zulus, by a plain woman. The narrative of a journey through the Zulu country, South Africa*, London, n.d., c. 1866, (repr. Merrett, Patricia L., (ed.), Pietermaritzburg, 1995).

Bates, H.W., *Illustrated travels: A record of discovery, geography, and adventure*, 6 vols., London, 1869–75.

Bennett, Ian H.W., *Eyewitness in Zululand: The campaign reminiscences of Colonel W.A. Dunne, South Africa, 1877–1881*, London and Novato, 1989.

Bird, John, *The annals of Natal, 1495 to 1845*, 1, Cape Town, c. 1855.

Bosman, Col. Walter, *The Natal rebellion of 1906*, London, 1907.

Brandis, D., 'Forestry in Natal', *Kew Bulletin*, D1-5, 1895.

Brooks, Henry, *Natal, a history and description of the colony*, London, 1876.

Brooks, S., 'Playing the game: The struggle for wildlife protection in Zululand, 1910–1930', Queen's University, Canada, master's dissertation, 1990.

Brown, N.E., 'John Medley Wood, 1827–1915', *Kew Bulletin*, 1915, pp. 417–19.

Bryant, A.T., *The Zulu people: As they were before the white man came*, Pieter-maritzburg, 1967 ed.
— *Olden times in Zululand and Natal*, London, 1929.

Bryden, H.A., 'The extermination of great game in South Africa', *Fortnightly Review*, 1894, pp. 538–51.
— 'On the present distribution of the giraffe, south of the Zambesi, and on the best means of securing living specimens for European collections', *Proceedings of the Zoological Society of London*, 1891, pp. 445–6.

Buckley, T.E., 'On the past and present geographical distribution of the large mammals of South Africa', *Proceedings of the Zoological Society of London*, 7 March 1876, pp. 277–93.

Callaway, Rev. Canon, *The religious system of the Amazulu*, Cape Town and London, 1890.

Casalis, Rev. Eugéne, *The Basutos*, London, 1861.

Cumming, R. Gordon, *Five years' hunting adventures in South Africa*, London, c. 1850.

Curson, H.H. and Hugo, J.M., 'Preservation of game in South Africa', *South African Journal of Science*, 21, 1924, pp. 400–24.

Drummond, Hon. W.H., *The large game and natural history of south and south-east Africa, from the journals of the Hon. W.H. Drummond*, Edinburgh, 1875, (repr. Salisbury, 1972).

'Encephalartos woodii', *Kew Bulletin*, 1914, pp. 250–51.

Eldridge, M.J. (ed.), *Records of Natal: Government House Despatches, vol. 1, 1845–1846*, Pretoria, 1987.

Erskine, St V.W., 'Journey of exploration to the mouth of the River Limpopo', *Journal of the Royal Geographical Society, London*, 1869, 39, pp. 233–76.
— 'Third and fourth journeys in Gaza, or southern Mozambique, 1873 to 1874, and 1874 to 1875', *Journal of the Royal Geographical Society, London*, 1878, 48, pp. 45–128.

Findlay, F.R.N., *Big game shooting and travel in south-east Africa*, London, 1903.

FitzSimons, F.W., *The natural history of South Africa*, 3 vols., London, 1920.

Gardiner R.N., Captain Allen F., *Narrative of a journey to the Zoolu country in South Africa*, London, 1836, Cape Town, 1966 reprint.

Gassiott, H.S., 'Notes from a journal kept during a hunting tour in South Africa', *Journal of the Royal Geographical Society of London*, 22, 1852, pp. 136–40.

Gray, Stephen (ed.), [Charles Rawden Maclean], *The Natal papers of 'John Ross'*, Pietermaritzburg, 1992.

Grout, Rev. Lewis, *Zulu-land; or, life among the Zulu-kafirs of Natal and Zulu-land, South Africa*, London, n.d., c. 1863.

Gurney, John Henry, 'On birds collected in the colony of Natal, in south-eastern Africa', *The Ibis*, ser. 1, vol. 2, 1860, pp. 203–21.
— 'On some additional species of birds received in collections from Natal', *The Ibis*, 1861, pp. 128–36.
— 'A third additional list of birds received from Natal', *The Ibis*, 1862, pp. 25–39.
— 'A fourth additional list of birds received from Natal', *The Ibis*, 1862, pp. 149–58.
— 'A fifth additional list of birds from Natal', *The Ibis*, 1863, pp. 320–32.
— 'A sixth additional list of birds from Natal', *The Ibis*, 1864, pp. 346–61.
— 'A seventh additional list of birds from Natal', *The Ibis*, 1865, pp. 263–76.
— 'An eighth additional list of birds from Natal', *The Ibis*, 1868, pp. 40–52.
— 'A ninth additional list of birds from Natal', *The Ibis*, 1868, pp. 460–71.
— 'A tenth additional list of birds from Natal', *The Ibis*, 1873, pp. 254–9.

Harris, Sir William Cornwallis, *The wild sports of southern Africa*, London, 1841 ed.

The history of the collections in the Natural History departments of the British Museum, 1–2, London, 1904 and 1906.

Harvey, William, *The genera of South African plants*, London, 1868 ed. by Hooker, J.D.

Holden, Rev. William C., *History of the colony of Natal*, London, 1855, Cape Town, 1963 reprint.
— *The past and future of the kaffir races*, London, c. 1866.

Hornaday, William T. and Haagner, Alwin K., *The vanishing game of South Africa*, Permanent Wild Life Protection Fund, bulletin no. 10, New York and Pretoria, 1 September 1922.

Instructions regarding formation of natural history collections, Cape Town, 1904.

Isaacs, Nathaniel, *Travels and adventures in eastern Africa* (Herrman, L., ed.), Van Riebeeck Society, 2 vols., Cape Town, 1936.

Ingram, J. Forsyth, *The Colony of Natal: An official illustrated handbook and railway guide*, London, 1895.

Jackson, Jean, *Beyond the pale*, London, 1960.

Kingston, W.H.G., *Hendricks the hunter: A tale of Zululand*, New York, 1880.

Kirby, P.R. (ed.), *Andrew Smith and Natal: Documents relating to the early history of that province*, Van Riebeeck Society, 36, Cape Town, 1955.
— *The diary of Dr Andrew Smith, director of the expedition for exploring central Africa, 1834–1836*, Van Riebeeck Society, 1, Cape Town, 1939 and 1940.

Le Roux, Servaas D., *Pioneers and sportsmen of South Africa, 1760–1890*, Salisbury, 1939.

Leslie, David, *Among the Zulus and Amatongas: with sketches of the natives, their language and customs; and the country, products, climate, wild animals, etc. being principally contributions to magazines and newspapers* (Drummond, Hon W.H., ed.), Glasgow, 1875.

Leverton, B.J.T. (ed.), *Records of Natal*, 1–6, Pretoria, 1984–1990.

Lindley, Augustus F, *After Ophir; or, a search for the South African gold fields*, London, c.1870.

Lucas, Thomas J., *Camp life and sport in South Africa*, London, 1878 (repr. Johannesburg, 1975).

Ludlow, Captain W.R., *Zululand and Cetewayo*, London, 1882.

McLeod, Lyons, *Travels in eastern Africa; with the narrative of a residence in Mozambique*, 2 vols., London, 1860.

Merrett, Patricia and Butcher, Ronald (eds.), *The hunting journal of Robert Briggs Struthers, 1852–56, in the Zulu kingdom and the Tsonga regions*, Pietermaritzburg, 1991.

Mitford, Bertram, *The gun-runner: A tale of Zululand*, London, 1893.

Monteiro, Rose, *Delagoa Bay: Its natives and natural history*, London, 1891.

Moodie, D.C.F., *John Dunn, Cetywayo and the three generals*, Pietermaritzburg, 1886 (reproduced privately, 2006).

North, Marianne (Symonds, Mrs J.A., ed.), *Recollections of a happy life,* 2 vols., London, 1892.

Plant, Robert, 'Notice of an excursion in the Zulu country', *Hooker's Journal of Botany,* 4, 1852, pp. 257–65; and a note on R.W. Plant in *Hooker's Journal of Botany,* 4, 1852, pp. 222–3.

Pridmore, Julie (ed.), *The journal of William Clayton Humphreys*, Pietermaritzburg, 1993.

Pringle, *The conservationists and the killers: The story of game protection and the Wildlife Society of Southern Africa*, Cape Town, 1982.

Reitz, Col. Deneys, 'The forests of northern Zululand', *Journal of South African Forestry Association*, 1, October 1938, pp. 28–29.

Returns of the British Museum, London, 1857, 1891, 1894 and 1895.

Rickard, C. (ed.), 'Charles Barter: Natal diary, 14 August 1852 – 26 April 1853', honours dissertation, University of Natal, Pietermaritzburg, 1975.

St George, H., *Failure and vindication, the unedited journal of Bishop Allard, O.M.I.,* Durban, n.d.

Samuelson, R.C.A., *Long, long ago,* Durban, 1929.

Selous, F.C., *A hunter's wanderings in Africa, being a narrative of nine years spent amongst the game of the far interior of South Africa containing accounts of explorations beyond the Zambesi, on the River Chobe, and in the Matabele and Mashua countries, with full notes upon the natural history and present distribution of all the large mammalia,* London, 1881 (reproduced Alberton, South Africa, 1999).

Sharpe, Bowdler, R., 'On the birds of Zululand, founded on the collections made by Messrs. R. B. and J.D.S. Woodward', parts I and II, *The Ibis*, 1897, pp. 400–22 (containing the brothers' account of their 1894 Zululand collecting trip) and pp. 495–517.

Spohr, Dr O.H. (ed.), *Ferdinand Krauss: Travel journal, Cape to Zululand: Observations by a collector and naturalist, 1838–40,* Cape Town, 1973.

Stuart, James and Malcolm, D. McK. (eds.), *The diary of Henry Francis Fynn compiled from original sources,* Pietermaritzburg, 1951 (1986 ed.).

Vaughan-Kirby, Frederick, 'Game and game preservation in Zululand', *South African Journal of Science*, 1916, pp. 375–96.
— *In the haunts of wild game: A hunter-naturalist's wanderings from Kahlamba to Libombo,* Edinburgh, 1906.

Ward, Rowland, (ed.), *The great and small game of Africa,* London, 1899.

Ward, Rowland, *Records of big game,* London, 1896 and 1899 eds.

Webb, C. de B. and Wright, J.B. (eds.), *The James Stuart archive of recorded oral evidence relating to the history of the Zulu and neighbouring peoples*, 1–6, Pietermaritzburg, 1976–2003.

Webb, Fleur (ed.) (trans.), *Adulphe Delegorgue's travels in southern Africa*, 1–2, introduced by Alexander, Stephanie and Webb, Colin, Pietermaritzburg, 1990 and 1997 (first published in Paris in 1847).

'The wild fauna of the empire', *Journal of the Society for the Preservation of the Fauna of the Empire, 2*, 1905, pp. 9–18.

Wilkinson, Mrs, *A lady's life and travels in Zululand*, London, 1882 (repr. Pretoria, 1975).

Wood, John Medley, *Natal Plants,* 1–6 (vol. 1 with Evans, Maurice S.), Durban, 1899–1912.
— *A preliminary catalogue of indigenous Natal plants*, Durban, 1894.
— 'Revised list of the flora of Natal', *Transactions of the South African Philosophical Society*, 17: 2, 1908, pp. 121–280.
— 'A chat with J. Medley Wood ALS', *Agricultural Journal*, 6: 2, 26 June 1903, pp. 345–7.

Woodward, R.B. and J.D.S., 'Description of our journey in Zululand, with notes on its birds', *The Ibis*, 1897, pp. 400–22 and 1898, pp. 216–28.
— 'Further notes on the birds of Zululand', *The Ibis*, 1898, pp. 216–28.
— *Natal birds (including the species belonging to Natal and the eastern districts of the Cape Colony),* Pietermaritzburg, 1899.

5. LATER WORKS

Aylward, Bruce and Lutz, Ernst (eds.), *Nature tourism, conservation, and development in KwaZulu-Natal, South Africa*, Washington, 2003.

Ballard, Charles, *The house of Shaka: The Zulu monarchy illustrated,* Durban, 1988.
— *John Dunn: The white chief of Zululand,* Johannesburg, 1985.
— Conference paper published as: 'The role of trade and hunter traders in the political economy of Natal and Zululand, 1824–1880', *African Economic History*, 10, 1980, pp. 3–21.
— 'The transfrontiersman: The career of John Dunn in Natal and Zululand, 1834–1895', University of Natal doctoral thesis, 1980.

Barnes, Bill, *Giant's Castle: A personal history,* Johannesburg, 2003.

Beinart, William, review article, 'Empire, hunting and ecological change in southern and central Africa', *Past and Present*, no. 128, August 1990, pp. 162–86.

Berglund, A., *Zulu thought-patterns and symbolism*, Johannesburg, 1976.

Brooke, R.K., 'More on the Woodward brothers', *Bokmakierie*, 36: 2, 1984, pp. 28–9.

Brookes, Edgar H., and Webb, Colin de B., *A history of Natal*, Pietermaritzburg, 1979 ed.

Brooks, Shirley J., 'Playing the game: The struggle for wildlife protection in Zululand, 1910–1930', master's dissertation, Queen's University, Canada, 1990.

Bruton, M.N. and Cooper, K.H., *Studies on the ecology of Maputaland*, Grahamstown and Durban, 1980.

Bulpin, T.V., *Lost trails of the Transvaal*, Johannesburg, 1989 ed.
— *Natal and the Zulu country*, Cape Town, 1977.
— *Shaka's country: A book of Zululand*, Cape Town, 1952.
— *To the shores of Natal*, Cape Town, c. 1954.

Carruthers, Elizabeth Jane, 'Dissecting the myth: Paul Kruger and the Kruger National Park', *Journal of Southern African Studies*, 20: 2, 1994, pp. 263–83.
— 'Game protection in the Transvaal, 1846 to 1926', doctoral thesis, University of Cape Town, 1988.
— 'The Pongola Game Reserve: An eco-political study', *Koedoe*, no. 28, 1985, pp. 1–16.

Clancey, P.A., 'On the contribution of the Woodward brothers', *Bokmakierie*, vol. 35, no. 3, 1983, pp. 56–8.
— *The rare birds of southern Africa*, Johannesburg, 1985.

Craig, Adrian and Hummel, Chris (eds.), translated by Michael Roberts, *Johan August Wahlberg: Travel journals (and some letters) South Africa and Namibia/Botswana, 1838–1856,* Van Riebeeck Society, 2nd ser., no. 23, Cape Town, 1994 for 1992.

Cubbin, A.E., 'An outline of game legislation in Natal 1866–1912 (i.e. until the promulgation of the Mkhuze Game Reserve), *Journal of Natal and Zulu History,* no. 14, 1992, pp. 37–47.
— *Empangeni: Aspects of the 19th century,* Empangeni, 1994.
— *History of Richards Bay, 1497–1970s*, Empangeni, c. 1998.
— 'On the trail of John Ross', *Kleio,* no. 27, 1995, pp. 63–9.

Desmond, R. *Dictionary of British and Irish botanists and horticulturalists,* Basingstoke, 1994.

Dictionary of South African Biography, vols. 1–5, Pretoria, 1968–87.

Du Plessey, S.F., 'The past and present geographical distribution of the Perissodactyla and Artiodactyla in southern Africa', master's dissertation, University of Pretoria, 1969.

Duminy, Andrew and Guest, Bill, (eds.) *Natal and Zululand, from earliest times to 1910: A new history,* Pietermaritzburg, 1989.

Ebedes, Hym, Vernon, Carl and Grundling, Irma, *Past, present and future distribution of elephants in southern Africa,* Pretoria, 1991.

Ellis, B., 'Game conservation in Zululand (1824–1947)', honours dissertation, University of Natal, 1975.

Ellis, Beverley, 'Game conservation in Zululand, 1824–1947', *Natalia,* nos. 23/24, December 1993/94, pp. 27–44.

Goetzsche, Eric, *The father of a city,* Pietermaritzburg, n.d.

Goodman, P.S. and Tomkinson, A.J., 'The past distribution of giraffe in Zululand and its implications for reserve management', *South African Journal of Wildlife Reserves,* 17, 1987, pp. 28–32.

Gosnell, Peter J., *Big Bend: A history of the Swaziland bushveld,* 2001.

Greaves, Adrian, *Isandlwana,* Johannesburg, 2001.

Guest, Bill, *A century of science and service: The Natal Museum in a changing South Africa 1904–2004,* Pietermaritzburg, 2006.

Gunn, Mary, and Codd, L.E., *Botanical exploration of southern Africa,* Cape Town, 1981.

Gush, Reg, *Mkhuze – The formative years; The story of the Mkhuze Game Reserve, KwaZulu-Natal,* Hilton, 2000.

Guy, J.J., 'A note on firearms in the Zulu kingdom with special reference to the Anglo-Zulu War, 1879', *Journal of African History,* 12: 4, pp. 557–70.

Guy, Jeff, *The destruction of the Zulu kingdom,* London, 1979.
— 'Ecological factors in the rise of Shaka and the Zulu kingdom', in Shula Marks and Anthony Atmore, *Economy and society in pre-industrial South Africa,* London, 1980, pp. 102–19.

Hackel, Jeffrey D. and Carruthers, E. Jane, 'Swaziland's twentieth century wildlife preservation efforts: The present as a continuation of the past', *Environmental History Review,* fall 1993, pp. 61–84.

Hale, Frederick, *Norwegian missionaries in Natal and Zululand: Select correspondence, 1844–1900,* Van Riebeeck Society, 2nd ser., no. 27, Cape Town, 1997 for 1996.

Harrison, E.R., *Memories of early Matubatuba and district,* Mtubatuba, 1989.

Hattersley, A.E., *More annals of Natal with historical introductions and notes,* Pietermaritzburg, 1936.

Hedges, D.W., 'Trade and politics in southern Mozambique and Zululand in the eighteenth and early nineteenth century', doctoral thesis, University of London, 1978.

Howard, Peter C. and Marchant, Athol N., 'The distribution and status of some large mammals on private land in Natal', *Lammergeyer,* no. 34, August 1984, pp. 1–58.

Jackson, P.B.N., 'The capture of Johnny Mullins', in McCracken, Donal P. (ed.), *Ireland and South Africa in modern times,* Durban, 1996.

Kemp, Bernard Harley, 'Johan William Colenbrander, A history of his times and the people and events with which he was associated, 1879–1898', doctoral thesis, University of Natal, 1962.

Knight, Ian, *The anatomy of the Zulu army frrom Shaka to Cetshwayo,* London and Pennsylvania, 1995.

Krige, E.J., *The social system of the Zulu,* Pietermaritzburg, 1936.

Laband, John, *Rope of sand: The rise and fall of the Zulu kingdom in the nineteenth century,* Johannesburg, 1995.

Loch, Ron and Quantrill, Peter, *Zulu victory: The epic of Isandlwana and the cover up,* London and Pennsylvania, 2002.

Maclean, G.L., *Roberts' birds of southern Africa,* 6th ed., Cape Town, 1993.

McCracken, Donal P., 'Dependency, destruction and development: A history of indigenous timber use in South Africa', in Lawes Michael J., Eeley, Harriet A.C., Shackleton, Charlie M. and Geach, Bev G. S. (eds.), *Indigenous forests and woodlands in South Africa: Policy, people and practice,* Pietermaritzburg, 2004, pp. 277–83.
— 'Fraternity in the age of jingoism: The British imperial botanic and forestry network', in Benedikt Stuchtey (ed.), *Science across the European empires 1800–1950,* Oxford University Press, 2005, pp. 49–62.
— *Gardens of empire: Botanical institutions of the Victorian British empire,* London and Washington, 1997.
— 'The indigenous forests of colonial Natal and Zululand', *Natalia,* no. 16, 1986, pp. 19–38.
— *Natal the garden colony: Victorian Natal and the Royal Botanic Gardens, Kew* (with Patricia A. McCracken), Sandton, 1990.
— *A new history of the Durban Botanic Gardens,* Durban, 1996.
— 'Qudeni: The early commercial exploitation of an indigenous Zululand forest', General paper, *South African Forestry Journal,* no. 142, September 1987, pp. 71–80.

McLachlan, G.R. and Liversidge, R., *Roberts' birds of South Africa,* 4th ed., Cape Town, 1982.

MacKenzie, J.M., *The empire of nature: Hunting, conservation and British imperialism,* Manchester, 1988.

Marwick, C.W., *Kwamahlati: The story of forestry in Zululand,* Department of Forestry bulletin no. 49, Pretoria, 1973.

Mentis, M.T., 'Distribution of some wild animals in Natal', *Lammergeyer,* no. 20, 1974, pp. 1–68.

Minnaar, A. de V., *Empangeni: A historical review to 1989,* Empangeni, 1989.
— 'Nagana, big-game drives and the Zululand game reserves (1890s–1950s)', *Contree,* 25, RAU, April 1989.

— *Ushukela: A history of the growth and development of the sugar industry in Zululand: 1905 to the present,* Pretoria, 1992.

Newman, Kenneth, *Newman's birds of southern Africa,* Cape Town, 2002.

Papini, Robert, 'Rainbirds and power in the Zulu kingdom story', in Connerty, P.E., Eisenhauer, B. and Spencer, B.M., *A flight through time: To celebrate the 22nd International Ornithological Congress, Durban 1998,* Durban, 1998.
— 'Some Zulu uses for the animal domains: Livestock (imfuyo) and game (izinyamazane)', in *Zulu treasures of kings and commoners: A celebration of the material culture of the Zulu people,* KwaZulu Cultural Museum and the Local History Museum, Durban, 1996.

Pearse, R.O., *Joseph Baynes, pioneer,* Pietermaritzburg, 1981.

Phillips, E. Percy, 'A brief historical sketch of the development of botanical science in South Africa to botany', *South African Journal of Science,* vol. 27, 1930, pp. 39–80.

Player, Ian, *Zululand wilderness: Shadow and soul,* Claremont, 1997.

Poland, Marguerite and Hammond-Tooke, W.D. (artwork by Leigh Voigt), *The abundant herds: A celebration of the cattle of the Zulu people,* Vlaeberg, 2003.

Pooley, Elsa, *The complete field guide to trees of Natal, Zululand and Transkei,* Durban, 1993.

Pooley, Tony and Player, Ian, *KwaZulu-Natal: Wildlife destinations,* Halfway House, 1995.

Pridmore, J., 'The impact of the European traders on Port Natal, 1824–1834: A look at environment and society', Environmental Conference paper, University of Natal, 1992.

Pringle, John, *The conservationists and the killers,* Cape Town, 1982.
— 'The distribution of mammals in Natal', part 2, 'Carnivora', *Annals of the Natal Museum,* 23, 1977, pp. 93–115.

Quickelberge, Clive, *Collections and recollections; The Durban Natural History Museum, 1887–1987,* Durban, 1988.

Rolando, S.C., 'Natal veterinary services, 1874–1912', University of Natal, master's dissertation, Pietermaritzburg, 1990.

Raymond, E.T., *Disraeli: The alien patriot,* London, n.d.

Roberts, A., *The birds of South Africa,* Johannesburg, 1940.

'Roberts VII species list', www.fitzpatrick.uct.ac.za/docs/birdname.html, accessed on 8 March 2004.

Rose, M., 'The oldest game reserve in Africa', *African Wildlife,* 31: 6, 1978, pp. 16–21.

Rowe-Rowe, D.T., *The carnivores of Natal,* Natal Parks Board, Pietermaritzburg, 1992.
— *The ungulates of Natal,* Natal Parks Board, Pietermaritzburg, 1994.

Schrire, B.D., 'Centenary of the Natal Herbarium, 1882–1882', *Bothalia,* 14: 2, 1983, pp. 223–36.

Sidney, J., 'The past and present distribution of some African ungulates', *Transactions of the Zoological Society, London,* 30, 1965, pp. 1–397.

Skinner, J.D. and Smithers, R.H.N., *The mammals of southern Africa subregion,* Pretoria, 1990.

Smith, Alan, 'The trade of Delagoa Bay in Nguni politics, 1750–1835', in Thompson, Leonard (ed.), *African societies in southern Africa,* London, 1969, pp. 171–89.

Smith, Alan Kent, 'The struggle for control of southern Moçambique, 1720–1835', doctoral thesis, University of California, Los Angeles, 1970.

Smith, C.A., *Common names of South African plants,* Botanical Survey Memoir no. 35, Pretoria, 1966.

Spencer, Shelagh O'Byrne, *British settlers in Natal, 1824–1857,* 1–7, Pietermaritzburg, 1987–2001.
— 'Green are the hills of Natal: Early Irish settlers in Natal, 1824–1862', *Southern African-Irish Studies,* 2, 1992, pp. 191–213.

Strey, Rudolph G., 'The father of Natal botany: John Medley Wood', *Natalia,* no. 7, 1977, pp. 43–5.

Stuchtey, Benedikt, *Science across the European empires, 1800–1950,* OUP, 2005.

Turner, Noleen, 'The pervasive influence of plant names in Zulu onomastics', *Nomina Africana,* 14: 2, 2007.

Van Jaarsveld, Albert, *Mtunzini: A history from earliest times to 1995,* 1, Mtunzini, 1998.

Vincent, J., 'The history of Umfolozi Game Reserve, Zululand as it relates to management', *Lammergeyer,* 2, 1970, pp. 7–49.
— *Web of experience: An autobiography,* Mooi River, 1989.

INDEX

aardvark 13

African society 22, 24, 26, 37, 65–77

Afrikaners 18, 35, 44, 56, 59, 60, 67, 161, 168

Angas, George French 19, 21, 44

Anglo-Zulu War 54, 60, 80, 83, 94, 111

ant-bear 26

baboon 12, 26, 66, 108, 166

Baldwin, William Charles 18–19, 21–22, 24, 26, 43, 45–53, 57, 60, 63, 69, 73–74, 86, 93

Barter, Catherine 26, 33, 42, 48, 52, 63, 123, 169

Barter, Charles 19, 57, 59, 73

Beningfield, Sam, Frank and Reuben 83–84, 161

Bhambatha 76, 117

birds 47, 50–51, 65, 69–71, 93, 100–102, 112–13, 115, 144, 148

blesbok 16, 44, 55, 112

blue buck 55, 108

Boers see Afrikaners

Bowker, Col. James Henry 'Butterfly' 92, 95, 99

British Museum 63, 106

Bryant, Dr A.T. 65–68, 70–71

Buckley, T.E. 12, 17, 19–21, 26

buffalo 5, 12–13, 16–17, 20, 28, 33, 43–44, 50–51, 55, 60, 66, 112, 133, 165–67

bushbaby 71

bushbuck 11, 20, 44, 66, 108, 112, 165, 166–67

bushpig 12, 26, 51, 55, 66, 108, 165–66

Byrne settlers 50, 96

Campbell, Dr George 167, 169

Casalis, Eugène 67

caracal 23

Cardew, Col. F. 38–39, 114, 145

Cato, George 53–54, 93

Cato, Joseph 14, 20, 44, 60, 72, 86

cattle 12, 14, 16, 62, 156

Cetshwayo kaMpande, King 15, 44, 54, 60, 69, 72–73, 76, 79, 83

cheetah 108

Chelmsford, Lord 15, 44

Clarke, Marshall 86, 103, 119, 121–23, 142–43, 147, 154, 156

cobra 66

Cowie, William 14–15, 33, 38, 44–45, 50, 54, 57, 72, 75

crocodile 12, 24, 49, 60, 65–66, 71, 81, 167

Curson, Dr H.H. 162, 167

Davies, G.H. 37, 76, 130, 135–36

Delagoa Bay see Maputo

Delegorgue, Adulphe 18, 24, 50, 57, 69, 80, 95, 101

Dingane kaSenzangakhona, King 33, 51, 67–68, 71–72, 76, 79, 82, 154

Dinuzulu kaCetshwayo, King 56

dogs 22, 24, 26, 48, 51–52, 55, 62, 66, 79, 81, 158

Drummond, Hon. William Henry 12, 16, 19–22, 24, 26, 45, 47, 50–51, 53, 55, 57, 68, 74, 79, 83, 93, 100, 103, 107–108, 158

duiker 11, 20, 44, 66, 108, 112, 166–67

Dukuduku 15, 32–33, 38–39, 76, 163

Dunn, John 18, 35, 50, 57, 59–60, 75, 79, 83, 100, 104, 114

Dunn, Samuel 130, 134

Durban 5, 12–13, 16, 18, 21, 24, 44–45, 50, 53–54, 56, 59, 73, 80, 82, 134, 165

Durban Botanic Gardens 22, 97–98, 155–56

eland 13, 20, 50–51, 65–66, 107, 112, 140

elephant 5, 12–16, 18, 24, 44, 50–51, 54–56, 60, 66, 74, 82, 99, 112, 125

Ellis, Charles 18, 44, 57, 108

Emthonjaneni 56, 59, 61, 75, 129, 154, 156

Empangeni 39

Entumeni 32, 38

Eshowe 12, 38, 54, 61, 75, 77, 83, 85, 104

Farewell, Francis 44

Findlay, F.R.N. 19, 44, 56, 66, 163

firearms 12, 18, 49–50, 63, 79–84

forests 5, 31–39, 114, 135, 169

Foxon, Cuthbert 33–34, 81, 86, 121, 134, 141–42 144

Frere, Sir Bartle 84

Fynn, Henry Francis 12, 70, 72

Fynney F. 141

Fynney, Oswald 21, 164, 167

Gardiner, Captain Allen Francis 12, 48, 71, 74, 79

genet 108, 166

Giant's Castle Game Reserve 121, 126

Gingindlovu 80

giraffe 24–25, 28, 66

Green, Frank 18, 61, 105, 164

ground hornbill 5

grysbok 112

Gush, Reg 141

Guise, C.D. 119, 142, 163

gunpowder see firearms

Harris, R.H.T. ('Fly') 167–68

hartebeest 55, 107

Havelock, Sir Arthur 72, 111, 142, 147

Hely-Hutchinson, Sir Walter 60, 69, 96, 106, 119–20, 121–22, 125, 142, 155–56, 158

hippopotamus 5, 12, 17–18, 28, 44–46, 50–51, 60, 66, 81, 108, 112, 143, 148

Hlabisa Game Reserve and area 17, 19, 61, 63, 75, 108, 112, 125–26, 164–65

Hlathikhulu 32–33

Hluhluwe Game Reserve and area 17, 19, 21, 26, 105, 122–27, 135, 164, 168

Hogg, Piet 46, 50, 53, 54–55, 57

Hooker, Sir Joseph 99

hyena 11, 14, 23–24, 26, 48, 51, 60, 63, 65–66, 107–108, 166

Imfolozi (Umfolozi) Game Reserve and area 19, 21–22, 26, 69, 72, 119, 122–24, 127, 131–34, 148, 163, 166, 168

impala 20, 60, 108, 112, 166–67

Ingwavuma 34, 57, 61, 75, 151, 164

Inyalazi 126

Inyanda 130

Inyoni Flats 104

ivory 5, 12–13, 15–16, 18, 27, 37, 44–45, 55, 70, 72

jackal 14, 24, 66, 70, 107–108

Jamrach 107–108

Kew Gardens 97, 106, 111, 114, 142

Kingston, W.H.G. 85, 95

klipspringer 20, 108, 112, 165–66

Kosi Bay 26, 32, 34, 109, 136, 149

kudu 12–13, 20, 44, 60, 66, 112, 134,158, 165–67

Lebombo Mountains 12, 14, 20–21, 24, 26, 44, 46, 53–54, 75, 85, 123, 125–26, 142

leopard 5, 12–13, 16, 22–24, 48, 51, 55–56, 66, 69–70, 107, 149, 166

Leslie, David 16–17, 22, 24, 26, 47, 50, 51–52, 54, 56–57, 67, 75, 79, 93, 154

lion 5, 12–14, 16, 22, 26, 30, 48, 51, 60, 63, 66, 70, 107–108

Lourenço Marques see Maputo

Lower Umfolozi 15, 18–19, 32, 61, 63, 75, 82, 122–23, 125, 147, 158

Ludlow, Captain 15, 44, 84

McKen, Mark 96–97

Mahemane bush 62

Mahlabatini 61, 130–31, 148–49

Makhathini Flats 33, 70, 123, 136,

145, 147

malaria 52, 54

Maphelana 15, 32–33, 67, 166

Maputa River 15, 24

Maputaland 5, 11–12, 14–16, 18, 21–22, 24, 33, 37, 51, 54, 57, 61, 68, 75, 86, 109, 122, 158

Maputo 13, 15–16, 21, 62, 69, 71–72, 82–83, 109, 134

Mbhekamuzi 72, 105

Mbulazi kaMpande 19, 74

Melmoth 83, 104

Mfolozi River 12, 14–15, 18–19, 24, 32–33, 47, 52–53, 69, 74, 84–85, 98, 104–105, 126, 133, 147, 154

mission stations (Zululand) 38, 63, 104–105, 133

Mitchell, Charles 38–39, 143

Mitford, Bertram 61

Mkhuze Game Reserve and area 18–21, 53, 57, 75, 82, 86, 125–27, 141, 151, 164–65, 166–68

monkeys 12, 26, 66, 108, 166

mongoose 108

mosquitoes 18, 52–53

Mozambique 13, 20, 55, 158, 167

Mpande kaSenzangakhona, King 13, 24, 60, 69, 71–73, 154–55

Msunduzi 21, 53, 148

Mthunzini 12, 34, 104–105, 163; see also Umlalazi

museums 95, 108–109, 121, 124, 161

nagana 154, 156, 158

Natal Game Protection Association 161

Natal and Zululand Game Protection Association 162

Natal Parks, Game and Fish Preservation Board 168

Natal Plants 96

Ndondakusuka 26, 45, 60, 69

Ndumo Game Reserve and area 21, 61, 75, 93, 127, 167

Ndwedwe 19, 61, 75, 147

Newmann, A.H. 21, 44, 57

New Republic 35, 56, 86, 161

Ngome 32, 34–35, 37, 56, 76, 116

Nhlophenkulu 19

Nkandla 31–32, 35, 37, 61, 63, 75, 76, 116, 136, 163, 169

Nongoma 37, 105, 147

North, Marianne 65, 95

Nquthu 39, 61, 76, 114

Nsele, Dikidiki 165

Nseleni 18, 53

Ntambanana 163–64, 167

Ntombela, Magqubu 168

nyala 19, 21, 44, 53, 60, 62, 95, 108, 112, 149, 166–67

Ongoye 12, 18, 32, 36–38, 46, 60–61, 71, 96, 98, 100, 104

oribi 112

Osborn, Melmoth 81, 111, 142–43, 149

ostrich 67

oxwagon 5, 46, 53

pangolin 11

Peters, Dr Wilhelm 20, 101

Pettie, W.E. 130, 133–34

Phongola River 13, 15–16, 18, 21, 24, 32–33, 37, 46–47, 60–61, 63, 85–86, 125, 158, 151, 167

Pierce, Catherine 60

Pietermaritzburg 13, 72

Plant, Robert 14, 51–52, 67, 70, 97–101

Player, Dr Ian 168–69

Plomer, William 61

Pongola Game Reserve 61, 121–22, 127, 165

Pongola–Mkuze Game Reserve 119, 123, 125–27, 154

porcupine 66

Port Durnford 39, 169

Port Natal see Durban

Porter, Captain Harold 168

Proudfoot, James 52, 57, 107

Qhudeni 31–32, 34–35, 37–39, 76–77, 114, 116, 135, 169

rabbit 112

reedbuck 11–12, 20, 44, 50, 66, 108, 112, 165–67

Reitz, Colonel Deneys 77, 167, 169

rhinoceros 5, 12, 13, 18–19, 22, 24, 28, 44–45, 55, 60, 66, 70, 108, 112, 125, 166–67

Richards Bay see Umhlathuze

rinderpest 12, 156, 158

roads 79, 84–86

roan 112

Robinson, John 122

Rorke's Drift 86

Ross, John 65

Royal game 113

Royal Geographical Society 111

Sabi–Crocodile area 19, 124

St Lucia Game Reserve and area 12, 14–15, 18–22, 26, 32, 44, 46–47, 51, 75, 81, 86, 94–95, 98, 105, 108, 122, 124–25, 127, 134, 165–69

Saunders, Charles 12, 18, 21, 54, 86, 108–109, 124, 142, 145, 149, 154–55, 158, 163

sawmills 34, 37

Selous, Frederick Courteney 21, 62–63, 121, 167

serval 108, 166

Shaka kaSenzangakhona, King 24, 51, 72

Shepstone, Arthur 132, 147, 149

Shepstone, Sir Theophilus 72

Silvertson, Sigurd 129–30, 133

Sim, T.R. 116, 135

snakes 12, 24, 65–66

Sodwana Bay 32

springbok 13, 16, 112

Steel, Nick 169

steenbuck 20, 44, 66, 108, 112, 165–66

Stevenson-Hamilton, Col. James 121, 165

stinkwood 5

Struthers, Dr Robert Biggs 22, 24, 51, 53, 57

Stuart, James 67

suni 44, 63, 108, 112

Swaziland 13, 24, 56, 73, 123, 126

Tongaland 22, 33, 54, 67, 73, 98, 121–24

trading stores 24, 61

transport riders 153

traps 66

tsetse fly 69, 154, 167

Tsongaland see Tongoland

Tugela River 5, 12, 18, 24, 31, 45, 53, 63, 79, 83, 85–86, 104

Turnbull, Alexander 72, 145, 147

turtles 26, 109

Tweedie, David D. 130, 132

Ubombo 12, 19, 21–22, 33, 54, 61–62, 65, 75, 82, 86, 116, 122, 148, 157, 164

Ulundi 24, 60, 85

Umango 105

Umbanda 149

Umbonambi 105

Umdletshe Game Reserve and area 122–25, 127, 159, 165

Umfolozi see Imfolozi

Umhlathuze 12, 14, 18, 24, 46, 86, 100, 104

Umlalazi 12, 24, 26, 49, 52, 61, 100, 105; see also Mthunzini

Umvoti 30

Usuthu River 15, 20–21, 33, 52, 61, 74, 147, 149,167

Varndell, C.H. 44, 121

Vaughan-Kirby, Frederick 19, 26, 121, 123, 131, 154, 161–63, 167

Vincent, Colonel Jack 165

Wahlberg, Johan August 24, 26, 49, 52, 55, 72, 80, 95, 101

Walmsley, Captain Joshua 57, 80

Warren, Dr Ernest 108, 162

warthog 26, 165, 167

waterbuck 44, 66, 108, 112, 125, 165–66

White, John Alfred 46, 57, 67, 73, 81, 94, 109

wildcat 108

wild dog 12, 23–24, 26, 66, 132–34

wildebeest 13, 16, 21, 42, 44, 55, 60, 66, 108, 112, 148,165–67

Windham, William 38, 129

Wissell, von 24, 61, 62–63

Wood, John Medley 71, 96, 156–57

Woodruff, Edmund Aureal 35

Woodward, John and Robert 101, 104–106

yellowwood 5, 32, 34, 37

zebra 21, 55, 65–66, 107–108, 112, 142, 165–67

Zoological Society of London 19, 95

Zululand Lands Delimitation Commission 108

Zululand Police 39, 57, 130–31, 141, 164–65